AF600316

SPANISH MODERNISM AND THE POETICS OF YOUTH

From Miguel de Unamuno to *La Joven Literatura*

LESLIE J. HARKEMA

Spanish Modernism and the Poetics of Youth

From Miguel de Unamuno to *La Joven Literatura*

UNIVERSITY OF TORONTO PRESS
Toronto Buffalo London

Toronto Buffalo London
www.utorontopress.com

ISBN 978-1-4875-0196-9

Library and Archives Canada Cataloguing in Publication

Harkema, Leslie, author
Spanish modernism and the poetics of youth : from Miguel de Unamuno to *la joven literatura* / Leslie J. Harkema.

(Toronto Iberic series ; 31)
Includes bibliographical references and index.
ISBN 978-1-4875-0196-9 (hardcover)

1. Spanish literature – 20th century – History and criticism. 2. Youth in literature. 3. Modernism (Literature) – Spain – History – 20th century. 4. Unamuno, Miguel de, 1864–1936 – Criticism and interpretation. I. Title. II. Series: Toronto Iberic; 31

PQ6072.H37 2018 860.9'35242090941 C2017-904299-8

This book has been published with the assistance of the Frederick W. Hilles Publication Fund of Yale University.

University of Toronto Press acknowledges the financial assistance to its publishing program of the Canada Council for the Arts and the Ontario Arts Council, an agency of the Government of Ontario.

Canada Council for the Arts Conseil des Arts du Canada

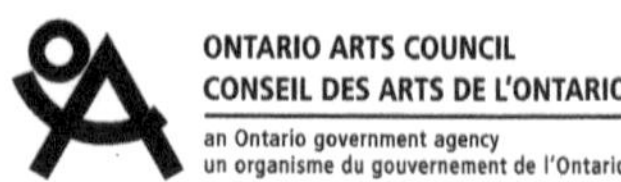

Funded by the Government of Canada Financé par le gouvernement du Canada

For my parents

Contents

Illustrations

Acknowledgments

This book has taken shape over the course of several years, and many individuals and institutions have supported it at various stages of its development. In the first place, I owe a tremendous debt of gratitude to Christopher Maurer, who enthusiastically encouraged my ideas in their most embryonic form, and who has been a dear mentor to me both during and after my time as a doctoral student. I also wish to thank Alan E. Smith for guiding the project at its earliest stage, for challenging me and helping me to grow as a critic and a reader of poetry. Later on, the readings and commentary that chapters of the manuscript received from Matthew I. Feinberg, Javier Krauel, Alberto Medina, Nelson Orringer, and Gayle Rogers strengthened my arguments and improved my writing. Two anonymous readers from University of Toronto Press also offered excellent suggestions that have made this a better book.

The opportunities to share my work and exchange ideas with colleagues at conferences and speaking engagements and in other settings enriched this study enormously. My thanks to Ângela Fernandes, Santiago Pérez Isasi, and Elisabete M. de Sousa for organizing the conference "Repensar Unamuno," held at the University of Lisbon in October 2014; to Nicolás Fernández-Medina and the Spanish and Italian Modernist Studies Forum at Penn State University for inviting me to speak at the Penn State Comparative Literature Lunch Series in September 2015; and to the participants and attendees of the colloquium "The Aesthetics of Youth in Modernist Spain," held at Yale University in November 2016.

I am furthermore grateful to the students in the graduate seminar I taught during the fall semester of 2013 titled "The Aesthetics of Youth in the Spanish Silver Age," for their engagement with the topic and their insightful discussions of some of the texts I analyse in these pages. For their encouragement and guidance, I thank my current and former colleagues in the Department of Spanish & Portuguese at Yale: Rolena Adorno, Roberto González Echevarría, Aníbal González-Pérez, K. David Jackson, Paulo Moreira, Kevin Poole, and Noël Valis. I am particularly indebted to Susan Byrne, without whose unfailing moral support this book would never have come to fruition.

In its earliest iteration, this project was supported by grants from the Fulbright Program, the Graduate School of Arts and Sciences at Boston University, and the Boston University Humanities Foundation. At Yale University, further research was made possible by funding from the Whitney Humanities Center and the MacMillan Center for International and Area Studies. I am grateful to the directors and staff at the Casa Museo Unamuno, the Residencia de Estudiantes, and the Fundación Gerardo Diego for facilitating my research in Spain. I particularly wish to thank José García Velasco, who welcomed me to the Residencia and showed early enthusiasm for this project, and Ana Chaguaceda Toledano, for the support she has lent me from her post as director of the Casa Museo Unamuno. Flor Hernández, Clemente Bernal Pérez, and Francisco Javier del Mazo Ruiz always make me feel at home at the Casa Museo, and I thank them for their assistance with numerous requests made in person and over e-mail.

I am grateful to University of Toronto Press and the two editors I have been fortunate to work with there: Siobhan McMenemy, who first showed interest in this book, and Mark Thompson, who skillfully guided it to its final form. My thanks, as well, to Frances Mundy for overseeing the production process, and to Anne Fullerton for her excellent copyediting work. The Frederick W. Hilles Publication Fund at Yale also provided instrumental financial support for the publication process.

During my time at Yale, I have been fortunate to be surrounded by brilliant female colleagues across several disciplines who have inspired me and made me a better scholar. I am grateful to Marijeta Bozovic, Marcela Echeverri, Briallen Hopper, Noreen Khawaja, and Joanna Radin for their friendship, humor, encouragement, and fierce commitment to our shared vocation of teaching and learning. I likewise offer my deepest thanks to friends farther away: to Victoria Livingstone for our many conversations about literature and translation and life in general, and to Wan Tang for her buoying spirit and warm collegiality. Above all, I am grateful to my family – my sister Lindsay, her husband David, and my parents, Laurie and Jack Harkema – for their constant love and support.

A Note on Translation

Unless otherwise indicated, all translations from Spanish and French are my own. When citing a secondary source originally published in a language other than English, I provide only the English translation.

Abbreviations

CMU	Archive of the Casa Museo Unamuno, Salamanca, Spain
E	Miguel de Unamuno, *Ensayos*. 7 vols. Residencia de Estudiantes, 1916-1918.
OC	*Obras completas*, by Dámaso Alonso, Gerardo Diego, or Federico García Lorca as specified in the text.
OCE	Miguel de Unamuno, *Obras completas*. Ed. Manuel García Blanco. 9 vols. Escelicer, 1966.
OCT	José Ortega y Gasset, *Obras completas*. 10 vols. Taurus, 2004-2010.
PCMV	José Moreno Villa, *Poesías completas*. Ed. Juan Pérez de Ayala. El Colegio de México/Publicaciones de la Residencia de Estudiantes, 1998.

SPANISH MODERNISM AND THE POETICS OF YOUTH

From Miguel de Unamuno to *La Joven Literatura*

Introduction

Spain, Modernism, Youth

In the spring of 1916, Madrid's Residencia de Estudiantes – a still relatively new centre for the cultivation of higher education in Spain that would house Federico García Lorca, Salvador Dalí, Luis Buñuel, and several other luminaries of Spanish art and literature in the following years – published the first volume of the collected essays (*Ensayos*) of the prolific novelist, poet, professor, and public intellectual Miguel de Unamuno (1864–1936). The series, which would comprise seven volumes when completed, was made up entirely of short essays and articles that Unamuno had published in various journals between 1894 and 1906, with one inclusion from 1911. An anthology of sorts, it selected from the author's expanding body of work the reflections on Spanish culture that he and the editors deemed most important at the time, not only because they bore witness to Unamuno's intellectual trajectory, but because of their pedagogical value: these essays were considered to be works of cultural criticism with which the educated readers that made up the Residencia's target audience ought to be familiar. One of the most important sectors of this intended readership was made up of young people – those young students who came to the Residencia and participated in the cultural life that it fomented, as well as others throughout Spain. Though today the *Ensayos* do not figure among Unamuno's most well-known publications, this collection of essays constitutes a highly significant point of contact between Unamuno and younger generations of Spanish artists, particularly those who lived and studied at the Residencia during the decades before the Spanish Civil War forced its closure. One telling example of the impact the *Ensayos* had on these young readers appears in a letter from García Lorca to his friend Adriano del Valle from September 1918, just after the sixth volume was published. Lorca writes, "¿Ha leído V. los últimos ensayos de Unamuno? Léalos; gozará extraordinariamente" ("Have you read the latest of Unamuno's essays? Read them; you will enjoy them a great deal") (García Lorca, *Epistolario* 52–3). Two decades later, as philosopher María Zambrano reflected on the significance of Unamuno's work, she referred to the Residencia collection as the "summa" of his early thought. The poet Gerardo Diego also looked back and singled out the *Ensayos* as texts that had shaped Unamuno's legacy among younger Spanish writers, encouraging and inspiring "tantas almas en formación" ("so many souls in formation") (Diego, "Presencia" 67).

Though the texts collected in the *Ensayos* deal with a range of topics, from contemporary politics to Spanish and Latin American literature to religious faith, one topic appears repeatedly in the collection and becomes a dominant theme: the nature of youth. Throughout the seven volumes Unamuno invokes youth repeatedly, as a foil to age-old, restrictive traditions; as the defining characteristic of a sector of Spanish society with the potential to effect change in political and intellectual arenas; and as the condition and source of artistic creativity. Indeed, the five essays that make up the first volume of the *Ensayos*, originally published in 1895 and later collected as *En torno al casticismo* (*Regarding the Cult of Authentic Tradition*),[1] culminate with a call for a resurgence of youth: a *true* youth ("verdadera juventud") that might oppose and defeat the reign of traditionalism that Unamuno sees as the source of late nineteenth-century Spain's cultural decadence. Other essays like "La juventud 'intelectual' española" ("'Intelectual' Spanish Youth"), "Viejos y jóvenes" ("The Old and the Young"), and "Almas de jóvenes" ("Souls of the Young") make young people the direct object of their reflection, acknowledging the power they weild in society as those who may either conform to the ways of their elders, or depart from them and inaugurate change. Several essays are written in the second person singular, addressed to a young reader whom the essayist encourages to think independently, to break away from convention in order to forge his or her own unique perspective on the world. Throughout the collection, youth appears as a site of possibility, of growth and discovery unfettered by the patterns and narratives that have reigned over Spain's past. Indeed, rather than speaking of youth as one stage in the process of growing up, as a chapter in a story, Unamuno likens it to poetry, or to a poetic mode of existence. As he writes in "Almas de jóvenes," "Si un poeta no es un espíritu … al que sentimos vivir, es decir, fraguarse día a día su sustancia, ¿qué es un poeta? Y si un joven no es así, ¿qué es juventud?" ("If a poet is not a spirit … that we feel living, that is, forging its substance day by day, what is a poet? And if a young person is not like that, what is youth?") (*E* 5:29–30).

In this book, I argue that the Unamuno of the turn of the century – the author of *En torno al casticismo*, of the other essays collected in the *Ensayos*, and of his first volume of poetry, *Poesías* (1907), among other publications – decisively shaped the conception of youth that would dominate Spanish literary production throughout the next several decades and flourish especially at the Residencia and in the work of a group of writers that called themselves *la joven literatura*. Though these writers are better known today as members of the "Generation of 1927" in Spanish letters, the name they chose for themselves indicates just how central the idea of youth was to their aesthetic thought and practice. Far from a phenomenon unique to Spain, this interest in youth reflects a broad cultural fascination with adolescence in early twentieth-century European society and in European modernism. Newly conceived as a stage of life different and distinct from both childhood and adulthood, adolescence became an emblem of the new era that would be inaugurated with the turn of the century, as well as a powerful source of inspiration for intellectuals concerned with shaping that imminent future. The artists studied here, like modernist artists elsewhere, embraced the power and hopeful futurity that youth came to represent. In Spain and among these writers, however, the concept also held particular potency as an antidote to historical narratives that had prevailed during the previous century – narratives of imperial decline and of Spanish belatedness. Against the linear conceptions of time and development that informed such accounts of Spain and its position in the world, youth represented a malleable and open-ended temporality that might depart from, renovate, reinterpret, or rearrange the narratives of the past.

In the pages that follow, I propose that Unamuno and his successors saw youth as a lyrical state that stood outside of history and cast a critical light on its ordering of events. For them, the power of youth was a poetic power, a capacity to resist or subvert the syllogistic logic of narrative progression (and of progress itself, in a positivistic sense), and to imagine alternative configurations of experience. While many of the works associated with a modernist treatment of youth belong to the prose genre of the *Bildungsroman* (one thinks of James Joyce's *A Portrait of the Artist as a Young Man* or Robert Musil's *Young Törless*), in early twentieth-century Spain the link between art and youth is most prevalent in debates about poetry and the essence of "poetic" art. This is not to say that it does not appear in works of fiction, but rather that in critical work and literary discourse of the period, youth is rhetorically aligned with the poetic. Related to this phenomenon in criticism is the fact that many Spanish modernist artworks that thematize youth also strongly critique or completely reject narrative temporality insofar as it corresponds to linear chronology. The writer Manuel Altolaguirre, one of the youngest members of *la joven literatura*, gets at this aesthetic understanding of youth when he describes the particular "youthfulness" of Unamuno's work, in an essay from 1940:

> Se dice y opina con frecuencia que la obra de Unamuno es vieja, que Unamuno es un viejo también. Yo no comparto esta opinión, que por lo demás no me parece denigrante. La juventud de don Miguel de Unamuno es más vegetal que humana, depende de sus flores. Era joven, vigoroso, claro, radiante y su obra a nadie puede aprovecharle mejor que la juventud. (103)

> (It is often said and thought that Unamuno's work is old, and that Unamuno is an old man as well. I do not share this opinion, which in any case does not seem to me to be an insult. Don Miguel de Unamuno's youth is more vegetal than human; it depends upon the blooming of its flowers. He was young, vigorous, clear, radiant, and his work can benefit no one better than the young.)

For Altolaguirre, the value of Unamuno's work lies in the way it defies the linear form of development that marks human life. Rather than blossoming and fading once, his perennial youth blooms over and again with each reading and each discovery by yet another young reader.

Today perhaps even more than in Altolaguirre's time, Unamuno is rarely thought of as young. The stature he reached by the end of his life, along with the image of him that emerged from his literary canonization over the course of the twentieth century, make it difficult to think of him as anything other than an imposing elderly man with white hair and a piercing, owlish stare. And yet, if one ventures beyond this received image and the most-studied of Unamuno's works, youth appears as a constant topic of interest and reflection. In one sense, this is not all that surprising, given that the writer spent most of his career as a professor and administrator at the Universidad de Salamanca, where the cultivation of adolescent students was his daily concern. The importance that he attributed to the concept of youth extends well beyond these professional duties, however. His call for the rejuvenation of Spanish culture at the end of *En torno al casticismo* is just one articulation of a desire for innovation and a critique of received authority that spans all of his early work. For these reasons, the thoroughly modernist stance that Unamuno assumed in praising the subversive, poetic nature of youth profoundly influenced the course of Spanish literature in the early twentieth century.

Unamuno's vision was so influential in giving shape to Spanish modernism because he linked Spanish culture and artistic creation to youth at a time when the concept was highly charged, and endowed with immense evocative power within a society increasingly aware of its own age. As Matei Calinescu notes in *Five Faces of Modernity*, the historical consciousness that underlies the idea of the modern lends itself to an anthropomorphic conception of civilization that, relying on a view of time as linear and irreversible, interprets the development of the human race according to the metaphor of the life stages of a single human being. Calinescu points out that the metaphor appears vividly in the *Querelle des Anciens et des Modernes* of the seventeenth century, and that according to Francis Bacon, the Moderns were in fact older than the Ancients, because they lived during a later stage when the increase of knowledge and technical capability had brought mankind to a greater level of maturity (Calinescu 24–6). This idea dovetails easily with the Enlightenment's concept of progress, with Comtean positivism (in *Discours sur l'esprit positif*, Comte repeatedly links the positive spirit to "maturité"), and with positivist receptions of the theories of Darwin or Haeckel, where a teleological view of history is quite literally concerned with anthropomorphism, *making-into-man*. During the last decades of the nineteenth century, however, this metaphor experienced a crisis. With the increasing growth of industry, progressive, quantifiable, capitalist time no longer corresponded to the personal and biological time of the individual. As a result, according to Calinescu, the analogy of the individual life and the life of the human race lost its viability. There is a sense, however, in which the metaphor's descriptive power persisted. As technological and scientific progress began to acquire connotations of decadence, artists and writers viewed Western civilization itself as ossified and senile. Modernity had grown old.

According to this metaphorical conception, the problem of history's aging could not be solved by the adult world. The bourgeois ideal of the employed adult (male) citizen, sustaining his family and contributing to capitalist society, only signalled the inevitable decline of old age and death. In Calinescu's words, "progress *is* decadence and decadence *is* progress. The true opposite of decadence – as far as the biological connotations of the word are concerned – is perhaps regeneration" (156). In the Spanish context, this emphasis on regeneration as opposed to decadence is held to be the central preoccupation of the members of the so-called Generation of 1898, of which Unamuno is considered a key member: writers and intellectuals concerned with the state of the nation at the end of the nineteenth century, supposedly in response to the loss of the Spanish-Cuban-American War and its last overseas colonies. (Here it should be remembered that a purportedly representative generational text like Unamuno's *En torno al casticismo* was written three years before that war.) Yet if one takes a step back and considers Spain within the broader context of intellectual life in Europe at the time, the type of turn-of-the-century *regeneracionismo* articulated by Unamuno appears as a commentary on the aging of history itself. In choosing to search out the elements of Spanish culture and society that might contain the seeds of a new youth, he not only offered an alternative to the narrative of decline and the cultural stagnation that he observed in his own country, but also activated a concept that thinkers across Europe were drawing on to imagine ways of approaching the modern world differently. Walter Benjamin, in a brief text titled "Experience" that he wrote as a young student just a couple of years before the publication of Unamuno's *Ensayos*, declared that the members of his generation knew "something different, which experience [*Erfahrung*] can neither give to us nor take away: that truth exists, even if all previous thought has been an error. Or: that fidelity shall be maintained, even if no one has done so yet" (*Selected Writings* 4). In Benjamin's life and work, this intransigent posture before the world-weary skepticism that the adult "philistine" calls "experience" evolves into an approach to history that "stops telling the sequence of events like the beads of a rosary," subverting the hegemonic account of the past, and therefore, the present (*Illuminations* 263).[2] There is something of Benjamin's historical materialist in the Unamuno of *En torno al casticismo*, who returns to the story of Spain's development and searches for a glimpse of a forgotten youth that would explode its traditionalist casing. Youth, newly conceived in Benjamin's and Unamuno's early twentieth-century European society as radically different from age (and thus also its antidote), suggested that it might be possible to resist the old narratives of personal, social, and national development, and chart a new course.

An illuminating example of the opposition between youth and age in Unamuno's modernist thought appears in the poem "Cuando yo sea viejo" ("When I Am Old"), included in the opening section of his first book of poetry, *Poesías* (1907). Grouped with other introductory poems that all address possible future readers, "Cuando yo sea viejo" stages an imagined debate between the poet himself and the next generation of artists. While the title, when translated to English, is nearly identical to that of a poem written fifteen years earlier by W.B. Yeats,[3] there is nothing in Unamuno's composition of the nostalgia that pervades the Irish poet's musings about nodding by the fire in "When You Are Old." Unamuno does not imagine how a poetically invoked "you" will look back longingly on love lost in some quiet, sad, and soporific future. Instead, he attempts to anticipate how he himself will change when he reaches old age. The poem opens with a portrait of the poet as an old man:

Cuando yo sea viejo,
– desde ahora os lo digo –
no sentiré mis cantos, estos cantos,
ni serán a mi oído
más que voces de un muerto
aun siendo de los muertos el más mío. (*Poesías* 70)

(When I am old,
– I'm warning you now –
I won't feel my songs, these very songs;
to me they will sound
like the calls of a dead man,
though of the dead, the most mine to be found.)

As he ages, the poet asserts, he will lose the ability to respond to his own poems in a heartfelt way. Instead, he will attempt to delineate their significance rationally and retain interpretive authority over them. It becomes clear that his growing older will inevitably result in his betrayal of his present self: "renegaré del alma que ahora vivo" ("I will renounce the soul that I live now"), he writes, and what is more, "no comprenderé ni aun a mis hijos" ("I won't understand even my own children") (70). At this point the gap between generations opens, dividing the imagined future poet from the one who composes

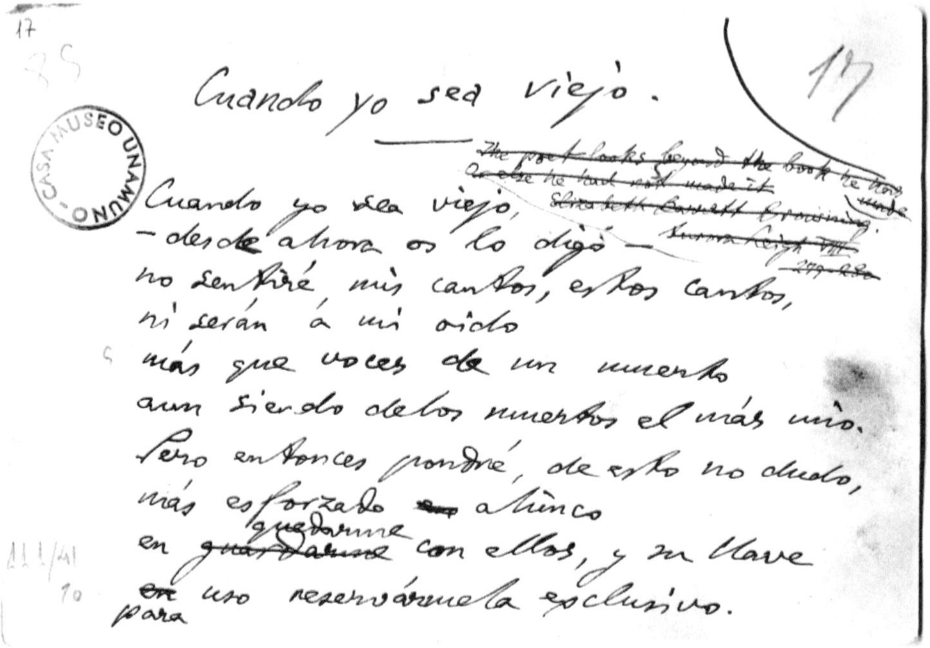

0.1 The opening lines of the poem "Cuando yo sea viejo," included in the full manuscript of *Poesías* (1906). The epigraph, crossed out, is taken from Elizabeth Barrett Browning's *Aurora Leigh*, and reads, "The poet looks beyond the book he has made / Or else he had not made it." Universidad de Salamanca. Casa-Museo Unamuno.

the poem, and from his future readers. Subsequently the focus shifts to these readers, and they become the new locus of authority for the poem's interpretation. While the lyrical subject of voice sympathizes with this younger generation, the imagined older poet refuses to relinquish control of his work to them. An argument ensues. The young people insist that Unamuno's poems are expressions of youth, and that, therefore, *they* are the ones best equipped to understand them. In response, the old poet becomes enraged and indignant, basilisk-like ("hecho un basilisco") in his anger, and full of "senil impaciencia" ("senile impatience") (71).

Eventually the lyrical subject breaks in to confirm that the young will win the debate:

Y yo protestaré, cual si lo viera,
pero estará bien dicho.
El alma que aquí dejo
un día para mí se irá al abismo;
no sentiré mis cantos;
recogeréis vosotros su sentido. (71–2)

(And I will protest, I can just see it now,
but you'll have proven your case.
The soul that I put down here
will fade one day into the abyss;
I'll no longer feel my songs;
you will be the ones to recover their sense.)

The poet here repeats his earlier statement and adds to it: he will someday cease to feel the meaning of his poems, and at that time it will be up to his readers to harvest the significance planted in them, gathering and reconstructing it with an enthusiasm to match that of the writer's own youth. With this statement, a baton has been passed. The poem concludes with a reaffirmation of the value of youth as receptor and even arbiter of artistic work. For the first time in this poem, the poet refers to his readers not as children ("niños") but as youths ("jóvenes"), and acknowledges their authority for evaluating his verse. He even goes so far as to tell them that if they have to, they should argue against him:

arguïd contra mí conmigo mismo
pues os declaro
– y creo saber bien lo que me digo –
que cuando llegue a viejo,
de este que ahora me soy y me respiro,
sabrán, cierto, los jóvenes de entonces
más que yo si a este yo me sobrevivo. (72)

(invoke me to argue against me,
for I say to you
– and I know of what I speak –
that when I grow old,

of the person I now am and live and breathe
the young men of then will know, better than I,
to judge whether I will have survived this me.)

Like the poem that preceeds it in *Poesías*, "Para después de mi muerte" ("For After My Death"), "Cuando yo sea viejo" is ultimately a poem about the passing of time and the writer's turn to literature as a stay against his own mortality. While undoubtedly exemplifying the existential concerns with death that appear throughout Unamuno's work, however, the poem also represents an effort to bridge a generational gap between adults and young people that was becoming a more prominent social reality even as the poet wrote these words. In this book I maintain that the next generations of Spanish poets did read and respond to his work much as Unamuno asks them to in this poem, and as the dialogic character of much of his writing requires. They did not simply revere him; at times they argued against him. Yet they recognized the energy of his writing as their own, identifying it with their own youthful state and with a youthful timelessness that many of them, like Unamuno, saw in art.

All of this is not to say that the poem successfully safeguarded Unamuno from the vicissitudes of age he describes in it. Twenty years after the publication of *Poesías*, in fact, the situation staged in "Cuando yo sea viejo" seemed to occur in real life, though the subject under debate was not Unamuno's poetry, but that of the seventeenth-century Spanish poet Luis de Góngora. In 1927 Unamuno, living as an exile in France in protest of the dictatorship of Miguel Primo de Rivera, received an invitation to participate in the commemoration of the three-hundredth anniversary of Góngora's death that the young writers back in Spain were planning. The older writer politely declined, citing the political circumstances that, at the time, preoccupied him completely. But in the manuscript of a book that he was revising that spring and summer, *Cómo se hace una novela* (*How to Make a Novel*), he had much harsher words for the young generation:

> Y ahora en estos días mismos de principios de junio de 1927, cuando la tiranía pretoriana española se ensoece más y el rufián que la representa la vomita [*sic*], casi a diario, sobre el regazo de España las heces de su borracheras [*sic*], recibo un número de *La Gaceta Literaria* de Madrid que consagran a don Luis de Góngora y Argote y al gongorismo los jóvenes culteranos y cultos de la castrada intelectualidad española. (*Manual* 200)[4]

(And now in these first days of June, 1927, when the praetorian Spanish tyranny continues to degrade itself and the ruffian that represents it vomits the dregs of his drunkenness, almost daily, upon Spain's lap, I receive an issue of Madrid's *La Gaceta Literaria*, which the pretentiously learned youths of Spain's castrated intellectual class dedicate to Don Luis de Góngora y Argote and to *gongorismo*.)

It should be noted that the cited cause of Unamuno's anger here is a particular issue of the literary journal *La Gaceta Literaria* – not the initial invitation that had been sent to him that spring, signed by the poets Jorge Guillén, Pedro Salinas, Dámaso Alonso, Gerardo Diego, Federico García Lorca, and Rafael Alberti. The reasons for the older writer's frustration with the journal will be discussed in chapter 3 of this volume. For now, it is enough to note that here in Unamuno's 1927 text, the old "basilisk" from "Cuando yo sea viejo" seems to re-emerge. Belligerent and impatient, Unamuno is unwilling to accept the literary tastes of a group of writers much younger than he. The anti-*gongorismo* he expresses here and elsewhere, in fact, has led critics to proceed with caution in the very few attempts that have been made to study his legacy among the writers of *la joven literatura*.[5]

In this book I contend that there is a different story to be told about the relationship between Unamuno and these young writers, and between Unamuno and the youth of modernist-era Spain in general. It is a story more about continuity than about generational divides. It is a story about the Unamuno who was a key point of reference for several young writers, most of them poets, who emerged on the Spanish cultural scene in the midst of a changing Europe and rapidly evolving youth cultures in the 1910s and 1920s. These young writers eventually engaged in various ways with the ideological and political conflicts that marked the 1930s in Spain and Europe, conflicts that themselves often made use of the rhetorical power of youth. As the argument I make here traces Unamuno's influence in places that it is not often expected to be, it also requires a focus on relatively understudied areas of his writing – namely, his short essays and poetry. Though today Unamuno is known as a novelist and his narrative production is the most frequently commented-upon area of his work, his essays and poetry were just as if not more familiar to the younger writers who read him in the early decades of the twentieth century. The timely publication of the *Ensayos* by the Residencia directed their collective attention to the writings the series contained and canonized, and their own poetic interests led them to study and follow Unamuno's lyrical production, from *Poesías* to the works he composed in the 1920s, contemporaneously with their own. Though the topic of youth does emerge in Unamuno's early narrative (perhaps most suggestively in *Nuevo mundo*, a drafted novel that remained unpublished until 1994), it is in his essays that he speaks most explicitly about it, linking it consistently to poetry, or more accurately, to *poiesis*, the Greek word for creation that he chose as the initial title for *Poesías*. This expansive definition of poetry was embraced by the successors of Unamuno singled out for study in this book: José Moreno Villa, Gerardo Diego, José Bergamín, and Ernesto Giménez Caballero. All of these writers, in diverse and at times divergent ways, affirmed the particularly poetic nature of youth. In order to understand their various interpretations of this resemblance, and the interpretations of Unamuno's work from which they stem, we must read beyond the most studied areas of his work, and read him not as a representative of the "Generation of 1898" – a label that, if extant at the time, did not become the dominant rubric for interpreting Unamuno until later in the twentieth century. Instead, we must read him as a prolific writer and public figure who was an active shaper of Spanish culture throughout the early twentieth century up to the beginning of the Civil War, and as a major representative of the intellectual currents prevalent throughout Europe at that time.

Reading Unamuno in this way opens up new avenues for placing Spanish literary production of the period known as *La Edad de Plata* ("The Silver Age," which for the purposes of this book I date from 1895 to 1936) in conversation with the wider field of modernist studies. While critics including Anthony Geist and José B. Monleón, Andrew A. Anderson, C. Christopher Soufas, José Luis Rodríguez García, Susan Larson, Gayle Rogers, and others have offered insightful analyses of the possible connections and divergences between the cultural production of the Spanish Silver Age and the trends and tendencies of European modernism, no study has as yet approached this topic through a consideration of the relationship between modernist art and youth. The existing work on this relationship, which has focused primarily on the modernist *Bildungsroman* written in English, French, and German, has created a rich conversation about narratives of modernity and national development to which Hispanism, in my view, has much to contribute.[6] At the same time, for Hispanists, placing the cultural production of the Spanish Silver Age against the backdrop of changing ideas about modern youth creates new ways of understanding the wide range of

Unamuno's work and how it shaped the writing of his immediate successors in Spain – those who first encountered him when they were young themselves, and who would appropriate the language of youth in their own literary self-fashioning.

Modern Youth in Europe and Spain

If youth and age and the differences between them are as old as human civilization itself, there is a particular fascination with youth that is a product of modernity, and that persists and continues to evolve in our time. Robert Pogue Harrison has named this phenomenon "juvenescence," a term by which he refers to a neotenic capability of human civilization to preserve and indeed develop "youthful" traits of past eras. According to Harrison, juvenescence has manifested itself since the Second World War in the global dominance of the United States, a country that has founded its identity on youth and newness. Already in 1961, the Spanish philosopher José Luis Aranguren registered something like Harrison's notion of juvenescence in an essay on postwar youth ("postwar" referring, for Aranguren, to both the Second World War and the Spanish Civil War). His study of what he calls "the general *juvenilization* of society" (my translation, original emphasis) leads him to reflect, in the essay's postscript, on the synergy between old and young as a defining characteristic of late twentieth-century modernity (Aranguren 11, 52). In this book I focus on the precursor to Aranguren's mid-century youth, the youth of the turn of the century, the First World War, and the interwar period, which in turn emerges from the social, cultural, and intellectual context of the nineteenth century. Both Harrison and Aranguren are conscious of this history, and note the influential role within it of G.W. Hegel, who memorably conceived of the development of world civilization as analogous to the life of an individual, with an infancy, youth, and maturity. Though Hegel was by no means the first to use this analogy, he shaped its application to modern thought by making it geographical. He cast human history as the biography of Spirit as it travelled through time and also through space, moving from its infancy in the East towards the adulthood of the West, of Europe.

Within this Hegelian matrix, Spain has always occupied a dubious position, and an ambiguous age. Situated at the Western extreme of the European continent, it is also the closest part of that continent to Africa – a proximity that facilitated its historical connections to Islam, Arabic cultures, and what Hegel considered the Orient. While its unification as a modern, Christian nation at the end of the fifteenth century predated that of other European countries (Germany and Italy in particular) by centuries, in the post-Enlightenment period its very age made it seem incapable of reaching a mature modernity. The decadence of the Spanish empire under the later Habsburg and Bourbon kings, the persistence of the Inquisition, and the notoriety of Spanish arrogance (what the French called *la morgue castillane*) fed the Black Legend that cast the nation as obscurantist and recalcitrant, and eventually as incapable of adaptation to the modern world. Immanuel Kant's depiction of the Spaniard in *Anthropology from a Pragmatic Point of View* (1798) as "whole-heartedly devoted to the laws, especially those of his old religion," as well as "centuries behind in the sciences" (178), must be understood in the light of the philosopher's earlier definition of immaturity (*Unmündigkeit*) as the lack of Enlightenment, the "inability to use one's own understanding without the guidance of another" (*Political Writings* 54). The question of Spain's relationship to knowledge, enlightenment, science, reason – the essence of maturity within German idealism – and to the continent that purported to embody all of these things, Europe, came to hold central importance for the Spanish intellectuals of the nineteenth and early twentieth centuries. In 1902, economist and politician Joaquín Costa asserted that Spain was underage ("menor de edad") when compared to its more developed, enlightened, self-governing neighbours to the north.[7] Later in the twentieth century, José Ortega y Gasset, heir to Costa's regenerationist thought, affirmed this view of Europe as more advanced, rational, and scientific. In their desire to Europeanize Spain, Costa and Ortega responded to the sentiment, encapsulated in the adage "Africa begins at the Pyrenees,"[8] that continued to highlight the country's liminal position as part, but also not part, of the European continent. If stages of development could be mapped onto geography, Spain found itself, at most, in a position of adolescence.

In these very same years, however, adolescence was acquiring a new cultural status and gaining social agency. Just as modernity's privileging of youth over adulthood has its cultural roots in romanticism (the angst of Goethe's *Werther*, and the reverence for the innocence and mysterious wisdom of childhood found in Wordsworth), a number of social changes in the nineteenth century contributed to the emergence of a new definition of this life stage in the *fin-de-siècle*. These included the institution of military conscription, the rise of secondary education, and the creation of child labour laws. Together, these elements effectively carved out a space for a new stage in the life of the individual. Youth became a period of enhanced personal independence combined with prolonged economic dependence, and young people (particularly young men of the middle and upper classes) were able to experience this age as a time for study and leisure, a period of relative autonomy still free from the full responsibilities of adulthood.[9] With the turn of the century, this new social reality manifested itself in a wide range of organizations created by or for young people, and was reflected in art and literature. The German Wandervogel (f. 1896) offered adolescents an escape from urban life and into nature, while the British Boy Scouts (1906) and the Spanish Exploradores modelled after them (1912)[10] promoted discipline and allegiance to one's country. Simultaneously, J.M. Barrie's *Peter Pan* (1904) fantasized about the possibility of never growing up, and novels like Joyce's *Portrait* (1916) or Spanish novelist Ramón Pérez de Ayala's *A.M.D.G.* (1910) depicted a multifaceted adolescence suspicious of the adult world.[11] Patricia Meyer Spacks, John Neubauer, and other critics of the period's literary representations of youth all point to the pivotal importance of American psychologist G. Stanley Hall's monumental study *Adolescence* (1904), an early and extremely comprehensive analysis of this stage of life in the terms of modern social science. In the preface to the book, Hall articulated the interest in youth that permeated Western culture at the time, asserting that adolescence was "the most fascinating of all themes, more worthy, perhaps, than anything else in the world of reverence, most inviting study, and in most crying need of a service we do not yet understand how to render aright" (xviii).

The excitement and concern that Hall expressed stemmed from his belief in the analogy between individual development and the history of civilization. Influenced by Haeckel's theory of recapitulation, he was convinced that adolescence marked a key stage in human life, a "new birth" and a period of tumultuous change that contained much more potential for future development than the "plateau" of adulthood (xiii, 50). He also understood this analogy in especially nationalized terms, seeing a clear connection between adolescence and the "youth" (relative to Europe) of his native United States. In Spain, a similar link between youth and national progress had been prevalent in the progressive intellectual community since the mid-nineteenth century, though it coexisted with anxiety about cultural belatedness. Mariano José de Larra wrote in 1836 of the need to create a "joven España" by renovating Spanish society and Spanish literature so as to solidify a new and modern national character on the level of its European neighbours (Larra 438–9). Later in the century, a series of student protests against the restriction of academic freedom in the university provided an opportunity for further reflection on youth by progressive intellectuals. The debate known as the *cuestión universitaria* arose in the 1860s as new intellectual currents – above all the philosophy of German idealist Karl Christian Friedrich Krause, introduced in Spain in the previous decade by Julián Sanz del Río – began to pose a threat to the established religious and political order. The student revolt of "La Noche de San Daniel" ("Saint Daniel's Night") in April 1865 was the first of several conflicts between young supporters of progressive reform and the reigning authorities. Through such uprisings, university students contributed to the cause that succeeded in overthrowing the monarchy with the Glorious Revolution of 1868. Though, as historian Eduardo González Calleja stresses, conservative youths were quick to organize their own protests against the liberal and republican regimes of the following six years (*Rebelión* 64–8), the idea of youth as a force for social change had acquired a central rhetorical role in liberal interpretations of the state of the Spanish nation and the direction it should take in the future.

Francisco Giner de los Ríos, a professor of law at Madrid's Universidad Central and a disciple of Sanz del Río, considered youth to be a crucial factor in the progressive transformation of Spanish society that Krausist idealism envisioned. In his 1870 essay, "La juventud y el movimiento social" ("Youth and Social Movement"), he looked back on the Glorious Revolution with mixed feelings, acknowledging the important contribution made by a new generation eager to join the fight against the old ways (209), yet also expressing disappointment that their enthusiasm seemed to have faded. The reason for this, he argued, was that young people in Spain had not been educated in a way that allowed them to pursue true reform. As Giner saw it, an inclination towards social change was innate to the spirit of youth, but at his present time only a limited number of individuals in Spain were capable of making such transformation a reality. While he affirmed that the power of the future "beat in the heart" of young people in general, he maintained that (due to the relative underdevelopment of Spain as a modern nation) only a select few ("los mejores") were capable of the discipline and dedication necessary to create change (217). By singling out this minority, Giner effectively made it more "youthful" than the rest of its generation, more faithful to the true essence of what it meant to be young and more capable of bringing about the progressive amelioration of Spanish political and intellectual life. This idea of a special, somehow *younger* youth would be central to the philosophy of education that Giner implemented when he founded the Institución Libre de Enseñanza (Free Educational Institution, ILE) in 1876, in response to renewed restrictions placed on academic freedom by the government of the restored Bourbon monarchy. As a small organization created on principles that opposed the restrictions of the political establishment, the ILE made good use of this minoritarian rhetoric to shape its mission to reform Spanish education. Many of the most prominent Spanish intellectuals of the late nineteenth and early twentieth centuries formed part of its community – among them Antonio Machado, who studied at the ILE and years later penned a poem addressed precisely to a younger youth: a "juventud más joven."

This poem, which appeared as "A una España joven" ("To a Young Spain") in the inaugural issue of the journal *España* in January 1915, provides one account of the young people of Machado's generation, men who had been "adolescentes" at the turn of the century. As Michael Predmore has argued, the poem casts a critical eye on this youth of yesterday, the youth of a failed century punctuated by the so-called "disaster" of 1898, as Machado looks ahead to a new youth of tomorrow that will achieve the regeneration of Spain his own cohort failed to produce (Predmore 26–7). Though his poem critiques the young Spaniards of the turn of the century, it also reflects the rhetorical weight that the descriptor *young* continued to gain during those years. The prevailing division in the artistic and literary circles of the late 1890s and early 1900s was between those known as the *gente joven* or *gente nueva*, and their elders, the *gente vieja*. The latter represented the literary establishment and considered themselves the curators of the tradition (Unamuno refers to them as "los tradicionalistas" in the opening pages of *En torno al casticismo*), while the former included a range of younger writers, from street-dwelling bohemians to more straight-laced intellectuals, united in their search for ways to break with the conventions of the foregoing century.[12] Titles of various periodical publications founded during these years, such as *Vida Nueva* (1898), *Revista Nueva* (1899), *Gente Vieja* (1900), *Juventud* (1901), or *Arte Joven* (1901), attest to this generational divide. While these publications and literary groups were forming, the turn of the century also brought the creation of the first political youth organizations in Spain: the first socialist youth division (founded in Bilbao in 1903); the radical republican *jóvenes bárbaros* (1904) of politician Alejandro Lerroux, also a member of the *gente nueva*; and the Carlist Batallones de Juventud (Madrid, 1902; Barcelona, 1903). Already in 1896, Unamuno had noted the propagation in various sectors of Spanish life of organizations focused on youth; though, as in *En torno al casticismo*, he doubted that what he considered to be *true* youth could be found among them: "Hay juventud carlista, conservadora ortodoxa y conservadora heterodoxa, fusionista, republicana de varios colores y colorines, meramente literaria, es decir, meramente cómica, artística, científica, erudita … toda clase de juventudes y ninguna joven" ("We have a Carlist youth, orthodox conservative and heterodox conservative youths, fusionist youths, republican youths of various colours and shades, merely literary youth, that is, merely theatrical, artistic, scientific, or erudite youths … every kind of youth imaginable, and none of them young") (*E* 3:56).

These various youth organizations frustrated Unamuno because they categorized and put labels on youth, and in so doing, placed limits on its unique freedom. For Unamuno, as for other artists of his time, youth stood for as-yet unrestricted possibility; it was imbued with an optimism that set it apart from cynical maturity, as well as a nonconformist willingness to challenge tradition and the status quo. Formalized youth organizations violated this adolescent freedom of thought and action; as John Neubauer has argued, the "sudden sprouting" of these organizations across Europe undermined the contemporary aesthetic fashioning of youth as rebellious and unconventional by forcing the individual "back into bonds" (11). Unamuno was highly sensitive to this social reality throughout the early twentieth century, criticizing the false youth of groups from the turn-of-the-century *modernistas* to the Spanish *ultraístas* and other avant-garde movements that formed during and after the First World War. For this famously idiosyncratic writer and thinker, collectivization, especially when aligned with militant rhetoric, threatened the creativity of true youth. This view likewise informed his criticism of the right-wing youth configurations that formed in the 1920s and 1930s, from Mussolini's *giovinezza* to the Juventudes de Acción Popular (JAP), the youth division of the Confederación Española de Derechas Autónomas (Spanish Confederation of Autonomous Right-Wing Groups, CEDA).

Fascist paramilitary organizations like the Opera Nazionale Balilla in Italy and the Hitler Jugend – or later, the Francoist Frente de Juventudes in Spain – represent an extreme example of ideologized youth: intellectually regimented, controlled, and altogether unlike the nonconformist youth envisioned by many modernist writers including Unamuno. But the difference between these two treatments of youth goes beyond the divide between artistic representation and social reality that Neubauer points out. They correspond to two opposing modes of social imagination: one that structures and orders social life according to an already-defined narrative; and another that disrupts and challenges the existing order, proposing novel alternatives to the course charted by convention. Paul Ricoeur aligned these two different modes of imagining reality with ideology and utopia.[13] Ideology, as a system of ideas that lends order – and, at its most pathological, dissimulates that which does not conform to the order it imposes – is at work in the early twentieth century's efforts to control and discipline youth, efforts that are often, though not always, aligned with nationalism. Unamuno was especially critical of this tendency in modern civilization, referring to it in 1900 as *ideocracia* – government by ideas. By contrast, the kind of youth he celebrates in his writing is utopian, in the sense that Ricoeur gives this term. At once critical and creative, it breaks through the hardened walls of tradition and discovers new, previously unconsidered possibilities, in realms of thought and action spanning politics, religion, and art. As early twentieth-century youth found itself stretched between the collective and the individual, between the supposed freedom and agility of adolescence and the demands of national progress – or, in a formulation Spanish pedagogue Federico de Onís offered in 1915, between "disciplina y rebeldía" ("discipline and rebellion") – Unamuno's particular poetics of youth would resonate with younger Spanish readers in various ways. For poets like José Moreno Villa and Gerardo Diego, it provided a model of the modern artist's posture before the poetic craft and the poetic tradition. Ernesto Giménez Caballero linked Unamuno's exaltation of youth to the experimentation of the literary avant-garde and ultimately to fascism, while José Bergamín saw Unamunian *poiesis* as exemplifying aesthetic and moral values that informed both his reading of the literary work of his peers and his support for the Second Republic.

It is important to note here that although in early twentieth-century European culture youth could stand for everything from heroism, duty, and strength to delinquency, subversion, or poetic genius, the rhetorical use of the term most often pertained to a restricted sector of the population. As Pierre Bourdieu pointed out later in the century by declaring that youth is "just a word" ("la jeunesse n'est qu'un mot"), a term used more to draw certain boundaries and blur others than to name any essential quality (*Questions* 143), in the space of one society multiple youths coexist whose experiences may or may not coincide. The successors of Unamuno that I examine in this book belong predominantly to the youth that the French sociologist associates with students, those whose status and educational pursuits enable them to live a quasi-ludic existence of intellectual independence and economic security (145). Heirs to the ILE's liberal tradition and beneficiaries of the educational initiatives and institutions that grew out of it (above all the Residencia de Estudiantes), they enjoyed the leisure and time for intellectual work still unavailable to many young people in the Spain of their day. At the same time, as members of the minority Giner had described in 1870, they were charged with a responsibility that had been handed down through the generations: the responsibility to create a new Spain. Luis García Montero has written of the young men of the Generation of 1927 that theirs was a youth "that could not dedicate itself solely to breaking the literary and social norms of the bourgeoisie, because first it had the obligation to consolidate the State, to fill in the holes of a lived and suffered history, to take up the legacy of its great-grandfathers, grandfathers, and fathers" (2, my translation). This obligation – a national obligation to be sure, and in many ways an obligation to a nation that did not yet exist – shaped the way these writers viewed modernity. Among the many considerations that can be brought to bear on Spanish modernism's practice of "representing distance" from the supposed centre of modernity, Europe (Geist and Monleón xviii), is an acknowledgment that Spain's marginality was perceived not only in terms of geography, but also in terms of development, as a function of under-ripeness. This developmental distance gave Spanish writers of the Silver Age space to weigh the value of "growing up" on the individual and national levels, and indeed, to critique its implications for modernity itself.

For the half of Spain's young population that was female, this distance was greater still, as contemporary conceptions of femininity effectively did not offer a female adulthood. Most women did not have the same access as their male counterparts to such "rites of passage" as higher education and the pursuit of a career, and in the eyes of the masculine cultural establishment they retained a mysterious, childlike innocence throughout life, an association strengthened by maternity and child-rearing. As Elizabeth Abel, Marianne Hirsch, and Elizabeth Langland note in the introduction to *The Voyage In: Fictions of Female Development*, "historically, only the masculine experience of separation and autonomy has been awarded the stamp of maturity" (10). They point out that, for an early twentieth-century thinker like Freud, women were incapable of achieving adulthood, destined to "remain culturally marginal, passive, dependent, and infantile" (10). As elsewhere in Europe, the patriarchal values of Spanish society reinforced such beliefs, insofar as they continued to limit twentieth-century female adulthood to the realm of the home and to the role of wife and mother. Still, there are many examples from the Spain of the 1910s and 1920s of women who challenge this model, including the students of the Residencia de Señoritas (Young Women's Residence, f. 1915) directed by María de Maeztu; female writers and artists such as Carmen de Burgos, Concha Méndez, Ernestina de Champourcín, Rosa Chacel, or Maruja Mallo; and Unamuno's own self-described "discípula," María Zambrano.

Yet it remains the case that in early twentieth-century Spain the choice between growing up and refusing to do so, accepting or rejecting the values of social autonomy aligned with adulthood, assuming authoritative maturity or subverting that authority with a vindication of youth, was by and large only available to men. As a result, while the women named above were often involved in the same aesthetic – and political – debates as their male contemporaries, rarely in their work do they thematize youth as the men can and do. This does not mean that a concern with youth is not present in their thought, but rather that it appears in areas outside their writing, or in oblique ways that only become explicit later on. For these reasons, female writers do not appear as central figures in this study – though there is much material for further research to be done on this front. Chacel's *Memorias de Leticia Valle* (*The Memoirs of Leticia Valle*, 1945), for example, is a novel of anti-formation that applies her early avant-garde distortion of narrative chronology in *Estación. Ida y vuelta* (*Station. Round-trip*, 1928) to the story of an adolescent girl in a small town and her quasi-Oedipal negotiation of relationships with adults both male and female. Chacel wrote this novel several years after the end of the Civil War, and well after the modernist moment studied here. In this sense, *Memorias de Leticia Valle* is probably best aligned with the postwar *Bildungsroman* in Spain, a genre that includes works by both men and women, and in which the novel of formation becomes a vehicle for protest against hegemonic Francoist models of development.[14] In terms of relationships with Unamuno and the reception of his work by female writers, it is impossible not to acknowledge María Zambrano's extensive engagement with his thought. The reflections on Unamuno's *oeuvre* that this philosopher penned from exile in 1940, collected and published by Mercedes Gómez Blesa in 2003, depict a writer and thinker at the height of the European thought of his time. Zambrano's involvement with the university student protests against the dictatorship of Primo de Rivera in the 1920s make her an important figure in the Spanish youth movement that I analyse in chapter 3 of this book. Still, and despite the fact that her later reflections on Antigone provide rich material for an analysis of the trials of female development informed by Unamuno's legacy,[15] in the years before the Civil War, youth appears as a concern in Zambrano's social and political activity, but not in her writing.

Insofar as both male and female Spanish writers of the early twentieth century rebelled against the values that Abel, Hirsch, and Langland refer to as "separation and autonomy," Spanish modernism's poetics of youth may also be illuminated by the insights from feminist theory that these critics bring to bear on modern literature and its treatment of development. If modernist production broadly vindicated the "young" or the "new" in opposition to old paradigms, Spanish artists' questioning of the teleological orientation towards an ideal of adulthood that was assumed to be male allowed for a reassessment of the "masculine" qualities associated with maturity. The rejection of *Bildung* and its strictures revealed the ways it was ill-fit to describe the experience of the modern individual, and that disconnect, which Hirsch calls the "lack of harmony between inner and outer life" (47), was felt by both men and women. Of course, this rejection was not uniform across the thought of all Spanish modernists. Though José-Carlos Mainer noted in his seminal study *La Edad de Plata* that youth was a "valor absoluto" ("absolute value") during the period (231), the ways in which individual artists and intellectuals in early twentieth-century Spain approached this value were diverse. Many turned to youth in an ideological mode, attempting to make it the basis of a new order closely tied to national values (fascism's exaltation of masculine youth provides the extreme example of this approach). Others, however, preferred to celebrate it as a symbol and source of utopian freedom, ever resistant to and escaping from the forces of formation, narration, and control.

Make It Young

Any discussion of youth and art in early twentieth-century Spain must make reference to José Ortega y Gasset's influential essay "La deshumanización del arte" ("The Dehumanization of Art," 1925), where Ortega uses the term "arte joven" to describe writers and works from across Europe that he sees as inaugurating a new artistic age. Announcing "el hecho indubitable de una nueva sensibilidad estética" ("the unquestionable fact of a new aesthetic sensibility") (*OCT* 3:364), the author examines the artistic consequences of a radical shift of authority from the old to the young in society at large. While in his own youth it had been common for adolescents to affect an age beyond their years, he observes, "hoy los chicos y las chicas se esfuerzan en prolongar su infancia, y los mozos en retener y subrayar su juventud" ("today boys and girls strive to prolong their childhood, and young men work to retain and accentuate their youthfulness") (384). While this statement registers the change in views of youth that manifests itself in the modernist *Bildungsroman* (Mao 10–11), Ortega's essay also reveals the proximity of the concepts of youth and novelty in modernist thought, as he uses the terms "arte joven" and "arte nuevo" interchangeably throughout the text. Indeed, the essay exemplifies how the adjective "young" functioned in early twentieth-century Spanish cultural discourse as its ubiquitous cousin "new" did in modernist production broadly: as an immensely versatile marker of difference whose lack of a precise definition made it a ready rhetorical weapon and a catch-all for developments of almost any kind.[16] From Machado's poem for "una España joven" to the 1918 manifesto of the avant-garde movement *ultraísmo* that addressed itself to any young writers whose work expressed "un anhelo nuevo" ("a new desire") to the *joven literatura* of the 1920s (whose critical reception and self-image owed much to Ortega's essay), youth was a common denominator. If critics of modernism have often (if somewhat anachronistically) invoked Ezra Pound's dictum "Make It New" as a slogan for the period, Spanish cultural production of the Silver Age might be described as consumed by a drive to "Make It Young."

Part of the attraction of youth in Silver-Age Spain was the fact that it offered an alternative to the decadence of an old world, a decadence felt throughout late nineteenth-century Europe and especially so in a country acutely aware of its own imperial decline. If accounts of Spanish backwardness originating from Protestant countries in Northern Europe and from the United States cast the Iberian country's enduring Catholicism and authoritarianism as the trappings of decay and old age throughout the nineteenth century, the loss of colonial territories culminating in 1898 seemed to confirm this account. Read against foreign attitudes like that represented by what Richard L. Kagan has called "Prescott's Paradigm," the allegorical depictions of the First and Second Spanish Republics as a young girl ("La Niña Bonita") reflect a desire to counter this reputation of age and infirmity with iconography that cast departure from monarchical rule as rejuvenation. But for some, youth also held a deeper philosophical and aesthetic appeal that extended beyond national or historiographical concerns. This understanding of artistic youth was vividly present in the cultural debates between the *gente vieja* and the *gente joven* at the turn of the century, particularly in the journal *Arte Joven*, founded a quarter century before Ortega published "La deshumanización del arte." In its inaugural issue, organizers Pablo Picasso and Francisco de Asís Soler sought to define artistic youth in such a way that it might be distinguished from biological age, and even historical period. Whereas Ortega would later assert that history alternated between "tiempos de viejos" and "tiempos de jóvenes" (*OCT* 3:149), the editors of *Arte Joven* insisted that the best art was always young. In doing so they articulated a post-romantic association of youth with the timeless value of art – what Charles Baudelaire, in his mid-nineteenth-century reflections on aesthetic modernity, had called its "eternal half." As Picasso and Soler wrote in their editorial introduction,

> Lo que tenga fuerza suficiente para resistir los embates de lo nuevo, lo que se mantenga firme e incólume, a pesar de la tormenta, no es viejo: es joven, joven siempre, joven aunque cuente mil años de existencia.
>
> Virgilio, Homero, Dante, Goette [*sic*], Velázquez, Ribera, El Greco, Mozart, Beethoven, Wagner … éstos son los jóvenes eternos, cuantos más años pasan más grandes son, crecen en vez de perecer y mientras el mundo exista existirán ellos: son los inmortales. (Picasso and Soler 2)

> (Whatever has the strength to resist the buffeting of the new, whatever stands firm and undamaged, is not old: it is young, forever young, young although it counts a thousand years of existence.
>
> Virgil, Homer, Dante, Goethe, Velázquez, Ribera, El Greco, Mozart, Beethoven, Wagner … these are the eternal youths, who grow greater with the passing years. They grow instead of perishing, and as long as the world exists they will exist: they are the immortals.)

For Picasso and Soler, the best art is intrinsically and eternally young. Though they affirm that this aesthetic youthfulness involves rupture and critique of past models, they also base their project on an ideal that, they maintain, extends throughout the ages. Unlike the concept of "arte joven" that Ortega would describe decades later, here youth is not primarily a generational category, or a term used to mark a new trend. For Picasso and Soler, it is an absolute quality that enlivens great works of art.

One of the young writers involved in the production of *Arte Joven* was the poet Bernardo G. Candamo, an admirer of Unamuno who maintained a steady correspondence with the professor in Salamanca at the turn of the century. Candamo introduced his *maestro* to the journal, and Unamuno responded favourably, sending three sonnets to be printed in its second installment – though they appeared with so many errors that they were reprinted in the following issue.[17] The simple fact that he contributed suggests that Unamuno was, or wanted to be, "young" in the sense that the editors gave the term in the inaugural issue. Moreover, his writing in one of the poems he sent, "Niñez" ("Childhood"), reflects a stance that is consonant with the publication's concept of youth. This attitude is markedly distinct from the nostalgia that pervades Machado's early poetry on youth, or that which appears in Rubén Darío's well-known refrain, "Juventud, divino tesoro, / ya te vas para no volver" ("Youth, you heavenly treasure, / you depart and will never return"). While Darío and Machado accept the passing of youth as an inevitable – if lamentable, even tragic – reality, in "Niñez" Unamuno portrays the value of early life as capable of transcending chronology.

Though the sonnet is undeniably pastoral, imagining childhood as a place of respite (and specifically as Bilbao, the site of Unamuno's own earliest years), it is not melancholic or nostalgic. This childhood, though past, is not absent, as the opening lines of the poem make clear: "Vuelvo a ti, mi niñez, como volvía / a tierra a recobrar fuerzas Anteo" ("I return to you, my childhood, as Anteus / would return to the earth to gather his strength") (Unamuno, *Poesías* 320). The memories of early life are an aid for the poet's battle in the modern world, a source of strength. He describes childhood as a guide and a wellspring of happiness ("manantial de mi alegría"), and most of all, a source of hope for the future. "Siempre que voy en ti a buscarme," he writes, "súbeme de alma a flor mi edad primera / cantándome recuerdos, agorera, / preñados de esperanzas y de consuelo" ("Whenever I go to find myself in you / the first stage of my life rises up in my soul, / singing of memories and telling the future / of remembrances filled with solace and hope"). The juxtaposition of "recuerdos" and clairvoyance in the term "agorera," used here as in the Latin *augurium* or English *augury* and without the negative valence often given to it in Spanish, reinforces the forward-looking stance of the poet. To be sure, the praise for childhood in this sonnet recalls the romantic vision illustrated in a line that Unamuno loved and quoted often, Wordsworth's "The child is the father of the man." The twentieth-century poet nevertheless converts this ideal of youthful innocence (what Wordsworth calls "natural piety") into an active mode, one that does not merely respond with wonder to the beauty of the exterior world, but generates power and fuels the poet's engagement – and struggle – with modern existence.

"Niñez" reflects a modernist shift very much present in Unamuno's thought during these years, a subversion of the hierarchical relationship between innocence and experience, youth and maturity that romanticism had mourned, but ultimately preserved. While still focusing on childhood, it realizes the passage that Stephen Burt has identified in English-language verse, from a "nineteenth-century poetics of childhood" to a "modern poetics of adolescence," from representations of innocence to an aesthetic of youthful agency (Burt 12). In this poem and throughout Unamuno's turn-of-the-century writing, categories of age based on chronology are refigured as opposing elements in dialectical tension: childhood represents the irrational aspects of existence – imagination, emotion, faith – that strive against the maturity of reason in the modern world. In this way, youth and age operate as functions of Unamuno's modernist resistance to the privileging of rational autonomy in post-Enlightenment thought. As C. Christopher Soufas has rightly pointed out, this writer's work exemplifies a critique of the "autonomous thinking subject" of the modern European philosophical tradition, a critique that is central to modernism itself (Soufas 16–17). While his philosophical works *Del sentimiento trágico de la vida* (*On the Tragic Sense of Life*, 1912) and *La agonía del cristianismo* (*The Agony of Christianity*, 1924) articulate this critique at length, it is also present in his earlier writing, and particularly in his writing of and about poetry. The struggle between the rational and the irrational that he saw as integral to post-Enlightenment experience especially informed his understanding of *poiesis*, the Greek word by which poetry stands for artistic creation writ large. Unamuno saw *poiesis* as embodying this struggle, this *agonía*, for the poetic mode uses language and reason to testify to a realm of experience that lies beyond these things. In a poem, the known and constituted gesture towards what is intuited and undefined; the (chrono)logical order of words on a page exists in tension with alternative patterns of aural resonance and achronic emotion. Taking these characteristics to be emblematic of modern art, Unamuno could consider all forms of creative activity – writing in any genre, and even civil and political action – to be poetry.[18]

For Unamuno, poetic creativity in any sphere of life was a form of rebellion against a modern world rendered prosaic. In this, his concept of *poiesis* fits the description recently offered by Anthony J. Cascardi and Leah Middlebrook, as a mode of thought and practice that exists in opposition to the Hegelian understanding of modernity as progressive "prosification" (xv). If, for Hegel, the waning of the poetic was the inevitable result of the development of civilization towards the plenitude – or maturity – of all-encompassing reason, then poetry represented an earlier, younger stage of humanity's lifespan. This resistence to the teleological pull of modernity towards reason and maturity also shaped Unamuno's view of Europe and Spain's relationship to it, a view in which he departed from Joaquín Costa and openly clashed with Ortega.[19] Although in *En torno al casticismo* he encouraged Spain's young people to look across the Pyrenees and draw inspiration from other European nations, during the decade following the initial publication of that work he increasingly questioned the unnuanced admiration for Europe as the paragon of science and development to which many of his Spanish predecessors and contemporaries ascribed. As Soufas argues, the critique of rational autonomy in Unamuno's work and that of many other Spanish writers of the Silver Age engages the aesthetic and philosophical foundations of European modernism, in a manner made possible by Spain's very marginality to the European centre. Zambrano observed this in her predecessor when she wrote that the rector of the Universidad de Salamanca "estaba de acuerdo con su tiempo en su disidencia" ("he was of his time in his dissent from it") (43). Unamuno was "of his time" in the sense that he like many other European thinkers – Henri Bergson comes especially to mind – was aware that his time was somehow out of sync: that chronology did not line up with personal and psychological development, that modernity and progress were dubious terms, and that *Bildung* in its various forms might not, in the end, be desirable.

In resisting the rationalistic model of European modernity, Unamuno challenged a teleological orientation towards a kind of civilization held up as mature, and embraced Spain's comparative "immaturity." In this regard, his stance resembles that of another "peripheral" modernist, Polish writer Witold Gombrowicz, whose novel *Ferdydurke* (1937) and later diaries (written from his exile in Argentina, a "young" country that Unamuno dreamed of visiting) deride and critique the European centre's pretensions to maturity. But Unamuno's particular modernism is not only a rejection of European adulthood. It is also a celebration of youthfulness, understood more than anything as the site of struggle between the rational and the irrational, the ongoing battle between the knowledge of experience and the hope of innocence. Through the interest in *poiesis* that deepened in him during the first years of the twentieth century, this agonic notion of youth shaped both his writing and his legacy in Spain.

Bridging the Generation Gap

How does Unamuno's turn-of-the-century understanding of youth and poetry pass into the consciousness and writing of his successors in later decades? The following chapters endeavour to answer this question by studying these later artists' work, their criticism, and their interactions with Unamuno on and off the page. It is a task that necessarily challenges traditional divisions and biases in the study of early twentieth-century Spanish literature. While many scholars have written about the (at times turbulent) relationships of the young writers of the 1920s with their mentors Juan Ramón Jiménez and José Ortega y Gasset, critics usually address Unamuno's contact with this group (if at all) in a cursory, anecdotal fashion.[20] Of course, Unamuno was older than Jiménez and Ortega, and had been a mentor – or in a Bloomian view of influence, an adversary – to both of them. His date of birth makes him seem further removed from *la joven literatura* than these more immediate predecessors. But there is more to their separation than simple chronology. The fact that so little critical attention has been paid to a possible relationship between Unamuno and these younger writers is in large part due to their belonging, not only chronologically but also historiographically, to two different generations. Over the course of the twentieth century, Unamuno increasingly came to be seen as the ideological figurehead of the Generation of 1898, while the literary production of the 1920s was identified with – and reduced to – a select group of poets involved in the events held in Góngora's honour in 1927, Ortega y Gasset's concept of dehumanized art, and an understanding of poetic purity inflected by Ortegan *deshumanización*.

While numerous Hispanists have critiqued the generational model, often pointing out that it confines Spanish literature to a narrowly national context and impedes comparative analyses, it continues to condition the ways figures within each of the "generations" are read.[21] In the decades following Unamuno's death, also those of Franco's dictatorship, both the establishment in Spain and its critics abroad cast the Generation of 1898 as representing a conservative form of Spanish nationalism founded on the memories of the country's glorious past and the existential blow dealt by the loss of its last colonial holdings to the United States. Unamuno's fate was to be converted into the leader of this group. While early accounts of the generation simply included him in their lists of members (and in at least one case, actually excluded him), later studies identified him unequivocally as its dominant figure and guide.[22] The generation that Unamuno was taken to represent was portrayed as highly nationalistic, concerned with ethical, philosophical, and spiritual questions about Spanish identity whose answers they sought in the country's imperial past. The critic Guillermo Díaz-Plaja disseminated the idea that unlike their contemporaries the *modernistas* (led by Unamuno's supposed archrival Darío),[23] the members of the Generation of 1898 were serious writers who had little interest in aesthetic frivolity and wrote primarily in prose. In the 1970s, even as scholarship moved towards more critical approaches to the Francoist mythology that supported this characterization, the characterization itself persisted, making the writers of the Generation of 1898 appear ideologically suspect.[24] A group of philosophers and prose writers with seemingly reactionary views of the nation – and Unamuno first among them – could have little to do with the group of young, innovative poets that made up the Generation of 1927.

This was exactly the sentiment expressed during the mid-twentieth century by many of the anthologists and critics of the 1927 group, which also received titles such as the "Generation of 1925," the "Generation of the Dictatorship" (that of Primo de Rivera), and the "Generation of the Republic." While Dámaso Alonso, in his 1948 essay "Una generación poética (1920–1936)," insisted that the members of his generation had not sought to break away from the older masters (Alonso 659–60), any affinity linking them to the figures of the Generation of 1898 – particularly Unamuno and Antonio Machado – would soon be denied. Critics drew on the framework provided by Ortega's "La deshumanización del arte" and the concept of poetic purity promoted by Juan Ramón Jiménez to characterize the Generation of 1927 as apolitical, playful artists far removed from the concerns of their serious and more socially conscious forebears.[25] While the younger artists undoubtedly appropriated the value of purity in poetic craft, or *poesía desnuda* (naked or denuded poetry) that Jiménez insisted on, as well as the Mallarmean notion of *poésie pure*, critics consistently paired this concept with Ortegan dehumanization, ascribing to the generation a programmatic effort to segregate art from social life that made the evident politicization of many members of the group after 1927 difficult to account for.[26] As a result, the all-too-human political and religious topics that Machado and Unamuno addressed in their writing seemed completely out of touch with the trends of the 1920s. Machado's wide recognition as a poet and his pro-Republican stance in the Civil War (along with the elegy he wrote in the wake of Federico García Lorca's death in 1936) eventually reinstated his connection to the Generation of 1927, especially as critics looked back upon the group as representative of an alternative, liberal Spain destroyed by Franco. Meanwhile, any connection between these writers and Unamuno all but disappeared.[27] The situation remains nearly the same today. As recently as 2007, in the introduction to his anthology of Spanish avant-garde poetry and the Generation of 1927, critic Andrés Soria Olmedo dedicated ample space to the influences of Jiménez and Ortega, yet mentioned Unamuno only in a passing reference to the publication of his *Ensayos* by the Residencia (*Las vanguardias* 47, 50–5).

This critical history ignores the fact that Unamuno was also a poet, and that the younger writers read and related to him as such. Several of them dedicated essays to his verse in later years, among them Luis Cernuda, who identified him as "el mayor poeta que España ha tenido en lo que va de siglo" ("the best poet Spain has had in this century") (*Prosa* 350). As noted earlier, many of them familiarized themselves with Unamuno's thought by reading the short essays collected by the Residencia beginning in 1916. Nevertheless, essays like these and Unamuno's poetry in general continue to be among the less-studied areas of his work.[28] One consequence of this neglect is that critics have overlooked the central importance of youth in these texts, the tie between youth and poetry that Unamuno articulates in his essays, and the fact that many of his writings from the turn of the century are addressed to young people.

Another factor that may explain the gap in scholarship surrounding Unamuno and the writers of the so-called Generation of 1927 is the fact that Unamuno was not in Spain, physically, at the time when this group of writers reached its heyday. His denunciation of Primo de Rivera's dictatorship forced him into exile in 1924, and after a short time on the island of Fuerteventura (and despite receiving a pardon),

Unamuno chose to continue his expatriation in France: first in Paris and ultimately in the Basque village of Hendaye, where he remained until the dictatorship fell in 1930. Though, as the letters of José Bergamín, Gerardo Diego, and others demonstrate, Unamuno was not absent from the minds of the younger writers, neither was he present among them, as others like Ortega and Jiménez were. Futhermore, his refusal to subject his writing to the dictator's censorship meant that his voice was not as prominent in the Spanish press as it once had been (though he continued to publish in France and Latin America, and collaborated in clandestine publications like *Hojas Libres*, edited by Eduardo Ortega y Gasset, brother of José). In addition to the physical distance imposed by exile, the zealous political stance that informed Unamuno's expatriation and his impatience with "purist" or apolitical aesthetics back home – as demonstrated by his tirade in *Cómo se hace una novela* – have been seen to distance him from the group then known as *la joven literatura.*

The members of *la joven literatura* themselves, however, had always considered the rector of the Universidad de Salamanca to be one of their poetic predecessors. Gerardo Diego indicated as much when he chose twenty-three of Unamuno's poems to open the first edition of his highly selective but trans-generational *Poesía española. Antología, 1915–1931* (1932). In his introduction to the anthology, Diego acknowledges the existence of stylistic "abismos" between the poets included, and not only between writers of different generations like Unamuno and Jorge Guillén, but even between those of more-or-less the same age. Still, he insists on the presence of "una idealidad común" ("a common ideal") that unites them (*Poesía española* 10). This shared ideal remains undefined in Diego's anthology, though he implies that the affinity is of an aesthetic nature. In "Una generación poética," Dámaso Alonso accounts for the same bond in another way, which might complement Diego's view. This member of *la joven literatura* grounds the affinity in historical coincidence, comparing the literature of the early twentieth century to that of the so-called Spanish Golden Age: "Hay que ir al Siglo de Oro, y precisamente allá por los años 1580 y tantos, cuando fray Luis y San Juan de la Cruz viven aún y Góngora y Lope son jóvenes … para encontrar algo semejante a la confluencia de generaciones poéticas en la que hemos vivido" ("One has to look to the Golden Age, particularly to the 1580s, when Fray Luis and Saint John of the Cross are still alive and Góngora and Lope are young … to find something like the confluence of poetic generations that we have lived through") (Alonso 675). Such a comparison, contrived as it may be, illustrates Alonso's conception of the various generations of writers of the Spanish Silver Age as living within a shared historical moment, merely seen from different vantage points. Indeed, in different ways they all bore witness to the nation's burgeoning and halting modernization at the beginning of a new century. Moreover, they all lived during a time when an increasing social and cultural awareness of the gap between the old and the young was endowing youth with new cultural capital and artistic value. Paradoxically, it was this generation gap that joined them.

This book seeks to examine the aesthetic and historical origins of the perennial youth that Manuel Altolaguirre attributed to "Don Miguel," and to demonstrate how in Unamuno's own lifetime, younger artists were able to reap the fruit of the vision he had sown at the outset of the century. In the first chapter, I take a close look at the formation of this Unamunian concept of youth during the twelve years following the initial publication of *En torno al casticismo* in 1895. I argue that during this time Unamuno's work undergoes a movement towards poetry and the poetic mode as the means of expression most consonant with his thought about and interest in what it means to be truly young. The year 1904 is an important and symbolic turning point in this process, as Unamuno's fortieth birthday both marks the temporal end of his own youth and serves as a catalyst for him to expand on the topic in his writings. Well before that date, however, youth had appeared frequently in his writing as the antidote to the rigid structures of an aged society, the force that might dismantle such structures and rearrange the constituent elements of Spanish society in order to renew it. Reading many of the essays later collected in the Residencia's edition of the *Ensayos*, I identify three main facets of youth in Unamuno's turn-of-the-century thought: the religious, wherein youth is tied to the pre-dogmatic early Christian church and becomes representative of the dynamic relationship between belief and doubt that he sees as the condition of true faith; the political, where the writer, while viewing most political parties with scepticism, associates youth with (his own understanding of) socialism, opposing it to the senility of the political and economic policies of the Bourbon Restoration; and finally, the properly poetic, where youth stands for the independence of the poet from aesthetic schools or trends – accompanied, however, by an ability to dialogue with and ultimately transform the poetic tradition. The publication of *Poesías* in 1907 marks the "coming of age" of Unamuno's own poetics of youth.

Unamuno's emergence as a poet and the appearance of his first book of verse came at a time when his stature as an intellectual figure was growing in Spain, making him a much sought-after speaker and, indeed, drawing the attention of many young minds. In 1906 he had his first encounter with Alberto Jiménez Fraud and José Moreno Villa, two men who would go on to shape the culture of the Residencia de Estudiantes (Jiménez Fraud as its director, Moreno Villa as a resident tutor during a span of twenty years). In chapter 2, I analyse the fashioning of Spanish youth by the Residencia during its first decade – years in which the First World War had a great impact on the idea of heroic youth throughout Europe – and in the particular case of Moreno Villa's poetry. The publication of Unamuno's *Ensayos* by the Residencia during this decade provides an important channel through which the writer's early ideas on youth reach the readers of a new postwar generation, while Moreno Villa's personal interactions with those texts and with Unamuno himself find echoes in his own writing, which takes creative inspiration from the experience of adolescence. The idealization of youth in Moreno Villa's poetry and at the Residencia, however, separates youth and art from politics, curiously replicating Spain's neutrality in the European conflict.

In chapter 3, I trace the appropriation and development of the concept of "juventud" in the art of the 1920s by writers who self-consciously participated in the fashioning of *la joven literatura*. Foremost among these is Gerardo Diego, orchestrator of the 1927 commemoration of the tercentenary of Luis de Góngora's death, and editor of *Antología. Poesía española, 1915–1931*, which provided an influential roster of "la joven poesía" and its immediate predecessors. As a critic himself, Diego paid careful attention to Unamuno's evolving poetic production during these years, and while more approving of his predecessor's later poetry than his early verse, in his own poetry he draws especially on the "humanity" of Unamuno's writing, out of vogue as that was assumed to be in the 1920s. Through Diego, the view of youthfulness as a necessary characteristic in modern poetry becomes a fundamental element (and a point of contention) in the representation of the Góngora celebrations of 1927, and in the consolidation of *la joven literatura* in that year. Youth as a trope in these writers' editing of journals (like *Verso y Prosa: Boletín de la Joven Literatura*), in their own poetry, and in their criticism is central to a modernist reconfiguration of the Spanish poetic tradition that responds to the vision put forth by Unamuno in the early years of the century. At the same time, the exiled Unamuno's prominence as a key figure for student protests of Primo de Rivera's dictatorship challenged the young poets of the period to think more deeply about the relationship between their "young" art and politics.

The fourth and final chapter of this book deals with developments in the aesthetic discourse of youth as art becomes politicized in the Spain of the final years of Primo de Rivera's dictatorship and the inauguration of the Second Republic. Here I focus on two writers, Ernesto Giménez Caballero and José Bergamín, who both share an ardent and vocal admiration for Unamuno but differ radically in their political views. Giménez Caballero represents a right-wing interpretation of youth rooted in an ultranationalist reading of *En torno al casticismo*. The concept of *juventud* that he promoted first as part of the Spanish avant-garde, with a series of articles and surveys in *La Gaceta Literaria*, and later in fascist works like *Genio de España* (*Genius of Spain*, 1932), is militant, responding directly to Unamuno's turn-of-the-century call for a revolutionary new youth, yet departing from his predecessor as it espouses an increasingly rigid ideological and political program. By contrast, Bergamín, who would later serve as president of the Alianza de Intelectuales Antifascistas (Alliance of Anti-Fascist Intellectuals) during the Spanish Civil War, develops his predecessor's thought by tying art to an eternal youth that comes to recall Unamunian *intrahistoria*: a tradition that both transcends and underlies chronological time. Ultimately, Bergamín attempts to preserve the nonconformist, utopian vision present in Unamuno's thought by moving away from the language of youth. He incorporates the youthful aesthetics cultivated in the 1920s into leftist political positions in the 1930s, editing the idiosyncratic-yet-influential journal *Cruz y Raya*. For Bergamín, Unamuno represents the paradoxical combination of creative, poetic youth with the resilient maturity of political resistance.

With the sobering reality of the outbreak of the Civil War, Unamuno is also a figure that accompanies Bergamín, Moreno Villa, Altolaguirre, and many of their colleagues into exile – a kind of marginalization that, while retaining something of the adolescent's rebellion, brings the youth of Spanish modernism to a close. Yet these writers, as they seek out a means of poetic survival in the diaspora, also allow for what Altolaguirre referred to as "supervivencia": the stage that a writer passes into "cuando deja de ser joven" ("when he ceases to be young")

(Altolaguirre 88). In the conclusion of this book, I briefly point out the ways that the members of *la joven literatura* continued Unamuno's own legacy of exile, and suggest how a critical approach that places tropes of youth and age at the centre of its analysis can reshape our understanding, not only of Unamuno, but also of the literature of the Spanish Silver Age in general. Indeed, a re-examination of this period, when Spanish artists wrestled with and celebrated notions of immaturity and adolescence, reveals how vital both Unamuno and Spain are to any discussion of modernism and youth.

Chapter One

Unamuno's Poetics of Youth, 1895–1907

Over the last several decades, the work of numerous scholars has created a rich picture of Miguel de Unamuno as a writer and a public figure in early twentieth-century Spain. While Unamuno has long been best known as the author of novels like *Niebla* (*Mist*, 1914) and philosophical treatises like *Del sentimiento trágico de la vida*, the diversity of his work in a range of literary genres is now well acknowledged. The publication of a great deal of the writer's vast correspondence as well as several collections of his contributions to newspapers and periodicals throughout his life has filled out this picture. Moreover, the discoveries of several previously unpublished and unknown manuscripts have recontextualized his published works and illuminated the development of his thought in new ways. Within the body of research spurred by these publications and discoveries, two areas are of particular interest for the present study. The first is the recovery of the figure critics have called "el joven Unamuno": the Unamuno who was a student at Madrid's Universidad Central in the 1880s and a young professor at the Universidad de Salamanca in the 1890s, an incipient novelist and poet, and a voracious reader of philosophy whose political affiliations migrated from Basque nationalism to an idiosyncratic socialism as he himself moved physically from his hometown of Bilbao to a career in Castile. What is known today of this young Unamuno is thanks to the work of scholars including Laureano Robles, Jean-Claude Rabaté, Adolfo Sotelo Vázquez, Paolo Tanganelli, Bénédicte Vauthier, and the contributors to the volume *El joven Unamuno en su época* edited by Theodor Berchem and Hugo Laitenberger. The second area of research comprises new readings of and approaches to Unamuno's poetry. In some of the most recent of these contributions, Javier Blasco, María Pilar Celma, and Ramón González have underscored the modernist poetics that Unamuno shared with his European contemporaries and with Hispanic *modernistas*, while Ana Urrutia Jordana has elucidated the intimate connection between poetics and politics in Unamuno's thought, particularly during his exile in the 1920s. The developments in these two fields of investigation have shown that the common conception of Unamuno as a novelist and philosopher, which bases itself primarily on prose works he wrote in middle age or later, is incomplete when divorced from the author's poetic production, and from the formative intellectual period of Unamuno's youth.

In this chapter I push these observations further, to argue that poetry and youth are not only necessary parts of a complete picture of Unamuno and his work, but that they are fundamental to what makes Unamuno a vital figure within European modernism, and an influential shaper of modernist thought in Spain. Youth and poetry are in fact closely interrelated in his work. Focusing on a period that overlaps with and follows that of "el joven Unamuno," I contend that these two concepts form the crux of a transition in Unamuno's life and work that coincides chronologically with the turn of the century and with his own passage into middle age. This confluence constitutes the basis of multiple, unequivocally modernist aspects of the writer's thought: his critique of rational autonomy, his questioning of historical time and of progress, and his call for radical reinterpretation of tradition in both artistic and social realms. Unamuno's intellectual trajectory in the last decade of the nineteenth century and the first decade of the twentieth has often been understood as hinging on the personal crisis he underwent in the spring of 1897. This crisis has been interpreted either as his last, unsuccessful attempt to regain the Catholic faith of his childhood, or as the definitive trading of a rationalist philosophical stance for one of irrationalism. While I do not disagree altogether with either of these characterizations, I follow critics like Francisco Arias Santos and Jean-Claude Rabaté in finding the stark division of Unamuno's life and work into pre- and post-crisis positions inadequate to describe changes that in fact took place over several years, and misleading in that it de-emphasizes the continuities in the writer's work during this period. One of the most striking of these continuities, I maintain, is the concern with youth, consistently present in his writing from the first publication of the essays of *En torno al casticismo* in 1895 through to the appearance of his first book of poetry, *Poesías*, in 1907.

Critics of Unamuno's poetry often comment that he discovered the genre late in life, and it is true that when *Poesías* appeared, Unamuno did not consider himself young in a chronological sense. Forty-three years old at the time, in the first poem of the collection he referred to his lyrical compositions as "flores de otoño" ("flowers of autumn"). In fact, in terms of a boundary that he himself had drawn repeatedly in the foregoing years, his fortieth birthday had marked the end of his youth. Already in 1900 he was anticipating this dreaded milestone, writing to Bernardo Candamo in December of that year, "Acabo de cumplir treinta y seis, de aquí a cuatro llegaré a los cuarenta, en que con la perfecta madurez empieza la oscilación espiritual, a esos cuarenta del dogmatismo cerrado. ¡Quiera Dios que mi frecuente trato con jóvenes, los estudiantes, y el tener que vivir con ellos, de ellos y para ellos, me preserve de esa oscilación terrible!" ("I just turned thirty six, four years from now I will arrive at forty, the time when along with perfect maturity comes spiritual wavering, at the forty years that mark the onset of dogmatism. May God grant that my frequent interaction with young people, the students, and my having to live with, by, and for them, keep me from that terrible wavering!") (Blázquez González 315). If forty could be considered the age at which one reaches full maturity, for Unamuno this arrival did not bring sound judgment and wisdom, but rather moral weakness and intellectual laziness, a reliance upon principles that have been systematized and locked in place.

The approach of forty and its attendant "dogmatismo cerrado" became something of an obsession for the rector of the Universidad de Salamanca in the first years of the century.[1] His conviction that spiritual feebleness and narrow-mindedness are unavoidable characteristics of age also appears, if in less personal terms than in his correspondence, in the essay "Viejos y jóvenes (Prologómenos)" ("The Old and the Young [Preliminary Thoughts]") from 1902. In this text Unamuno argues that men between the ages of forty and sixty who occupy positions of authority – "el político A" and "el literato B" are the hypothetical examples he gives – are those least likely to perceive the potential of the young. He insists categorically that the old, no matter how insightful or well-meaning, "no saben lo que quieren los jóvenes ni pueden entenderlos" ("do not know what young people want nor can they understand them") (*E* 4:49). But in stating this he faces a problem: what will happen to him when he must count himself among the old? This worry seems to have been the driving force behind the composition of his unfinished essay "Mi confesión" ("My Confession"), uncovered and published by Alicia Villar Ezcurra in 2011. Intended as the introduction to a book to be titled *A la juventud hispana* (*To Hispanic Youth*), the text opens with a dedication to "los jóvenes de los pueblos todos de lengua española siempre que sean de veras jóvenes" ("the young people of all Spanish-speaking communities, as long as they are truly young") (*Mi confesión* 13).[2] There, after addressing this select audience characterized by "true" youth, the author expresses his fear that he will soon cease to possess this attribute: "temo dejar de serlo y antes de que esta desgracia me sobrevenga, quiero hacer un alto en mi carrera, recoger y entrojar en estas páginas los pensamientos que he ido echando en escritos de ocasión" ("I fear I will soon cease to be so, and before that disgrace befalls me, I want to pause in my journey, gather the thoughts I have been putting forth in occasional writings, and store them in these pages") (13).

This reiterated anxiety about turning forty suggests that a resistance to aging and maturity is as central to the thought of the turn-of-the-century Unamuno as his fear of death and desire for immortality – undoubtedly related concerns that have been underscored time and again in analyses of this period in his life. Critics have frequently turned to the "joven Unamuno" of the 1890s in attempts to understand these philosophical or theological preoccupations, usually focusing on his religious doubts and the crisis of 1897. But they have not sufficiently recognized how crucial the concept of youth itself was to this seminal period in the writer's career, precisely because it offered an alternative to the linear conception of time and human development that led inexorably to death. At the turn of the century, as Unamuno's efforts to dismantle certain hegemonic historical narratives led to a broader questioning of narrative form, his writing repeatedly expressed a resistance to maturity and age, understood as finality, immobility, and the absence of creativity. His analysis and re-interpretation of Spanish history in *En torno al casticismo* attempted to subvert an account of the nation's past that had culminated in cultural stagnation and decadence, while the series of novels or *nivolas* that he composed between 1895 and 1907 spurned the even progression and tidy closure of the nineteenth-century narrative of formation in favour of self-conscious narratives whose protagonists fail or refuse to grow up. Underlying all of his work at this time is a resistance to dominant narratives in philosophy that framed the history of civilization as a process of maturation from pre-rational superstition to enlightened, autonomous rationality. Rejecting the teleological historical vision of German idealism, and particularly the Hegelian account of history as progressive rationalization and prosification, Unamuno chose to vindicate the poetic – an in-between, adolescent state where reason and the irrational coexist in dynamic, productive tension. As he began to compose actual poems, lyrical texts in which narrative momentum is offset and subverted by rhyme and aural structure, this form of creative youthfulness became the paradigm that structured his thinking not only about the relationship between reason and faith, but also about Spanish politics and nationhood, and the writing of poetry itself. In this way Unamuno's aversion to the idea of growing old reflects a deeply modernist questioning of the teleology of modernization, and a search for novelty and regeneration that values artistic creation – *poiesis* – for its ability to disrupt and transcend chronological time.

En torno al casticismo and the "Soul-Nation" Allegory

Though he was in his thirties by the mid-1890s, there is an adolescent character to the Unamuno of the turn of the century, whose career, thought, and work began to branch out into new areas in these years. This time in the writer's life in some ways recalls the "new birth" that G. Stanley Hall described in *Adolescence* – not in the sense of a decisive change or conversion with which some critics have been wont to describe Unamuno's 1897 crisis, but in that it was a period of discovery and expansion. Unamuno's thinking in these years led him to embrace a paradigm of continual movement, of rupture and recombination, critique and creativity that he associated on numerous occasions with both youth and poetry. This paradigm would inform his later work and constitute an important part of his thought and the legacy he left to subsequent generations. And yet, understanding this "poetics of youth" in the early Unamuno requires an analysis of his turn-of-the-century writing on its own terms – apart, especially, from the notion of the Generation of 1898 and the critical framework that was imposed on it retrospectively.

It is fitting, then, to begin by reflecting on *En torno al casticismo*, a work usually considered to be a cornerstone of the ideas of the Generation of 1898, despite the fact that these essays were originally written three years before that date, and make no direct reference to the political situation in Cuba that would lead to the Spanish-Cuban-American War. Though in this work Unamuno does acknowledge the global sphere of empire and its role in the constitution of the Spanish nation, he chooses to focus predominantly on the history of that nation's development within the local context of the Iberian Peninsula. In fact, his analysis limits itself to one region – Castile – that is of interest to him because of its role in the creation of the modern State. In the essayist's reading of Spanish history, Castile was both responsible for the unification of the Peninsula and also the origin of traditions, social doctrines, and disciplinarian order that he consistently identifies throughout the work as old: "la vieja idea castellana," ("the old Castilian idea"), "vieja cepa castellana" ("old Castilian stock"), "la vieja *morgue castillane*" ("old Castilian arrogance"). Against the age of this Castilian social order, Unamuno contrasts a youthfulness that may be glimpsed fleetingly in Spanish history, but that, he argues, has largely been suppressed and has faded over time, to the point that youth seems to be absent from modern Spanish society.

Indeed, if one traces the historical and narrative thread of Unamuno's analysis through the five essays of *En torno al casticismo*, they appear together not only as a history of the Spanish nation, but as the story of Spain's aging. Unamuno begins to tell this story by decrying the decadence that dominates Spanish society in the late nineteenth century. In the opening essay, "La tradición eterna" ("The Eternal Tradition"), he launches a stinging attack on cultural conservatives and so-called "traditionalists," members of the dominant intellectual class of the day whom he characterizes as old: "Abominan del presente con el espíritu senil de todos los *laudatores temporis acti*; sólo sienten lo que les hiere, y como los viejos, culpan al mundo de sus achaques … la dócil sombra del pasado la adaptan a su mente, siendo incapaces de adaptar ésta al presente vivo" ("They reject the present with the senile spirit of all *laudatores temporis acti*; they only feel what cuts them, and like old men, blame the world for their discomfort … they adapt the helpless shadow of the past to their minds, incapable of adapting their minds to the living present") (*E* 1:50). Against this senile, nostalgic, dogmatic traditionalism and its account of Spanish history, Unamuno pledges to focus on what he calls *intrahistoria*, the unofficial, unrecorded history embodied not in the stories of wars, politicians, and kings, but in the quiet lives of the rural agrarian class. As several critics have noted, through this concept of *intrahistoria* the author of *En torno al casticismo* imagines something akin to the romantic *Volksgeist*, the spiritual link between people and land that naturalized the nineteenth-century process of nation building.[3] In Unamuno's account, however, the history of this bond is cast not as a reassuring narrative of formation, but as an undesirable aging. Rather than simply offering a comforting story of national origins for a country mourning its imperial losses, Unamuno's line of argument sets out to critique a process of aging that he sees as defining the history of Spain and producing the *casticismo* of his present day.

As it rereads Spanish history and its account of national development, *En torno al casticismo* anticipates the early twentieth-century "crisis of historiography" that C.A. Longhurst has aligned with a modernist aesthetics of the novel throughout Europe and in Spain (Longhurst 50–5). In these 1895 essays, Unamuno draws on modernity's analogy between the lifespan of an individual and the development of a civilization, invoking a connection between personal time and national time that provided the basic structure for the *Bildungsroman* in the nineteenth century. Yet the way he employs this trope departs significantly from nineteenth-century conventions. In a recent study of the coming-of-age tale in British novels of the early twentieth century, Jed Esty has referred to this link between the individual and the national as the "soul-nation allegory." Drawing on Mikhail Bakhtin's theory of the *Bildungsroman* as unfolding in "national-historical time," Esty argues that this allegory breaks down in modernist works of the British Age of Empire because "relatively stable temporal frames of national destiny gave way to a more conspicuously global, and therefore more uncertain, frame of social reference" (6). Though *En torno al casticismo* is not a novel, this crisis of national-historical time is also apparent in Unamuno's text. There, however, the crisis is not caused by an expansion of empire and the hegemony of unlimited, open-ended capitalist time, but rather by the contraction of empire and a critique of the national framework as a product itself of capitalism. Rather than questioning narrative structure as a result of an encounter with time and space beyond the nation, these essays actively seek to undermine a national narrative built upon imperial expansion, a narrative based on a rigid set of doctrines and orders that Unamuno sees as having accelerated the nation's aging and all but stamped out its youth.

The second through fifth essays of *En torno al casticismo* trace the history of this aging, from the late fifteenth century to Unamuno's present. In the second essay, the author considers how the civilizations of the Iberian Peninsula passed through the puberty ("pubertad") of their configuration as a modern nation with its centre in Castile (*E* 1:67). In the essayist's account, the "forja de las grandes nacionalidades" ("forging of the great nationalities") (67) is a process that European civilizations underwent in the transition from the Middle Ages to the early modern era, and it resembles puberty because it results in the physical – if not necessarily spiritual – adulthood of the body politic. In the third and fourth essays, Unamuno depicts the early detrimental effects of the adulthood of the nation on a potentially youthful Spanish culture. He describes the writers of sixteenth- and seventeenth-century Castile as constrained by the limitations of an inquisitorial and imperialist regime, pointing especially to the mystical writers Teresa de Ávila, San Juan de la Cruz, and Fray Luis de León as repressed and angst-filled, oppressed by the weight of their society, which forced them to become highly introspective, like insecure teenagers too timid to venture out into the world. (By way of contrast, Unamuno cites the earlier example of Francis of Assisi in Italy, freely travelling the "juvenil campiña" ["youthful countryside"] as he carries out a mission primarily of social works, not internalized reflection [164].) Though passionate and often valiant, these religious writers from Spain – all of them poets, two predominantly so – are limited by their own "inquisición inmanente" ("immanent Inquisition") (162), the disciplinarian control that they instinctively impose on themselves in a reflection of the external control of the Spanish Church. Even Fray Luis, whose humanism Unamuno portrays as vibrant and rebellious, full of subversive potential, is in the end too oppressed by the atmosphere of his time to counter the forces of discipline and intellectual control, the ever-aging religious and political structures that dominate his society.

In the last essay, "El marasmo actual de España" ("Spain's Current Stagnation"), Unamuno reflects on how the country has ultimately arrived at a complacent, lifeless senescence by the end of the nineteenth century. He complains of a spiritual aridity that grips his country: "No hay frescura ni espontaneidad, no hay juventud" ("There is no freshness nor spontaneity, there is no youth") (197–8). While in other parts of Europe young people are forming groups and editing publications, he finds no such equivalent in Spain. All life seems to be dominated by the "vieja idea castellana castiza" ("the old traditionalist Castilian idea") (1:74). Given the intensity of Unamuno's critique of this cultural senility and stagnation, it comes as no surprise that he concludes with a call for a youth that would break the restricting mesh of Spanish traditionalism, embrace new influences from elsewhere in Europe, and vindicate a part of the nation's identity that had been suppressed throughout the centuries, buried and devalued as modernity plodded on and grew ever older:

> ¡Ojalá una verdadera juventud, animosa y libre, rompiendo la malla que nos ahoga y la monotonía uniforme en que estamos alineados, se vuelva con amor a estudiar el pueblo que nos sustenta a todos, y abriendo el pecho y los ojos a las corrientes todas ultrapirenaicas ... avive con la ducha reconfortante de los jóvenes ideales cosmopolitas el espíritu colectivo intracastizo que duerme esperando un redentor! (*E* 1:218–19)
>
> (May a true youth, brave and free, breaking the net of mesh that stifles us and the uniform monotony in which we are regimented, turn lovingly to study the populace that supports us all, and opening its lungs and its eyes to all types of currents from beyond the Pyrenees ... revive with the soothing shower of ideal, cosmopolitan young people the truly pure, collective spirit that slumbers awaiting its redeemer!)

This closing invocation of youth posits that it is possible to break away from the soul-nation allegory, to subvert the linear progression of historical time and the aging of modernity (and Spain), and to create new understandings of the Spanish people, their past, and their relationship to Europe. If influenced by thinkers like Herder and Taine, *En torno al casticismo* is more than a post-romantic or even a naturalist account of a national spirit. It is a modernist call for a radical reinterpretation of tradition, a questioning of the narrow historical narrative preserved and perpetuated by the *casticista* establishment, and a reconfiguration of Spanishness. The explicit critique of received history and the implicit critique of linear narration that appear in these essays from 1895 were foundational for Unamuno's subsequent writing of both nonfiction and fiction. Indeed, they found a particularly aesthetic expression in his engagement and experimentation with the genre of the novel.[4]

The (Anti-)Development of the *Nivola* and the Turn to Poetry

In May of 1895, while the first essays of *En torno al casticismo* were appearing in *La España Moderna*, Unamuno wrote his first letter to Leopoldo Alas (Clarín), one of the foremost literary authorities of the day. As Unamuno insinuates at the end of the letter, it was intended as a way to ingratiate himself with Clarín in hopes of gaining some attention from the powerful older writer.[5] Nonetheless, this first correspondence is charged with generational conflict, not least because the pretext Unamuno uses to write the letter is to correct the definition of the word *adolescente* that Clarín had given in a review published earlier that spring. In a move inevitably conditioned by the tensions between *gente joven* and *gente vieja* that dominated Spanish cultural discourse at the time, Unamuno jumps at the chance to clarify the proper definition of the term. In his review, Clarín had attempted to relate the word to the Castilian verb *adolecer* (to suffer), but in his letter Unamuno makes use of his linguistic knowledge to point out that the two terms are not actually etymologically related. He tells Clarín that, instead of a time of painful trial, adolescence should be understood as a period of possibility and growth. Citing the Latin, he writes, "*ad-olescere* es crecer, aumentar, desarrollarse, cobrar vigor. Y su subfijo *-escere* más bien que frecuentativo debe decirse que es incoativo como *arborescere*, empezar a hacerse árbol, ir haciéndose árbol" ("*ad-olescere* means to grow, to become larger, to develop, to gain strength. And the suffix *-escere* is not frecuentative but rather inchoative, as in *arborescere*, to begin to turn into a tree, to start to become a tree") (Alas, *Epistolario* 46). Adolescence is the period in which the self begins to put down roots, and extend its branches. Moreover, Unamuno insists, the term describes someone who "se halla *en la edad de la energía*, en el vigor potencial que se despliega, de los catorce a los veintitrés años" ("finds himself *at the energetic age*, in the midst of the vigorous potential that unfolds between fourteen and twenty-three") (47, original emphasis). This is a much more positive view of adolescence than the one Clarín had given, and Unamuno clearly appears here as an advocate for the young.

Although Clarín's letters to Unamuno have not been preserved, it is evident from Unamuno's next letter to him that the older writer responded right away. On May 31 Unamuno writes with enthusiasm and thanks Clarín for his comments, but also stands firm and continues to push the debate about *adolescencia*. It seems that Clarín had cited, as a counter example to Unamuno's theory, the fact that some Roman writers had used the word to refer to men in their thirties or even older. Unamuno replies that these writers were not referring to an actual age in years, but rather to the vitality and continued growth of these older men (Alas 50). This distinction between biological and spiritual age was something Unamuno was likely thinking about quite a bit at the time, as he worked on a new project that he describes in his letter: a story about a young man arriving in the big city, Madrid, and questioning his deeply-held childhood faith. From Unamuno's description, the story sounds very much like a coming-of-age tale. He writes to Clarín that its young protagonist

> va al mundo, choca con uno y con otro, tiene que luchar y lucha y sus energías y sentimientos morales van desfalleciendo, y siente cansancio y que el mundo le devora el alma. Entra un día en una iglesia a oír misa y el recinto, las luces, los niños junto a él ... el ambiente todo, le trasporta a sus años de sencillez, le saca de las honduras del alma estados de conciencia enterrados en su subconciencia, le vuelve a una edad pasada, le evoca por asociación un mundo de pureza *adolescente*. (54)
>
> (goes out into the world, has brushes with this person and that, has to fight and does fight and his energy and moral sentiment begin to wane, and he feels tired and that the world is devouring his soul. One day he goes into a church to hear the mass, and the space, the lights, the children next to him ... the whole atmosphere transports him to a simpler time, it brings up from the depths of his soul states of mind that had been buried in his subconscious, it returns him to a past age, it evokes by association a world of *adolescent* purity.)

The italicization of *adolescente* refers back to the earlier discussion, and indicates that Unamuno uses it with his own meaning in mind: this adolescence signifies potential, energy, and vigor. His association of this adolescent state with purity is somewhat unexpected, for childhood is usually the life stage considered most "pure" and least sullied by exposure to the world. Unamuno's usage suggests that this purity is not innocence, but rather a superior moral condition; a spiritual purity not necessarily linked to a particular stage of life, yet seemingly only accessible to those who have passed beyond childhood.

The project that Unamuno describes in his letter to Clarín is *Nuevo mundo*, a novel manuscript that he composed between 1895 and 1896 but never attempted to publish. Although it did not appear in print during the writer's lifetime, the work displays many of the characteristics that would define his later *nivolas* – most notably the presence of a multilayered narrative frame that destabilizes the relationship between author and character, and the inclusion of paratexts that further undermine the integrity of the story told in the main text. Still, at least in its first sections, the story outlined in the manuscript does appear to take the form of a traditional *Bildungsroman*. It tells the story of Eugenio Rodero, a young man who travels from his childhood home in the country to the capital in order to attend university. In the city, Rodero experiences several rites of passage: the loneliness of modern urban alienation, a sexual initiation of sorts through a brief relationship with the maid at his boarding house, and the crisis of faith that Unamuno mentions in his letter to Clarín. There are many clear similarities between Eugenio's experience and Unamuno's own time as a student in Madrid. However, these parallels come to an end with the scene in which Eugenio visits a church and finally has the spiritual breakthrough that brings him to the "mundo de pureza *adolescente*" that Unamuno describes in his letter. This is the "nuevo mundo" of the work's title.

As I have argued elsewhere, at this point *Nuevo mundo* breaks completely with the *Bildungsroman* model, and Eugenio's aging process seems to cede to a state of perpetual adolescence (Harkema 47). His life now ceases to follow the standard course of a bourgeois entrance into adulthood (and the course of Unamuno's biography), with its passage from home to school to workplace. Deserting all sense of a planned course of action, Eugenio leaves his job and travels to Argentina, spends some time there and falls in (and then out of) love, and eventually returns to Spain and gets involved in the publication of a literary journal. The peregrinations of this part of the story, which as it progresses seems increasingly more like a working draft than a finished novel, anticipate the meandering style of the final section of the text, where the narrator inserts a rambling essay by Rodero in lieu of a traditional conclusion. Instead of what Rodero refers to in his essay as "la condenada letra autoritaria, el viejo y tradicional texto" ("the authoritarian letter, the old and traditional text") (69), the reader is given the protagonist's own voice. By way of introduction to the closing essay, the narrator intervenes to affirm the value of this voice, and to explain that he has decided not to impose his own criteria upon it by editing Eugenio's text:

> Pensé un momento aprovechar el siguiente ensayo de Eugenio Rodero para un trabajo coherente y justificado, reduciéndolo a la lengua y el pensamiento comunes, traduciéndolo a la lógica social, pero deseché al punto tal tentación, impiadosa hacia mi pobre amigo. Dar coherencia a su ensayo era quitarle vida, era destruir la libre marcha de su asociación de ideas, era restituir lo sugestivo con lo instructivo. (64)

> (For a moment I thought I would turn the following essay by Eugenio Rodero into a coherent and justified work, reducing it to common language and thought, translating it to social logic, but I quickly discarded such a temptation, so impious toward my poor friend. To give coherence to his essay was to take away its life, to destroy the free flow of its association of ideas, to exchange suggestion for instruction.)

With this statement, it becomes clear that Unamuno's interest is not in telling the linear story of Eugenio's life, but in the unique nature of his character – his indefinitely prolonged adolescence. In addition, the writer is concerned with the ethical dimension of his own role, as author, in representing his protagonist. Creating a "coherent" version of Eugenio's text would be a betrayal of the youthful spirit that infuses his thought, a spirit characterized especially by its freedom and its refusal to adhere to "social logic." Imposing narrative structure would mean, among other things, privileging a socially-agreed-upon chronological order, the logic of linear time.

In *Nuevo mundo*, the adolescent voice of Eugenio Rodero is freed from the strictures of narration and given full agency, and as a result the work expands essayistically in various directions and does not come to a neat end. This undercutting of the narrator's (and author's) authority, tamed and refashioned as a contest rather than the narrator's voluntary ceding of editorial control, would become the hallmark of Unamuno's *nivolas* later on. His first published novel, *Paz en la guerra* (*Peace in War*, 1897), written concurrently with *Nuevo mundo*, retains a formal composition rooted in the novelistic traditions of the nineteenth century (particularly in that it is narrated in the third person by a speaker whose authority is not questioned). *Amor y pedagogía* (*Love and Pedagogy*, 1902) and *Niebla*, meanwhile, both highlight the constructed nature of their stories through the use of paratexts and, in the latter case, a fictionalized battle between author and protagonist. What is more, both of these later novels may be read as *Bildungsromane* gone awry. *Amor y pedagogía* makes the pathological dangers of controlling the development of the young its central theme, as it recounts main character Avito Carrascal's determination to "make" a genius and the disastrous effects his ambition has for his son Apolodoro, who commits suicide at the end of the novel. With *Niebla*, the question of the meta-fictional relationship between author and work merges with the generational strife between old and young, as the ill-fated protagonist Augusto Pérez contends with a much older Unamuno for control over his own story. Here too, both biological and narrative forms of development are cut short with the protagonist's death. From the 1890s on, then, Unamuno's novelistic production was consistently concerned with questioning the link between individual, narrative, and historical development that had been so common in nineteenth-century fiction. As Germán Gullón has observed, even the less-formally-experimental *Paz en la guerra* subtly subverts the conventions of the realist novel and the nineteenth-century

Bildungsroman as it recounts the coming of age of its adolescent protagonists Ignacio Iturriondo and Pachico Zabalbide in the midst of the third Carlist War. Instead of reproducing the traditional paradigm of maturation through an encounter with the outside world, this novel, as Gullón puts it, "turns in on itself," deserting the sequential flow of historical events in favour of an intra-historic vision ("*Paz en la guerra*" 42–4). *Nuevo mundo* and Unamuno's subsequent novels carry this process of modernist interiorization one step further, turning its reflection on the process of writing itself.

The treatment of adolescence in *Nuevo mundo* makes clear that Unamuno's earliest novels and his creation of the *nivola* participate directly in modernism's transformation of traditional concepts of formation.[6] In their explicit rejection of the narrative structures that dominated the genre during the nineteenth century, *Amor y pedagogía* and *Niebla* offer departures that are just as, if not more, radical than the aesthetic innovation of Joyce's *Portrait* and other modernist *Bildungsromane*. As Luis Álvarez Castro, María Pao, and others have indicated, this rejection of nineteenth-century realist aesthetics would prove to be an important point of reference for later Spanish novelists, particularly the avant-garde writers of the 1920s. Some of these later novelists would even connect the subversive techniques employed by Unamuno to the topic of youth, as this life stage grew even more visible and exalted in that decade. Yet this reception is difficult to trace, in part because *Nuevo mundo* remained unknown during the period, and in part because with the publication of *Niebla* the concept of the *nivola* was associated primarily with a modernist critique of realism via metafiction and not with the genre of the coming-of-age tale. Precisely because Unamuno so successfully destroyed the model of the *Bildungsroman* in his early novels at the beginning of the century, later novelists of the Spanish avant-garde do not foreground the theme of growing up, though works like Antonio Espina's *Pájaro Pinto* or Antonio de Obregón's *Hermes en la vída pública* (discussed in chapter 4) do incorporate elements of the youth culture that flourished especially in the 1920s – sports, dance, and film – into their theoretical and metafictional questioning of traditional narrative development.

As the example of the aborted novel *Nuevo mundo* shows, the kind of youth that Unamuno was interested in representing at the turn of the century defied the parameters of the novel, at least as it had traditionally been conceived in the nineteenth century. Between the composition of *Nuevo mundo* in 1895 and the publication of *Niebla* in 1914, however,

Unamuno began to write verse. In poetry, he discovered a genre more appropriate to the spirit of youthfulness that narrative forms could depict only partially at best. Lyric better embodied the conception of youth that he was cultivating in the 1890s because it was capable of preserving the multifaceted character of adolescent experience that linear narrative accounts inevitably betrayed. As Unamuno's dreaded fortieth birthday approached and passed, poetry provided him with a means to preserve his youth – in the realm of art if not in time – and in some ways, to discover youth for the first time. In 1906 he wrote about this revelation to José Ortega y Gasset, one of several younger intellectuals he corresponded with during these years: "Ahora … hago versos. En lo que va de año he escrito de ellos más que en todo el resto de mi vida. Estoy hecho un chiquillo; en nueva primera" ("Right now … I am writing poems. So far this year I have written more of them than in all the rest of my life. I am like a little child; in a new beginning") (Robles, *Epistolario completo* 39).

In his autobiographical work *Recuerdos de niñez y mocedad* (*Memories of Childhood and Youth*), published two years later, Unamuno explains more about the nature of this sense of rejuvenation linked to poetry. Looking back on the years of his adolescence, a time he remembers as spent reading philosophy and trying to devise his own "*nuevo* sistema filosófico" ("*new* philosophical system," original emphasis), he reflects, "¡Y todavía, por entonces, no había escrito un verso! A lo cual se debe, sin duda, que haya más tarde casi abandonado la metafísica por la poesía, que me parece más honda metafísica" ("And at that time I still had not written a single line of poetry! Which undoubtedly explains why I later abandoned metaphysics almost completely for poetry, which seems to me to be a deeper metaphysics") (*OCE* 8:145). As a young man Unamuno had immersed himself in the writings of Kant, Hegel, and Spencer, inspired by them to attempt to contrive his own metaphysical system that might give a rational account of the world and his own experience within it. In describing this period of his life, he often says he turned to philosophy in order rationalize faith, and this indeed seems to have been the goal of a manuscript he composed in 1886 titled *Filosofía lógica*. In 1908, by contrast, he understands poetry as offering a richer depiction of reality than philosophy can offer, one that accounts for both that which is rational and that which lies beyond reason.

In this turn away from a strictly rational metaphysics to the metaphysics of poetry lies Unamuno's principal departure from his early philosophical influences, and especially from Hegel. As Robert Patrick

Newcomb has recently noted, critics have tended to disregard or downplay Hegel's influence on Unamuno, often in order to emphasize his affinity to Søren Kierkegaard. But the depth of the German philosopher's influence on Unamuno's thought is undeniable. Citing the many references the Spanish writer makes to Hegel's work, Newcomb demonstrates just how fundamental Hegelian structures like mirror images and dialectical oppositions are in Unamuno's writing. Still, he acknowledges that the depth of this influence "did not preclude Unamuno from questioning certain features of Hegel's system, particularly its aspiration towards a totalizing rationality" (21). In other words, it was not the whole of Hegelian thought or method that Unamuno rejected, but its end goal, its belief in the eventual, full revelation of reason as identical to and coextensive with reality. Ultimately unwilling to negate the reality of irrational aspects of experience, of feeling unsubordinated to thought, Unamuno could not accept Hegel's conception of the progressive rationalization of the world. Like Kierkegaard, author of the analeptic, pseudonymous work *Repetition*, Unamuno understood reason as a force perpetually contending with the irrational, and recognized this tension both in religious experience and in artistic creation. It is worth recalling here that Hegel's aesthetic philosophy projected that art would somehow come to an "end" in the modern era. Such a notion of finalizability, the idea that art would reach a point at which its social function had been completely fulfilled, ultimately clashed with Unamuno's view. If in *Nuevo mundo* he rejected the strictures of traditional narrative form in order to represent the nonlinear, polyvalent experience of adolescence and its challenge to the rationality of the adult world, with his turn to poetry, to *poiesis*, he discovered a mode of writing free from the rationalizing ends of philosophy.

In the essay "La ideocracia" ("Ideocracy"), published in 1900 in the triptych *Tres ensayos*, Unamuno commented on his early interest in poetry, casting it as a possibly puerile infatuation that he nevertheless preferred to the more serious work of academic scholarship. He writes, "Cuando amigos oficiosos me aconsejan que *haga* lingüística y concrete mi labor, es cuando con mayor ahínco me pongo a repasar mis pobres poesías, a verter en ellas mi preciosa libertad, la dulce inconcreción del espíritu, entonces es cuando con mayor deleite me baño en nubes de misterio" ("When meddling friends advise me to *do* linguistics and solidify my work, that is when I am most driven to work on my poor poems, to pour my precious freedom – the sweet diffusion of the spirit – into them, that is when with greatest delight I bathe myself in clouds of mystery")

(208). Poetry here stands from freedom from concretion, from the definition and order and the absence of mystery that the professional, adult world demands. This is not mere escapism; Unamuno's praise for the indefinite, unfinalizable character of poetry is of a piece with the whole of his turn-of-the-century thought. The resistance to the maturity of totalizing reason that informed his intellectual shift from philosophy to poetry lies at the core of the poetics that he articulated in the poems eventually collected in *Poesías*. As a genre that suspends the syllogistic momentum of rational argument, lyric poetry creates a space in which intellect and emotion can meet on equal grounds. "Piensa el sentimiento, siente el pensamiento" ("Think the feeling, feel the thought"), Unamuno implores his reader, or himself, in the first line of his "Credo poético" ("Poetic Creed"), the second poem of the collection. For him as for other twentieth-century poets and critics, this concordance of thought and feeling is what makes poetry a deeper form of metaphysics. Critics such as Javier Blasco and José Ángel Valente have noted the similarities between the poetics Unamuno lays out in his credo and the critical writings on metaphysical poetry produced subsequently by T.S. Eliot and, in Spain, Luis Cernuda.[7] Yet what is distinctive about Unamuno's view of poetry as a "deeper" metaphysics is that it does not only pertain to literary craft. His understanding of *poiesis* extends beyond lyric poetry and literary creation, to inform his understanding of religion in the modern age, of Spanish national politics, and of the cultural establishment. In each of these areas of his thought, the youthful dynamism of the poetic counters the process of solidification, the hardening of rational systems converted into dogma, that Unamuno identified with *la ideocracia*.

All That Is Fluid Hardens to Stone

Unamuno's refusal to accept Hegel's totalizing conception of reason provides further insight into the subversive historical vision that he puts forth in *En torno al casticismo*, and that appears again in the essays that make up his *Tres ensayos*, "¡Adentro!" ("Inward!"), "La ideocracia," and "La fe" ("Faith"). Stephen G.H. Roberts has recognized the importance of Unamuno's philosophy of history in his writing and in the voice he crafted as a modern public intellectual in Spain, rightly describing this vision as originating in the contrast between *historia* and *intrahistoria* that runs throughout the 1895 essays. Roberts follows general critical consensus in interpreting this contrast as an opposition of quotidian events to eternal values. However, it may also be understood in terms of a distinction between temporal events that become part of a historical narrative (the hegemonic story of History) and those aspects of life that do not form part of this narrative, and in fact defy its logic of temporal order and progress. The resurgence of youth that the essayist imagines at the end of *En torno al casticismo* is an intra-historic phenomenon because it subverts the process of aging that defines the story of Spain's national history. As in the case of his *nivolas*, the dissident character of Unamuno's approach to history lies in his challenge to existing narrative structures, especially those that rely on the allegorical connection between the life stages of an individual and the development of modern civilization. In essays like "La fe" and "La ideocracia," Unamuno juxtaposes a Hegelian understanding of history as a narrative of progressive rationalization and maturation with an alternative conception of the relationship between reason and irrationality as a perpetual and ahistorical struggle. In describing this struggle, or *agonía*, he consistently employs images of movement, energy, and fluidity, which contrast sharply with the stasis that comes with the triumph of reason, represented repeatedly in his turn-of-the-century writing with images of shells, scabs, exoskeletons, and ossification. (In *En torno al casticismo* it appears as the "capullos casticistas" ["traditionalist cocoons"] from which modern youth must break free.) Against a temporal process of aging, characterized by solidification, the author of *Tres ensayos* advocates for an eternal dynamism that he again aligns with youth.

This alternative view of history has its origin in Unamuno's own biography, and particularly in his personal wrestling with religious faith. In *Recuerdos de niñez y mocedad* he alludes to the allegorical relationship between an individual life and the trajectory of human history as a way to reflect on his religious upbringing: "Si la vida del hombre es trasunto y resumen de la vida del linaje humano, no puede tenerse por verdaderamente hombre quien no haya por lo menos pasado por un período sinceramente religioso" ("If the life of a man is the image and summary of the life of the human race, one cannot be considered a man if he has not passed through a period of sincere religiosity") (*OCE* 8:146). The implication here is that maturity in both individuals and in human civilization is predicated on and preceded by a period of credulity. Religious belief is associated with the pre-rational innocence of childhood, which eventually comes to an end when the person (or the civilization) reaches an age of reason. Many accounts of Unamuno's biography – his own and those of others – reference this link between religion and childhood. His religious crisis of 1897, for example, is often described as dominated by memories of growing up under the care of a devoutly Catholic mother, and an anguished desire to rediscover the unwavering faith of his childhood. Many – again, including Unamuno himself – have stressed the significance of his wife Concha's words of comfort to her husband on the night of the crisis, "¿Qué tienes, hijo mío?" ("What is the matter, my child?"). These maternal words address Unamuno as the child that, in that moment, overcome with grief over the illness of his hydrocephalic son Raimundín and an acute awareness of his own mortality, he perhaps wished to be once more. In Emilio Salcedo's biography of Unamuno, the image of childhood remains vivid in the writer's mind in the days following this episode, as he leaves home and seeks refuge in a nearby convent, where he prays with his face to the wall "como en castigo infantil" ("like a child being punished"), and searches for the faith he had felt so strongly as a young boy (Salcedo 90). This connection maintained between faith, the security of childhood, and the fervent and unquestioning belief of the pious altar boy led critics such as Antonio Sánchez Barbudo to conclude that Unamuno never achieved true faith after 1897, when his attitude towards religion became endlessly restless and founded on paradox.

However, such a conclusion depends on a definition of faith that Unamuno rejected, because it assumes that religious belief is static and unchanging. Three years after publishing his *Recuerdos*, in an interview with the journal *Coenobium*, Unamuno reflected on the crisis he experienced in 1897 and remarked, "Si la fe de la infancia está viva, no se puede conservar intacta … Creí entonces volver a la fe de mi infancia; ¡imposible! Como dijo uno de los nuestros, se pierde la virginidad de la fe para adquirir la maternidad de la razón. Pero quizás se pueda permanecer madre y virgen" ("For the faith of childhood to live, it cannot stay intact … I thought then that I was returning to the faith of my childhood; impossible! As one of our own said, one loses the virginity of faith in order to acquire the maternity of reason. But perhaps it is possible to remain both mother and virgin") (Unamuno, *De la desesperación* 88). On the one hand, he acknowledges that it is impossible to retain the faith of childhood, recognizing that reason will inevitably pose questions that will require religious belief to change and adapt. But on the other hand, reason need not drown faith out. Unamuno draws on the Catholic doctrine of the virgin birth to suggest that the mysteries of faith may also dialogue with rationality. The fusion in this statement of nineteenth-century liberal progressivism[8] and religious dogma illustrates quite elegantly the understanding of faith that appears throughout the Basque writer's work from 1895 to 1907, which founds itself on the coexistence – and mutual strife – of reason and mystery, experience and innocence, maturity and childhood. Such a conception defies the Hegelian understanding of human history as a process of progressive rationalization, and the historical narrative that equates modernization and progress with secularization.

This in-between, ever-forming kind of religious belief is what Unamuno refers to as true faith – and particularly as young or youthful faith – even before the crisis of 1897. In *Nuevo mundo*, he calls it "fe en la fe misma" ("faith in faith itself") as he depicts Eugenio Rodero's experience at the church service where he both remembers his childhood faith and manages to do away with its rational strictures, which he calls "los viejos dogmas" ("the old dogmas"). The tautological character of the formulation "fe en la fe misma" underscores its imperviousness to rational argument, a resistance that it uses as fuel in an ongoing process of discovery and creation rather than as scaffolding for ideological positions: "la santa fe, fe en la fe, la que crea lo que no vemos, la que hace el dogma, lo aviva, lo trasforma, lo mata y lo resucita" ("holy faith, faith in faith, the one that creates what we do not see, that makes dogma, brings it to life, transforms it, kills it, and resurrects it") (*Nuevo mundo* 57). A very similar characterization of faith appears in the essay "¡Pistis y no gnosis!," published in January of 1897, a few months before the famous crisis. In this brief article, Unamuno links the dynamism and creativity of faith directly to youth. There he describes youth as a stage of life in which the self is awakened to a range of future possibilities that stimulate the imagination: "Es la juventud, cuando es realmente joven, la edad en que las infinitas tendencias de nuestro espíritu se cruzan y entrecruzan cual activo enjambre" ("Youth, when it is really young, is the age when the infinite tendencies of our spirit crisscross and intermingle like bees in a hive"). As such, the essayist argues, it is, or should be, "la edad de la fe verdadera, del entusiasmo creador" ("the age of true faith, of creative enthusiasm") (*OCE* 3:682).

In all of these examples it is youth – not childhood – that is the age of true faith. Though Unamuno retains reverence for the innocent and unquestioning belief of the child, this is not the model he chose in writing about this topic. He stressed energy and flexibility as the most important qualities of faith, qualities that endow it with agency and an ability to contend with the forces of reason that seek to confine and control it.

Whereas childlike faith is passive and thus can easily be oppressed by these forces, youthful faith is capable of resistance. Unamuno develops this distinction in "¡Pistis y no gnosis!" and in "La fe," which reproduces and adds to the text of the earlier essay. Central to his argument in both of these texts is the opposition he sets up between the Greek terms *pistis* – which he identifies as the pure, undogmatic faith "in faith itself" – and *gnosis*, knowledge based on theological (i.e., rational) formulations. While he unequivocally identifies *pistis* with youth and the hope for the future that it represents, *gnosis* pertains to that which is past and already established. It is the rational ordering of the experience of faith, and it is a product of age.

To illustrate the difference between these terms, Unamuno describes the role each has played in the history of Christianity. His account of this history clearly reflects his reading of various liberal Protestant thinkers, and in particular, the influence of Adolf Harnack's *History of Dogma* (*Lehrbuch der Dogmengeschichte*, 1886–9).[9] Following the German theologian, he begins his account with the early Christian church: "Acababa de pasar Jesús por el mundo, donde quedaba aún el perfume de su huella y el eco vivo de sus palabras de consuelo … Jóvenes las comunidades cristianas esperaban la próxima venida del reino del Hijo de Dios e Hijo del Hombre … Sentíanse henchidas de verdadera fe, de la que con la esperanza y el amor se confunde, de lo que se llamó *pistis* (πιστης)" ("Jesus had just passed through the world, where the perfume he left in his wake and the living echo of his words of consolation still hung in the air … Young, the Christian communities awaited the imminent coming of the kingdom of the Son of God and Son of Man … They were swollen with true faith, the one that blends with hope and love, that was called *pistis* [πιστης]") (*E* 2:224–5). Though they represent the infancy of Christianity, Unamuno describes these communities as young, not as infantile or childlike. The intensity of the hope that he attributes to them endows these believers with vigor and agency unlike the passivity and helplessness of children.

The faith of these early Christian communities is motivated by visceral responses to tangible realities: the "perfume" of Jesus' presence and the echo of his words. Yet the physical and emotional character of *pistis* does not preclude the involvement of the mind. Though secondary to the initial exuberance of the believers, intellectual attempts to make sense of the experience of Christ soon materialize, in a notably disordered fashion. The essayist writes, "Daba cada cual a su esperanza la forma imaginativa o intelectiva que mejor le cuadrara" ("Each one gave his hope the imaginative or intellectual form that best suited him"), stressing the diversity and flexibility of the interpretations of the early church fathers, who even enjoyed, he insists, "la santa libertad de contradecirse" ("the holy freedom to contradict themselves") (225). A protean fluidity reigns over these intellectual processes, which take shape and then morph into new forms according to the energy provided by the believer's hope. Ultimately, the image Unamuno employs to describe the community of faith is a hot, plasmic substance like lava: "aquella masa de anhelos y de aspiraciones, hirviente de entusiasmo" ("that mass of desires and aspirations, bubbling with enthusiasm"). As in the description of youth that opens "¡Pistis y no gnosis!," this image casts the early church as a site of multiple potentials, a wide range of possible interpretations of Christianity that have not yet taken on a definitive shape.

As the religion begins to age and faith becomes formalized, however, this changes. Again staying close to Harnack's outline of the history of dogma, Unamuno chooses to describe it as the cooling and hardening of the lava of *pistis*:

> A medida que el calor de la fe iba menguando y mundanizándose la religión, iba la candente masa enfriándose en su superficie y recubriéndose de costra, que le separaba más y más del ambiente, dificultando su más completa aireación ... Aparecieron puntos de solidificación y cristalización aquí y allí. La juvenil *pistis* fue siendo sustituída [*sic*] por la *gnosis* (γνῶσις), el conocimiento, la creencia, y no propiamente la fe; la doctrina y no la esperanza. Empezóse a enseñar que en el conocimiento consiste la vida; convirtiéndose los fines prácticos religiosos en principios teóricos filosóficos. (226)
>
> (As the heat of faith lessened and the religion became mundane, the surface of the sizzling mass began to cool and form a crust that separated it more and more from the atmosphere, impeding its aeration ... Spots of solidification and crystalization appeared here and there. The youthful *pistis* was increasingly substituted by *gnosis* [γνῶσις], knowledge, belief, and not properly faith; doctrine rather than hope. It began to be taught that life depends on knowledge; the practical ends of religion were converted into theoretical philosophical principles.)

This metaphor of solidification aligns the history of Christianity with a process of aging similar to that described in Unamuno's account of

Spanish history in *En torno al casticismo*. Here the youth of *pistis* fades gradually and is replaced by the rational maturity of *gnosis*. In Unamuno's reading of religious history, full maturity is finally reached with the creation of the Nicene Creed in 325 C.E. After this moment, he writes, "la fe fué para muchos creer lo que no vieron, adherirse a fórmulas: *gnosis* … Así pasa una juventud" ("for many faith came to be believing in what they had not seen, subscribing to formulas: *gnosis* … That is how youth comes to an end") (227). According to Harnack, the Helenization of the Jewish tradition in early Christianity had been a process of intellectualization, a shift from lived and felt religion to philosophical abstraction. For Unamuno, this shift represents the entrance of Christianity into a rigid and undesirable adulthood. As in *En torno al casticismo*, this process of aging leads to a state of decay and senility in Unamuno's present, where the Church has become an immobile, dogmatic institution founded on traditions that are incapable of adaptation to the modern world. To the author of "La fe," even old church buildings have come to represent a worn-out, lifeless, rotting faith; he describes Notre Dame des Victoires in Paris as "el cementerio del fetichismo, donde éste hiede en su seca osamenta" ("the cemetery of fetishism, where its dry bones reek of superstition") (236).

Unamuno surely had statements like the one I have just quoted in mind when he wrote to Bernardo Candamo in March of 1900 that "La fe" would cause a great scandal among Spanish Catholics. In this letter, however, he adds that the implications of his argument extended beyond an attack on the church, telling Candamo, "y tenga en cuenta que en esto de católicos incluyo a casi todos nuestros librepensadores y anarquistas, a los ideócratas todos … Aborrezco toda etiqueta, pero si alguna soportase, sería la de ideoclasta, rompeideas" ("and keep in mind that when I say Catholics I include almost all of our freethinkers and anarchists, all of the ideocrats … I hate all labels, but if I were to put up with one, it would be the label of ideoclast, breaker of ideas") (Blázquez González 248–9). This statement points to an important conceptual link that joins "La fe" and the essay that precedes it in *Tres ensayos*, "La ideocracia." Unamuno's concept of *ideocracia* describes the product of rationalizing processes like the triumph of *gnosis* in his account of historical Christianity, and it also closely resembles modern definitions of ideology. Unamunian *ideocracia* is significantly similar to ideology as defined by the early Marx, who in turn drew on Feuerbach's critique of religion to cast it as an intellectual abstraction distinct from and at odds with material reality. In "La ideocracia," Unamuno draws on

Marx's *Capital* and Schopenhauer's *The World as Will and Representation* to suggest that ideas are a kind of currency, a representation of wealth and an instrument of exchange. As with the creation of paper money in an advancing capitalist society, to the extent that ideas are separated from the direct experience from which they were "mined," their value depends increasingly on the imprint, the signature of the wise person who endorses them, as does the stamp of the Banco Español on the *peseta* (*E* 2:203). Dedication to the currency rather than to the commodity it ought to represent – that is, the intellectual labour of real human beings – alienates and immobilizes. A world measured by ideas and not by humanity is a coldly rational place, where formulas and dogmas encase and confine individual people, keeping them from interacting freely with and having compassion towards one another. Unamuno writes,

> La lógica justicia, reina en el mundo de las ideas puras, ahoga a las obras de misericordia que brotan del amor, soberano en el mundo de los puros espíritus. En vez de verter éstos y fundirlos en un espíritu común, vida de nuestras vidas y realidad de realidades, tendemos a hacer con las ideas un cemento conjuntivo social en que como moluscos en un englomerado quedemos presos. (208)
>
> (Logical justice, queen of the world of pure ideas, suffocates the works of compassion that sprout from love, the sovereign of the world of pure spirits. Instead of pouring our own spirits out and merging them in a common spirit, life of our lives and reality of realities, we tend to use ideas to make a kind of connective social cement, in which we become trapped like mollusks in conglomerate.)

Instead of allowing thought to crystallize and solidify as *ideocracia*, Unamuno insists, the intellectual atmosphere must be kept flexible, breathable. The contrast here between fluid "spirit" and cemented ideas illuminates certain aspects of the essayist's thought, particularly in relation to Marx. Unamuno's argument against *ideocracia* clearly resembles Marx's critique of ideology, particularly as it develops in writings beginning with the *Critique of Hegel's 'Philosophy of Right'* and leading up to *The German Ideology*. Following Feuerbach, this critique opposes ideology to material reality and seeks to invert the hierarchical relationship that makes the latter predicate to the former.[10] Unamuno's argument in "La ideocracia" is quite similar, but at the same time, the imagery of the passage cited above signals an important discrepancy between Unamuno's thought and Marxist orthodoxy. While the authors of the *Communist Manifesto* assert that "all that is solid melts into air," Unamuno's writing proposes an inversion, something like "all that is fluid hardens to stone."[11] With this comes a metonymic link between the processes of solidification and those of age, rife with physical and tactile associations: the stiffening of joints, the hardening of the arteries, or the fossilization of an ancient bone. Such images suggest a departure from one of Marxism's most Hegelian aspects: its reliance on a teleological narrative of development. Whereas Marx and Engels herald their conception of a change of physical state (solid to gas) as a symbol of the self-destruction of the bourgeoisie, an outcome they view as desirable, Unamuno seeks to critique, disrupt, and arrest the hardening process that is modernity's progressive aging.

While "La fe" and "La ideocracia" sketch out a view of historical time characterized by a process of solidification in which faith and creativity struggle against the ever-hardening dogmatic tendencies of reason, "¡Adentro!" advocates for an alternative temporality. Unlike the two essays that follow it in *Tres ensayos*, this one is written in the form of a letter addressed directly to a young person. In it the essayist urges his young addressee to form a strong sense of self, apart from the dictates of the adult social world that he (the implied reader is male) is beginning to enter. "En vez de decir, pues, ¡adelante!, o ¡arriba!, di: ¡adentro!" ("Instead of saying forward! or upward!, say inward!") (196), Unamuno declares. Eschewing the militaristic exclamation "¡Adelante!" – soon to be adopted by youth organizations like the Spanish Exploradores – and the progressive aspiration to new intellectual heights (later also used by Nationalist soldiers) implied in "¡Arriba!," the essayist asks the young person not to focus on a goal, but to practice introspection, to observe and learn. A linear trajectory is replaced by an interior dynamism, an atmosphere in which to forge new perspectives on the world. In this way, "¡Adentro!" prepares its young reader to face and fight against the problems of an aging modern society that Unamuno describes in the second and third essays of the book. As María Pilar Celma has noted in the case of Unamuno's poetry, the effect of the intimate form of second-person address employed here is to create a dialogic mode in which the reader is empowered to engage with the text and with the ideas of the author (Blasco, Celma, and González 286). In the case of an essay directed specifically to a young person, this empowerment also encourages youth to question and dialogue with the authority of the adult world.

Less a didactic list of things one must do to succeed than a building-up of the young reader's spirit, the essay is an invitation to self-reflection.

The central message that the essayist seeks to convey in "¡Adentro!" is that his young reader need not harness his imagination or desires in order to follow an already-marked-out path in life. As he puts it,

> Cuando la vida es honda, es poema de ritmo continuo y ondulante. No encadenes tu fondo eterno, que en el tiempo se desenvuelve, a fugitivos reflejos de él. Vive al día en las olas del tiempo, pero asentado sobre tu roca viva, dentro del mar de la eternidad; al día en la eternidad, es como debes vivir.
>
> Te repito, que no hace el plan a la vida, sino que ésta se lo traza a sí misma, viviendo. ¿Fijarte un camino? El espacio que recorras será tu camino; no te hagas, como planeta en su órbita, siervo de una trayectoria. (*E* 2:186–7)
>
> (When life is full, it is a poem of continually undulating rhythm. Don't chain your eternal core, which unfolds through time, to passing reflections of it. Live day by day in the waves of time, but anchored to your living rock in the sea of eternity; day by day in eternity, that is how you should live.
>
> I repeat, a plan does not make a life; rather, life makes its own plan, by living. Chart out your path? Whatever space you travel will be your path; don't be like a planet in its orbit, slave to a trajectory.)

According to the essayist, a life – and especially a young life – is a poem, not a clearly determined, linear path. The critique of historical time and progress that Unamuno develops in the later essays is anticipated here in his wish that his young reader refuse to conform to pre-existing notions of how his experience should be ordered. What matters are not the dead ideas that already structure the world (its *ideocracias*), but the young person himself, whom the essayist calls an "idea viva," a living idea. If he must have set ideas, Unamuno writes, "tenlas como los huesos, dentro, y cubiertas y veladas con tu carne espiritual, sirviendo de palanca a los músculos de tu pensamiento, y no fuera y al descubierto y aprisionándote como las tienen las almas-cangrejos de los dogmáticos, abroqueladas contra la realidad que no cabe en dogmas" ("have them like you have bones, on the inside and covered by your spiritual flesh, serving as levers for the muscles of your thought, and not on the outside, exterior and imprisoning you like the ideas of the crab-like souls of dogmatic people, hardened against a reality that does not fit into dogmas") (191).

The hard exterior that Unamuno associates with *gnosis* and *ideocracia* elsewhere in *Tres ensayos* appears in the opening essay as the shell that forms around the souls of old people, converting them into crustaceans. Youth, however, remains free of such contraints: it is flexible, nimble, strong, and able to interact freely with the outside world. To Unamuno's mind, this youthful vitality and flexibility needed to serve as a guiding emblem for modern Spain, if the old age of entrenched national traditions was to be countered. Indeed, this is the model that informs his thought on Spanish "regeneration" in many of his early essays on politics and culture. The following sections of this chapter demonstrate how in these writings, as Unamuno endeavours to combat the progressive solidification of various national dogmas, his work exemplifies a modernist pursuit of novelty by way of recombination: the explosion of the old casings of Spanish society and a rearrangement of its constituent parts.

The Youth of Socialism

In his recent book *Novelty: A History of the New*, Michael North points to two basic categories into which understandings of renovation can be divided. He groups the concept of renovation central to Christianity along with the cultural notions of renaissance and revolution as forms of a cyclical "novelty by return" (41). Unamuno's tendency to present youth as an eternal value that may reappear in or burst onto a given historical moment owes much to such conceptions of the new. But in his turn-of-the-century writing on politics Unamuno also imagines youth according to the other model that North offers: that of recombination. North identifies this model with modern science as initiated with Bacon and Descartes, tracing its origins to Lucretian atomism (50–4). Within this conception, novelty arises from rearrangement, as a new substance is formed through the creation of new relationships among its components. For Unamuno, recombination was the essence of a youthful interaction with an existing tradition, and it exemplified the kind of re-reading that he believed modern Spanish society needed to undergo. Just as atoms may be rearranged on the molecular level to form a new compound, Unamuno held that Spanish society ought to be broken down to its constituent parts and reconfigured. To the rigidity of national and cultural *ideocracias*, he opposed the possibility of creative reorganization. One of the contexts in which this model appears is in his call for the disassembly and reorganization of existing ties in Spanish culture between political and religious power. Beginning with his brief affiliation with the Spanish Socialist Party in the mid-1890s, the young Unamuno saw socialism as a means to just such a reconfiguration.[12]

As we have seen, in his turn-of-the-century writings on faith, Unamuno identifies reliance on dogma as the fundamental problem of modern religion: the loss of Christianity's youth occurs when faith becomes formalized and institutionalized, blended with Hellenic philosophy and Roman law. With regard to Spain, he saw the historic intertwinement of political authority and religious confession as a main source of the country's decadence in the modern era. Unlike the private reflections contained in his *Diario íntimo* (1897), where he wrestles with theology, doctrine, and biblical texts, in essays written for a broad Spanish audience like "La fe" and his later "Religión y patria" (1904), he aims his critique primarily at the systematization and reduction of faith that occurs through the union of Church and State. The continued hegemony of the centuries-old alliance between these two powers in the Spain of the Bourbon Restoration had produced what Unamuno called a "régimen de mentira" ("regime of lies"), a disingenuous structuring of public life based on "la vieja máquina" ("the old machine"), the age-old marriage of the altar and the throne (*Nuevo mundo* 103). This continued alliance, he maintained, was detrimental to both religious belief and to politics.

To the Unamuno of the 1890s, socialism presented itself as an exciting alternative to the Restoration's old machine. First drawn to politics through his interest in Basque nationalism, he paid growing attention to the movement in the early years of the decade, joining the Agrupación Socialista de Bilbao in 1894. In that year he declared in a letter to Valentín Hernández, editor of the association's journal *La Lucha de Clases*, that he believed socialism to be "la religión de la humanidad" ("the religion of humanity") (*OCE* 9:477). In his interpretation, socialism re-combined faith and politics by exploding the old alliance of Church and State and creating a new formation. While doing away with the structures of power that prevailed in European society, it allowed for the flourishing of values that would be central to the concept of faith he wrote of a few years later: hope, energy, and creative diversity of interpretation. The wording of Unamuno's description of the movement in the letter to Hernández is indicative in this regard: he writes of "el socialismo que inició Carlos Marx con la gloriosa Internacional de Trabajadores y al cual vienen a refluir corrientes de otras partes" ("the socialism that Karl Marx initiated with the glorious International Workingmen's Association, upon which currents from other places come to converge") (477). As Jon Juaristi has pointed out, this sentence is far from a declaration of Marxist orthodoxy (222). In addition to its emphasis on a perceived doctrinal plurality in the socialist movement (not unlike the variety in the "masa informe" of early Christianity in "¡Pistis y no gnosis!" and "La fe"), the description stresses its transnational character. The critique of nationalism that Unamuno sees in socialism is a vital part of his writing over the next years, not only in his analysis of the Spanish nation in *En torno al casticismo* (where he identifies the creation of "las grandes nacionalidades" as a root cause of modern Europe's old age), but also in several subsequent essays.

This early enthusiasm for the "religion of humanity" is, of course, an idiosyncratic interpretation of socialism, one more in line with Unamuno's personal intellectual concerns at the time than with Marx's thought, or with the directions the socialist movement was taking in Spain. The discrepancy between his interpretation and the inflexible ideological program that the leaders of the Socialist Party in his country hoped to advance would lead to tension, conflict, and the university professor's eventual break with the organization. The interest he took in the early church in 1897 might represent a search for historical models of the kind of politics that he had imagined socialism could inaugurate. Manuel Urrutia has affirmed that "¡Pistis y no gnosis!" establishes a parallel between these early Christian communities and socialism (*Evolución* 68). Indeed, the idea finds support in the New Testament, particularly chapters two and four of the book of Acts, which Unamuno cites specifically in his *Diario íntimo* under the heading "Cuestión social" (*Diario íntimo* 122). Like the young Louis Althusser of "The International of Decent Feelings," the Unamuno of the 1890s was able to imagine socialism as the realization of Christian values. The Spaniard, despite his eventual break with the Socialist Party, would retain this personal understanding of a deep connection between socialism and religion for several years beyond his own youth.

Unamuno's personalized view of the intersection of a new political order and religious tradition comes to light especially in a poem probably written several years after he left the party, "En la Catedral Vieja de Salamanca" ("In the Old Cathedral of Salamanca"). Though it is undated, it seems likely that it, like most of the poems in *Poesías*, was written between 1899 and 1906 – perhaps in 1904, the year he wrote the ode "Salamanca" that appears alongside it, in the section titled "Castilla." In any case, "En la Catedral Vieja" combines Unamuno's concern for political and religious innovation with the language of aging and rejuvenation, as the poet surveys the loneliness of a religious building fallen into disuse, and then imagines it being filled with a new faith for the modern world, a faith that would breathe life back into it. The closing stanzas express the hope towards which the entire poem builds:

Quiera Dios, vieja sede salmantina,
que el pueblo tu robusto pecho llene,
florezca en tus altares
un nuevo culto,

y tu hermoso cimborrio bizantino
se conmueva al sentir cómo su seno
renace oyendo en salmo
la Marsellesa. (*Poesías* 100)

(May God grant, old Salmantine seat,
that the people fill your robust chest,
may a new rite flourish
in your altars,

and your beautiful, Byzantine dome
be moved when it feels its breast
revive upon hearing the psalm
of the Marseillaise.)

Though the poet speaks of rebirth in these last lines, what he actually suggests is the joining of previously disparate elements: a twelfth-century cupula and the Marseillaise – Catholicism and Republicanism. The poem's presentation of the revolutionary hymn as the psalm of a "nuevo culto" establishes an alternative combination of politics and religion. At the same time, the combination that it proposes is a joining of the present with a much earlier period in the history of civilization, a moment when humanity and Christianity were "younger." Significantly, Unamuno looks to the old cathedral of Salamanca, whose construction began in the twelfth century and reflects an initial Romanesque design, instead of the much larger and more ostentatious "new" cathedral, built between the sixteenth and eighteenth centuries and, as such, a product of a later, more advanced or "mature" historical stage.

That Unamuno continued to view socialism as the antidote to the Restoration's "vieja máquina" is confirmed in an article he published in *La Lucha de Clases* in May of 1907. The brief piece is titled "Socialismo y juventud" ("Socialism and Youth"),[13] and in it Unamuno argues that what links these two terms is a disposition towards generosity. He makes his case by contrasting youth with old age and childhood:

> Si juventud quiere decir algo más que el contar tal o cual número de años de vida, significa, sin duda, una redundancia de esta vida misma, redundancia que la lleva a derramarse y darse a los demás. Los viejos, séanlo de años o de espíritu, pues hay quien nace viejo y hay quien se conserva siempre joven, los viejos son egoístas, y lo son también los niños. Aquéllos necesitan ahorrar una vida que se les escapa; éstos ir atestorando una vida para mañana. Mas así que el hombre llega a la edad en que ha de hacer otros hombres, el amor le despierta el corazón y su vida pugna por darse y derramarse. (*OCE* 9:925)
>
> (If youth represents anything more than counting a certain number of years of life, it undoubtedly represents an abundance of that life, an abundance that causes life to overflow and give of itself to others. Old people, whether they are old in years or in spirit – for there are those who are born old and those who stay young forever – old people are selfish, and so are children. The former are compelled to save what remains of a life that is escaping from them; the latter, to store up a life for tomorrow. But when a man arrives at the age of making other men, love awakens his heart and his life strives to give of itself and pour itself out.)

Unamuno concludes, "El que en su juventud no se siente socialista de corazón, es que no es de veras joven" ("If one does not feel himself to be a socialist at heart in his youth, he is not truly young") (926). While both children and the elderly are selfish, youth enjoys a sense of prodigality that leads it to give of itself and to create – indeed, to procreate. In very broad terms, this distinction between avarice and generosity corresponds to Unamuno's views on economic policy at the turn of the century, and on the relationship between the various regions of Spain. With regard to the economy, Unamuno favoured free trade over protectionism, which he saw, especially in the 1890s, as a product of the "old machine" of bourgeois capitalism and a form of national selfishness (Pérez de la Dehesa 23–6; Urrutia, *Evolución* 46–9). The efforts to protect the interests of a particular region that he increasingly observed in Catalonia and the Basque Country in the first years of the twentieth century also struck him as selfish – though, as we shall see, in this case he attributed the avarice to childishness, a youth that had failed to blossom.

The relationships sketched out in "Socialismo y juventud" between youth, age, and childhood provide a useful framework within which to revisit a shift in Unamuno's political posture that Pérez de la Dehesa and Urrutia have associated with the repercussions of the crisis of 1897, and which the former in particular characterized as a move "de la decentralización al centralismo" ("from decentralization to centralism") (158). Focusing on a change of perspective to which Unamuno himself called attention in his 1905 essay "La crisis actual del patriotismo español" ("The Contemporary Crisis of Spanish Patriotism"), Pérez de la Dehesa asserts that the writer underwent a radical ideological shift in almost every area of his political thought around 1900. Urrutia affirms this idea, while providing a more nuanced picture of Unamuno's intellectual evolution during these years. While his writing indicates that in the new century his allegiances began to become more centralist (in ways that are surprising when compared to his earlier stances, and often problematic when viewed from a twenty-first-century perspective), this transition is not simply an about-face. An approach to Unamuno's turn-of-the-century politics that considers his conception of youth reveals a more continuous and coherent development. In the first decade of the twentieth century, his critique of the nationalist "vieja idea castellana castiza" from *En torno al casticismo* did not fade. Nor did the belief, which he put forth in "La crisis del patriotismo" ("The Crisis of Patriotism," 1896), that the northern and eastern coasts of the Iberian Peninsula were sites of potential rejuvenation for Spain. Unamuno did, however, become more critical of a kind of regionalism that he viewed as false youth or puerility because it repeated the same process of nationalization he had critiqued in Castile's history, one that promoted collectivized conformity and exclusivity rather than the openness and generosity he saw in socialism.

In "La crisis del patriotismo," published in the anarchist journal *Ciencia Social* about a year and a half into his official membership in the Socialist Party, Unamuno put forth a critique of nationalism clearly informed by his political thinking at the time. The essayist denounces

Spain's military efforts to retain economic control of Cuba (the conflict that would end with the "Disaster" of 1898), and takes advantage of this troublesome situation to comment on economic and political changes taking place back on the Peninsula as well. He writes that nationalism, "cuando no es hijo de la fantasía literaria de los grandes centros urbanos, suele ser producto impuesto a la larga por la cultura coercitiva de los grandes terratenientes" ("when it is not the child of the literary fantasy of the great urban centers, is usually a product imposed over time by the coercive culture of the great landowners") (*E* 3:34). A product of commercial interests concentrated in cities and among the wealthy, and even reinforced in bourgeois reading material, nationalism is clearly suspect in this text. Efforts to construct what Benedict Anderson has called an "imagined community" create a false patriotism with no connection to the personal experience of the citizen, nor to a broader sense of humanity. Yet the essayist argues that in his time this nation-based patriotism is weakening as it is stretched between two stronger poles: on the one hand, a universal sense of "la gran Patria humana," and on the other, the local "patria chica." The strengthening of regionalism presents an opportunity for the reconfiguration of the country through Hegelian dialectics. As the "antítesis de la vieja tesis patriótica doctrinaria" ("antithesis to the old, doctrinary patriotic thesis"), it poses a heterodox challenge to traditional nationalism, but also anticipates a "síntesis final," a new arrangement that results in a better, stronger unification: regionalism is "la diferenciación que prepara la integración suprema" ("the differentiation that makes way for the ultimate integration") (41–2).

This ultimate integration is not merely a return to nationalism. For the Unamuno of 1896, socialism has shown that the modern nation, protagonist of nineteenth-century European history, is now an inadequate, out-of-date formulation that must cede to a new way of imagining community, balanced between a sense of universal belonging to the human race and a commitment to and affection for the region where one lives. Drawing on the concept of *intrahistoria* that he had developed the year before, he insists that the bourgeois model of nationhood is an inauthentic historical product. Its counterpoint is to be found among the working class, which in late nineteenth-century Spain was still overwhelmingly agrarian:

> Es una de las concepciones más erróneas la de estimar como los más legítimos productos históricos las grandes nacionalidades, bajo un rey y una

> bandera. Debajo de esta historia de sucesos fugaces, historia bullanguera, hay otra profunda historia de hechos permanentes, historia silenciosa, la de los pobres labriegos que un día y otro, sin descanso, se levantan antes que el sol a labrar sus tierras y un día y otro son víctimas de las exacciones autoritarias. (36)
>
> (One of the most misguided conceptions is that which views the great nationalities, ruled by a king and a flag, as the most legitimate historical products. Beneath this history of fleeting events, a boisterious history, there is another, deep history of permanent realities, a quiet history, that of the poor laborers who rise before the sun every day, without rest, to work their land and who are victims every day of extortion by the authorities.)

Upon reading these words it is worth recalling the end of "El marasmo actual de España," where Unamuno describes a new Spanish youth, made up of those who will turn their attention to "el pueblo" and draw on its intra-historic resources in order to break the country out of its senile inertia and monotony. In "La crisis del patriotismo," the essayist imagines the pulling apart of the Spanish nation and its territories as a first step in a process of rejuvenation, and places hope in regionalism's ability to resist the selfishness of the centre that paternalistically maintains control over the periphery.

When Unamuno returned to this topic nine years later, in "La crisis actual del patriotismo español," he openly stated that his thinking had changed, and poignantly couched the shift in terms of his own maturation. Now past his fortieth birthday, the author of this text looks back on "La crisis del patriotismo" and also *En torno al casticismo*, which he calls "un ensayo de estudio del alma castellana" ("an attempt to study the Castilian soul"). Of these earlier essays he writes,

> Me fueron dictados por la honda disparidad que sentía entre mi espíritu y el espíritu castellano. Y esta disparidad es la que media entre el espíritu del pueblo vasco, del que nací y en el que me crié, y el espíritu del pueblo castellano, en el que, a partir de mis veintiséis años, ha madurado mi espíritu. Entonces creía, como creen hoy no pocos paisanos míos y muchos catalanes, que tales disparidades son inconciliables e irreductibles; hoy no creo lo mismo. (*E* 6:137–8)
>
> (They were dictated by the deep disparity I felt between my spirit and the Castilian spirit. And this disparity is the same one that separates the spirit

> of the Basque Country, from which I was born and in which I grew up, and the spirit of Castile, in which, from the age of twenty-six, my spirit has matured. At the time I believed, as do not a few of my countrymen and many Catalans today, that such disparities are irreconcilable and insurmountable; I do not believe this any more.)

Pérez de la Dehesa sees this final comment as evidence of Unamuno's radical change of outlook. Indeed, the essayist continues with a highly polemical statement, declaring that at the root of Catalan, Basque, and even Galician regionalism "no hay sino anticastellanismo" ("there is nothing more than anti-Castilianism") (138). Nevertheless, even as he recognizes that he now feels a greater affinity with the Castilian spirit, Unamuno maintains his earlier geographical association of central Spain with age. The periphery is still the site of youth: the Basque Country, of course, is the land of his childhood, and of his early political affiliations with Basque nationalism and the Agrupación Socialista de Bilbao. Castile, by contrast, has been the site of the ripening of his spirit, a ripening he also associated during these years with the arrival of the closed-minded dogmatism of age.

It is difficult to determine whether Unamuno considered this maturation to be a good thing, especially when one considers the various writings from the first years of the twentieth century that display his anxiety about turning forty. In any case, if his opinion had changed, it had not simply reversed. By no means did he now consider Castile to be youthful. In "La crisis actual," the critique of Castilian hegemony is as strident as ever, and cast into greater relief than in *En torno al casticismo* by the contemporary historical context to which it responds. The impetus for the writing of this essay was the *Cu-Cut!* incident of 25 November 1905, a much-commented-upon occurrence in which the Guarnición de Barcelona used military force to stamp out separatist sentiment in the capital of Catalonia, while the authorities did nothing to stop them. Earlier that fall, the *catalanista* journal *Cu-Cut!* had printed a cartoon ridiculing the army. On 25 November, members of the military retaliated by attacking the journal's editorial offices, causing significant destruction and damage. In "La crisis actual," Unamuno takes up his pen to decry this military action, while urging the Catalan nationalists not to follow the centralists' intolerant example. As Colette and Jean-Claude Rabaté note in their biography of Unamuno, this article is at its core a defence of freedom of expression and a critique of the military's interference in political matters (253–4). The freedoms that the writer sought to defend would only be further restricted in the aftermath of the incident, however, with the passage of the *Ley de Jurisdicciones* in early 1906. This law gave the Spanish army the right to prosecute offences to the unity of the "patria," the flag, and indeed, the army itself. The ongoing debate surrounding this law is the subject of Unamuno's subsequent essays "La patria y el ejército" ("The Fatherland and the Army") and "Más sobre la crisis del patriotismo" ("More on the Crisis of Patriotism"), which appeared, like "La crisis actual," in the journal *Nuestro Tiempo* in the first months of 1906.

Even as these essays condemn the government's anti-Catalan censorship and the involvement of the military in politics in general, they also reflect Unamuno's fear that the regionalist movements were also becoming unthinkingly doctrinaire and hostile to free speech and divergent viewpoints. He comments that these movements seem defensive and self-involved, more interested in rejecting whatever is Castilian than in promoting and disseminating their own unique heritage. As they embark upon a process of nationalization on a smaller scale, they travel the same path that has led to Spain's decadence: isolation within the shell of the *ideocracia* commonly called patriotism. Unamuno warns that Catalonia and the Basque Country must not follow in the same direction. If, in his view, Castile showed "generosity" in imposing itself on the rest of the Peninsula and unifying it in the late fifteenth century (a highly contentious claim, to be sure), it is now old and power-hungry, and must be challenged. In "La crisis actual," though the essayist criticizes what he sees as cowardice in the regional nationalisms, he also stresses his sympathy with them. He acknowledges that they feel a deep aversion – "y la siento también yo" ("and I feel it, too"), he adds – towards "casi todo lo que pasa por castizo y genuino" ("almost everything that passes for traditional and authentic") (6:140). As in *En torno al casticismo*, this pseudo-authenticity originates in Castile and runs through all of its culture. It is up to the coastal regions to denounce such superficiality and, more importantly, propose something better. Unamuno repeatedly asserts that the regionalists need to conquer the centre. Spanish national history, he argues, has for too long been centrifugal; "tiene que ser ahora centrípeta" ("it has to be centripetal now") (144).

In this call for the periphery of the Iberian Peninsula to impose itself upon the centre, Unamuno imagines geopolitical relations in terms of the human traits of generosity and avarice. Inspired by his opposition to protectionism in economics and an enthusiasm for the transnational confluence he saw in socialism, his idea of political selflessness leads to a reading of Spanish history that fails to sufficiently denounce the use of military force and other forms of violence by Castile on the Peninsula and by Castile-led Spain in the Americas. A twenty-first-century critique of this deficiency must be balanced, however, by an acknowledgment of Unamuno's fierce anti-military and anti-nationalist stance at the time, one which perhaps made it possible for him to imagine a cultural "imperialismo sin emperor, difusivo y pacífico" ("imperialism without an emperor, diffusive and peaceful") in "La crisis actual" (144), or, in an uncollected poem from the time,

> Una bandera sin empresa alguna,
> bandera toda blanca,
> para que cada uno se imagine
> ver en ella sus armas
> refulgir puras. (*OCE* 6:793)

> (A flag without any emblem,
> a flag left totally blank,
> so that each one might imagine
> his own coat of arms there
> shining pure.)

This image of a blank, white flag, an image that suggests a utopian politics of unity in diversity, appears in an untitled and undated poem dedicated to youth.[14] The ideal politics for Unamuno was one of youthfulness, as "Socialismo y juventud" suggests: a youthfulness characterized by a tendency to overflow the container of the self, to give from a surplus of energy and creativity. Just as he hoped to see the Catalans practice this kind of youth by "catalanizing" Castile in "La crisis actual," he would soon call for Spain to do the same with respect to the European continent, to *españolizar Europa*.

Though the Basque writer had imagined in 1896 that Spain's "crisis of patriotism" would create opportunities for the coastal regions to inject youthfulness into the country's political and cultural stagnation, in 1905 this potential had not translated into reality. In Unamuno's view, the regionalist movements had turned inward and become sectarian rather than giving of themselves, imposing their distinct cultural personalities on the Spanish nation and precipitating its rejuvenation. These feelings seem to have been reinforced when he travelled to

Catalonia to speak in the Ateneo Enciclopédico Popular in Barcelona in October of 1906. A poetic record of this trip appears in the section of *Poesías* titled "Cataluña," which includes three poems: "La catedral de Barcelona" ("The Cathedral of Barcelona"), "Tarrassa," and "*L'aplec de la protesta*" ("The Protest Meeting"). Taken as a unit, they reflect the concerns that weighed on Unamuno that fall of 1906 and in the years preceding it, as well as a mixture of admiration and disillusionment. In "La catedral de Barcelona," a poem dedicated to Joan Maragall and likely read in this Catalan poet's presence during the trip (Rabaté and Rabaté 264), there is a sustained desire for a transnational "patria universal" – here identified with the cathedral, whose "espíritu católico" ("catholic spirit") unites people from various nations and languages, yet without erasing their linguistic and cultural difference. "Tarrassa" describes a young Catalan girl as a symbol of hope for her home province, "un lirio humano henchido de promesas" ("a human lily filled with promise"), and as the poet implies when he thanks God for the encounter "en nombre de mi patria" ("in the name of my homeland"), for Spain in general (*Poesías* 114–15).

"*L'aplec de la protesta*," however, reveals a very different take on Catalonia's youthfulness: it expresses the poet's disillusionment with regional nationalism. Unamuno composed this last poem in response to his experience at a rally in protest of the *Ley de Jurisdicciones*. Though he had denounced this law in "La patria y el ejército" and "Más sobre la crisis del patriotismo," and thus had sympathy for the cause of the rally, Unamuno's poem expresses great disappointment with the Barcelonese, whom the poet calls "niños." It is difficult to determine what it was, exactly, that inspired the writer's antipathy at the rally and in the city in general, but an article that he published in Buenos Aires' *La Nación* after his trip does provide some clues. In this article, the author focuses on what he perceives as the superficiality of Barcelona, which he carefully distinguishes from rural Catalonia. The capital is a city of façades, attentive to appearances but neglectful of human needs (he notes how typhus spreads because the city has not invested in an adequate drainage system),[15] and overly concerned with the impression it makes on foreigners while ignorant of other parts of Spain. He concedes that the atmosphere is much more pleasant than in Castile, and notes more sarcastically that the Barcelonese have an "envidiable educación cívica en las masas, que les hace celebrar reuniones políticas a veces de muchísima gente, como la que presencié en la Plaza de Toros el domingo 21 de octubre de este año, en medio del mayor orden y del más pacífico entusiasmo" ("an enviable civility in large groups, which allows them to hold political meetings at times of a great number of people, like the one I witnessed in the bullring on Sunday the 21st of October of this year, in the midst of the greatest order and most peaceful enthusiasm") (*OCE* 1:259). He continues,

> Entusiasmo más sensual que apasionado, más estético que poético – es decir, recreativo – ; entusiasmo que se vació en gran parte en un agitar pañuelos blancos, diciéndose para sí cada espectador: "¡Oh, qué hermoso!," y yo, al salir de aquel mitin monstruo, del que llamaron *aplec de la protesta*, iba parodiando a aquel sacerdote egipcio cuando habló a Solón de los griegos, diciéndome para mí mismo: ¡ay, barceloneses, barceloneses, siempre seréis unos niños! (259)

> (An enthusiasm that is more sensual than passionate, more aesthetic than poetic – that is, recreational – ; an enthusiasm that expended itself mostly in the waving of white handkerchiefs, while each spectator said to him or herself: 'Oh, how beautiful!' And I, when I left that monstrous meeting that they called *aplec de la protesta*, went parodying that old Egyptian priest when he spoke to the Greek Solon, saying to myself, Oh, Barcelonese, Barcelonese, you will always be children!)

Like the Greeks as described by the Egyptian in Plato's *Timaeus*, in Unamuno's view the inhabitants of Barcelona are childlike in that they praise their own culture and remain willfully incognizant of the achievements of others. (In this, in fact, they resemble the Castilian traditionalists described in *En torno al casticismo*, who turn away from Europe.) Such an attitude signals to Unamuno that they will never develop spiritually into the generosity of youth, for they refuse to look outside themselves. In so doing they not only fail to work towards a universal harmony between peoples; they also sacrifice their own freedom of conscience. The large political gathering, which Unamuno attributes with irony to civic propriety ("educación"), is in his view the indoctrination of the people in mass mentality.

In the poetic version of Unamuno's account of the *aplec*, his tone becomes more sarcastic, and his words provide more insight into his distinction in the article between "estético" and "poético." As it parodies the patriotic character of the rally, *"L'aplec de la protesta"* could be a passage from a mock epic. It begins amidst the applause following a series of speeches against the new law, when one member of the crowd pulls out a handkerchief and begins to wave it: "brotó un pañuelo / y al punto se pobló la gradería / de blancas flámulas" ("a handkerchief sprouted / and immediately the stands were filled / with white pennants") (*Poesías* 116). The poet describes this ripple effect with a somewhat ridiculous extended simile:

> Diríase una banda de gaviotas
> después de haber pasado a flor del océano
> cuando alza el vuelo
> y un momento se agita a ras del agua,
> templando la partida. (116)
>
> (As when a flock of seagulls,
> after passing over the surface of the ocean,
> rises in flight
> and for a moment flutters just above the water,
> delaying departure.)

This epic flourish communicates the heightened drama of the moment for the onlookers. The scene before them manages to orchestrate the emotions of the crowd and produces the collective exclamation: "¡Oh, qué [*sic*] es hermoso!" ("Oh, how beautiful!") (117). Just as one handkerchief sets a flock of "pennants" waving, a single sense of awe and admiration consumes the entire crowd. All of one mind, they surrender to the spectacle, and the show becomes the true protagonist of the gathering: "Fue el triunfo de la estética / ¡el espectáculo!" ("It was the triumph of aesthetics! / The spectacle!") The poet documents this "fiesta para los ojos" ("feast for the eyes"), and mimics the somewhat simplistic enthusiasm of the crowd with mock astonishment: "fue la protesta!" ("it was the protest!") (117). But he cannot help becoming serious at the end of the poem, questioning the value of the spectacle as it ends. He comments, "Momento de hermosura … ¡bien! ¿y el fruto?" ("A moment of beauty … Good! And its fruit?"):

> Y al salir …
> . . . .
> sentí en mi pecho
> la voz grave del mar de mi Vizcaya,

la que brizó mi cuna,
voz que decía:
¡seréis siempre unos niños, levantinos!,
¡os ahoga la estética! (117–18)

(When I left …
. . . .
I felt in my chest
the grave voice of the sea of my Biscay,
the one that rocked my cradle,
a voice that said:
You will always be children, Levantines!
You drown in aesthetics!)

The Barcelonese people resemble children captivated by a pretty scene, but who in the process lose their individual capacity for critique. The spectacle of the *aplec* offers them a means to express a patriotic sentiment, but does not empower them to change their sociopolitical situation as individuals. "*L'aplec de la protesta*" thus denounces an instance of what Walter Benjamin would refer to later (though in a very different context) as the aestheticization of politics (*Illuminations* 41).[16] The poet's disgust here anticipates the indignation that he would voice whenever he saw political rhetoric stamping out freedom of thought in Spain, be it by direct censorship or propaganda. In this case, Unamuno reads the situation as another example of how nationalism, on the level of the country or the region, inhibits the development of a people, in this case making them childishly self-centred rather than endowing them with the agency necessary for them to express and truly give of themselves; that is, to act youthfully in the political realm.

Perhaps Unamuno was thinking of his trip to Catalonia when he distinguished youth from both adulthood and childhood in "Socialismo y juventud" a few months later, in May of 1907. In any case, the image of the Barcelonese as children drowning in aesthetics while a decrepit Spain crumbles around them speaks a great deal to his view of artistic movements back in Madrid at the turn of the century, which he also scorned as he immersed himself in the writing of poetry for the first time. In this, the distinction between "estético" and "poético" – the former superficially sensual while the latter is regenerative, "recreativo" – illuminates a link between his concept of youth in politics and his views on what might constitute truly young art.

A Change of Rhythm

Just as faith and socialism are continuous and evolving elements in Unamuno's writing from the 1890s through the first decade of the twentieth century, so too his interest in rhythm – a poetic device that also serves in his writing as a metaphor for the vitality of cultures and artistic movements – is a recurring presence in his essays during these years. For the Unamuno of the turn of the century, the stagnation of Spanish culture requires a change of rhythm, and more than that, a complete reconfiguration: a transformation of its very chemical make-up. In the opening of the essay "La juventud 'intelectual' española" ("'Intellectual' Spanish Youth"), the fourth and last of the series of essays he published in *Ciencia Social* in 1896, he uses the Greek term *metarrhythmisis* to describe this desired "'cambio de ritmo' o sea transmutación de íntima estructura" ("'change of rhythm,' that is, transmutation of inner structure") (*E* 3:47). The word has theological resonance, as it is used in the Eastern Orthodox Church to describe the transformation undergone by the bread and wine in the celebration of the Eucharist, comparable to transubstantiation (Greek: *metousiosis*) in Roman Catholic doctrine (Meyendorff 203–5). Here, however, Unamuno layers onto this concept an understanding of renewal borrowed from contemporary chemistry. Drawing from the German chemist Lothar Meyer's *Les theories modernes de la chimie et leur application à la mécanique chimique* (French translation, 1887–1889), to which he directs his readers in a footnote,[17] Unamuno envisions the needed change in Spanish society in terms of isometric compounds. Such compounds, though they all contain the same elements in equal proportions, differ in their various properties "hasta el punto de ser cuerpos totalmente diversos" ("to such an extent that they are completely different substances"). The reasons for this difference are to be found in the arrangement of the compounds' constitutive atoms, which, the essayist asserts following Meyer, "se reduce a una diferencia en ritmo molecular" ("comes down to a difference in molecular rhythm") (*E* 3:48).

Unamuno sees in this concept of molecular rhythm a metaphorical means to describe the relative energies of different cultures. Invoking the first law of thermodynamics, he observes that "hay pueblos que *andan fríos*, otros que *se están caldeados* y otros por fin – ¡terrible estado! – que *se están fríos*, dormitando en monorítmicas [*sic*] oscilaciones, en verdadero estado de cristalización, estado en que parece se mueven las moléculas a batuta y compás, todas a un tiempo y en una dirección todas" ("there are cultures that are *active but cold*, others that are *inactive but warm*, and still others – terrible state! – that are *inactive and cold*, slumbering in monorrhythmic oscilations, a true state of crystallization, a state in which it seems that the molecules move to a single beat, all at the same time and in the same direction") (50). It is not difficult to guess to which of these categories Spain belongs, in Unamuno's view. According to the essayist, this cultural monotony extends to all sectors of Spain's intellectual life. All of Spain – and most urgently, its young people – needs to undergo "una sacudida en las más íntimas y entrañables palpitaciones de su ser" ("a shaking-up of the deepest and innermost palpitations of its being") (47–8). As it takes its images from contemporary molecular physics, this essay clearly envisions novelty in the terms of recombination that North has described. Once again, however, Unamuno ties the possibility of innovation explicitly to the young: it is youth that needs to be "metarritmizada."

Why does Unamuno single out the younger sector of Spanish intellectuals? Given the disdain for old age that appears repeatedly in his writing during these years, this critical attitude towards youth might seem inconsistent. Yet as in his views of regional nationalisms in the political realm, in the cultural sphere, and especially with regard to poetry, Unamuno sees false youth in any collective mentality that limits free expression for the individual and, consequently, keeps emerging artistic trends from producing real change.[18] In this regard, the artistic trend that received the brunt of his criticism was *modernismo*. His relationship to this Hispanic literary movement is complex, and made more so by critical debates regarding its definition, extension, and relationship to modernism more broadly. Here I focus on Unamuno's own use of the term, which was largely negative and usually refers to the literary culture of Madrid, despite the origins of the movement in Latin America and the important influence of Catalan *modernisme* in the Peninsular variety.[19] In his opinion, the novelty that *modernismo* offered to Spain was a superficial one: a veneer of stylistic affectation that did not attempt to rearrange the most basic elements of the poetic tradition.

Though "La juventud 'intelectual' española" does not mention the *modernistas* by name, it provides an illuminating picture of how cultural life in *fin-de-siècle* Spain appeared to Unamuno. The predominant image in the essay, which also appears in a number of his writings over the next several years, is that of "la charca nacional" ("the national pond"). Santos Juliá has interpreted this motif in the work of the turn-of-the-century Unamuno as a form of reactionary late romanticism that deplores the present state of society without offering an alternative, and thus tells us more about Unamuno than about the society he purported to depict. That the allegory he develops based on this image bears the imprint of the writer's subjectivity is undoubtedly true, but from a literary perspective this makes it extremely useful, as it supplies a backdrop against which to understand both Unamuno's critiques of *modernismo* and his own developing poetics. Indeed, with the focus on rhythm that opens the essay and the essayist's imagining of Spanish society as a pond in which various forms of wildlife produce song, the poetic serves throughout "La juventud 'intelectual' española" as an implicit barometer for the cultural wellbeing of the nation.

An illuminating factor in Unamuno's vision of modern Spanish culture in this essay is the role intergenerational dynamics play within it. In the essayist's description, the *charca* is populated by frogs and tadpoles at various stages of development who chirp in unison to create the soporific drone that a swamp exudes on a summer evening. The old frogs – "viejas ranas" – represent the ensconced Spanish cultural establishment. Below them in the water are obsequious tadpoles ("renacuajos") anxiously awaiting the day that "les crezcan las patas y se les borre el rabo" ("their feet will grow and their tails will disappear") (*E* 3:52). Exemplifying a cultural sycophantism that Unamuno would lambast later in his essay "Ramplonerías!" (1905), these youngsters – organized, the essayist declares, in hierarchical order according to the length of their tails – are disloyal to their youth in wishing only for the approval of their elders and the security of adulthood. A bird that crosses the sky above, singing a song to freedom, openness, and light ("a la libertad, al aire abierto y a la luz"), symbolizes new currents of thought from beyond the nation's borders – but the insular Spanish frogs refuse to hear its song, splashing in the swamp to disturb the bird's reflection and cover up its voice (53). The essayist later makes explicit the connection between this hierarchy based on age and the Restoration government, with its capital in what he calls "el Sahara de Madrid." In this urban desert, he writes, "la centralización política ha recojido [*sic*] a los más de los jóvenes que se las buscan" ("political centralization has absorbed the majority of the young people looking to make a living") (56). He immediately goes on to cite the range of youth organizations that have sprung up in Madrid, "toda clase de juventudes y ninguna joven" ("every kind of youth imaginable, and none of them young") (56), displaying his keen distaste for the collectivization and pseudo-militarization of youth that was occurring in Spain as throughout Europe at this time.

Notably, he also associates this with political centralism. As he observes how the Restoration government regiments youth in all areas of life, whether political, cultural, or intellectual, he insists that such regulation annhiliates youthfulness itself.

What is absent in the allegory of *la charca* (and from Madrid's cultural life in Unamuno's view) is a positive image of true youth to correspond to those the essayist employs in essays like "La fe" and "Socialismo y juventud." Such an ideal cultural youth might be represented by a hypothetical tadpole able to escape from the swamp and chirp to the beat of its own drummer, as it were,[20] perhaps in harmony or counterpoint with the foreign bird in the sky. In a later poem that revisits this allegorical scene, "A la corte de los poetas" ("To the Court of the Poets"), Unamuno in fact imagines that the tadpoles sprout wings, turn into larks, and fly away. These protean amphibians-turned-birds manage to leave the rigid hierarchical system and narrow-mindedness of the pond behind. Yet ultimately the poet doubts the viability of such a solution in his contemporary Spain: "Pero, ¡no!, nuestras ranas son sesudas, / no les tienta el volar" ("But, no! Our frogs are sensible, / flying does not tempt them") (*Poesías* 77).

The only manuscript of "A la corte de los poetas" preserved in the archives of the Casa Museo Unamuno is the one that appears in the full compilation of *Poesías*, so it is impossible to know for certain what year it was composed. However, the title that Unamuno gives it does provide a chronological marker, as it alludes to an anthology of *modernista* verse published by Emilio Carrere in 1905, *La corte de los poetas*.[21] With this allusion, Unamuno applies the allegory of the *charca* that he had developed a decade earlier to the poetry scene in Spain during the first years of the century – notably, at the time when he himself was writing more and more verse. It would seem that in Unamuno's view, contemporary Spanish poetry – particularly that represented in Carrere's anthology – maintains the hierarchy of "viejas ranas" and servile "renacuajos." As Marta Palenque has observed, in his editorial choices and his introduction to *La corte de los poetas*, Carrere does not distinguish between nineteenth-century predecessors and his contemporaries, either in terms of chronology or of poetic style; "on the contrary, he establishes a sort of continuity between the great poets of the nineteenth century (in his opinion Campoamor 'the divine,' Zorrilla, Rivas, Bécquer, and Espronceda) and the contemporary ones" (Palenque xxi, my translation). Such reverence for the poets of the previous century would likely have irritated Unamuno, especially as he sought to forge an iconoclastic

– or ideo-clastic – poetics of his own. It is telling that he includes "A la corte de los poetas" in the introductory section of *Poesías*, along with five other poems that serve as a sort of manifesto, a summary of his own poetic stance. In this last poem of the section, Unamuno presents himself as a poet who rejects both the old ways and the false youth of new trends.[22]

Carrere gave Unamuno further motive to dislike his collection by including the work of José Zorrilla in it. For the Basque writer, Zorrilla – a famed and revered bard much beloved by the middle class – epitomized the old cultural hegemony of the past century. In a well-known passage from a letter to poet Juan Arzadun, Unamuno derides Zorrilla's popularity: "Sólo aquí puede pasar por gran poeta Zorrilla, encarnación de la vacuidad sonora y tarareante" ("Only here can Zorrilla, that incarnation of sonorous and humming vacuousness, pass for a great poet") (cited in García Blanco, *Don Miguel* 44). What most annoys him in Zorrilla's verse and in contemporary Spanish poetry at large is the plodding beat that disguises a lack of content and poetic ingenuity, and a formulaic character that suffocates what little aesthetic value might remain. This is a problem of excessive prescriptivity, of attending too strictly to patterns of rhyme and metre. In the notes on poetry and translation that he includes in *Poesías*, Unamuno deplores the "oído preceptivo tradicional en España" ("prescriptive ear that is traditional in Spain") (*Poesías* 325). The rules that govern Spanish poetry are overly rigid and doctrinaire, constituting another form of *ideocracia* wherein theory dictates and constrains practice.

For Unamuno, nineteenth-century Spanish poets like Zorrilla represent the old molecular structure of a culture that must be broken apart into its constitutive elements and reassembled. Still, if Zorrilla and the traditionalism that he represented frustrated the Basque poet, the latter did not find the kind of rhythmic rejuvenation he desired in more recent poetic trends. There too, his preferences placed him at odds with the poets revered by his contemporaries. While he might have concurred with Paul Verlaine's provocation against prevailing trends in nineteenth-century France, "prends l'éloquence et tords-lui son cou!" ("take up eloquence and wring its neck!"),[23] he remained unconvinced by the French Symbolists and Parnassians that the *modernistas* admired. He saw these trends as limiting the artist to a narrowly literary environment like the proverbial ivory tower that separates the intellectual from broader social life. In a letter to Candamo from 1900 he expresses these concerns with reference to Rubén Darío: "Tiene un valor positivo muy grande, pero carece de toda cultura que no sea exclusivamente literaria … Sin sentido filosófico y hasta metafísico, ético, científico y religioso del mundo se podrá ser un *homme de lettres,* pero no un gran escritor" ("He has a very great positive value, but he lacks all culture beyond the exclusively literary … Without a philosophical, and even metaphysical, ethical, scientific, and religious sense of the world one can be a man of letters, but not a great writer") (Blázquez-González 261).

This attitude towards the early Darío cannot be written off as a manifestation of Unamuno's avowed "Francophobia" or his wish to retain a Hispanic cultural hegemony in Latin America, both of which are nevertheless evident elsewhere in his writing.[24] The critique is rooted in his own poetics. Unamuno's "Credo poético," the second poem included in *Poesías* and his version of the Horatian *ars poetica,* offers insight into the "deeper metaphysics" he found in poetry as it dialogues with Verlaine's "Art Poétique." The French poet had famously championed "la musique avant toute chose / … / sans rien en lui qui pèse ou qui pose" (*Oeuvres* 150), identifying nuance and musicality as the highest values in his art. In "Credo poético," by contrast, Unamuno resists Verlaine's celebration of intangible music, arguing that poems need to have form and weight: "algo que no es música es la poesía, / la pesada sólo queda" ("poetry is something that is not music, / only verse with weight endures") (*Poesías* 67). Some early reviewers of *Poesías* – and more than a few estimations of the collection since – did not hesitate to affirm that Unamuno's poetry was indeed *pesada,* clunky and tiresome,[25] but of course the poet's words here are not an enjoinder to write pedantries. They counter Verlaine in order to claim that the poet must begin his work from concrete, material existence observed by an alert and open mind. Unamuno's allergy to *ideocracia* appears once again, as he priveleges the reality of experience over the imposition of preconceived ideas:

> No el que un alma encarna en carne, ten presente,
> no el que forma da a la idea es el poeta
> sino que es el que alma encuentra tras la carne
> tras la forma encuentra idea. (67)
>
> (Not he who embodies in body a soul,
> nor he who gives form to idea, bear in mind;
> the poet rather finds soul through the body,
> and through form, idea finds.)

Here imagined as a sculptor, the poet works with concrete material – sensory images and language – to create something that transcends them, but does not tailor his words or feelings to fit an already-defined notion, style, or form. Material reality – the flesh – is primary, while ideas are secondary, developed through the work and not imposed upon it from the start.

The understanding of poetic creation in "Credo poético" as the sculpting of experience lay at the heart of Unamuno's critique of the Spanish *modernistas*, whom he saw as distracted by Verlainean musicality and Darío's literary allusions from the weighty, generative work of *poiesis*. In his estimation, the young writers in Spain who emulated these poets had little sense of their own artistic vocation, little of the enthusiasm and passion that were central to his understanding of true religious faith and of socialism's approach to politics. Instead, these youths were insecure, quicker to imitate others, whether elders or peers, than to strike out on their own. Even the most counter-cultural forms of aesthetic self-fashioning struck him as conventional at base. In "La juventud 'intelectual' española" he remarks on the "juventud de los bohemizantes, el detritus del romanticismo melenudo" ("youth of the bohemianizers, the detritus of the long-haired romantics") – *melenudo*, long-haired, was one of his preferred epithets for the *modernistas* in Madrid – as "borrachos que cultivan el arcaico convencionalismo de tronar contra los convencionalismos siendo convencionales hasta el tuétano" ("drunks who cultivate the archaic conventionalism of raving against conventionalisms while being conventional to the core") (*E* 3:59). A decade later, in an article published the same month as "Socialismo y juventud," he reflects on how, as they grew older, the *modernistas* had continued without direction or fervor, and that many, on or about their thirty-fifth birthday, had given up their juvenile ways in order to become "buenas personas calculadoras y razonables" ("good, calculating, and reasonable people") (*OCE* 7:1304). The ease with which these one-time rebels conformed to serious, rational maturity, assuming positions of social respectability, suggests that they had never been truly young. They never set out to transform their society through critical and creative work, but merely hoped to ensure their own security within the status quo.

Poesías, then, represents Unamuno's attempt to rejuvenate Spanish poetry by different means than those of *modernismo*. In presenting his own first collection of verse, Unamuno works against the grain, as Manuel Álvar observes (*Poesías* 39). The culmination of his thinking about Spanish culture and poetics during the preceding decade, *Poesías* runs counter to its contemporary literary world by questioning dominant views of what poetry ought to be like, and by putting forth alternative rhythms and patterns of thought. As they resist the limitations that might be imposed upon them by tradition or by contemporary trends, the poems of *Poesías* constitute Unamuno's own attempt at *metarrhythmisis*, a disruption and reconfiguration of turn-of-the-century Spanish verse. Many of them present a change of rhythm in the most literal sense: as if guided again by modern chemistry, the poet breaks traditional metres down into their constituent stressed and unstressed syllables, and puts them together in an unfamiliar order to jostle the reader awake. An excellent example of this practice is "Música," a poem that outrightly refuses to sound or scan in an agreeable manner:

¿Música? ¡No! No así en el mar de bálsamo
me adormezcas el alma;
no, no la quiero;
no cierres mis heridas – mis sentidos –
al infinito abiertas,
sangrando anhelo. (*Poesías* 249)

(Music? No! Not like that – don't lull my soul
to sleep in a sea of balsam;
no, I do not want it;
don't close up my wounds – my senses –
lying open to infinity,
bleeding desire.)

Echoing a critique that he also articulates in a review of Manuel Machado's *Alma* (1901), the poet rejects the soporific effects of verses meant merely to be pleasing to the ear. He works to keep his reader as alert as he himself strives to be. Punctuated by sharp exclamations of "¡No!" and "¡sí!, ¡sí!," as well as uncomfortable images and collisions of stress – "que mi mano / sus huesos crujir haga" ("that my hand / might make its bones creak," 249) – the poem denies the reader the peaceful experience its title might suggest, choosing instead to startle and provoke.

Elsewhere in the collection, recombination occurs on a thematic level. The book contains several of the religious and political poems analysed earlier in this chapter, as well as scenes from domestic life; meditations inspired by the "musings" of the English Lake Poets;[26] and translations from English, Catalan, and Italian. As such, its contents already display a much wider range and greater juxtaposition of topics than was typical of *modernista* collections. What is more, some individual poems show Unamuno interacting with the Spanish tradition that precedes him much in the manner that T.S. Eliot describes in "Tradition and the Individual Talent" with yet another chemical analogy. As with the introduction of a piece of platinum into a chamber containing oxygen and sulphur dioxide, Unamuno, as a "new poet," catalyses an alteration in the "*whole* existing order" of the poetic canon prior to his appearance (Eliot 15). Whereas Eliot makes the "mature poet" the protagonist of his essay, however, Unamuno again resists the idea of rational autonomy that informs such a concept of maturity. The poem "No busques luz, mi corazón, sino agua" ("Don't Search for Light, My Heart, but Water") illustrates this with a stiking rearrangement of images and philosophical ideas present in the work of his predecessor Fray Luis de León.

"No busques luz" presents a reconfiguration of relationships between the human soul, knowledge, the natural world, and the divine as it subtly dialogues with Fray Luis' writing. In the opening lines of the poem, a description of the poet's soul as bewildered and confused, having lost its capacity for discernment and true orientation ("tino"), instantly calls to mind the sixteenth-century poet's ode "A Francisco Salinas," dedicated to a professor of music at the Universidad de Salamanca, where both men preceeded Unamuno by three centuries. In his ode, Fray Luis describes how his soul recovers its "tino" upon listening to the music of Salinas' organ, which induces a spiritual ascent through the spheres to God – the source of divine, celestial music, and of supreme enlightenment. In Unamuno's text, this neoplatonic vision of the universe is inverted and complicated. Predictably, he does not share Fray Luis' interest in music, choosing instead to focus on the role of light as a metaphor for knowledge of the divine (present in the ode to Salinas as "luz no usada" ["uncommon light"]). It is clear from the title of "No busques luz" that the modern poet rejects this metaphor. Referring to the sun not as source of life but as a blind executioner ("ciego verdugo"), he urges his soul, imagined as a tree, to flee the light and let its roots take refuge in the ground, where water, darkness, and mystery will nourish it. Whereas for Fray Luis the poet's true self was revealed and re-discovered through an ascent that distanced him from the material world, Unamuno writes that this upward movement is antithetical to self-understanding.

Ultimately, "No busques luz" replaces the idea of separation between the mundane and the earthly in Fray Luis' poem with an image of interdependence. In its final lines, the tree that represents the poet's soul appears planted on the banks of a still pond, bending over the water to see the starry night sky and its branches reflected together on its surface. Pondering this scene, the poet muses,

> Y esta misma agua mansa
> . . . .
> sustancia es de los cielos de que llueve,
> y el cielo mismo, el cielo en que se mueve
> el coro de las luces siderales,
> verás, si miras bien, cómo se asienta,
> y cómo en el vacío
> la Tierra sobre el cielo se sustenta;
> el cielo está a tus pies, corazón mío. (214, ll. 88–97)
>
> (And this same still water
> . . . .
> is the substance of the sky from which it rains,
> and the sky itself, the heaven that displays
> the chorus of the sidereal lights,
> you'll see, if you look close, how it comes to rest,
> and how in the emptiness
> the Earth rises up above the sky;
> heaven is at your feet, heart of mine.)

These lines produce an image that counters the rigid conglomerate of ideas described in "La ideocracia." Through the natural cycle of precipitation and the play of reflections on the surface of a lake, heaven and earth are joined in a process of constant transformation. In this poem, Unamuno rearranges old neoplatonic oppositions between spiritual purity and "fallen" matter, as well as philosophical and religious associations of light with knowledge and the divine. He argues that it is only by penetrating within – not ascending on high – that one arrives at the mystery of the divine and the knowledge of the self. In so doing, he contests in poetic form modernity's teleological orientation towards enlightenment, replacing its unidirectional movement with a constellation of ideas and experiences in a new ordering. "No busques luz" thus enacts a kind of ideo-clasm, a disruption of the reigning ideologies of the Spanish tradition, that the poet undertakes elsewhere in

Poesías through experimental rhythm, critique, and a near-constant use of the dialogic mode.

In the last analysis, dialogism, understood in the Bakhtinian sense of a text in conversation with a range of others both past and future, is perhaps the most fundamental characteristic of this collection, written by a late-blooming poet longing to retain contact with his own younger self and with the young people who would come after him. The prevalence of second-person address and the imperative and subjunctive moods in the poems of *Poesías* reinforce their author's rebellion against what the Western philosophical tradition had identified as a state of maturity: the autonomy of reason. To be sure, it can be argued that this gesture simply repeats a romantic move, especially as exemplified by the British romantics that Unamuno had read. Still, the Spanish poet's engagement with future generations, particularly in "Cuando yo sea viejo," displays an aesthetic self-consciousness rooted in the intellectual and social contexts of the modernist period. *Poesías* is a work that extends beyond itself to engage with other poets, with realms of experience not traditionally considered "poetic," and especially, with the reader. As this chapter has shown, a similar stance infuses Unamuno's essays, which engage the reader in a more discursive fashion and often rework ideas also present in the poetry. The implicit argument of "No busques luz," for example, owes much to "¡Adentro!," and lends many of its images to the later essay "El secreto de la vida" ("The Secret of Life"). Both of these essays, along with "La fe," "La ideocracia," "Viejos y jóvenes," "Religión y patria," "La crisis del patriotismo," "La crisis actual del patriotismo español," and "La juventud 'intelectual' española" were selected for inclusion in the Residencia de Estudiantes edition of Unamuno's *Ensayos* in the mid-1910s, and thus made available to the generations immediately following Unamuno's own. In many cases, the encounter with the *Ensayos* was accompanied by a reading of *Poesías*. Through such encounters the essayistic and poetic texts of the turn-of-the-century Unamuno found the interlocutors that their discourse so avidly seeks.

The responses of these subsequent writers, whose cases and contexts I take up in the chapters that follow, were not those of blind submission to a master. In "Cuando yo sea viejo" Unamuno entreated his readers to use his work to argue against him, and in subsequent decades his successors did just that. What is more, they argued with him from their own positions of youth. Writing out of a sense of what being young meant in the immediate time and place of their youth and in the context of their own work, they offered correctives to Unamuno's vision and, indeed, in some cases put his ideas to use in ways he could not foresee and of which he did not necessarily approve. Such appropriations, however, are unavoidable in the reception of texts that so directly invoke and provoke their audience, that offer themselves as ideas to be used. "Me daría por pagado si lograra sugerir *una sola idea* a *un solo* lector" ("I would consider myself repaid if I manage to suggest *one single idea* to *one single* reader"), Unamuno writes at the end of *En torno al casticismo* (*E* 1:218, original emphasis). The following chapters chart some of the ideas that the turn-of-the-century Unamuno who wrote these texts inspired in his successors – along with the Unamuno who, off the page, continued to write, teach, critique his contemporary Spanish society, and correspond with young people.

Chapter Two

The Heroic Age: The Residencia de Estudiantes, José Moreno Villa, and Spanish Adolescence During the First World War

Though the political, economic, and cultural changes brought on by the First World War transformed Spanish society much as they did those of other European nations, the fact that Spain remained neutral in the conflict often causes this impact to be overlooked.[1] Far away from the trenches, Spain once again seemed to be behind the times, looking on as the more sophisticated countries went to war (albeit a war that would call that very sophistication into question). In his memoirs, Juan Ramón Jiménez recalled an evening in July 1914 when he, José Ortega y Gasset, Federico de Onís, and Alberto Jiménez Fraud gathered on Madrid's Paseo de la Castellana – just steps away from the Residencia de Estudiantes, then located on Calle Fortuny – to read news of the declarations of war. Jiménez wrote that on that night he had the impression of living "en los trasmuros del mundo" ("on the outskirts of the world") (*Guerra en España* 121). Politician and pedagogue Luis de Zulueta expressed a similar sentiment in a talk he gave in late 1915 at the Residencia, by that time situated at the new campus that Jiménez had named "La Colina de los Chopos" ("The Hill of the Poplars") for the trees he had planted there. In that talk Zulueta also bemoaned Spain's air of provinciality, comparing it to a sleepy "pueblo" cut off from the bustling metropolis of Europe (*La edad* 108). Yet as he spoke to the adolescent students that made up his audience, he affirmed that they could still contribute to the events that were transforming the continent, by way of a "nuevo pacifismo heroico":

> Tiene la juventud española deberes muy especiales, deberes muy urgentes que cumplir. España está en paz; afortunadamente, está en paz. ¡Ojalá lo esté siempre! Pero … preciso es que nosotros, aprovechando

previsoriamente la paz de que gozamos, nos esforcemos en trabajar como si estuviéramos en guerra … fomentando la riqueza y la cultura del país, haciendo una España nueva que pueda incorporarse mañana a esa nueva Europa cuyos cimientos, amasados con sangre, se están ahora echando a lo largo de las trincheras. (143–4)

(Spanish youth has very special, very urgent duties to perform. Spain is at peace; fortunately, it is at peace. That it might always be so! But … we, looking ahead and taking advantage of the peace we enjoy, must make an effort to work as if we were at war … promoting the wealth and culture of the country, making a new Spain so that tomorrow it may join that new Europe whose foundation, mixed with blood, is being laid right now in the trenches.)

The optimism of Zulueta's words, still possible at this point in the war – or perhaps made possible by Spain's physical and political distance from the battlefields – is full of dramatic irony for the twenty-first century reader. Zulueta cannot foresee the difficulties that will plague the efforts to forge a new Europe after the devastation of the First World War, nor can he know that even as he gave this lecture tensions and divisions were arising in Spanish society that would bring it to its own civil conflict twenty years later.[2] In 1915, he can present Spanish neutrality as a privileged position of security and peace that allows the young people of his nation to cultivate a kind of heroism that transcends the present conflict. This praise for the patriotic wartime contributions of young people to national interests parallels the celebration of heroic youth promoted during these years in England, France, or Germany, and thus suggests that Spain's neutrality did not preclude its participation in the broad cultural currents that affected all of Europe in the mid-1910s. Zulueta's exaltation of heroic *pacifism*, however, is a surprising endorsement of Spain's neutral position, for it fails to acknowledge a well-documented cultural reality within the country: the fact that, though the nation technically stayed out of the conflict, in practical terms Spain and its people were far from indifferent to it. Debates between *aliadófilos* (a group that included progressives, liberals, and most of the intellectual community) and *germanófilos* (traditionalists, the aristocracy, the military, and the Church) raged in the press, and port cities on the coasts were inevitably implicated in the economics of the war.[3] Spain was not truly neutral, and some intellectuals viewed such a claim as farcical, accusing Prime Minister Eduardo Dato's administration

– and later that of Álvaro de Figueroa, Count of Romanones – of tacitly supporting the Central Powers. Prominent among these critics was Unamuno, whose unexplained dismissal from his post as rector of the Universidad de Salamanca in the spring of 1914 aggravated his virulent attacks on the Spanish government and its handling of the war.[4] It might be argued that Zulueta's conciliatory stance in his lecture recalls Ortega's efforts early on to find a third voice in Spain's domestic debate, one based on a "neutralidad activa" (Menéndez Alzamora 295). But by late 1915, Ortega had also given his support to the Allies, and his journal *España* was to become the foremost organ for anti-German views in the country. Why, then, does Zulueta (himself an *aliadófilo*) stress to his young audience that Spain is at peace? And what, exactly, is the work that he would have them do as the war is waged elsewhere?

The questions that arise from Zulueta's lecture, which was published the next year with the title *La edad heroica* (*The Heroic Age*), get at the heart of the identity of the Residencia de Estudiantes and the image of Spanish youth that it promoted during the first decade of its existence, the second of the century. In this chapter, I argue that the Residencia's fashioning of youth develops emphases on creativity, artistic individuality, and poetic interiority drawn from Unamuno, but that it also incorporates them into a discourse of patriotism and discipline comparable to those found in other parts of Europe in the years leading up to the First World War. It embraces the radical potentiality of youth that appears in an essay like Unamuno's "La fe" as the ability to create new realities ("crear lo que no vemos"), but directs that possibility towards a pseudo-military project of nation building to be undertaken by a select cultural elite. It thus departs significantly from the critique of nationalism expounded in Unamuno's early writings, and from his association of youth with political opposition to the Restoration regime. The early poetry of José Moreno Villa provides an illuminating example of these dynamics at the Residencia, demonstrating the extent of Unamuno's interaction with and intellectual influence on that community, as well as the ways in which it revised and tempered some of his views, particularly in relation to political engagement and critique. Indeed, the wartime nationalization of youth led the Residencia's project of cultural and pedagogical reform to lose touch with political realities, for in the case of this pedagogical institution to fall in line with the nation was, in multiple senses, to claim neutrality.

In the 1910s, the Residencia found itself caught between the modernizing liberal mission that it had inherited from the Institución Libre de

Enseñanza and the need to ensure its own survival within a State not entirely sympathetic to such aims. Born out of opposition to government restrictions on intellectual freedom in the first years of the Bourbon Restoration, the ILE presented itself as an alternative to traditional education in Spain, independent of the State's political and religious interests.[5] In this context, the declaration in article 15 of the ILE's statues that it would be "completamente ajena a todo espíritu e interés de comunión religiosa, escuela filosófica o partido politico" ("completely separate from the spirit and interests of any one religious community, philosophical school, or political party") was nevertheless inevitably political: it amounted to a *non serviam* directed to the Spanish State.[6] The Residencia proudly continued in this tradition, but the growing prestige and acceptance of new pedagogical methods in the twentieth century, marked by the founding of the Junta para Ampliación de Estudios e Investigaciones Científicas (JAE) in 1907, changed its relationship to the government. Striving both to represent the best of a modernized Spain and to situate itself at the height of European culture (as exemplified by its emulation of the English residential colleges at Oxford and Cambridge), it wavered between rupture and conservation, between the endeavour to be on the cutting edge of intellectual and artistic life and the need to protect and perpetuate its own liberal tradition. As Alison Sinclair has put it, the Residencia occupied "a curious middle-ground" in early twentieth-century Spanish society ("Telling It" 744).

In its everyday operations, the Residencia aimed to offer an atmosphere conducive to reflection and learning, removed from the rest of society so as to focus completely on the formation of its young residents, viewed as a select minority, the seedlings of the new nation. These young minds were to be nurtured at a distance from the ways of the *ancien régime* that still held sway over Restoration society, and also separated out from that society as an elite enjoying privileges that early twentieth-century culture associated with youthfulness: higher education, study, sports, and leisure. Rather than political activism, the *residentes*' work consisted of learning and self-reflection – a regimen that proved amenable and artistically fruitful for the various poets who would live there as tutors or students in the 1910s, including Jiménez, Moreno Villa, Jorge Guillén, Emilio Prados, and Federico García Lorca. Yet it also marked a divergence between political and poetic youth that would shape the following decades of the Residencia's work. While for the Unamuno of the first decade of the century youth had been inextricably bound to a critique of nationalism and the Restoration regime, at the Residencia it was to be a tool for the creation of a new Spain. This project would require it to assume a strictly apolitical posture.

Unamuno did figure as a major influence on the intellectual and moral disposition of the Residencia, or what its director Alberto Jiménez Fraud called "el espíritu de la casa." Not only had the Basque writer's ideas informed the outlook of many of the educators involved with the direction of the Residencia, but he also spent time there in personal contact with the students. The Residencia was his preferred place to stay whenever business took him to Madrid, and from its founding in 1910 he paid regular visits and delivered lectures there. Such was his involvement in the daily life of the centre during these visits that Jiménez Fraud called him "el perfecto residente" ("the perfect resident"), remembering how he would rise early and set up his "escuela" ("school"), spending the morning interacting with the students (*Historia* 445). José García-Velasco has suggested that the Spanish liberal tradition as it was constructed and exemplified by the Residencia based itself on a synthesis of the influences of Unamuno and Ortega y Gasset ("Alberto Jiménez" 37). While Unamuno clearly had a formative impact on Ortega himself in his early years, by the time the Residencia was established the disagreements between the two regarding Spain's relationship to Europe had made them intellectual antagonists. Yet each man made his mark on the Residencia through his physical presence and his writings. Significantly, both of them had works published by the Residencia during the first decade of its existence. Ortega's *Meditaciones del Quijote* (1914) was the first text published in its series "Ensayos," which reached the height of its activity with the seven volumes of Unamuno's collected essays.

In addition, both men shaped the way youth was conceived at the Residencia, and subsequently projected to the nation. Ortega's argument for the Europeanization of Spain demanded that it achieve a national identity on par with those of other European countries, and fomented a view of Spanish young people as those who would accomplish this task – a heroic generation comparable to the young men that were heading off to war in the belligerent countries. By contrast, Unamuno's vindication of youth as the radical, poetic opponent to a teleological understanding of modernization informed the individual perspectives of many within the Residencia community, fortifying their sense of personal originality and social nonconformity. The case of Moreno Villa, a

2.1 Photograph of Miguel de Unamuno in the garden of the Residencia de Estudiantes, 1913. Universidad de Salamanca. Casa-Museo Unamuno.

poet and painter who was involved in the life of the Residencia in its early years of existence and lived there from 1917 to 1937, is especially illustrative in this regard. While he formed part of Ortega's intellectual circle, during the 1910s this young artist was also developing a poetics that drew inspiration from Unamuno. Moreno Villa has often been seen as the poetic bridge between the Spanish writers of the turn of the century and *la joven literatura* of the following decade, and thus his case presents one means of approximation between Unamuno and those even younger writers. In order to understand the later context, however, it is necessary to examine the less-studied early years of the Residencia, the prelude to the much-mythologized period when Lorca coincided there with Dalí and Buñuel, when they staged plays and gave concerts, and Moreno Villa looked on, as he put it in the title of one of the chapters of his autobiography, "En presencia de la eterna juventud" ("In the Presence of Eternal Youth").

While many studies of the First World War period in Spanish cultural history have focused on the so-called Generation of 1914, led by Ortega, the Residencia provides a richer and more vivid picture of how Spanish intellectuals – at least one group of them, congregated in a place of undeniable cultural influence – imagined youth during these years. One of the primary questions that this chapter seeks to address is how the Residencia, founded on an anti-establishment tradition and often seen as something like the headquarters of the Spanish avant-garde, came to idealize youth in such a way that cast it as transcendent and heroic, but also carefully circumscribed it within certain intellectual, artistic, and social realms – and in some cases, the very walls surrounding its campus. In one sense, this can be explained by its *institucionista* heritage: the ILE had distanced itself from a political environment hostile to its mission, and the Residencia maintained this distance as a fundamental part of its own work. However, in its own historical moment the Residencia's retreat from political life, and to some extent from social concerns more broadly, turned it into a kind of Never-Never Land, an Arcadian space dedicated to imagining an alternate reality that lost the posture of noncompliance and critique that had characterized its predecessor. In this context, Unamuno's ideas about youth held a profound, but also partial, resonance. Where the author of *En torno al casticismo* had distinguished between a deep *intrahistoria* and a superficial *historia* and called on young people to reconnect Spain to its intra-historic roots, his immediate successors at the Residencia also embraced an ideal of youth as an eternal source of renewal for the culture, and of young people themselves as untainted by the country's past and thus capable of redirecting its history. The somewhat paradoxical result was an elegant defence of the heroism of youth on an aesthetic and intellectual level, which nevertheless segregated itself from the political realm and from the intense debates in the country regarding the First World War, effectively reproducing Spain's neutrality with regard to the European conflict.

Unamuno in Málaga

The story of Unamuno's relationship with the Residencia begins in August of 1906, when he gave a series of lectures in the southern costal city of Málaga.[7] A group of young students there, known as the *peña de Málaga* (Málaga club), worked to organize the event and received the rector of the Universidad de Salamanca with enthusiasm. Jiménez Fraud and Moreno Villa were among them. In a letter dated 7 July 1906, Jiménez Fraud wrote to Unamuno in anticipation of his visit, expressing hopes that his lectures would invigorate and inspire the other young people of the Andalusian city:

> La nota fresca la encontramos en la gente joven, pero pasada una cierta edad, todos están conformes (incluso los jóvenes) en que hay que ser sesudo, discreto y compuesto. ¡Qué peso el de estos señores prácticos y de experiencia a quienes vamos a pedirle [*sic*] un pedacito de vida a cambio de otro muy grande que le damos, y que nos responde con un consejo grave y una sonrisa protectora!
>
> Pero hay un grupo de muchachos ansiosos de comunicarse con usted y esta ansia, que ya corre entre muchos, parece que nos ha modificado en pocos días ... ¿Podremos dejar alguna simiente en Málaga? (Jiménez Fraud, *Residentes* 123–4)

> (The fresh perspective is to be found among the young people, but after a certain age everyone [even the young] decides that they must be sensible, discreet, and put-together. How tiresome are those practical, experienced men, whom we ask for a little piece of life in return for the large one we give them, and who answer with a solemn word of advice and a protective smile!
>
> But there is a group of boys who are eager to communicate with you and this eagerness, already shared by many, seems to have changed us in just a few days ... Will we manage to plant a seed in Málaga?)

Jiménez Fraud's words reflect the growing generation gap in early twentieth-century European culture, as they point to a fundamental animosity between youth and adulthood, and take for granted that seriousness and condescension are undesirable characteristics inextricably linked to age. His practical and experienced adult calls to mind Walter Benjamin's "philistine," smiling haughtily from behind his mask of worldly knowledge. Nevertheless, though Jiménez Fraud writes to a man decades older than he, the author of this letter is clearly confident that in this debate Unamuno is on his side – the side of the young. For Jiménez Fraud, the imminent presence of the older writer in his hometown is a beacon of promise for the cultural life of his region, an opportunity to sow its ground with seed and encourage new growth. Indeed, within a few short years he would carry this newfound passion for reform and for youth with him to Madrid and the Residencia.

The topic of reform came up repeatedly in the lectures Unamuno gave in Málaga that August. In the first talk, delivered in the Teatro Cervantes, he spoke about education, reiterating ideas that he had developed in his essays of recent years regarding Spain's cultural stagnation and the need to encourage the young (echoes of "Viejos y jóvenes" and even the much earlier "La juventud 'intelectual' española" are discernible in the speech). But the appeal that Unamuno held for the young men of Málaga went beyond his arguments. As he addressed the challenges facing the country's young people, it was his manner, his independence of thought and spirit that caught the attention of the adolescents in his audience. In their later memoirs, both Jiménez Fraud and Moreno Villa recall this aspect of Unamuno's character and the way it thrilled them as young men. Jiménez Fraud remarks on how Unamuno's fierce individualism and "extremos paradójicos" ("paradoxical extremes") attracted the attention of many young people (*Residentes* 54). Similarly, in a later memoir Moreno Villa recalls the way Unamuno captivated him at twenty, writing that in the first years of the century "apasionaba a la juventud por lo que tenía de revulsivo e inconforme, de voz bíblica y fondo poético" ("he thrilled the young with his galvanizing and nonconformist character, his biblical voice and poetic depths") (*Los autores* 17).

Neither of these retrospective accounts presents unequivocal admiration for Unamuno – in fact, Moreno Villa prefaces his comment by stressing that as an older man, he can no longer view his predecessor as he once had. He looks back and distances himself from his own youthful experience, perhaps as one sheepishly and self-consciously remembers one's idolization of a childhood hero. But the formative impact of this encounter in 1906 on both Moreno Villa and Jiménez Fraud is undeniable. As subsequent letters to Unamuno confirm, that fall Jiménez Fraud was brimming with plans to continue what had been started in Málaga, which he associated not only with the rector from Salamanca's cultural and intellectual activism, but also with the bonds of friendship formed among the young members of the *peña* – a group dynamic that anticipated the kind of community life he would cultivate later at the Residencia.[8] Moreno Villa, for his part, took an immediate interest in Unamuno's poetry. In his first letter to Unamuno, dated 8 September 1906, he asks the older writer to send him copies of two poems that he had apparently read to the youngsters of Málaga during his stay: "El Salmo a la Desesperación" ("Psalm to Desperation") – a possible reference to one of the "salmos" included in *Poesías*, perhaps "Salmo I" – and "otra que Vd. nos leyó dirigida a su perro que nos causó gran impresión" ("another that you read to us addressed to your dog that made a great impression on us") (Robles, "Doce cartas" 63). The latter is a reference to "Elegía en la muerte de un perro" ("Elegy Upon the Death of a Dog"), also from *Poesías*. In his next letter, from 16 October, the young *malagueño* writes of the "tirantez de ánimo que usted nos dejó al partir" ("the spiritual tension that you left with us when you departed"), and affirms that he is now following the older writer's work with interest (63). Elsewhere, on multiple occasions, he used the verb *espolear* (to urge, to spur on) to describe the effect that Unamuno's presence had on him, prodding and provoking, inciting him to action.[9]

Among the seeds planted during Unamuno's trip to Málaga was the seed of Moreno Villa's personal poetics. In an essay he wrote about forty-five years later, titled "Algo sobre poesía" ("Something About Poetry"), the Andalusian writer looks back on the origins of his poetic vocation and remarks that from the beginning he was guided by "un afán de *densidad*, que en gran parte le debo a Unamuno" ("an obsession with *density*, that I owe in good part to Unamuno") (*PCMV* 38, original emphasis). As he describes this poetic density, he points specifically to two texts that sparked this interest: the essay "¡Adentro!" and "Elegía en la muerte de un perro."

> Densidad por adentramiento en la vida psíquica y, si se quiere, metafísica. Dos obras de Unamuno encontraron adherencia en mí por aquellos años:

> su ensayo 'Adentro', y un poema titulado 'En la muerte de un perro', que me mandó manuscrito y leí a mis amigos en Málaga.
>
> Con este poema empecé o aprendí a preguntarme y a preguntar a las cosas, que es el modo de ir adentrándose en ellas. La pregunta es la barrena de la inteligencia. (38)
>
> (Density by way of penetration into psychic and, if you wish, metaphysical life. Two works by Unamuno caught my attention in those years: his essay 'Inward,' and a poem titled 'Upon the Death of a Dog,' which he sent me in his own hand and which I read to my friends in Málaga.
>
> With that poem I began or learned to ask questions of myself and of things, which is the way to penetrate into them. The question is the intellect's drill.)

Moreno Villa goes on to cite some of the questions that appear in Unamuno's elegy, stressing the connection they reveal between interrogation and the poetic craft. Like many of the poems from *Poesías* studied in the previous chapter, "Elegía en la muerte de un perro" is full of questions. The poet rhetorically asks his deceased dog about the nature of the "el otro mundo," the world that comes after death, and his questions are charged with broader existential uncertainties. At one point he also observes that in life the dog would look at him and seem to ask, "¿a dónde vamos, mi amo?" ("Where are we going, owner?") (Unamuno, *Poesías* 210). This question about direction and purpose underlies the entire poem. Like "No busques luz, mi corazón, sino agua," it questions the neoplatonic element in Christian thought that orients human life towards an otherworldly heaven devoid of material existence. When he considers the idea that "El otro mundo es el del puro espíritu" ("The other world is the one of pure spirit"), the poet immediately exclaims, "¡Oh terrible pureza, / inanidad, vacío!" ("Oh, terrible purity, / inanity, emptiness!") (209). Through the interrogative mode, the elegy addresses these reflections and the many questions they prompt not only to the dog, or to God, but also to the reader. In so doing, the poet forces the reader to question the nature and limits of his or her own existence, much as Unamuno does by other means in the novel *Niebla*, which he wrote not long after composing this elegy.[10]

For Moreno Villa, the state of personal questioning elicited by "Elegía en la muerte de un perro" is what defines Unamuno's poetic concept of density. Elsewhere in "Algo sobre poesía" he refers to the substantial quality of Unamuno's verse, a weightiness that he finds lacking in the more "ethereal" (Moreno Villa's term) poetry of Rubén Darío and Juan Ramón Jiménez (*PCMV* 40). But above all, it is the phonic (though not etymological) link between the Spanish *denso* (dense) and *adentro* (within) that seems to shape Moreno Villa's thought here. Unamuno's exhortations to his young reader in "¡Adentro!" reinforce this link, as he encourages the adolescent to look inward, not upward or forward, in order to find inspiration and a sense of self. Moreno Villa's concept of dense, substantial poetry enacts the inward movement Unamuno calls for in the essay, using the "barrena," the drill of interrogation, to penetrate into reality – the reality of the self, of other people, and of things. The need for the tool implies that all of these are made up of dense substance in themselves – that they are not easily understood but rather mysterious, resistant to logical reason. In order to reach the interior of the self and the world, one must use a fine instrument, the gimlet of the lyric.

In the fall of 1906, after Unamuno's visit, Jiménez Fraud and Moreno Villa parted ways, though the enthusiasm for the rejuvenation of Spanish culture awakened in them in Málaga that summer had bonded them and their *peña* together, and they would eventually reunite in Madrid. Jiménez Fraud made his way to that city and to the ILE, where he studied with and apprenticed himself to Giner de los Ríos. In 1910, Giner asked him to serve as the director of a new student residence intended to address the limitations of university education in Spain by offering a select group of young men the opportunity to live and study in a community that would supplement and enrich their academic pursuits. Meanwhile, Moreno Villa returned to Freiburg im Breisgau, at the edge of Germany's Black Forest, where he had been studying chemistry. He had been sent there in 1904, in accordance with the wishes of his father, a wine merchant in Málaga who planned to enlist him as an analyst in the family business. The time abroad and the self-reflection it prompted during Moreno Villa's adolescent years, however, would ultimately lead young Pepe to choose a different path, that of art and literature. It was a path that would eventually take him, as well, to the Residencia de Estudiantes.

A Muscular Youth

In the Madrid of the early 1910s, intellectual life, prominently led by José Ortega y Gasset, continued to focus on the need to "regenerate" Spain. As he built on and responded to the ideas of Joaquín Costa and Unamuno, Ortega began to focus on a program of national development that he spoke of in the conclusion of his landmark speech, "Vieja y nueva política" ("Old and New Politics").[11] In this speech, given in March of 1914 at the inauguration of a new association for young Spanish intellectuals, the Liga de Educación Política (League for Political Education), he asserted that Spain had not yet achieved the status of a fully-fledged modern nation like that of other European countries. In order to achieve such a status, it needed to undergo a process of "nacionalización" (*OCT* 1:736). Tatjana Gajic has cogently described Ortega's project of nationalization as "a revitalization of the collective consciousness of the Nation" that would allow for a new basis of recognition between the Spanish people and the State (199). What Gajic does not emphasize is the primary role Ortega assigns to youth in this process. If the Ortega of "Vieja y nueva política" is careful to distinguish "nacionalización" from "nacionalismo," in which he detects an imperialist thrust, he nevertheless defends a vision for Spain that, like the nationalisms developed by European intellectuals such as Henri Massis in France or Giovanni Papini in Italy, bases itself on the potential of the young generation. In particular, the philosopher's creation of groups and associations like the Liga de Educación Política and Joven España (founded in 1910) clearly contributed to the creation of what María Dolores Gómez Molleda has called "la joventud política 'de las aulas'" ("'classroom' political youth"): a sector of the young Spanish population that eschewed direct involvement with political parties in favour of developing the intellectual strains of *regeneracionismo* and pedagogical work ("Juventud y política" 8).

In "Vieja y nueva política," the language Ortega uses to define his "new politics" is especially striking. Distinguishing between "la España oficial" ("official Spain") and "la España vital" ("living Spain"), he proposes a contrast between the old establishment and the robust vigor of youth that recalls Unamuno's "Viejos y jóvenes." In the final line of the speech, he introduces an image that clothes the trope of Spain's underdevelopment in the language of evolution, and would provide the title of his 1921 book *España invertebrada* (*Invertebrate Spain*). What Spain should strive to be, and what the young generation can help it to become, is "una España vertebrada y en pie" ("a vertebrate, upright Spain") (737): a more developed, autonomous, and sturdy country with a backbone, capable of standing on its own two feet.

Ortega may have drawn his vertebrate/invertebrate metaphor from Unamuno (the latter had used it in his 1902 essay "El individualismo español"). Be that as it may, in the context of 1914, such images of bodily strength were especially potent. As Europe headed towards an unprecedented military conflict, concepts of duty and discipline derived from muscular Christianity were garnering attention in Spain. Historian Andrew McFarland has shown that beginning in the late nineteenth century the ILE, along with other organizations and individuals, advanced the idea that Spain's regeneration would come through the cultivation of athleticism and physical exercise. This idea fit naturally with Krausist and *institucionista* philosophy, which stressed a holistic approach to education and the idea of an intimate connection between the individual and society at large, but as McFarland points out, it was also inspired by the exposure to British sport and muscular Christianity that many ILE instructors gained while studying abroad (618).[12] Throughout Europe, the prevailing image of youth was shifting from that of late nineteenth-century bohemianism and nonconformity to one of nationalized, dutiful strength: a much-cited example of the latter is the 1912 survey *Les Jeunes gens d'aujourd'hui*, compiled by Massis and Alfred de Tarde. Following this shift, Spanish educators and intellectuals began to place greater emphasis on training and discipline. Ortega's own *Meditaciones del Quijote*, addressed to readers younger than the author, reflects this trend. Composed in the summer of 1914 and written in a diaphanous prose that contrasts oddly with the dark times ahead, the work opens with a call for the imposition of a hierarchy of values to remedy what the author sees as Spain's cultural backwardness. As Gajic has shown, the identification of these values, which drives Ortega's hermeneutical approach to *Don Quijote*, would inform the plan for nationalization, or national vertebration, put forth in "Vieja y nueva política."

Ortega's insistence in *Meditaciones* on the need for hierarchy – a framework or backbone that might support the body politic – forms part of a broader cultural and political vision within which he assigned a central leadership role to "minorías intelectuales." This phrase, which also appears in "Vieja y nueva política," hearkens back to the view of social change as driven by a select group of young people that Giner had put forth in 1870. Indeed, it resonated with the ILE's project of cultivating young minds to drive liberal reform that would re-make the Spanish nation. Neither Giner nor Ortega conceived of this minority as a reflection of existing social hierarchy, but rather as a means to contest old concentrations of power. Nevertheless, it remained the case that the young people who might fill this role were separated out from the rest of the population, and given a new status and responsibility. Ortega in particular envisioned a new social stratification and what he would come to call a "nueva aristocracia" – a concept that, despite significant contextual differences, can be compared to the notion of intellectual aristocracy adhered to by the Bloomsbury Group in England during the same period. Raymond Williams' view of Bloomsbury as a "fraction" of an upper class seeking to reform its society while tacitly maintaining class distinctions does find some parallels in the intellectual circles of Madrid in the 1910s. However, whereas Leonard and Virginia Woolf or John Maynard Keynes (who would later make a celebrated trip to the Residencia de Estudiantes) were motivated by a liberal individualism connected only loosely to the State, in Spain the construction of "minorías" was of a piece with Ortegan nationalization. These minorities – to be formed from the new generations of young men just coming of age – were charged with the duty of turning their country into a strong, modern nation.

Influenced by the intellectual leadership of both Giner and Ortega, the educational centers that grew out of the ILE in the early twentieth century were highly receptive to their views on youth, the nation, and the role of "minorías." With the founding of the JAE in 1907, the pedagogical principles of Giner's *institucionismo* had given rise to several new places of learning and research: the Centro de Estudios Históricos, the Instituto-Escuela, and the Residencia de Estudiantes, among others. Drawing on the anti-establishment posture of Giner de los Ríos in his founding of the ILE, these centers saw themselves and their work as cultivating an alternative intellectual tradition within Spain, a progressive project of reform that dovetailed easily with Ortega's ideas. Many affiliates of these institutions formed part of the Joven España group and the Liga de Educación Política. Moreno Villa, in fact, was a member of both.

Upon his return to Spain from his studies in Germany, Moreno Villa – now a burgeoning poet – took a job at the Centro de Estudios Históricos (CEH). He worked there between 1912 and 1916, and his memories of his time there reveal a close association between the scholarly work of the centre, dedicated to liberal reform in Spain, and a wider discourse of militarization proper to the years of the First World War. Moreno Villa describes the CEH as "un gran campo de batalla" ("a great battlefield"), viewing it as a place dedicated to the fight for knowledge and filled with soldier-scholars who were no less men of action than the military heroes fighting in the trenches to the north (*Memoria* 98). The enemy against which these scholars fought was ostensibly ignorance, but in political and cultural terms it was also the ensconced, reactionary traditionalism of "la España oficial" that Ortega denounces in "Vieja y nueva política." Moreno Villa's text transmits a very appreciable sense that the scholars at the CEH were engaged in a civil conflict, contending for the power to redefine Spanish nationality. Here it bears remembering that Moreno Villa writes these lines from exile after the Civil War, and quite possibly traces the contours of this cultural battle according to political differences that became especially stark in the 1930s. Yet the military imagery also evokes the more immediate historical context of the First World War – an event, in any case, whose repercussions in Spain did shape and in some ways prefigure the later conflict. From his retrospective stance, Moreno Villa uses the earlier war as a means of situating himself and his colleagues in the struggle between "official" and "vital" Spain.

The ongoing battle for progress in which Moreno Villa sees himself participating, implicitly directed against an old Spain, was also central to the ethos of the Residencia de Estudiantes and the public image it projected. Run by men of Ortega's age and geared towards the education of a (literally) younger youth, students still in their biological adolescence, the Residencia might have seemed to embody the "juventud más joven" whose powers Machado extolled in "A una España joven."[13] In fact, a few months before that poem appeared in the first issue of *España*, the Residencia's annual program for the fall of 1914 employed a similarly fervent tone as it laid out the intstitution's goals and stressed its role in Spain's modernization. The program presents the Residencia as a student association that believes in "una futura y alta misión espiritual de España" ("a future and noble spiritual mission for Spain") ("Residencia" 85). The lines that follow this statement clearly demarcate the Residencia community's place within the generational dynamics of the time:

> La visión de los dolores de nuestra patria creó una generación pesimista que, aunque vivió entre negaciones y escepticismos, tuvo el valor de denunciar todas las falsas actividades que dirigían la vida española ... En la vanguardia de este grupo, creyente y luchador, queremos ocupar un puesto, nosotros que hemos nacido lo bastante tarde para tener la fortuna de crecer en una sana atmósfera de esperanza. (85–6)

> (The observation of the sufferings of our country created a pessimistic generation that, although it lived among negations and skepticisms, had the courage to denounce all of the false activities that controlled Spanish life ... Faithful and determined, we want to take up our place at the vanguard of this group, we who have been born late enough to have had the good fortune to grow up in a healthy atmosphere of hope.)

Stepping in to take the place of the worn-out, pessimistic generation whose frustration Machado's poem would express, the Residencia situates itself on the front lines of the battle for cultural reform. Within this conception of the educational centre as vanguard, the students gathered there become soldiers. They are strong, dutiful, and most important, undefiled by Spain's past: their late date of birth has allowed them to remain uncorrupted by the adult world that surrounds them. Their youth means that they are still malleable, capable of being formed into a new, stronger kind of citizen.

The Residencia's emphasis on physical education and athletics played an important part in its effort to cultivate a robust Spanish youth. This aspect of its pedagogical program was not only a product of *institucionista* approaches to the incorporation of body and mind in learning, but also an indicator of cultural and international status, as it replicated practices in the English residential colleges.[14] As art historian Carmen Sánchez has pointed out, the emblem chosen to represent the Residencia on everything from sporting jerseys to the covers of its publications, the *efebo rubio* or *atleta rubio* (blond ephebe or athlete), symbolized this vision of modern youth by linking it back to the origins of Western civilization. Representing the head, shown in profile, of an adolescent Greek male as portrayed in a statue dating from the fifth century B.C.E., the emblem connected the Residencia's outlook to a classical society that had celebrated and cultivated youth. The image perfectly embodied the centre's aspirations not only to enhance Spanish education, but also to establish itself on a European level (Sánchez 142). Evoking the holistic pedagogical philosophy of Greek *paideia*, the *efebo rubio* combined the concepts of learning, youth, and athleticism with the classical, and particularly Mediterranean, origins of European culture.[15]

The fashioning of a disciplined, national – and, to be sure, masculine – youth at the Residencia also occurred in its publications, many of which focused their reflections on individual development and the training of the will. The concept of heroism became a central element particularly in the series titled "Ensayos," inaugurated with Ortega's *Meditaciones*.

2.2 Cover of the first volume of Unamuno's *Ensayos* (Publicaciones de la Residencia de Estudiantes, 1916). Residencia de Estudiantes.

The figure of the hero presides over that text, where the philosopher asserts that "todos, en varia medida, somos héroes" ("all of us, in varying ways, are heroes") and that "ser héroe consiste en ser uno, uno mismo" ("being a hero means being oneself") (*OCT* 1:754, 816). Above all, for Ortega, a hero is someone who strives within his or her sphere of influence to "reformar la realidad" ("reform reality") (816). The heroic corresponds to an act of individual will independent of precedent or tradition that, like the deeds of Don Quijote, endeavours to bring about

2.3 Cover of *La edad heroica* by Luis de Zulueta (Publicaciones de la Residencia de Estudiantes, 1916). Residencia de Estudiantes.

change in the surrounding society. As such, Ortega's hero in some ways resembles the critical, nonconformist, ideo-clastic youth that Unamuno had written of in the preceding decades, in essays that the Residencia would soon reprint.

The image of the hero put forth in the works of the Residencia's "Ensayos" series was clearly developed with Spanish youth in mind. As is the case with the *Meditaciones*, the majority of the subsequent texts in the series address themselves directly to a young audience.

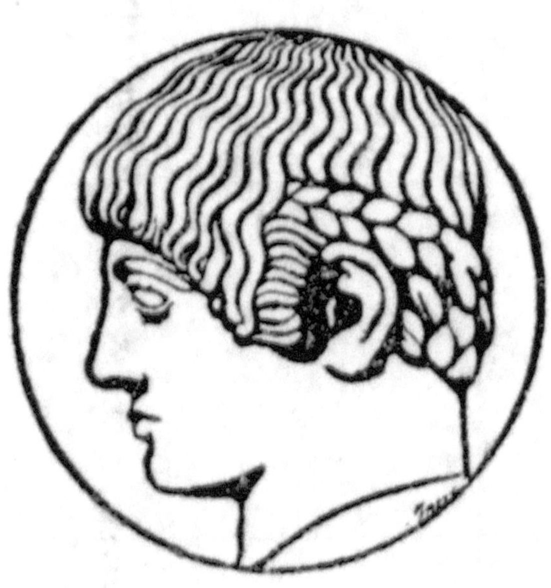

2.4 "Efebo rubio." Drawing by Fernando Marco for the logo of the Residencia de Estudiantes (1915). Residencia de Estudiantes.

Alberto Jiménez Fraud explicitly indicated that young people would be the particular focus of the Residencia's publications in a letter to Unamuno in December of 1913, where, excited about his new editorial endeavour and eager to have the older writer contribute to it, he writes, "Yo desearía que cada [publicación] fuere una lección de energía, de entusiasmo y de ímpetu para los jóvenes españoles, que prendiere en el espíritu de un estudiante de veinte años con una eficacia análoga a 'Los Héroes' de Carlyle, L'Avenir de la Science de Renan, etc." ("I would like each publication to be a lesson of energy, enthusiasm, and inspiration for young Spaniards, and that it would ignite the spirit of a twenty-year-old student with an effectiveness analogous to Carlyle's 'On Heroes,' Renan's L'Avenir de la science, etc.").[16] Jiménez Fraud's mention of Carlyle's book underscores the interest in the heroic that would appear time and again in the "Ensayos" series.

Indeed, heroism was the subject of a lecture given by Eugenio d'Ors at the Residencia in early 1915, subsequently published as *Aprendizaje y heroísmo*. This was the first in a series of lectures that would all follow a similar pattern: initially presented in person to an audience of young *residentes*, they were then edited and disseminated to the public as published works under the Residencia imprint, emblazoned with the image of the *efebo rubio*. D'Ors' main argument in *Aprendizaje y heroísmo* can be summed up by a comment Ortega makes in *Meditaciones*: "Nada impide el heroísmo – que es la actividad del espíritu – tanto como considerarlo adscrito a ciertos contenidos específicos de la vida" ("Nothing impedes heroism – which is the activity of the spirit – so much as considering it to be restricted to certain specific areas of life") (*OCT* 1:757). In his lecture, the Catalan writer tells his young listener (singular, and referred to throughout as "hijo mío" ["my son"]) that heroism stands for work well done, no matter in what trade, profession, or context. His words affirm the idea that intellectual pursuits can be heroic endeavours, and he emphasizes the importance of seriousness and dedication in all areas of life in a way that recalls the Krausist pursuit of universal harmony. At the same time, echoing Ortega and other voices within the European Generation of 1914, he stresses the need for rigor and self-control in achieving goals: "Tal vez ya es hora de rehabilitar el valor del *esfuerzo*, del *dolor*, de la disciplina de la voluntad" ("Perhaps it is now time to revive the value of *effort*, of *pain*, of the discipline of the will") (*Trilogía* 74, original emphasis). In this text, D'Ors' tone is decidedly paternalistic – encouraging, yes, but always intent to stress the need for hard work and seriousness in whatever task a young person takes up, whether the learning of a trade, academic study, or the development of the self. Without making any reference to contemporary domestic or international politics, his lecture reinforces the values of what we might call muscular youth: strength and integrity paired with discipline and a spirit of service to a higher goal. The critical or nonconformist valences of heroism are subdued in favour of a liberal ideal that equates individual work with the betterment of society.

With Federico de Onís' *Disciplina y rebeldía* and Zulueta's *La edad heroica*, youth becomes the express object of inquiry, as well as the embodiment of heroism *par excellence*. Both texts are more extravagant than d'Ors' lecture in their praise of youth as a time of special freedom and as-yet undefined possibility. Onís's opposition between discipline and rebellion approaches adolescent experience in a way reminiscent of Ortega's famous declaration in *Meditaciones*, "yo soy yo y mi circunstancia" ("I am myself and my circumstance") (*OCT* 1:757). Onís argues that the primary task of youth is to balance a sense of admiration for and submission to the exterior world (what he calls discipline) with the affirmation of one's own individuality against the dictates of that world (rebellion). Yet Onís' informal, intimate speech departs from the measured philosophical rigor of Ortega's meditations as he permits himself to wax lyrical about the beauty and excitement of youth. For Onís, this life stage is "precisamente la indefinición, la inconcreción ... la pura posibilidad" ("precisely the undefined, the inconcrete ... pure possibility"), and therein lies its unique value (*Disciplina* 19). While for this writer and teacher youthfulness means "aspirar a serlo todo" ("aspiring to be everything"), adulthood, by contrast, signifies an ominous future resignation, the pious acceptance of "la tragedia de nuestro destino" ("the tragedy of our fate") (32–3).

Despite the wartime context that directly frames Zulueta's series of lectures (there are three in all), he is even more strident than Onís in praising youth, viewing it as the golden age of possibility, of discovery, of love, and of aesthetic sensibility. Both writers take care to acknowledge that the best of modern pedagogy (like that of the ILE tradition) gives youth freedom rather than trying to control it. As Zulueta puts it, adults should not attempt to rein in (*efrenar*) the young, but rather expose them to higher goals and aspirations (*La edad* 18). In these lectures, planned with the express purpose of addressing the topic of youth, there is a noticeable shift in the attitude of the authors towards their young audience, as compared with those of Ortega and d'Ors. Perhaps because they address the experience of young people directly, Onís and Zulueta are more deferent, more enthusiastic, and less formal than their predecessors in the Residencia's essay series. It should also be noted that both men received Unamuno's guidance during their own relative youth at the turn of the century.[17] Their celebration and vindication of the adolescent period of life as unrestrained possibility is thus something they could well have learned from the rector of the Universidad de Salamanca as they were living it out.

All of these texts published by the Residencia between 1914 and 1916 reflect, in varying proportions, a combination of the opposing impulses of celebration and control that characterized attitudes towards youth in European culture in the early twentieth century, and which came together in the glorification of the image of the young soldier with the outbreak of the war. As Zulueta acknowledged, Spain was not at war, but its young men still had duties to their country and to the continent. While the Residencia's *efebo rubio* might be seen as the symbol of the "pacifismo heroico" that the author of *La edad heroica* calls for, it bears remembering that the ephebes of ancient Greece had not only been students; they were also soldiers in training, and they owed their allegiance to a concrete political entity. The situation of the students at the Residencia was more ambiguous, for again, the nation to which they were being prepared to give allegiance had not yet come into existence. The ILE and its offshoot organizations provided a foundation, but for the time being Spain was still governed by the old, if increasingly criticized political system of the Restoration, the regime that Ortega referred to as "la España oficial" and that years earlier Unamuno had called "la vieja máquina."

The Residencia as No Man's Land

The ambiguity of the image of youth promoted by the Residencia in its early years – muscular and soldier-like, but also pacifist – reflects a new series of relationships in the 1910s between liberal education, its *institucionista* origins, and the Spanish State. One the one hand, the creation of the JAE as a government-funded entity overseen by the Spanish Ministry of Public Instruction and Fine Arts[18] represented an achievement for the ILE community that would have been unthinkable a few decades earlier. It signified the penetration into the central government of pedagogical principles that had cost many university professors their jobs in the 1860s and 1870s. As such, the founding of the JAE was a milestone for liberal educational reform in Spain. On the other hand, however, it inevitably compromised the critical political posture that had characterized the ILE in its beginning. In order to continue its pedagogical work, the JAE (and the Residencia, which depended upon it) now needed the support – or at least, the tolerance – of the establishment. As a result, the Residencia was forced to distance itself from the ILE, in official terms if not in philosophy, and by the same token, to be accommodating to the government. One telling indication of the difference between the respective postures of the two institutions with regard to the State is that in 1911, just days after Giner had refused to allow King Alfonso XIII to visit the ILE, the monarch was warmly received at the Residencia. Giner himself only visited its grounds on one occasion, to hear Unamuno speak in 1914, before his death the following year (Onieva 299, Pérez-Villanueva 78).

While Jiménez Fraud's handling of the Residencia's relationship with the monarchy (and later, in the 1920s, with the dictatorship of Miguel Primo de Rivera) has been interpreted in different ways, either as a judicious and skillful balancing act or as an attempt to bolster the Residencia's aristocratic aspirations (in both Ortega's sense and in terms of existing social class),[19] it is undoubtedly true that it found itself in a delicate position, between the nonconformist posture of the ILE and a dutiful respect for the throne. Jiménez Fraud's desire to preserve the educational and cultural program of the Residencia converted the pointed rejection of political and confessional affiliations that its parent institution had voiced so loudly (and which the Residencia continued to affirm) into a claim of political neutrality necessary to its existence – and also in line with Spain's official policies regarding the First World War. In other words, the centre's survival as a partially State-dependent entity, as well as its aspirations to reform Spanish education and forge a new model of citizenship in its country, rested upon its ability to maintain the status of an innocuous no man's land in the political landscape of early twentieth-century Spain.

Along these lines, Jiménez Fraud's account of an exchange he had with Giner after the first visit of Alfonso XIII to the Residencia in 1911 is especially illuminating. In his *Historia de la universidad española*, a work that moves from scholarly writing to personal testimony as it interprets the more recent past, Jiménez Fraud recalls that when he met with Giner after the king's visit (off campus on the neutral ground of the Paseo de la Castellana) his esteemed mentor took his hand and exclaimed, "¡Criatura, qué responsabilidad!" ("My boy, what responsibility!") (440). While the author identifies Giner's own anti-monarchist views as the source of the emotion behind these words, he interprets them not as a statement of caution but as a charge. He says that Giner was referring to the great honour the king had bestowed upon "la modesta y apenas nacida Residencia" ("the modest and still newborn Residencia"), and that "había que devolverlo con inmenso esfuerzo para ser digno de él" ("I had to reciprocate it [the honor] with immense effort in order to be worthy of it"). Given the older pedagogue's attitude towards the State, however, one might just as well understand his comment to refer to a responsibility owed not to the king, but to the educational task itself, now complicated by a relationship with the monarchy. The reflection that Jiménez Fraud offers in the following lines suggests an awareness of this implication, as he turns to Giner's words to justify his actions:

> Nos separamos en silencio, y yo me alejé pensando, no sé por qué asociación de ideas, en una frase que con frecuencia repetía Giner, y era que la revolución había que hacerla en los espíritus y no en las barricadas, frase que en un ensayo suyo ampliaba en esta forma: 'Por su trágico aparato, las revoluciones imponen y amedrentan, y nos parecen que trituran las entrañas del mundo, cuando apenas arañan la superficie.' (440)

> (We parted in silence, and I walked away thinking, by I don't know what association of ideas, of a phrase that Giner repeated frequently, and it was that one had to fight for revolution in spirits and not in the barricades, a phrase that he expanded in this way in one of his essays: 'Due to their tragic mechanism, revolutions impose and intimidate, and it seems to us that they shake the foundations of the earth, when they only scratch the surface.')

That these are the words the Residencia's director turns to in this difficult personal situation eloquently illustrates the ideological transformations the *institucionista* project had undergone since its founding. The line that Jiménez Fraud cites here comes from an essay on anarchism that Giner wrote in 1899, in which he drew on an article by Unamuno in order to argue that no political program would bring about true change in Spanish society on its own.[20] While in this turn-of-the-century piece Giner was asking his fellow intellectuals to push for a moral transformation *beyond* politics (beyond even the most radical of political parties), Jiménez Fraud uses his words to justify stopping short of a confrontation with the State. The prioritization of interior ("espíritus," "entrañas") over exterior ("barricadas," "superficie") in these lines recalls Unamuno's distinction in *En torno al casticismo* between *intrahistoria* and *historia*. Here, however, the praise of subterranean, abiding truths over transient historical events is invoked to justify the preservation of the Residencia's separate, elite culture at the expense of its critical voice in the wider social arena.

The difference between Unamuno' evocation of the Castilian peasant and Jiménez Fraud's concern for the privileged urban student is significant, and it may be seen as a product of the maturation of the liberal project in Spain. If Unamuno's 1895 text comprised an attempt to dismantle the *casticista* thinking that continued to inform the Restoration system, in the 1910s Jiménez Fraud's aims were in some ways more modest. While speaking of vanguards and revolutions, he was in reality trying to find a *modus vivendi* for his institution within the system: not to demolish an old order, but to incubate a new one. Understanding the Residencia's project this way helps to explain the strikingly apolitical treatment of the First World War in Zulueta's *La edad heroica*, as well as the centre's official neutrality with regard to contemporary debates between supporters of the Allies and defenders of the Central Powers in the Spanish press.

The image of incubation is also apt, because it reflects the fact that the Residencia community's separation from the rest of Spanish society was not only intellectual, but also spatial. Especially with the creation of its new campus on "La Colina de los Chopos," the Residencia's mission of cultivating the youth of a new Spain was tied to the setting apart of spaces for learning, recreation, and physical exercise: dormitories, laboratories, and athletic fields. Michel Foucault identified the demarcation of separate space, which he called "enclosure," as an element in the historical development of methods of discipline, rooted in the transformation of "docile bodies" into soldiers. According to Foucault, enclosure delimits a "protected place ... a place heterogeneous to all others and closed in upon itself" (141). While the Residencia's liberal and pedagogical aims certainly differentiate it from the penal institutions that are the ultimate focus of Foucault's analysis, in its effort to educate an elite group of young men to be strong citizens and models of heroic pacifism, it did fashion itself as this kind of protected place. In so doing, it translated into spatial terms a division that was already present in Spanish culture and would become increasingly pronounced in the decade that followed: that between political activism and intellectual pursuits, social engagement and the pure, hermetic world of art. For the time being, within the Residencia's sphere youth would be most explicitly linked to the latter of these terms.

Moreno Villa's Tragic *Bildungsgedichte*

The situation of the Residencia community within a neutral space associated with heroism and vitality but not with politics created a uniquely fertile environment for the writing of poetry. Juan Ramón Jiménez, who moved to the Residencia in 1913 and soon took charge of editing its publications, stood at the centre of its poetic world. While at that post, he composed some of his most well-known collections, including *Diario de un poeta recién casado* (1916), *Eternidades* (1917), and *Piedra y cielo* (1919), as well as his prose work *Platero y yo* (1914). In these same years the young Moreno Villa was starting out on a quest for his own, singular poetic voice, one that would distinguish him from his predecessors and contemporaries. His early collections of poetry especially reflect his interest in a topic that, as he remarked later on, other writers at the time seemed not to have noticed: "la angustia del joven en la pubertad" ("the anguish of the young man during puberty") (*PCMV* 65). Even as he found himself in the midst of political debates about the war and the initiatives for cultural transformation launched by Ortega in the early 1910s, Moreno Villa was also immersing himself in a poetic exploration of the experience of adolescence.

Moreno Villa is now best known for his part-narrative, part-collage collection of poems *Jacinta, la pelirroja* (*Jacinta the Redhead*, 1929); for his extensive memoirs, with their depictions of Spanish artists and intellectual life during the pre-Civil War period and later in exile; and for an eclectic style that associated him with avant-garde movements in both poetry and painting. His first publications, composed decades earlier, reflect the inner life of a young man just emerging from adolescence. As he settled into life in Madrid and within the cultural milieu of the Residencia, he was also reflecting a great deal on the time he had spent in Germany between his seventeenth and twenty-second years, and how that experience had influenced his life's trajectory. As he describes it in his autobiography *Vida en claro* (*Life Made Clear*), his time in Freiburg had been filled with the internal drama and insecurity of youth, as well as a Dantean sense of having strayed from the straight path. "Comencé a sentirme solo, abandonado en la selva" ("I began to feel alone, abandoned in the forest"), he writes. "Ya de por sí es selvática la adolescencia. El amanecer sexual, con sus angustias, sus temores, sus anhelos infinitos, hunden el espíritu en una selva que se nos antoja sin salida" ("Adolescence is already forest-like in itself. Sexual awakening, with its anguish, fears, and infinite desires, sinks the spirit into a forest in which it seems to be trapped") (*Memoria* 72–3). The separation from his family and the isolation of living in a foreign country and speaking a new language shaped Moreno Villa profoundly at this age, and the confusion of youthful desires and anxieties that he felt in Germany eventually inspired the long poem "En la selva fervorosa" ("In the Fervent Forest"), a composition that takes up over half of this artist's second book of poems, *El pasajero* (*The Passenger*, 1914).

While Luis Cernuda later judged that Moreno Villa's first book, *Garba* (*Sheaf*, 1913), marked a turning point in modern Spanish poetry ("*Garba* inicia y separa" [1224]), this debut collection is often tentative, and conspicuously self-conscious in situating itself in relation to older writers. A section in *Garba* titled "Recreos" includes poetic sketches of figures from the preceding generation (Ramón del Valle-Inclán, Pío Baroja, Azorín, and Unamuno) rather similar to the sketches in prose in his later *Los autores como actores* (*Authors as Actors*, 1951) and the drawings of cultural figures that he published in various periodicals in the 1920s. The four poems are vignettes, offering an imagined glimpse or caricature of each writer with the matter-of-fact, somewhat wry tone that dominates in the collection. The amateurish exact rhymes used in all of them fall heavily on the ear, and in all except the last poem, dedicated to Unamuno, the first-person verb form foregrounds the presence of the poet in the construction of the sketch. In Moreno Villa's account of Unamuno, the existential preoccupations of the rector from Salamanca liken him to Don Quijote in his idealistic, ill-fated, and often ridiculous quests.[21] Moreno Villa's treatment is not overly reverent, but this comparison creates a telling link to an earlier poem in the collection titled "El nieto de Don Quijote" ("Don Quijote's Grandson"), which directly addresses the topic of generational succession. In it, the progeny of no less than Spain's most famous cultural icon declares, "Yo quiero ser su nieto, pero existir por mí, / que el mundo me respete por lo que yo le di" ("I want to be his grandson, but exist on my own. / Let the world respect me for what I myself have done") (*PCMV* 96). Together with the portrayal of Moreno Villa's predecessors later in *Garba*, the generational dynamics referenced here point to a thinly veiled personal anxiety – an especially transparent case of the anxiety of influence, perhaps – on the part of the poet.

In *El pasajero*, however, Moreno Villa becomes more secure in himself and his aesthetic project. Published, like Ortega's *Meditaciones*, just before the outbreak of war in Europe, *El pasajero* is the collection in which Moreno Villa comes of age as a poet. This, at least, is how it seemed to Ortega, whose laudatory prologue to the book heralded its author as "un poeta verdaderamente nuevo" ("a truly new poet") (*OCT* 1:664). About "En la selva fervorosa" in particular, the philosopher commented (with language that anticipates his argument in "La deshumanización del arte"), "hay allí una poesía pura. No hay en él más que poesía. Se halla extento de aquel *minimum* de realidad que el simbolismo conservaba al querer dar la *impresión de las cosas*" ("there one finds a pure poetry. There is nothing more than poetry in it. It is free of that *minimum* of reality that symbolism retained in order to give the *impression of things*") (1:679, original emphasis). Ortega's enthusiasm is surprising, given the highly autobiographical character of Moreno Villa's poem, which draws heavily on the author's time in Germany and would thus seem to be at odds with what Ortega would later call "dehumanized" art. But the philosopher did not dwell on this aspect of the text. As a reader, Ortega was impressed by the absence of mimetic referents in the poem, its creation of a self-contained allegorical world refracted into a wide range of sensory images. Indeed, this technique of poetic abstraction anticipates the "álgebra superior de las metáforas" ("superior algebra of metaphors") that Ortega would identify in the poetry of "arte joven" in his 1925 essay (*OCT* 3:864).

As a result of the greater interest placed on Moreno Villa's writing from the 1920s onward (the period of his artistic "maturity," which also coincides with the activities of the so-called Generation of 1927), critical accounts of "En la selva fervorosa" have been few, and the readings they offer superficial. It is customary for commenters to situate the poem and the book in which it appears within a first stage or period in the broader trajectory of the poet's work, to note the praise it received from Ortega, and to affirm the movement towards a new kind of poetry in Moreno Villa's early work as a precursor of trends that would blossom in the next decade.[22] Yet closer analysis of the text itself, apart from its role in a teleological account of Moreno Villa's developing *oeuvre*, is highly rewarding, for it reveals that a questioning of teleology and development lies at the heart of the work itself. An initial reading indicates immediately that "En la selva fervorosa" relies at least in part on a narrative structure: it presents itself as the story of a wandering pilgrim (the "passenger" of the book's title) and the tribulations of his soul, imagined as a tree within a great forest. What critics have thus far failed to note is that this narrative is a narrative of formation – or perhaps more precisely, of anti-formation. The poem narrates the growth of the young sapling, "raicilla que es apenas tajo" ("small root barely forming a stem") (*PCMV* 152), into an adult tree. At every turn, however, it attempts to delay and resist this process of maturation. On a formal level, the fact that the poem is made up of twenty-five cantos that could stand alone as shorter poems, each with its own metric and aural structure, attests to the poet's effort to slow narrative momentum wherever possible. As Manuel García Morente wrote in a review of *El pasajero* that appeared soon after its publication, "todo cumplirse, todo acabar, todo llegar, todo término es para [Moreno Villa] muerte y silencio" ("any fulfillment, any completion, any arrival, any ending is death and silence in Moreno Villa's view") (3).

García Morente describes an attitude towards endings that relates to the thematic presence of youth in "En la selva fervorosa." To borrow terms that Frank Kermode developed in a different but related context, in this poem imminence becomes immanence; linear history oriented towards a temporal ending is challenged by a sense of crisis emanating from the self. In Moreno Villa's forest, the dreaded end is not the Apocalypse, but "todo acabar" ("any finality"), and in particular, the finality that comes with the passage into adulthood. In an unpublished account of the origins of *El pasajero*, the poet writes that the collection was motivated by a preoccupation with "la fugacidad de todo" ("the fleetingness of all things"). He goes on to explain that at the time of writing the book he found himself in "esa lucha juvenil interna, sorda, con los sentimientos heredados, los conceptos adquiridos y las sensaciones de la carne" ("that internal, silent struggle of youth with inherited attitudes, acquired concepts, and the sensations of the flesh").[23] His concerns stem from the inevitable passing of time – a confrontation with the diachronic aspect of existence – and from the synchronic experience of multiple influences and desires felt simultaneously during the period of youth. As in contemporary modernist novels of formation like Joyce's *Portrait* or Ramón Pérez de Ayala's *A.M.D.G.*, Moreno Villa's "En la selva fervorosa" privileges the multivalent, internal life of the young person over the journey that will lead him to adulthood.

This complex relationship to temporality proved difficult to translate into poetic form. Later Moreno Villa recalled that as he searched for a means to express his youthful angst, he was inspired by an article Pérez de Ayala had written about the triumph of the short lyric poem over more extended forms.[24] Pérez de Ayala's doubts about whether contemporary poets were capable of writing long poems served as an "acicate" ("stimulus") for Moreno Villa, challenging him to resuscitate the form. In doing so, however, he faced a problem. As he put it, "los poemas largos se han sostenido siempre a base de un hilo narrativo, de un asunto; y yo no quería salirme de la lírica, echándome en la épica" ("long poems have always relied on a narrative thread, an argument; and I did not want to stray from the lyric and fall into epic"). In this desire to write a long lyric poem while resisting the epic mode, Moreno Villa's project resembles the one Federico García Lorca would later attribute to Luis de Góngora in the composition of the *Soledades*.[25] Yet the hybrid of narrative and lyric that ultimately took shape in "En la selva fervorosa" served Moreno Villa well in his attempt to depict the experience of adolescence, a life stage at once preoccupied with the process of growing up, the "story" of development, and consumed with interiorized self-analysis. The final structure of "En la selva fervorosa" provided him the opportunity to examine this transitional period at length, to plumb the depths of a jungle-like time of life.

Moreno Villa's contemplative interrogation of and penetration into his own adolescent experience in this poem exemplifies the "afán de *densidad*" whose origin he would later trace to Unamuno. Indeed, while the poem can be and was placed in dialogue with Ortega's contemporary ideas, under analysis Unamuno emerges as an important philosophical and poetic point of reference both in the text of "En la selva fervorosa," and in the conditions of its composition. As regards the latter, Moreno Villa traveled to Salamanca in late 1913 while he was composing the poems of *El pasajero*, and the impact of this trip is readily discernible in the collection. His letters to Unamuno reveal that one of the poems from the first part of the book, "Frente al retablo de San Miguel que hay en el claustro de la Catedral Vieja" ("Before the Image of Saint Michael in the Cloister of the Old Cathedral"), is the product of a trip he made with Unamuno to the same site that had inspired the older poet's "En la Catedral Vieja de Salamanca" years earlier (Robles, "Doce cartas" 64). Furthermore, in *Vida en claro* the writer recalls reading sections of the still-unfinished "En la selva fervorosa" to Unamuno, while the older writer in turn recited parts of the long poem that he, too, had begun to compose against the grain of prevailing trends: *El Cristo de Velázquez*.[26] Even before this encounter, however, Unamuno seems to have been the source of the central image that structures "En la selva fervorosa." In yet another, earlier letter to Unamuno dated 25 February 1913, Moreno Villa makes reference to an article that the older writer had published in *Los Lunes de El Imparcial* ("Doce cartas" 63). This article centers on the image of "la selva de nuestras almas" ("the forest of our souls") as a metaphor for modern society. Unamuno describes this forest as a living gathering of solitary individuals ("solitarios"), and he singles his reader out as one of its trees ("tú, que eres un árbol de esta selva") (Unamuno, "Intermedio"). In the piece, the writer creates a scene that is strikingly similar to the one Moreno Villa develops in his own *selva*. While in his letter Moreno Villa does not say he has read the article (only that Giner has recommended it to him), it seems quite likely that he consulted it in the following months. In any event, the image of the tree, with roots stretching down in the ground and branches swaying in the breeze and sunlight, is a favourite of the early Unamuno, and it appears in other texts that Moreno Villa likely knew. As indicated in the last chapter, it forms the basis of "No busques luz, mi corazón, sino agua," from *Poesías*, and it also figures prominently in Unamuno's essay "El secreto de la vida," which first appeared in July of 1906, just before his trip to Málaga.

In regards to the text of "En la selva fervorosa" itself, Unamuno appears as a point of reference at the outset of the poem, where Moreno Villa chooses lines from the Basque writer's 1911 sonnet cycle "En horas de insomnio" ("In Insomnolent Hours") as epigraphs: "Dejar un grito, nada más que un grito / aquel del corazón cuando le quema / metiéndosele el sol" ("To leave a cry, nothing more than a cry / that of the heart being burned / when laid bare in the sun") (*PCMV* 146).[27] As in "No busques luz," these lines set up an opposition between the light of the sun as a symbol of exterior objectivity and the interior, subjective space of the heart. This contrast prepares the reader for the opening canto of Moreno Villa's poem, which also recalls "No busques luz" as it presents a dialogue between the poetic voice and the poet's soul, which is imagined as a tree. As in Unamuno's poem, Moreno Villa's poet addresses his soul directly, endeavouring to counsel it and guide it through life's troubles. To this end, the *pasajero* asks after the source of his soul's unease, and receives a reply that invites him and the reader into the pages that follow: "Una selva en mis hondones siento" ("I feel a forest within me") (147).

From this point forward the poet's soul assumes the position of narrator, and the poem proceeds to record its sensations and emotions as it strives to take root and grow, but also encounters the dangers of the forest. These dangers consistently point to the passage of time as a force that, rather than facilitating growth, hinders and threatens. A woodcutter and his axe represent the greatest of these dangers; they are ominous intimations of mortality that contrast in their symbolism with a nearby river, the source of life: "Pasa el río – la vida – / y el leñador – el hacha – " ("The river passes – life – / and so does the woodcutter – the axe – ") (149). Where the medieval Castilian poet Jorge Manrique had described life as a river running passively and inevitably to the sea, Moreno Villa casts death as a violent intrusion lurking at every turn. Further threats come from the beasts that roam the forest: the poetic voice warns, "acabarán con la conciencia joven" ("they will finish off your young mind") (152) and "desgarrarán tu adolescente cuerpo" ("they will tear your adolescent body apart") (153). Despite the fears these threats instil, exuberant expressions of youthful ambition burst out periodically in the poem, as in the seventh canto, where the tree stretches its branches towards the sky and declares, "¡Arriba! ¡A perforar los siete cielos" ("Up! To pierce the seventh heaven!") (154). Yet with the aspiration to ascend and grow upward comes inevitable loss. This is underscored dramatically when the tree loses a limb (botanic and anthropomorphic) to the woodcutter's axe in the eighth canto:

Pero una tarde el hacha del leñador oscuro
hundióse penetrante en mis axilas.
Algo futuro y deseado
se desprendió de la conciencia viva,
y topando y chocando cayó donde las hojas amarillas
para quedar como algo externo, extraño,
aquella cosa que nutrió mi vida. (155)

(But one afternoon the dark woodcutter's axe
sank deep into my armpits.
Something hoped for in the future
was detached from living consciousness,
and fell, bumping and knocking, among the yellow leaves
to be left as something external, strange,
that thing that once nourished my life.)

Here, as throughout the poem, the protagonist laments the progressive narrowing of his selfhood, the limitation of his aspirations and increasing alienation, even from parts of himself, as he grows (literally) up. Hopes and desires fall away like chopped branches, reified tokens of what Unamuno would call a "yo ex-futuro": the memory of a possible self.

The soul's loss of innocence continues in cantos X through XX, which recount the trials of awakening sexuality and the adolescent subject's first experience of romantic love. Again, the poetic voice struggles with contradictory impulses – here the classic opposition of spiritual and physical desire. In canto XIII the "arborescent" protagonist, represented as gender-neutral in the earliest poems, assumes the human and masculine avatar of Saint George on his white horse, vanquishing the dragon of the flesh. Like Michael, this is a warrior saint, and the two have similar iconography, particularly in that they both appear slaying a reptilian foe.[28] As Saint George kills the beast in Moreno Villa's poem, he is a model of clear-headed action, virility, and moral authority, displaying "ímpetu, idea, / y un brazo viril" ("vigor, determination, / and a virile arm") (159). This image of belligerent masculinity can certainly be seen as a variant of the concept of the heroic soldier so present throughout Europe and in Moreno Villa's Madrilenian milieu in the year of *El pasajero*'s publication. At the same time, however, the hagiographical reference and religious overtones situate this adolescent battle of spirit against flesh within a theological, otherworldly sphere. Throughout "En la selva fervorosa," as he removes what Ortega called the "minimum" of reality from his poem, Moreno Villa elevates the trials of adolescence to the status of archetype. They come to illustrate the most fundamental questions of human existence, from the tensions between vitality and mortality to the entanglements of love and suffering (beautifully depicted through the iconography of Saint Sebastian in canto XVIII). This aesthetic sublimation is likely the reason that Moreno Villa's contemporaries stressed the universality of the poem – what García Morente described as its "fiel trasunto de la irremediable complejidad humana" ("faithful copy of our irremediable human complexity") – over its references to youth and adolescence.

Nevertheless, youth's radical otherness with respect to the adult world was the source of a peculiar, intriguing, and unsettling novelty that García Morente identified in the poem as he tried to describe and account for its "emoción inédita y desconocida aún" ("novel and as yet unknown emotion"). What "En la selva fervorosa" reflects is youth's own awakening awareness of its difference from and critical attitude towards the completeness of maturity: the realization that the onset of adulthood is not necessarily to be desired, and in fact might be cause for mourning. Like Onís in *Disciplina y rebeldía*, the poet views the conclusion of youth as a form of tragedy. The ominous closing canto of "En la selva fervorosa" suggests that for Moreno Villa the anguish of puberty was an existential anguish proximate to the "tragic sense of life" of which Unamuno had written in his famous philosophical essay, published two years before *El pasajero*. In this final canto, the young tree's story comes to a dismal end when a forest fire consumes its trunk, ushering it into a charred maturity:

Y en una noche azul, callada y encalmada,
la selva ardió.
Y cuando vino el alba, rosada y alocada
apareció
recto y mudo, en la cumbre, un carbón gigantesco
solitario,
con faz y cuerpo de hombre forzudo y principesco.
Sagitario
le corona en Estío con su diadema astral. (169)

(And on a blue, quiet, and tranquil night,
the forest burned.
And when dawn came, rosy and crazed,
there emerged
tall and silent, on the summit, a gigantic charred shape,
all alone,
with the visage and body of a man, tough and stately.
Sagittarius
crowns it in summer with its astral diadem.)

Beneath the cold gaze of a night sky whose stars signal the end of springtime, the tree has reached a seasoned adulthood. The poetic subject is no longer a sapling or an adolescent; it is a man. Enrique Baena has argued that the image of fire in these lines and elsewhere in the poem symbolizes the spiritual purification of Christian tradition. This may be so, but if it is the case such purification is not depicted as welcome or desirable, but rather as a torment from which the protagonist wishes to escape. In the second-to-last canto, the poetic voice calls out to God for rescue, but cannot be saved from the flames. Such images so startled Juan Ramón Jiménez that he composed a poem in response where he attempted to soften their impact by insisting that with the next spring, new green shoots would grow from Moreno Villa's scorched forest.[29] There is no sign of possible rebirth in the original poem, however. Its last lines leave no doubt that the tree, the youthful soul and protagonist of the story, has died, even if its mature incarnation manages to narrate the final line from the present. Within the poem's allegory, the fire's sudden destruction represents an inevitable reality: the passage of time, like the eventual arrival of a dawn that seems illogical and incongruent in the face of loss, brings youth to an end.

Editing Unamuno in 1916

The stark ending of "En la selva fervorosa" reinforces the poem's resistance to narrative propulsion towards an imminent demise, and its prioritization of the interior, immanent crisis experienced by the individual subject. In this, yet another connection to Unamuno's essayistic writing reveals itself, because the poem seems to respond to injunctions the rector from Salamanca makes in "¡Adentro!," the text Moreno Villa later cited as one of the sources of his interest in poetic *adentramiento*. Unamuno's warning in that essay against any conception of life as a linear trajectory resonates deeply with the thrust of Moreno Villa's poem, particularly when the essayist writes, "deja eso de adelante y atrás, arriba y abajo, a progresistas y retrógrados, ascendentes y descendentes, que se mueven en el espacio exterior tan sólo, y busca el otro, tu ámbito interior" ("leave the concerns with forward and backward, up and down, to progressives and retrogrades, those who are rising and those who are falling, those who only move in exterior space, and search out the other space, your interior realm") (*E* 2:196). In its attention to the various emotions, fears, and desires of the adolescent self, "En la selva fervorosa" enacts the inward turn that Unamuno encourages in his essay.

Whether or not Moreno Villa had "¡Adentro!" in mind when composing his long poem, he had the opportunity to read it (or re-read it) in 1916, when he stepped in for Juan Ramón Jiménez to edit the first three volumes of Unamuno's *Ensayos* at the Residencia. As he prepared the second volume, in which the essay appears, he wrote to his "maestro" in Salamanca: "Cada vez que sale un tomo me parece más feliz la idea ([de] Alberto Jiménez) de reunir esos trabajos dispersos. Vuelve uno a leerlos y se saca la impresión de que son actuales, frescos" ("With each volume that comes out the idea [Alberto Jiménez's] of bringing these dispersed essays together seems better to me. One rereads them and takes away the impression that they are current, fresh") (Robles, "Doce cartas" 66). Moreno Villa had begun overseeing the editing of the Residencia's publications at the beginning of 1916, when Juan Ramón left for North America on the wedding trip that inspired his *Diario de un poeta recién casado*. Jiménez Fraud seems to have been in charge of selecting the texts to be printed (Ribagorda, "Las publicaciones" 46), but Moreno Villa worked jointly with him (as did Juan Ramón, after his return)[30] to prepare a collection of Unamuno's essays that would become a point of reference for the young students of the following years.

Though the correspondence between Jiménez Fraud and Unamuno indicates that the *Ensayos* never sold as either of them had hoped they would, the younger writers that lived at or frequented the Residencia over the next two decades did read Unamuno in this edition, and referred to it by name in later reflections. Gerardo Diego wrote in 1943 of the influence that "los 'Ensayos' sobre todo" ("the 'Essays' above all") had on "tantas almas en formación y sobre la obra – ideas, estilo, inquietudes – de no pocos escritores de hoy" ("so many souls in formation and on the work – ideas, style, preoccupations – of more than a few of today's writers") ("Presencia" 67). In addition to the widespread influence of the *Ensayos* that Diego sees in the work of his contemporaries, the collection clearly formed part of the conception of Unamuno held by many of this writer's successors in the following decades. Moreno Villa's work preparing its first three volumes, then, is another, less-acknowledged aspect of his function as a bridge between the so-called Generations of 1898 and 1927, between Unamuno and *la joven literatura*.

The seven volumes of the *Ensayos* constitute one fifth of the publications the Residencia produced between 1913 and the outbreak of the Civil War, and they figured in the earliest plans for this editorial project. Jiménez Fraud writes in his memories of the Residencia that he believed the essays to be "lo más logrado" ("the finest") of Unamuno's work, texts in which one could find the main ideas the writer had presented in other genres, and in his opinion, "mejor desarrolladas" ("better developed") (*Residentes* 54). In addition to the summary of Unamuno's wide-ranging thought that the essays provided, their discursive style and the fact that many of them address themselves to younger readers would have made them an ideal choice for the Residencia's series. The collection displays the Basque writer's deep preoccupation with the concept of youth and the problems facing Spanish youth in particular at the outset of the twentieth century – the topics that had captivated the attention of Jiménez Fraud and Moreno Villa in their early years. Its compilation of so many essays explicitly concerned with youth provides an invaluable window into the largely unnoticed element in the Basque writer's turn-of-the-century work outlined in the previous chapter.

Still, the view from this window is partial. The essays included in the *Ensayos* collection come from only a few of the many publications to which Unamuno contributed in the 1890s and early 1900s. Most of them first appeared in one of two Madrid-based publications that had a broad, educated, middle- and upper-class readership: *La España Moderna* and *Nuestro Tiempo*.[31] The triptych *Tres ensayos* (included in volume two) and the four essays Unamuno published in *Ciencia social* in 1896 (volume three) are notable exceptions to this rule. Three other essays included were originally published in Madrid's *La Lectura*. While the early Unamuno's cultural, religious, and even political views – particularly as expressed in his evolving thoughts on "La crisis del patrotismo" – are represented in the selection, his contributions to other journals, such as *La Ilustración Española y Americana*, Barcelona's *Las Noticias, El Eco de Bilbao*, or *La Lucha de Clases*, do not appear (though, to be sure, many of the writings in this last journal appeared unsigned and would not be attributed to Unamuno for decades). Effectively, then, the collection mutes certain strains in Unamuno's early political thought (i.e., his socialism), and his contributions to journals published across Spain, while focusing on essays relevant to the Spain most proximate to the Residencia's situation and goals: a Spain centred in Madrid, where an idealized national youth comparable to those promoted throughout Europe at the time was being formed.

In light of these observations, and the sheer volume of Unamuno's turn-of-the-century writing, the extent to which the Residencia's edition of the *Ensayos* is truly representative of the early Unamuno is a debatable matter. Jiménez Fraud's assertion that the essays encompass and synthesize all of the writer's contributions in the genres of the novel, theatre, or poetry is clearly reductive, at least from a twenty-first-century standpoint. In any case, the brief prologue that Unamuno wrote to open the first volume of the collection stresses that the essays it contains are *not* representative of the state of the writer's thought in 1916. While asserting that his thinking has changed in many ways in the span of years since he wrote the essays, however, the author explains that he has decided not to revise them: "No va el que hoy soy yo a corregir al que fui" ("The man I am today will not correct the one I was") (*E* 1:11). He justifies his decision as an act of faithfulness to his earlier self, as well as to the interpretive capabilities of the reader: "acaso sirva a alguien lo que pensaba hace años en oposición a lo que hoy pienso y tanto o más que esto" ("perhaps what I thought years ago will be of use to someone, in contrast with what I think today and as much as or more than the latter") (12). He invites the reader to compare the Unamuno of the essays with the Unamuno of 1916, evaluate the ideas each presents, and draw his or her own conclusions.

Moreno Villa and his contemporaries had the opportunity to do just that. There are many ways in which the Unamuno of 1916 differed from the Unamuno of the turn of the century, and especially from the author of the earliest essays collected in the Residencia edition, but one of the most significant is his greater personal animosity towards the Spanish State in the wake of his abrupt dismissal from the rectorship of the Universidad de Salamanca in August of 1914. This slight caused an uproar in the intellectual community and was the source of great bitterness for Unamuno, who never received an explanation for his dismissal. Moreover, as Christopher Cobb points out in his anthology of the ex-rector's articles from the time of the First World War, it fueled an increase in his journalistic writing, where he polemicized openly against the Spanish government's policies. Unamuno published a great number of these articles in *España*, the same publication that advertised the successive appearance of the volumes of his collected essays between 1916 and 1919.[32] Thus his fierce attacks on the government could not have gone unnoticed by the intellectual community in Madrid that also formed the primary audience for the *Ensayos*.

In addition to Unamuno's campaign against Spanish neutrality under both conservative Prime Minister Eduardo Dato and his more liberal successor the Count of Romanones, during the war years Unamuno wrote extensively on the topic of education, attacking the poor quality of instruction and denouncing widespread incompetence among Spanish instructors. In May of 1916, just after the first volume of his *Ensayos* was published, he linked the two topics in an article that appeared in *España*, "La paz de la neutralidad pedagógica" ("The Peace of Pedagogical Neutrality"). There he asserted that the greatest danger for Spanish education was the institution's indifference towards the quality of its instruction, a position he regarded as unsustainable and cowardly, much like Romanones' continued stance of neutrality before the war. Here a similarity between the Unamuno of the 1910s and the Unamuno of the turn of the century does emerge. Just as in *En torno al casticismo* he had denounced the stagnation of Spanish cultural life and called for the opening of the country to fresh breezes from Europe, in 1916 he critiques both an inadequate educational system and isolationist politics that prevent Spain from taking a moral stand in the unprecedented conflict then engulfing the continent. In his prologue to the *Ensayos*, Unamuno insisted that, despite the many differences between his present and previous selves, he had remained faithful to the essence of his character. There is ample evidence to suggest his conviction that Spanish youth needed to be educated for the future and his rejection of the senile regime that inhibited that process should be counted among the aspects of his thought that were constant, despite the interval of years. For example, his article "Discípulos y maestros" ("Disciples and Masters"), also from May 1916, champions the role of young people in overturning an outdated society much as "Viejos y jóvenes" had. If the war had served as a catalyst for this generational revolution throughout Europe, Spain's neutrality had insulated the country from its rejuvenating effect. As Unamuno wrote in 1918, "Los ministros del actual Ministerio de Su Majestad … nos parecen ya, incluso los nuevos, los que lo son por vez primera, viejos, viejísimos, decrépitos, del antiguo régimen, de un siglo pasado, del siglo que acabó de acabar en 1914" ("The ministers of His Majesty's current Ministry … even the new ones, the first-timers, already seem old, extremely old, decrepit, belonging to the old order, to a past century, to the century that finally ended in 1914") (Cobb 205).

The Residencia as Arcadia

Unamuno's principled critique of the Spanish government in the wake of his dismissal from the rectorship at Salamanca was not lost on Moreno Villa. As a poet and painter of some acclaim, a contributor to *España*, a scholar of art history, and a boarder and tutor at the Residencia, the artist had his proverbial finger on the pulse of Spanish cultural life during the mid-1910s, as he would during the next decade as well. His personal encounters and exchanges with Unamuno in 1913 and early 1914 undoubtedly informed his own response to the events in Salamanca that August. As part of the ongoing reaction to the Basque writer's dismissal from his administrative post at the university, Moreno Villa dedicated a poem to him that appeared in December in the journal *Nuevo Mundo*. The poem, titled "A Don Miguel de Unamuno," was subsequently included in Moreno Villa's collection *Evoluciones* (1918) as "A un hombre sin tacha" ("To an Untainted Man"). In the later version, the body of the text is unchanged, but a two-stanza epilogue that appeared in *Nuevo Mundo* is missing. Addressed directly to "Miguel," this epilogue develops an image that first emerges in the ninth stanza of the body of the poem: "¡Pureza! Recio escudo / contra el dragon que arrastra / la inmundicia del mundo." ("Purity! Solid shield / against the dragon that drags behind him / the filth of the world.") In its original context, the purity of which the poet speaks refers to the unblemished whiteness of Unamuno's beard, evoked in the opening stanzas of the poem as a sign of his integrity. The shield and dragon correspond yet again to the iconography of the warrior saint Michael, also Don Miguel's namesake. The hendecasyllables of the dedication, more stately than the seven-syllable lines of the main text, depict Unamuno as a virtuous masculine hero similar to the one Moreno Villa imagines in canto XIII of "En la selva fervorosa":

DEDICANDO

Miguel, escudo y lanza firmes
te puso Dios, en poderosos brazos;
pero el supremo don fue tu pureza,
que destiló en el fondo de tu vaso

Por eso tiemblo al escuchar el verbo
sin rozaduras, aunque recio y áspero;
porque no son palabras, son … tu vida
dolorosa y triunfal de varón santo.

(**DEDICATION**

Miguel, God put a solid shield and a lance
in your hands, for use by your powerful arms;
but your purity was his most surpassing gift,
which he poured out in the bottom of your glass

For that reason I tremble when I hear
the unabrading although strong, surly voice;
for what I hear are not words, they are … your life,
the pain and the triumph of a holy man.)

In the context of its original publication, "A Don Miguel de Unamuno" is marked by politics and history, as Moreno Villa joins his voice with the intellectual community that denounced the government's treatment of Unamuno. His removal from the rectorship undoubtedly reminded someone like Giner, who wrote to him in the days after the incident, of the clashes between the State and the educational community in the 1870s. Yet Moreno Villa elevates these conflicts to an idealized, allegorical, and theological plane, much as he does with the topic of adolescence in "En la selva fervorosa." Unamuno becomes the archangel, paragon of virile heroism and righteousness. Aspects of dutiful, robust masculinity that were especially tied elsewhere in Europe to the image of young soldiers fighting in the First World War are here attributed to a man of fifty, whose white hair stands more as a testament to his moral virtue and imperviousness to corruption than to his age. In effect, Unamuno's purity endows him with the eternal youth of noble causes so revered during these early years of the war – a Spanish and older counterpart to England's Rupert Brooke, whose death in 1915 precipitated an outpouring of admiration and innumerable elegies. With the inclusion of "A un hombre sin tacha" in *Evoluciones*, however, the later version of the poem erases its historical markers – universalizing its meaning, perhaps, but also suppressing the political elements of its origin.[33]

There are very few direct references to the First World War in Moreno Villa's writings. Among his poems, there are three. Two of them also appear in *Evoluciones*: the third-to-last poem "Sentimiento de traslación" ("Feeling of Transference") and the penultimate "Tres víctimas de la Gran Guerra" ("Three Victims of the Great War"). In "Sentimiento de traslación," Moreno Villa contrasts the activities of a Spanish family in a seaside city – work and the sharing of a midday meal – with scenes from the war: the bloodstained waters of a maritime battle, trenches filled with corpses, and conflicts in the air. Each of the last five stanzas opens with the line "Y en tanto…" ("And meanwhile…"), an anaphora that enacts the overland movement of the title and signals the contemporaneous and ongoing suffering inflicted by the war in places distant from sunny Iberian beaches. Immediately following these scenes of violence and loss, "Tres víctimas de la Gran Guerra" offers a series of vignettes depicting women marked by the conflict: one Belgian, one French, and one German. By focusing here not on the fallen soldiers, but on innocent women on both sides of the battle whom it has scarred (the first woman has been raped; the second looses material belongings and seems to have lost her husband as well, though her son is spared; and the third has her lover taken from her), the poet reflects the disillusionment that spread throughout Europe as the war drew on.

The other reference to the conflict in Moreno Villa's poetic corpus occurs three years earlier, and shows a very different kind of concern for the fighting happening beyond Spain's borders. In the epigraph to *Luchas de "Pena" y "Alegría" y su transfiguración* (*The Battles of "Sorrow" and "Joy" and their Transfiguration,* 1915) – a collection of poems linked, like those of "En la selva fervorosa," by an allegorical and loosely narrative thread – Moreno Villa writes,

> En años de congoja y luchas universales se retrajo la musa al primitivo solar; no en huida, sino en busca de los otros combates intensos y humanas que la copla andaluza – directa flecha del alma – trasluce.
>
> Así nació esta condensada Alegoría, totalmente ajena en su exterior a las contiendas que afligen hoy, más [*sic*] fuertemente unificada en su meollo con las eternas pugnas. (*PCMV* 171)[34]

> (In years of distress and universal fighting the muse retreated to her primitive home; not fleeing, but rather searching out the other intense and human battles that Andalusian song – an arrow straight from the soul – reveals.
>
> Thus this condensed Allegory was born, on the surface totally removed from the conflicts that trouble our day, but at root strongly united to eternal struggles.)

Though averring that he is not trying to avoid the reality of war, the poet nevertheless says that he takes refuge in his poetry, and the poetry of his native region, Andalusia. This is a somewhat contradictory statement, and his decision to focus on the abstract rather than the concrete, the "eternal" rather than "external" battles – Unamuno's *intrahistoria* echoes again in these words – clearly had become less feasible by the time he wrote "Sentimiento de traslación" and "Tres víctimas de la Gran Guerra."

Yet the idea of refuge, linked to art and to the concept of eternity as opposed to progressive time, reappears in Moreno Villa's later writing. In the chapter of *Vida en claro* dedicated to his years at the Residencia he recalls his former home fondly, remembering "todo lo que tenía de maravilloso aquel refugio para un carácter como el mío, ansioso de tarea y harto de esas complicaciones materiales que entorpecen tanto en las casas" ("all of the marvels of that refuge for a character like mine, anxious to get to work and fed up with those material complications that so get in the way in [private] houses") (*Memoria* 104). While he marvels over the freedom from mundane tasks that living at the Residencia afforded him (he notes that a "fairy godmother" took care of all of these menial chores for him), he especially cherishes the idyllic atmosphere and the proximity to the students – "la juventud eterna" – that allowed his creative impulses to thrive. If, as James Valender has suggested, poetry was Moreno Villa's "ascesis" ("A propósito" 390), the Residencia was his Arcadia. In his autobiography he praises the physical location of the centre, removed from the city on its hill. "Ningún edificio ajeno podía molestarle" ("No outside building disturbed it"), he remarks, though he goes on to note at there was an asylum for women next door that "como cuña se metía en los terrenos adquiridos por la Residencia" ("stuck into the grounds acquired by the Residencia like a wedge") (*Memoria* 108). The physical penetration of an institution associated with the feminine and the irrational into the space of the Residencia signals by opposition the orderly, intellectual, and masculine character of the realm Moreno Villa identifies with eternal youth. In his writing, it is a hermetic space, closed off from threatening, uncontrollable forces. It is to the Residencia that the author recalls returning after a dark year spent working in the northern coastal town of Gijón, and after the failure of his relationship with a redheaded young woman from New York named Florence, the Jacinta of *Jacinta, la pelirroja*. Politics makes almost no appearance in the world of "la eterna juventud." When Moreno Villa's mind does, inevitably, stray to the Civil War that put an end to the institution's work, he stops himself and laments the "intrusión de las horas finales en el relato" ("intrusion of the last hours upon the story") (109), just as, in closing the chapter on his life at the Residencia, he laments having to move on: "me duele separarme de esta época llena de cosas" ("it pains me to leave this period full of things behind") (119).

Was the Residencia a refuge only from the tedious tasks of adult life and homeownership? Or did it shelter Moreno Villa, and its other inhabitants, from certain spheres of social reality as well? The educational institution's assumption of a neutral stance and distance from the debates between *aliadófilos* and *germanófilos* in the early years of the First World War suggests that this was the case, though this need not imply that the topic of the war was avoided there.[35] Turning inward upon itself, it endeavoured to create a space where young people could experience the kind of intellectual and cultural stimulation, camaraderie, and leisure that would enrich their individual development and, eventually, the new Spain of which Giner, Unamuno, and Ortega, in their various ways, all dreamed. Pursuing these goals, it avoided direct engagement with the political debates that dominated Spanish society in the 1910s (and later on) and constituted a world apart. The Residencia's insularity reveals an intentional distancing from the political realm – a reproduction in miniature of Spain's self-exemption from the war – and a subsequent complicity with the *status quo* that is at odds with its *institucionista* origins. Nonetheless, it also forms the foundation upon which the Spanish writers who lived there were able to develop aesthetic reflections about the relationship between youth and art, and incorporate the perspective of the adolescent, that recent product of modernity, into their own artistic creation.

Moreno Villa is perhaps the first Spanish writer to grapple with a twentieth-century understanding of adolescent experience in verse, and to allow it to shape his writing on both thematic and stylistic levels. While Unamuno had identified youth in the abstract with his own religious, political, and even poetic ideas, the poet from Málaga allowed the adolescent condition of incompleteness and changefulness to permeate all of his work. At one point in *Vida en claro*, Moreno Villa explains his prolonged stay at the Residencia by stating, "mi destino era la interinidad" ("the provisional was my destiny") (104). Literally a state of being "in the interim," *interinidad* rests not on stability but on transition. Rooted in Catholic theology, it stresses the provisional character of earthly life as opposed to the security that comes with death. In claiming this state as his destiny, however, Moreno Villa chose to live and work in unending transition. In this sense he is not simply an intermediary between two "generations" in Spanish literary history, but a poet who lives in the interstices: between narrative and lyric, life and art, innocence and experience. His interstitial, adolescent mode of writing is especially pronounced in "En la selva fervorosa," but it also informs his later work. In *Salón sin muros* (*Room Without Walls*, 1936), the poet comments on being an almost-fifty-year-old bachelor (still living at the Residencia): "Mi celibato me permite comer acá y allá, / concluir el mes con el último céntimo / y tener en suma cierta levedad juvenil" ("My solitude allows me to eat where I like, / finish the month on the last dime / and have, in sum, a kind of juvenile levity") (*PCMV* 413).

Moreno Villa's self-immersion in the *locus amoenus* (or Never Land) of the Residencia during a twenty-year period serves as an illustration of his attraction to a way of life distinct from that of the adult world – the static realm of bourgeois resignation that the later *residentes* Salvador Dalí, Federico García Lorca, and Pepín Bello would refer to as putrefied, *putrefacto*. The eternal youth he found at the Residencia allowed him to take the aesthetic interest in adolescence that pervades "En la selva fervorosa" and make it into the basis of a poetics. As I argue in the next chapter, the ties between poetry and youth forged at the Residencia in the 1910s – and the apolitical character they acquired there during that decade – also shaped the self-understanding of the young writers who frequented the "Colina de los Chopos" in the 1920s.

Chapter Three

"Un joven auténtico de 366 años": Fashioning a Young Literature

Unamuno's library, preserved at the Casa Museo Unamuno in Salamanca, includes a copy of British soldier-poet Rupert Brooke's *1914 and Other Poems,* which was published in London by Sidgwick & Jackson, Ltd. in 1917. There is an inscription inside the front cover that reads, "From J.E. Crawford Flitch / 1918." Crawford Flitch was a British Hispanist, a veteran of the First World War, and an enthusiast of Unamuno's work. In 1921 he published the first translation of *Del sentimiento trágico de la vida* into English, and in 1924 accompanied the Spanish writer on the island of Fuerteventura when he was exiled there by dictator Miguel Primo de Rivera.[1] The copy of Brooke's *1914* that Flitch gave to Unamuno six years before his exile shows signs of an attentive reading. Several lines of poems are marked, and a list of page numbers indicating those compositions that most interested the reader appears inside the back cover of the book. The first of these numbers corresponds to the sonnet "The Soldier." On the page where the sonnet appears, three vertical lines have been drawn to the left of the opening statement: "If I should die, think only this of me: / That there's some corner of a foreign field / That is forever England" (Brooke 15).

This annotation reveals a link between the young soldier of the First World War and the Unamuno of the 1920s, another poet who found himself separated from his homeland, though under a different set of circumstances. Upon reading the opening lines of Brooke's "The Soldier," the student of Unamuno's poetry inevitably hears the beginning of the first poem in his *Romancero del destierro* (*Ballads of Exile,* 1928):

> Si caigo aquí, sobre esta tierra verde
> mollar y tibia de la dulce Francia,

. . . .
llevad mi cuerpo al maternal y adusto
páramo que se hermana con el cielo. (*OCE* 6:743)

(If I should fall here, on this green earth,
in the cool, soft sweetness of docile France,
. . . .
carry my body to the maternal and austere
plateau that rises up to meet the heavens.)

This poem is dated 1925, and was written in Paris. Its basic argument is very similar to that of "The Soldier": if the poet should die on foreign soil, his connection to his country will remain. Years later, when accepting an invitation to join the Comité Rupert Brooke in 1930, Unamuno would confirm that he had the young Englishman's poem in mind when he wrote his own.[2] Yet in "Si caigo aquí…" Unamuno revises Brooke's resignation to being buried in a "foreign field" and asks that his body be taken back to Spain. While "The Soldier" describes the dust of the warrior's corpse as an extension of England itself – the physical remains of a young man "whom England bore" – Unamuno preserves a distinction between his bodily integrity and Spanish soil. Enumerating parts of his anatomy in a way that recalls his meditation on the body of Christ in the third part of *El Cristo de Velázquez*, the poet uses the anaphoric refrain "tape su polvo" ("may its dust cover") with regard to his eyes (l.23), feet (29), hand (33), chest (37), forehead (46), ears (49), and genitals (53). The distinction between dust and flesh, however subtle, reminds the reader that Unamuno's estrangement from Spain at the moment of composing "Si caigo aquí" arises not only from his physical distance from the country, but also from his fierce disagreements with the way it was being run by Primo de Rivera. While Brooke's poem is an ode of unwavering patriotism (the patriotism that made him an icon of heroic youth during the First World War), Unamuno's text shuns nationalism. He even goes so far as to ask that his corpse not be wrapped in the Spanish flag, "ese roto harapo gualda y rojo" ("that torn rag of red and yellow") (65), but in white linen ("un lienzo de blancura") (61). The burial the poet imagines is a reconciliation, a reunion of man and country long separated by national politics.

In one sense, Unamuno's impassioned critique of Primo de Rivera's dictatorship and the six-year exile that resulted from it also kept him at a distance from the Spanish literary and cultural scene in which the group of poets and writers that called itself *la joven literatura* coalesced. His exile and the political principles upon which it was founded prevented him from joining in the event that would come to form the basis of the generational identity of these artists: the three-hundredth anniversary of the death of the Baroque poet Luis de Góngora that they celebrated in 1927. As Cecilia Enjuto Rangel has pointed out, Unamuno's critique of the event was primarily motivated by politics, as he expressed his disapproval of its lack of political consciousness, its neutrality before Primo's oppression (167). In this regard the tercentenary continued in the vein of the dissociation between intellectual life and politics that held sway at the Residencia de Estudiantes in the 1910s. If Unamuno had been critical of Spanish leaders for remaining "neutral" in the First World War, he was bound to be even more impatient with Spanish artists who carried on with their work and play while an oppressive regime annulled parliament and the freedom of the press. This is not how critics have usually interpreted the abstention, however. Unamuno's non-participation in the tercentenary, together with the belligerent statements he made about it later in *Cómo se hace una novela* and his relative lack of interest in Góngora's work have consolidated the view that the exiled poet was far removed, not only geographically but also aesthetically, from the members of *la joven literatura*. My contention in this chapter is that this was not the case. While Unamuno was physically absent from Spain during the years in which this group reached the height of its collective activity, his ideas about poetry, artistic creation, and especially the link between these things and youth were very present in the younger writers' work, before and, increasingly, after 1927.

This presence of the exiled Unamuno as a point of reference for the young generation in Spain was in fact twofold. It comprised his literary legacy, with which the younger writers were familiar through their own readings of his work and personal contacts with him, but it also extended to the visibility that he gained as a political figure over the course of his exile. In terms of the literary connection, the lyrical and essayistic sensibility that guided José Moreno Villa in his approach to writing poetry about adolescence in the 1910s also resonated with the creative and critical outlooks of a group of writers eager to reinvigorate Spanish letters in the 1920s. Gerardo Diego, the main organizer of the Góngora tercentenary who would go on to edit the influential anthology *Poesía española. Antología, 1915–1931*,[3] employed an especially Unamunian vision of youth in his efforts to represent the artistic values of *la joven literatura*. From a broader cultural and historical standpoint, however, it is important to acknowledge that these artists' activities took place during a time of burgeoning political organization among Spain's university students, and that from the mid-1920s on, the exiled Unamuno was an increasingly celebrated and revered figure within that youth movement. Within a few years of the military coup that placed Primo in power in September of 1923, a sector of the rapidly growing student population began to criticize the dictatorship. Progressive and largely republican, they occupied the opposite end of the political spectrum from the pro-regime, Catholic youth organizations that also proliferated during these years, above all Primo's own Asociación de Estudiantes Católicos (AEC). The dictator blocked initial attempts by the anti-regime youth activists to organize as the Unión Liberal de Estudiantes (ULE), but by the 1926–1927 school year they formed the Federación Universitaria Escolar (FUE), looking to Unamuno as one of their models.[4] Now in his sixties, the former rector of the Universidad de Salamanca was once again affiliated with political youth.

The first chapter of the FUE was founded in Madrid in January of 1927, as Diego and the other organizers of the Góngora tercentenary were preparing their celebratory publications and sending out invitations. This coincidence suggests a new means of approaching the activities of *la joven literatura* in 1927 and the following years, one that focuses on the discourse of youth they developed and the central role Unamuno played in it. It is standard in literary criticism on the Generation of 1927 to acknowledge the increasing political awareness and politicization (along sometimes opposing ideological lines) that defines the group beginning in the late 1920s. How should their literary youth be understood in relation to the political versions of youth proliferating in the student organizations of these years? To be sure, the members of *la joven literatura* were no longer university students by the mid-1920s, but neither were they oblivious to the changing role of young people in the political world of interwar Europe. Santos Juliá has argued that the central question for young Spanish intellectuals around 1930 (he focuses, as I do here, on circles centred in Madrid) was a question of purpose: what were they creating art *for*? Irrespective of one's political leaning, the need to justify the creation of art and the pursuit of poetry was growing in urgency. If notions like Paul Valéry's "poésie pure" or Ortega's "deshumanización del arte" reaffirmed the modernist argument that art justifies itself, that it is autonomous and separate from life, Spain's artistic youth was compelled to interrogate and nuance these concepts. Juliá lists Malraux, Weil, Brecht, and Orwell as artists of the time whose work modelled the reunion of art and life, as it "fused with their lives" and became "the manifestation of life, its outward projection" ("Ser intelectual" 761, my translation). Among Spanish writers, these words describe no one better than Unamuno, and especially the Unamuno of exile. As Ana Urrutia Jordana has demonstrated, the author of *De Fuerteventura a París* and *Romancero del destierro* practices a "poeticization of politics," the transformation of contemporary events into sites of creation. In the prologue to the *Romancero* he writes, "la actualidad política es eternidad histórica y, por lo tanto, poesía" ("the political present is historical eternity, and therefore, poetry") (*OCE* 6:741). Drawing on the historical vision that had informed his thought since the turn of the century, Unamuno during these years saw political engagement as a form of *poiesis*, an activity embedded in history yet endowed with the capacity to transcend the historical. At the same time, as he lived out his six-year-long poetic act of political resistence, his exile catalysed an evolution in his own poetic writing that approximated him to the younger generation of poets in his homeland. In the following pages, I argue that the example of the exiled Unamuno deepened these young Spanish artists' understanding of what it meant to be artists – and particularly young artists – during these years.

Poetry and Politics, Purity and Humanity

In the spring of 1924, the French journal *Intentions* published a special issue titled *La Jeune littérature espagnole,* featuring the work of Dámaso Alonso, José Bergamín, Rogelio Buendía, Juan Chabás y Martí, Gerardo Diego, Antonio Espina, Jorge Guillén, Federico García Lorca, Antonio Marichalar, Alonso Quesada, Adolfo Salazar, Pedro Salinas, and Fernando Vela.[5] Though the roster of the group and its parameters would vary over the next several years, the publication provided an initial sketch of *la joven literatura*. Several of these names (Alonso, Diego, Guillén, García Lorca, and Salinas) would continue to figure in later lists and eventually be counted among the "canonical" members of the Generation of 1927. Yet as the *Intentions* roster indicates, from the beginning the concept of a literary youth traced boundaries distinct from those that the critical tradition would impose later on: this roster included prose writers (Chabás) and critics (Marichalar) as well as a figure like Bergamín, who despite being highly involved in the endeavours of the group in 1927 has received much less attention from scholars. Still, the fact that the young Spanish literature heralded by *Intentions* was predominantly made up of poets corroborated a contemporary view of new writing from Spain. In 1926 Marichalar, who had helped to organize the issue of the French journal, wrote in a piece for London's *The New Criterion*: "In all countries there is an age for prose-writers and another for poets ... in Spain, the present age is undoubtedly passing through the sign of the lyric" ("Madrid Chronicle" 357). This parceling of history into times for poetry and times for prose echoes Ortega y Gasset's claim that art passes through periods of age and youth, and it suggests that "La deshumanización del arte" was at the back of Marichalar's mind as he wrote the article. Indeed, when the first instalments of Ortega's essay appeared in *El Sol* in early 1924, his theory of modern "arte joven" was immediately applied to Spain's own literary youth. As Andrew Anderson has noted (*El Veintisiete* 26), the characteristics that Ortega attributed to young art in the early sections of his essay – incomprehensibility to the masses, abstraction, and rejection of the "old" aesthetic modes of the nineteenth century – were readily associated with these Spaniards. In an article titled "Nuestra joven literatura" ("Our Young Literature"), Melchor Fernández Almagro was quick to link the Ortegan view of the new art to the work of his contemporaries. When these young artists began to champion Góngora's poetry, famous for its difficulty and aristocratic, Latinate style, they reinforced these associations.

Two months before the publication of the special issue of *Intentions*, and just after *El Sol* printed the first sections of "La deshumanización del arte," Unamuno's exile began. On 21 February, Unamuno, escorted by police, left his home in Salamanca for Fuerteventura in the Canary Islands. He stayed on the island until July, when he escaped to Paris just after receiving a pardon from Primo. Choosing not to accept a pardon that he had not solicited, nor to return to a country where his writing would be subject to censorship, he stayed in the French capital for a year before ultimately relocating to the Basque village of Hendaye, just across the border from Spain. There he remained until the dictatorship fell in early 1930.

Exile placed Unamuno at the centre of public discourse once again, much as his dismissal from the position of rector of the Universidad de Salamanca had in 1914. His perpetual embattlement with Spain's political powers had once more brought retaliation from a government hoping to silence him. The members of *la joven literatura* were familiar with his divisiveness. In 1921, for example, Jorge Guillén experienced it firsthand when an article he had written was denied publication because it mentioned the professor from Salamanca (Ciplijauskaité, "Apostilla" 81–2). In an expression of political solidarity with "Don Miguel" just after the military coup in the fall of 1923, Antonio Espina affirmed the exemplary importance of Unamuno's resistance to Primo's new regime, declaring in an article published in *España*, "¡Unamunámonos!" ("Let us Unamunify ourselves!"). Beyond the literary realm, during his exile Unamuno inspired the university students who began to organize in opposition to the dictatorship. While Primo worked to frame his government as the antithesis to and solution for the old ways of the past (in this like other European dictators who seized power in the wake of the First World War), Unamuno encouraged Spanish students to see themselves – not a new regime – as the only true source of rejuvenation for their country. In the spring of 1925 he addressed "los estudiantes de España" in an open letter that was published in the anti-regime periodical *España con honra* (*Spain with Honour*). There he warned them that while Primo claimed to have put an end to the *ancien régime* of the Restoration, in reality his dictatorship was the culmination of that defunct order. Without the parliamentary system and the freedom of the press that had at least been able to hold endemic corruption and oppression in check before, the "gangrena" ("gangrene") could now spread unhindered (*Cartas del destierro* 117). In light of these considerations, Unamuno encouraged his young addressees not to be taken in by Primo's rhetoric, and not to act as young recruits to what was in reality an old and abhorrent cause.

The students were listening. As José López-Rey maintains in his book *Los estudiantes frente a la dictadura* (*Students Against the Dictatorship*, 1930), the exiled writer was ever-present in the thoughts of the young people at Madrid's Universidad Central who organized in opposition to their conservative Catholic counterparts and the dictatorship. López-Rey identifies Unamuno, along with the younger professor Luis Jiménez de Asúa (who would later serve as president of the Spanish Republican government in exile) as the two "maestros" of the student movement: "Anciano, el uno; joven, el otro; juveniles, los dos" ("One elderly; the other young; both youthful") (10). This focus on youthfulness as a quality shared by both the students and their chosen models summarizes a reciprocity that deeped in the last years of the 1920s. When student protests against Primo's educational policies initiated a strike that brought the university system to a standstill in 1928 and 1929, Unamuno wrote another open letter to the students, publishing it in his own journal

Hojas libres. Dated 17 March 1929, this letter was not only one of encouragement but also, and above all, one of praise. Unamuno congratulated the young people for refusing to become the dictator's sheep, and moreover, for taking the initiative to turn around and teach their professors how to be masters and leaders. (Indeed, many professors, including Ortega y Gasset, had followed the students' lead in joining the strike.) Such action and leadership on the part of the young was what Unamuno had called for not only in 1925, but also in 1914 and 1895, consistently arguing that Spain's future depended upon the initiative of the young, on the inversion of the dynamics of instruction between masters and disciples. Finally, here was a youth that seemed capable of saving Spain from the "régimen de mentira" that continued to exist under Primo. In closing, Unamuno asked them to do just that: "Salvad a España, estudiantes" ("Students, save Spain") (*Cartas del destierro* 300). The letter was talked about throughout the country, and especially in Madrid. Unamuno's son-in-law José María Quiroga Plá, a poet and collaborator in some of the projects of *la joven literatura*, wrote to him of the enthusiastic reception it received among the young people in the capital (Martínez Nadal 123). Responding for the students, FUE activists López-Rey, María Zambrano, and Carlos Díez Fernández wrote a warm letter in which they committed themselves to carrying out the mission with which Unamuno had charged them, declaring in the first line of their letter, "alma nuestra es la de tu carta" ("the soul of your letter is our soul") (López-Rey 146).[6]

The impact of Unamuno's voice in the late 1920s did not go unnoticed among the members of *la joven literatura*. Bergamín, whose relationship with the exiled writer is examined in greater depth in the next chapter, was personally acquainted with it through their sustained correspondence. But it was Rafael Alberti who perhaps most famously placed Unamuno at the crux of the aesthetic preoccupations of the time. As he writes in a well-known passage from his memoir *La arboleda perdida*,

> Poco o nada sabía yo de política, entregado a mis versos solamente en aquella España hasta entonces de apariencia tranquila. Mas de repente mis oídos se abrieron a palabras que antes no había escuchado o nada me dijeran: como república, fascismo, libertad … Y supe, a partir de ese instante, que don Miguel de Unamuno, desde su destierro de Hendaya, enviaba cartas y poemas … verdaderos panfletos contra el otro Miguel … que no más recibidos corrían como la pólvora por las tertulias literarias,

> las redacciones de los periódicos enemigos del régimen, las manos agitadas de los universitarios. (317–18)
>
> (I knew little or nothing of politics, wholly dedicated as I was to my poetry in a Spain that had until then seemed so calm. But all of a sudden my ears opened to words that I had never heard or that had never meant anything to me: like republic, fascism, liberty … And I discovered, in that moment, that Don Miguel de Unamuno, from his exile in Hendaye, was sending out letters and poems … veritable propaganda against the other Miguel … that, as soon as they arrived, spread like wildfire through literary circles, the offices of anti-regime newspapers, the restless hands of the university students.)

Alberti goes on to mention Ramón María del Valle-Inclán, who was jailed by Primo in 1929, but it is Unamuno whom he cites as the initial catalyst for a dramatic shift in his own artistic life, from an early time of complete separation between poetry and politics to a later stage when the two began to combine. In Alberti's account, the exiled writer provides the hinge between a period of purist aestheticism and another of social engagement – periods that have also defined the basic arc of the history of his generation as told by numerous critics, beginning with Dámaso Alonso in his essay "Una generación poética: 1920–1936" (1948). According to this history, the time of artistic purism fostered by the early mentorship of Juan Ramón Jiménez and Ortega y Gasset gives way, more or less in the pivotal year of 1927, to what Alonso calls "el demonio de la política" ("the demon of politics") (670). Despite Alberti's mention, Unamuno rarely figures in later versions of this narrative that, in following the general arc of Alonso's essay, also inevitably reproduce some of his nostalgia for the earlier years. Though near the end of the text Alonso refers to the shift in more positive terms, as the bursting-in of life on the previously cold and removed artistic world of his generation (673), it is difficult not to sense in his essay, and in other personal and critical accounts, an idealization of the first period as prelapsarian: a time of innocence preceding the tragically inevitable fall into the harsh realities of life. Moreno Villa's portrayal of the Residencia in *Vida en claro* as the Arcadian site of "eterna juventud" presents a similar vision. From such a perspective, political awakening is a loss of innocence and a coming of age, the exchange of carefree youth for the serious responsibilities of maturity. The instrumental placement of Unamuno and the university student resistance movement in Alberti's recollections, however, suggests that this coming of age for Spain's *joven literatura* was an initiation not into adulthood, but into a new understanding of youth.

Of course, the phenomenon that Juliá calls an "awakening to political consciousness" did not occur all at once, nor in the same way for each of the young writers. It is probably more accurate to speak of a gradual change in tone and focus, a shifting of emphases, than to imagine that political awareness hit *la joven literatura* like a thunderclap. In this regard, the subtle presence of Unamuno's literary legacy becomes especially important. The younger generation's familiarity with his work and their recognition of him as one of their poetic predecessors provided a backdrop for their understanding of his exile, and allowed their admiration for him to grow during this period. To begin to define the nature of Unamuno's example for the younger poets in the 1920s and early 1930s, it is illuminating to compare the trajectory of his relationship with them with that of another of their *maestros*, Juan Ramón Jiménez. Jiménez fostered the work of many younger poets in his journal *Índice* (1921–1922) and created close ties with several of them in the early 1920s. As the decade wore on, however, he channeled his energies into the ambitious project of refining and perfecting his (capitalized) "Obra." Withdrawn into the controlled spaces of his art and his home, and highly sensitive to any sign of disrespect, Jiménez quarreled and cut ties with almost all of his former protégés: among them Bergamín, Salinas, and Guillén. In the 1930s he positioned himself as the sole arbiter of poetic purity in his reviews and articles for the Spanish press, further alienating his younger admirers.[7] Meanwhile in France, Unamuno immersed himself in the task of fusing political dissent and poetic creation. His art, like the rest of his life, was an expression of protest that gained an audience beyond literary circles, in Spain and throughout Europe. In addition to *La agonía del cristianismo* and *Cómo se hace una novela*, he wrote *De Fuerteventura a París* and *Romancero del destierro*, and began the composition of his *Cancionero*, where he even began to experiment with techniques similar to those practiced by the young poets back in Spain.[8] This work from exile, in tandem with his many earlier writings, offered the younger generation another view of what it meant to write poetry, and of why it might matter for the cultural and political rejuvenation of modern Spain.

The prologue to *Romancero del destierro* offers a deeply considered reflection on the relationship between poetry and politics that engages the contemporary artistic world by wrestling with the term "poesía pura," a concept much discussed in Spain and in France during these years.[9] In this text Unamuno remarks that to him it makes no sense to speak of poetic purification, as if the purity of art could be engineered through some process of extraction. The type of purity that most compels him is one of intention. He understands the work of poetry as a bearing of witness to the complexities of personal and historical experience without subjecting his observations to rules and formulas, the dependence on which becomes a kind of poetic bad faith. Echoing an argument that he had made in the notes to his earlier collection *Teresa* (1924), he refuses to lay out doctrines that guided him in writing the poems of the book; instead he attempts to give his reader a sense of "el ámbito íntimo en que me brotaron" ("the personal space in which they sprouted") (*OCE* 6:742). In *Teresa*, written just before his exile and published after he had left Spain, he wrote that a poet "se atiene a postceptos y no a preceptos, a resultados y no a premisas, a creaciones, o sea poemas y no a decretos, o sea dogmas" ("holds to post-cepts and not to precepts; to results and not to premises; to creations – that is, poems – and not to decrees – that is, dogmas") (*OCE* 6:660). These last words appear in the passage that Gerardo Diego would later choose to represent Unamuno's poetics in his 1932 anthology.

Despite this commitment to non-dogmatic openness, however, the Unamuno of *Romancero del destierro* does allow his dislike for the terms *poesía pura* and *deshumanización* to colour his view of the young poets in Spain. The precept by which he especially refuses to abide in his prologue and throughout *Romancero* is the conceit that poetic purity requires the progressive elimination of the "human" from art. He makes this exceedingly clear in a poem from the collection dated 27 April 1927, which he indignantly addresses to a group of writers he calls "gongorinos de pega" ("phony Gongorines"):

> ¿Poesía pura? El agua
> destilada, no por obra
> de nube del cielo, pero
> de redoma.
> ¡Deshumanad!, ¡buen provecho!;
> yo me quedo con la boda
> de lo humano y lo divino,
> que es la gloria. (*OCE* 6:770)

(Pure poetry? Distilled
water, not made by the labour
of clouds in the sky, but
bottled.
Dehumanize! Good luck to you!
I'll be just fine with the wedding
of the human and the divine,
which is heaven.)

According to Luis Cernuda, the *gongorinos* might have been more in agreement with the poet than Unamuno was able to recognize. In an essay on Unamuno written after his death, Cernuda reflects on this "malhumorado poemita" ("ill-tempered little poem") and muses that the author's anger was probably provoked not so much by the youngsters' interest in Góngora as by "la deshumanización supuesta ... en ellos y de la cual sólo era responsable Ortega y Gasset, quien siempre entendió bien poco en cuestiones de poesía" ("their supposed dehumanization ... the sole source of which was Ortega y Gasset, who always understood very little in questions of poetry") (356). Cernuda distinguishes between the young writers' love for Góngora – which is ultimately a love for poetry, one shared with Unamuno in the general sense, if not in this specific case – and the dehumanization attributed to them. Indeed, the members of *la joven literatura* did not accept the notions of poetic purity and dehumanization uncritically. In his essay "El pensamiento hermético de las artes" ("The Hermetic Thought of the Arts"), José Bergamín revised Ortega's terminology, exchanging the verb *deshumanizarse* for *desvivirse* (to do one's utmost) – a term that implies passionate longing and suggests that if modern art takes a step back from life (*se des-vive*), it does not for this reason cease to be human.[10] A similar interest in nuancing contemporary theoretical categories famously appears in a letter from Jorge Guillén to Fernando Vela from 1926, later reprinted in Diego's *Poesía española*: "poesía pura, *ma non troppo*" (*Poesía española* 196). It was Diego who perhaps summarized the feelings of his peers most clearly when he stated in his 1928 lecture "La nueva arte poética española" ("The New Poetic Art of Spain") that "todos los poetas jóvenes de España ... desean también una poesía humana" ("all of the young poets of Spain ... also want a human poetry") (*OC* 6:210).

In the first part of this two-part lecture Diego offers one of his earliest accounts of Unamuno's importance for the poets of his generation.

He names Unamuno along with Antonio Machado and Juan Ramón Jiménez as three poets who can be considered masters and predecessors for the young poets. This is the case, he states, because they are all living poets, working and changing with continued energy and dynamism: "conservan en pleno vigor su capacidad creadora, de la que nos han dado recentísimas y conmovedoras muestras" ("they maintain in full force their creative capacity, of which they have given us very recent and very moving examples") (198). While careful to point out the differences between his peers and these three older poets, he affirms that each has offered an example for the younger writers, both in his poetry and in his writing about poetry. He mentions Unamuno's "prólogos, notas y ensayos" ("prologues, notes, and essays") (198–9), likely thinking of the paratextual sections of *Teresa* and *Romancero del destierro* as well as the *Ensayos*, all of which he knew well.[11] While he is critical of the writer's earliest poetry, Diego is lavish in his praise for the poems of exile, asserting, "no hallaremos en la poesía española inspiraciones más puras y hondas que las de su último libro, *Romancero del destierro*" ("in Spanish poetry we will not find purer or more profound inspirations than those of his last book, *Ballads of Exile*") (199). It seems that, in Diego's view, this work in particular provided the moving evidence of an older writer's persisting creative ability that he mentions earlier in the essay. As he concludes, the *Romancero* reflects a "purificación poética, lograda en la anciandad – una anciandad gloriosamente juvenil" ("poetic purification achieved in old age – a gloriously youthful old age") (200).

For the younger critic, the beauty and crystalline simplicity that Unamuno's writing in verse had acquired over time was what made it an example of pure poetry. The political element in *Romancero del destierro* did not compromise this purity: in fact, exile was what definitively turned Unamuno into a poet in Diego's view (200). It also made of him what several of the younger poets recognized for a time in Jiménez: an example. For Diego, Unamuno's example, like those of Jiménez and Machado, lay in a personal commitment to his art; but his was also moral example, one that conveyed "una voluntad de lucha" ("a will to fight") (203).[12] Diego's attention to the exemplarity of Unamuno here parallels the following that the expatriate was receiving at the same time from the student protesters of the FUE. And yet, his literary example was already longstanding. His importance for *la joven literatura*, and for Diego in particular, had been born well before his exile began.

Gerardo Diego, Student and Critic of Unamuno

As in the case of José Moreno Villa, Gerardo Diego's first encounter with Unamuno occurred while he was still a student. The two met when Diego came to Salamanca in 1914 to take his Greek exam (a native of Santander, he studied as an extern at the Universidad de Deusto, but had to fulfil the requirement in Salamanca). Years later he recalled the experience of being seventeen and sitting across the table from the famed professor, enjoying the comments that Unamuno made to such an extent that when he left the examination room, as he recalls, "sentí por única vez en mi vida que concluyese un examen" ("for the first and only time in my life I regretted finishing an exam") (Diego, "Presencia" 68). This early experience and others like it established a sense of respect and shared purpose that infuses all of Diego's later critical writing on Unamuno. Having witnessed the professor's insight into the workings of language firsthand, Diego was especially demanding in his assessment of Unamuno's poetry. At times he even used the poetry to argue against the poet's claims, as Unamuno himself had instructed his successors to do in "Cuando yo sea viejo": "arguïd contra mí conmigo mismo."

In a 1923 review of *Rimas de dentro* (*Rhymes from Within*), for example, Diego advocates for qualities in Unamuno's verses that the poet himself seems not to see. Discussing the first poem of the collection, "Caña salvaje" ("Wild Reed"), the reviewer cites the poet's claim that his writing is artless ("sin arte"), in order to suggest that this is in fact not the case: "Afortunadamente, el libro no cumple tan alarmante programa, y en las poesías hay plan, hay arte y hasta filigranas de rima interna y ensayos de música rítmica, si no siempre conseguida, patentemente buscada" ("Fortunately, the book does not carry out such an alarming proposal, and in the poems there is a plan, there is art, and there are even silvery threads of internal rhyme and attempts to create a rhythmic music that, if not always achieved, is clearly pursued") (128–9). Ever a sensitive and independent critic, Diego manages to perceive aspects of the aural structure of Unamuno's poetry that might go unnoticed if one were to take the author at his word. A marked shift in Diego's assessment of Unamuno's verse begins here, and it continues in a letter he wrote the next year to his friend José María de Cossío, who had published *Rimas de dentro* in his editorial series *Libros para amigos* (*Books for Friends*). While reading Unamuno's *Andanzas y visiones españolas*

(*Wanderings and Visions in Spain*, 1922), Diego writes to Cossío, "Estoy leyendo las *Andanzas* de D. Miguel. Las poesías a la ría de Bilbao y a un cementerio castellano son formidables. Me reconcilian con Unamuno poeta" ("I am reading Don Miguel's *Wanderings*. The poems to the river in Bilbao and to a Castilian cemetery are terrific. They win me over to Unamuno the poet") (Diego, *Epistolario* 52–3). Perhaps significantly, this letter was written just a couple months after Unamuno was exiled. Despite his general lack of interest in political matters,[13] Diego paid careful attention to Unamuno's poetry during the years of his expatriation, beginning in 1924.

This was a time in which Diego's own work was highly ambivalent in character. Avant-garde and formalist, innovative and drawn to tradition by turns, Diego's poetry spanned a gap that usually separated the new poets from writers of the past. In the late 1910s he had participated in some of the first experiments in Spanish *ultraísmo*, contributing to the journals *Grecia* and *Cervantes*, and he continued to be highly involved in the movement known as *creacionismo*, inaugurated by Chilean poet Vicente Huidobro and practiced alike by Diego's good friend Juan Larrea. Products of this involvement include his collections *Imagen* (*Image*, 1922) and *Manual de espumas* (*Manual of Sea Spray*, 1924). Concurrently, however, he was also writing poems dealing with everyday life or religious themes, composed in traditional stanzaic forms. It is this latter style that prevails in his collection *Versos humanos* (*Human Verses*, 1925).[14] As Diego freely admitted later, this collection of "human" poems bears the mark of Unamuno's influence ("Presencia" 68). The opening poem in the book even recalls the Unamuno of *Poesías*, in poems like "Credo poético" and "Denso, denso." While in his critical writing Diego dismissed Unamuno's early poetry, some of the main theoretical tenets of *Poesías* emerge as he describes the "poesía de circunstancia" ("poetry of circumstance") that is the focus of *Versos humanos*:

Poesía de circunstancia.
Trazo fino, leve perfil.
Que una lejana resonancia
envuelva el concreto marfil.

Que el vuelo bien cautivo siga
la órbita de una previa pauta.

No se cante el verso, se diga.
El cielo es largo y la hora cauta. (*OC* 1:207)

(Circumstantial poetry.
Slender line, light profile.
Let a distant resonance
envelop the solid marble.

Let the restrained flight follow
the curving of an earlier orbit
Don't sing the verses; say them.
Heaven is long and time, vigilant.)

This turn to poetry of circumstance is a freely-chosen submission to the tradition of the past, a return to old forms and modes – invoked as "Vieja estrofa" and "verdad madura" – that paradoxically takes the artist back to the classroom of his school days, as if he were a child once again, viewing the poetic tradition with fresh eyes. This voluntary apprenticeship, the decision to obey the rules of traditional versification and see what he can learn, exemplifies the "vuelta a la estrofa" ("return to the stanza") for which Diego and his peers are known. Yet it also afforded Diego another connection with Unamuno. As Diego later affirmed, he had been paying special attention to Unamuno's sonnets while composing *Versos humanos*. The older poet had written a great number of poems using this form, not only in his *Rosario de sonetos líricos* but also in *De Fuerteventura a París*. In fact, he read many of these sonnets to Diego when the younger poet paid him a visit in the French capital in September of 1924 (Diego, *Epistolario* 75).

Among the poems of *Versos humanos*, "El ciprés de Silos" ("The Cypress at Silos"), often considered Diego's most famous sonnet, stands out as an especially Unamunian poem. In it, the poet's attention centers on a tree at the monastery of Santo Domingo de Silos, a location that Unamuno had visited not long before he was exiled.[15] Perhaps this was why, as Diego recalls on multiple occasions, Unamuno kept a copy of "El ciprés de Silos" in his pocket while he was living in Hendaye. Or perhaps it was because this poem, too, echoes strategies that the poet from Salamanca had used already in *Poesías*. Much like Unamuno's ode "Salamanca" and a number of other poems from his first book of poetry, "El ciprés de Silos" opens with a series of epithets that serve to create an accumulation of images and at the same time postpone action:

Enhiesto surtidor de sombra y sueño
que acongojas el cielo con tu lanza.
Chorro que a las estrellas casi alcanza
devanado a sí mismo en loco empeño.

Mástil de soledad, prodigio isleño;
flecha de fe, saeta de esperanza.
Hoy llegó a ti, riberas del Arlanza,
peregrina al azar, mi alma sin dueño. (Diego, *OC* 1:230)

(Upright fountain of shadow and dreams
who troubles the heavens with your lance.
Stream that shoots, almost reaching the stars
winding round itself in a crazed advance.

Solitary mast, isolated marvel;
arrow of faith, missile of hope.
Upon you today, from Arlanza's banks,
chanced my wandering, ungoverned soul.)

Like Moreno Villa in "En la selva fervorosa," Diego turns to the Unamunian trope of the tree as analogue for the poet's soul. The vertical images of fountains and arrows lend themselves to the spiritual aspirations of the poet, himself taken aback, in his wandering state, by the bold rectitude of the tree. In the tercets, the poem enacts a kind of identification between poet and nature similar to the poetic technique that critic Concha Zardoya, writing on the pervasively human vision that distinguishes Unamuno's poetry, called "humanación."[16]

Cuando te vi, señero, dulce, firme,
qué ansiedades sentí de diluirme
y ascender como tú, vuelto en cristales,

como tú, negra torre de arduos filos,
ejemplo de delirios verticales,
mudo ciprés en el fervor de Silos.

(When I saw you, unrivalled, soft, resolved,
what desires I felt to let myself dissolve
into tiny crystals and ascend like you to the heavens,

just like you, dark tower of blade-like shingles,
example of vertical aspirations,
mute cypress amid the fervor of Silos.)

Beyond the stylistic similarities between this sonnet by Diego and several poems by Unamuno, this meditation on the desire for transcendence taps into the metaphysics of poetry that had drawn the older writer to the genre decades earlier. Like the tree it describes, the poem is an emblem of the kind of faith Unamuno had referred to as *pistis;* that is, faith based on fervent religious feeling and an impulse to create. Judging from the "Defensa de la Poesía" ("Defense of Poetry") that Diego offered to the other members of *la joven literatura* who gathered to commemorate Góngora in Seville in December of 1927, his own poetic theory rested on a belief in this Unamunian link between poetry and faith. Delivering that speech as part of the closing act of the tercentenary year, the culmination of the celebration of Góngora and a moment that sealed the unity of *la joven literatura,* Diego affirmed that writing poetry constituted an act of faith: "La Poesía existe, pues, por un acto de fe del poeta que la requiere y la busca, aun sabiendo que no la verá nunca" ("Poetry exists by an act of faith on the part of the poet, who needs it and searches for it, though he knows he will never see it") (*OC* 6:187). The statement alludes to the romantic conception of poetry exemplified in the Spanish tradition especially by Gustavo Adolfo Bécquer, but Diego follows it with a play on the verbs *creer* and *crear* that varies only slightly from Unamuno's own juxtaposition of these terms in his essay "La fe": "Creer lo que no vimos dicen que es la Fe. Crear lo que no veremos: esto es la Poesía" ("They say that believing what we have not seen is faith. Creating what we will not see: this is Poetry") (188). Diego, among many other things a religious poet,[17] seems to have found in Unamuno the same thing his poem identifies in the cypress at Silos: an example of transcendent aspirations.

The poetic affinity that developed between Diego and Unamuno in the early 1920s was perhaps sealed during the aforementioned visit that the former paid to the latter in Paris in September 1924. On that trip Diego brought with him his recently completed edition of the early seventeenth-century poet Pedro de Medina Medinilla's *Égloga en la muerte de doña Isabel de Urbina* (*Eclogue Upon the Death of Doña Isabel de Urbina*). He read it to Unamuno, who was captivated by one line, which expresses the kind of religious and existential anguish he had struggled with throughout his adult life: "Oh, cuán caro el mirar al cielo cuesta"

("Oh, how costly it is to look to the heavens") (Diego, *OC* 7:339).[18] In a letter to Cossío, Diego relates that after he finished with the eclogue, and after Unamuno read to him from *De Fuerteventura a París*, he made a request: "Le pedí autorización para reproducir versos suyos en mi futura Antología y me lo dio de buen grado" ("I asked for his permission to reprint poems of his in my future Anthology and he gave it to me gladly") (*Epistolario* 75). As Morelli has indicated (*Historia* 33), this is the first reference in Diego's letters to the project that would come to fruition years later as *Poesía española. Antología 1915–1931*, the anthology that would do much to define the Generation of 1927 for posterity and also trace its poetic genealogy. That Unamuno was to be included in the anthology's roster from its earliest conception confirms that even before the pivotal year of 1927 its editor already considered him an essential part of a new, twentieth-century Spanish poetic tradition. As Diego turned his attention to the Góngora tercentenary, the mark Unamuno had made on his critical sensibilities (and on those of his peers) would become especially apparent in their self-conception as rejuvenators of Spanish literary culture.

Gongorismo as Rejuvenation

Late in 1926, as he was striving to maintain his colleagues' interest and bolster their enthusiasm for the celebration of the three-hundredth anniversary of Góngora's death, Diego wrote to Cossío about a journal that appeared ephemerally that year, *Favorables París Poema*. Its editors were the Peruvian poet César Vallejo and the Spaniard Juan Larrea, who had met in Paris in 1924 around the same time that Diego paid his visit to the exiled Unamuno. (Diego and Larrea had in fact travelled to France together.) Only two issues of *Favorables* were published, one in July and one in October of 1926, but its intransigent vanguard stance and radical critique of dominant literary trends in Spain and the Hispanic world, as well as its international scope, distinguish the publication among its Spanish-language contemporaries and make it an undoubted point of interest within studies of the historical avant-garde. What Diego chooses to focus on in his letter, however, is the youthfulness that he sees as the basis of the journal's iconoclastic posture:

> La revista no es seria, ni quiere ser seria. Va en contra de la seriedad. Es una revista juvenil, de ataque, broma y humor, no reñidas estas cosas con el verdadero fervor y pureza lírica … Esto es lo que indignará a Juan

> Ramón, por ejemplo, o a Ortega o a Paul Valéry o a cualquier otro santón autoidólatra por el estilo. En esto se diferencian de un espíritu verdaderamente poético o perpetuamente juvenil, como un Apollinaire, un Góngora o un Larrea. (*Epistolario* 144–5)

> (The journal is not serious, nor does it want to be. It is against all seriousness. It is a youthful journal, one of attack, comedy, and humor, all of which need not exclude true lyrical fervor and purity ... This is what will offend Juan Ramón, for example, or Ortega or Paul Valéry or any other self-worshipping big shot like that. In this they are different from a truly poetic or perpetually youthful spirit, like an Apollinaire, a Góngora or a Larrea.)

In Diego's view, *Favorables* represents the essence of the poetic because it is perpetually youthful – that is, not serious. Poetic purity can exist in play, subversion, and critique; what sullies it is the artist's own inclination towards pride and self-aggrandizement. The purity of the lyric is founded on the willingness to experiment and the surrender of control. Taking oneself too seriously, as Jiménez, Ortega, and Valéry do in Diego's view, impedes this youthful spirit and makes these writers seem old, out of touch, and humorless. Though he does not question their abilities, he clearly believes their attitude towards their own work is out of step with artistic youth.[19] His irreverence before their authority resembles the generationally charged resistance to institutional power felt and acted on by many young people during the 1920s, from the partiers of Britain's "Bright Young Things" to the political protests organized by the FUE in Spain. But what is unique about Diego's personal rebellion is his inclusion of Góngora among the unserious, youthful poets. Spanish critics had either praised or reviled Góngora, the most notorious representative of Baroque *culteranismo*, for three centuries. Whether admired as prodigious or dismissed as a vacuous putting-on of airs, the ornate, Latinate, and labyrinthine style represented by his *Fábula de Polifemo y Galatea* and *Soledades* (both 1613) had not often been considered playful. Nineteenth-century critics, in particular, had scorned Gongorine ostentation. Foremost among them was Marcelino Menéndez y Pelayo, who judged Góngora's verbal complexity to indicate only deceit and vanity. While Diego generally respected the work of this critic, a fellow native of Santander, he departed from the master scholar on this point. Where Menéndez y Pelayo saw needless affectation, Diego saw experimentation and innovation, a ludic rearrangement of words that produced poetry rife with artistic and interpretive possibilities.

Diego's 1924 essay "Un escorzo de Góngora" ("A Foreshortening of Góngora") exemplifies the effort to present the poet in a novel way, asking the reader to approach Góngora's writing from an unconventional angle, as if the poet's body of work were a physical object placed in a new spatial relationship to the viewer. It begins by reviewing past interpretations of Góngora: that of the poet's contemporaries, who created the initial debate surrounding his work; the negative view of nineteenth-century critics epitomized by Menéndez y Pelayo; and the fascination with Góngora among writers of the *fin-de-siècle* like Rubén Darío, whose *Trébol* (1899) placed the Baroque poet in a literal dialogue with his contemporary Diego de Velázquez and a more figurative one with modern poetics. In each case, Diego distinguishes between the poet and the literary establishment that commended and repudiated him by turns, asserting that historically it had been other poets, not academic critics ("los eruditos"), who were most able to appreciate Góngora (*OC* 6:789). He then offers his own perspective, which reveals and foregrounds aspects of the poetry that had thus far gone unnoticed. At one point he notes how Góngora's "peculiar sintaxis" ("unique syntax") gathers and frames words and phrases in such a way that they suggest myriad potential readings beyond what they say literally. One can pull a line out of context and discover unexpected images and meanings made possible by the poetry's unique architectonics. In effect, what Diego finds here is novelty through recombination. The unusual juxtapositions manufactured by Góngora's hyperbaton and the reorganization of the poetry's constituent parts facilitated by the modern critic's fresh perspective become sources of endless renovation and possibility. This allows Diego to see Góngora's poems themselves as ageless: resistant to the passing of time and ever enlivened by new interpretations. If this is in fact true of Góngora's work, it follows that one generation's reading of the poet will be distinct from those of the past. Diego concludes by declaring his generation's right to its own Góngora, which, he maintains, "no es exactamente el que nos habían legado" ("is not exactly the one that has been passed down to us") (797).

Though it has not been acknowledged previously, this effort to create a new critical approximation to Góngora, to separate the poet from traditional readings of his work and literary trends that it inspired, corresponds remarkably closely to opinions Unamuno expressed on several occasions about how the seventeenth-century poet ought to be read and studied. This similarity has been overlooked due to the fact that Unamuno also more than once confessed his personal lack of interest in Góngora – not least when he declined the young poets' invitation to participate in the tercentenary activities. Indeed, he cited this lack of interest already in 1903, in his response to a survey on Góngora for the journal *Helios*, then edited by a young Juan Ramón Jiménez. It is true that in his statement for the survey Unamuno declared that he had tried, and failed, to read and understand Góngora. However, when read in context this declaration leads directly to a much more expansive reflection on artistic individuality. Musing over the distortions created when a single artist's name comes to stand for a style – as in the case of *gongorismo* – Unamuno writes, "tenemos los más de los españoles de algunas letras una idea más o menos clara del gongorismo: pero de Góngora no" ("most of us Spaniards with some literary education have a more-or-less clear idea of *gongorismo*: but not of Góngora") ("Sobre Góngora" 475).

The *Helios* survey had arisen due to a renewed interest in Góngora among the writers of the turn of the century, particularly after Darío published his *Trébol*. For Unamuno, the fact that Góngora had caught the attention of *fin-de-siècle* poets had more to do with the vague concept of a "Gongorist" style than with a true penetration into the Baroque writer's work. The phenomenon simply highlighted the similarities between the imitative tendencies he saw in *modernismo* and the idea, familiar to most Spanish readers, of "gongorismo" as shorthand for a kind of poetry that makes use of unnecessary difficulty in order to gain attention. For his part, Unamuno writes, he has no interest in perpetuating Góngora's use by the literary establishment as a touchstone of artistic partisanship. He refuses to "tomar a Góngora de achaque para despacharme a mi sabor contra los que no gustan de ciertas supuestas exquisiteces, más o menos gongorinos que ahora corren" ("use Góngora as a pretext to sound off against those who do not like certain supposed, more-or-less Gongorine subtleties that are in fashion right now") (476). Infused with the contrarian view of *modernismo* characteristic of the turn-of-the-century Unamuno, this comment attacks the literary-critical uses of Góngora more than Góngora's poetry itself. Unamuno urges the readers of *Helios* not to re-hash old debates about the value of *gongorismo*, but instead to find an original take on this poet. Notably, while he is not willing to take on the task, he does not put it past those younger than himself. Here the affiliation between youth and creativity that is so much a part of the turn-of-the-century Unamuno's thought comes to bear on the subject in question, as he concludes, "lo que sí deseo es que ustedes, los más jóvenes – pues por joven me tengo, – si se ponen a leerlo y estudiarlo, le saquen cuanta substancia poética contenga, aprendan en él cuanto de bueno pueda de él aprenderse y nos lo sirvan en odres nuevos" ("what I do hope is that if those of you who are younger – for I still consider myself young – if you set out to read him and study him, that you extract all of the poetic substance that his work contains, learn every good thing that can be learned from him, and serve him up to us in new wineskins") ("Sobre Góngora" 477).

While Diego and his peers did not form part of the original readership of *Helios*, they could have encountered similar statements by Unamuno elsewhere in his writing. In *Alrededor del estilo* (*On Style*, 1920), for example, he again comments on the phenomenon of *gongorismo*: "Del nombre propio de Góngora hemos hecho el término gongorismo para designar aquel estilo – es decir, aquel no estilo, aquel estilismo – de los que pretenden imitar a Góngora. Lo que no cabe decir es que Góngora fuese gongorista, ni siquiera gongorino: era Góngora" ("From the name Góngora we have created the term *gongorismo* to designate the style – that is, the non-style, the stylization – of those who set out to imitate Góngora. What one cannot say is that Góngora was a Gongorist, nor even Gongorine: he was Góngora") (*OCE* 7:909). In the letter Unamuno wrote in 1927, in response to the invitation to participate in the tercentenary, the distinction between Góngora and *gongorismo* appears once more: "No puedo decir que le conozca [a Góngora]. El gongorismo me lo veló siempre, impidiéndome el deseo de llegar a él. Porque Góngora era, seguramente, él, Góngora y no gongorista, ya que todo –ista es un otro que sí mismo" ("I cannot say that I know Góngora. Gongorism always concealed him from me, impeding any desire I had to get to him. Because Góngora was, surely, himself, Góngora and not a Gongorist, given that every –ist is someone other than himself") (*Cartas del destierro* 205).

Unamuno's repeated distinction between Góngora the poet and the literary style that developed in his wake gestures towards the unconventional approach to the seventeenth-century poet that *la joven literatura* promoted. Indeed, the initiative undertaken by Diego and his peers in the mid-1920s to resuscitate appreciation for Góngora's poetry responds perfectly to Unamuno's invocation in *Helios*. They set out to study the Baroque poet's work carefully, documenting their discoveries in a series of new editions and scholarly collections (even though, as Diego relates in the "Crónica del centenario" ["Chronicle of the Centenary"] that he published in late 1927 and early 1928, the majority of the planned texts never materialized). Honorary issues of several journals edited by members and affiliates of *la joven literatura* published critical essays and creative work that endeavoured to extract the poetic essence of Góngora's craft and put it to use in new contexts and artistic creations. Publications including *Verso y Prosa, La Gaceta Literaria,* and *Litoral* (and later Diego's *Lola,* the supplement to his poetry journal *Carmen*) all endeavoured to present Góngora from new angles and in new packaging – or wineskins, to use Unamuno's evangelistically inflected term.

Youth was a prominent feature of the majority of these honorary issues and the contributions to them by various young artists. *Litoral,* which appeared as a combined three-volume issue in October of 1927, incorporated it in a subtle yet pervasively thematic way. In addition to Góngora-inspired poetic contributions including Alberti's *Soledad tercera* (*Third Solitude*) or Diego's *Fábula de Equis y Zeda* (*Fable of X and Z*), the issue included more loosely affiliated poems from Manuel Altolaguirre, José Moreno Villa, Federico García Lorca, and Luis Cernuda, among several others. There was also artwork from Juan Gris, Picasso, Dalí, and other representatives of the kind of young art that Ortega y Gasset had described as "arte deshumanizado." Still other contributions in the plastic arts made young figures their subjects. Notably at odds with the focus on masculine youth that had dominated European culture in general and the Residencia de Estudiantes in particular during the First World War, the youths represented in these contributions were consistently female. Benjamín Palencia and Josep de Togeres sent drawings of female nudes, and Gregorio Prieto's sketch of a young woman reading Góngora on the beach (modelled on the poet Concha Méndez) united the image of the "nueva mujer" of the 1920s with the journal's maritime orientation (Neira 80). Manolo Hugué's sketch depicting the wide-eyed stare of a girl who seems to bite her lip in irresolution evokes innocence and vulnerability. But perhaps the most compelling visual representation of youth in the publication is Apel·les Fenosa's "Tête de Marthe Morère," a bust of an adolescent girl whose placid face and fine features make her seem especially delicate and lost in reverie. On the page that follows this image, Vicente Aleixandre's poem "Adolescencia" melancholically recalls the transitional experience of leaving childhood behind, apostrophizing, "Vinieras y te fueras dulcemente, / de otro camino / a otro camino" ("That you had come and gone unobtrusively / from another road / to another road") (Prados and Altolaguirre 11).

The tone set in this issue of *Litoral* is at once playful and pensive, aesthetically innovative and intellectually centred on the introspection that had linked poetry to youth for Moreno Villa in *El pasajero* a decade before. In contrast to this lyrical youth, the homage to Góngora in *Verso y Prosa*, the self-proclaimed *Boletín de la Joven Literatura*, features a mixture of critical essays, creative prose, and autobiographical testimony – and all of them together, in one case. While this issue did include poetry by Aleixandre, García Lorca, and Claudio de la Torre, as well as a brief fictional piece by Juan Chabás, it focused primarily on criticism. Marichalar and Cossío wrote about Góngora's famed obscurity and elevated language, while César Muñoz Arconada reflected on the musical qualities of the poet's verse. All of these articles concentrated on the poetry itself. By contrast, the up-and-coming avant-gardist Ernesto Giménez Caballero contributed a piece that reflects on the renewal of interest in Góngora from an autobiographical perspective, as the writer recalls (imagines?) the role the Baroque poet played in his own adolescence.

Titled "Primer amor. Y Góngora en el dancing" ("First Love. And Góngora at the Dance Hall"), Giménez Caballero's piece tells of a summer he spent as a teenager in the town of El Escorial, home to the monastery built by King Felipe II in the sixteenth century, with its famous archive and library. As Anderson has pointed out, the author makes use of this autobiographical frame to ground his own interpretive authority and stake his claim on Góngora (*Ernesto Giménez* 182–3). What is especially remarkable is that Giménez Caballero (or Gecé, as he called himself by this time) explicitly links his early encounter with Góngora to adolescent angst and infatuation. Setting the scene, he tells his reader that during the summer in question he was staying with his grandmother in El Escorial in hopes of improving a state of poor health. Though he was a sickly youth, a rebellious spirit was budding inside of him. As a working-class boy from Madrid, he viewed the well-to-do, bourgeois town with disdain: "Odiaba la burguesía de El Escorial. Y arrojaba – con toda la energía de mi gran debilidad física – bombas de Góngora sobre el monasterio" ("I hated the bourgeoisie of El Escorial. And – with all of the energy that my great physical weakness would allow – I hurled Góngora bombs at the monastery"). Here Giménez Caballero imagines Góngora as a literal weapon to be used against high society and the establishment. In reality, the "bombs" he says he threw were the notes he was taking as he read the poet's work in the library for two hours every morning, after spending another two hours in the art gallery, viewing paintings by El Greco. Giménez Caballero depicts his introduction to these artists during his periods of study as both the birth of an adolescent crush and a sexual initiation: "Entonces, nadie, apenas, pensaba en Góngora. Yo me lo encontré en sueños … Palpé los planos picassianos de la musa gongorina por la alcahuetería del Greco" ("At that time, scarcely anyone thought about Góngora. I found him in my dreams … I touched the Picassian planes of the Gongorine muse with El Greco for a pimp") (2).

The implication of Giménez Caballero's reflections becomes clear: Góngora was *his* first love; *he* loved Góngora first, before any other members of his generation took notice.[20] It would seem that he was also the first admirer that Góngora dumped. When the last part of his article jumps to the present, imagined as a dance hall where the Baroque poet now entertains a group of new suitors ("amiguitos"), Gecé becomes an embittered and jealous former lover. He claims to have gotten over Góngora, event to detest him, yet the fact that he keeps careful vigil over the scene, sipping rum in a corner, suggests otherwise. As he concludes this memory of his early "aventura" ("love affair"), he considers warning the poet's new suitors of the possible betrayal that lies ahead. But he fails to find the authority to speak, and lets his arguments trail off: "Pero amiguitos de Góngora … Nada. / Iba a enseñaros … Nada" ("But little friends of Góngora … Nothing. / I was going to show you … Nothing"). Setting the end of his piece in one of the most emblematic spaces of youth culture during the 1920s, the dance hall, Giménez Caballero uses youth rhetorically to support his personal claim on Góngora. The autobiographical mode that he employs here, along with the psycho-sexual subtext, approximate this article to the short fiction he was writing at the time, and especially to his collection of stories *Yo, inspector de alcantarillas* (*I, Sewer Inspector*), published the same year. Furthermore, the competitive edge that emerges in this text signals and anticipates the tension between Giménez Caballero and other members of the young generation that would only grow in later years.

Across the page from Giménez Caballero's teenage memories of Góngora in *Verso y Prosa*, an article by José Bergamín pays homage to the poet of the hour by turning to a fairy tale. For Bergamín, Góngora is the ugly duckling of Spanish Golden-Age poetry, the outcast that eventually turned out to be a graceful swan among a flock of quacking conformists. Riffing on a line taken from one of Góngora's defamatory sonnets about his contemporary Lope de Vega, the article, "Patos del aguachirle castellana" ("Ducks of the Castilian Backwater"), credits the poet from Córdoba with stirring up Spain's stagnant literary world in the early seventeenth century. Bergamín elaborates on Góngora's metaphors to suggest that at that time Spanish poetry had formed a still pool to which "los primeros patos casticistas" ("the first traditionalist ducks") would go to make their "académica algarabía" ("academic racket"). In Bergamín's account, they praise their pond as containing "las más cristalinas y trasparentes aguas poéticas del mundo" ("the clearest and most crystalline poetic waters in the world"), but in reality it is a site of decadence and decay. Góngora, however, manages to escape this suffocating atmosphere: "Abandona la charca para huir en más alto vuelo" ("He abandons the pond to flee to a loftier flight") (2).

At first glance, there is no direct connection to youth or youth culture in Bergamín's essay, besides the evocation of a children's story. Yet the image of the "charca" that he works with here does not originate only in Góngora's sonnet. It draws heavily on Unamuno's vivid use of this metaphor at the turn of the century, especially in the essay "La juventud 'intelectual' española." The ducklings of Góngora's time are predecessors to the senile *casticistas* that Unamuno famously denounced, while Góngora himself becomes the strange bird that Unamuno had imagined soaring away from the Castilian swamp, leaving behind the representatives of literary traditionalism and academic snobbery that he had likened to frogs and tadpoles in "A la corte de los poetas." Bergamín goes on to describe the author of the *Soledades* in highly Unamunian language, as an "hereje del dogma literario" ("heretic of [Spanish] literary dogma"). When he cites Unamuno directly a few lines later it becomes clear that the exiled writer is present in Bergamín's mind as he attempts to explain Góngora's poetic value. The conclusion of his article affirms a vision of the poet that recalls Unamuno's distinction between Góngora and *gongorismo*: "De la actualidad, – o actuación poética – de Góngora, da testimonio, durante tres siglos, como ahora, su presencia, su permanencia; suscitando siempre entusiamos y hostilidades. Admirar, comprender a Góngora ... no es ser gongorino ni gongorista, es ser persona; tener entendimiento y gusto de persona humana" ("The contemporaneity – or poetic activity – of Góngora is evidenced by his presence, his permanence, throughout three centuries as today; always exciting enthusiasm and hostility. To admire, to comprehend Góngora ... is not to be Gongorine or Gongorist, it is to be a person; to have a human person's understanding and capacity for pleasure"). In Bergamín's view, Góngora's ability to be simultaneously eternal and contemporary, and to spur discussions and debates in the present as he had for hundreds of years, is what differentiates him from the literary dogmatists of all ages and signals his persisting artistic youth.

Youth and Age in the Tercentenary

Bergamín was not the only one of the young *gongorinos* to employ tropes of old age and decay reminiscent of Unamuno's writing at the turn of the century. In the retrospective article "Balance del gongorismo" that Diego wrote for the honorary issue of *La Gaceta Literaria,* he also described Góngora as the hero that saved Spanish poetry from sinking into monotony at the beginning of the seventeenth century. As the Renaissance equilibrium of Fray Luis was fading away and the Spanish poetic lexicon was reaching its "madurez sazonada" ("seasoned maturity"), Diego writes, "el ejemplo de Góngora vino a atenuar la descomposición" ("Góngora's example came to slow the process of decomposition") (Morelli, *Gerardo Diego* 202). Diego's timeline corresponds closely to the account of the Spanish Golden Age that Unamuno offers in "De mística y humanismo," the fourth essay of *En torno al casticismo,* where he reads Teresa de Ávila, San Juan de la Cruz, and Fray Luis as writers struggling with the contradictions of the Castilian spirit "al sazonar en madurez" ("seasoning in maturity") (*E* 1:150). While Unamuno skipped directly from Fray Luis to the "morass" of contemporary Spain, Diego sees Góngora as a seventeenth-century example of the rejuvenation his predecessor was searching for. Moreover, Diego's imagining of how Góngora countered stagnation in Spanish verse once again recalls the imagery and argument of "La juventud 'intelectual' española." Especially important for Diego's vision of both Góngora and his contemporaries is the concept of *metarrhythmisis* that appears at the opening of that essay. In his copy of Unamuno's *Ensayos,* he marked the passage that explains this term, particularly noting the connection the essayist makes between a change in rhythm and molecular reconfiguration. Indeed, Unamuno's vision of rejuvenation through recombination is very similar to Diego's own approach to Góngora's work in his "escorzo," and to other critical perspectives among the writers of *la joven literatura.* Jorge Guillén, for example, wrote in his contribution to *La Gaceta Literaria* that Góngora had taken the components of the Spanish tradition and placed them in an entirely new order (Guillén, "Su originalidad"). For these poet-critics, the syntactic rearrangement that characterizes Góngora's writing serves as a metaphor for a relationship to the tradition as a whole. In this way, the Baroque artist's exemplary response to the poetic landscape of his time provides the "sacudida" that Unamuno desired for Spanish culture in 1896.

One further trope that appears in "La juventud 'intelectual' española" and that plays an important role in Diego's conception of artistic youth during the Góngora tercentenary is the distinction between true and false youth. In his account of the tercentenary Diego is keenly attentive to the traitorous falsity of a youth willing to pander to the tradition or the establishment in order to make a place for itself. He would have found ample support for this view in Unamuno's essay. In fact, in his copy of the third volume of the *Ensayos* he made note of a sentence that sums up the writer's sentiments on the matter: "Cosa triste una juventud a la caza de la recomendación y el cotarro (*coterie* en francés)" ("A youth always prowling for a good reference and a social set [*coterie* in French] is a sad thing") (*E* 3:56, original emphasis).

An effort to create a change of rhythm in the Spanish literary world; a rejection of previous critical traditions and of all academic posturing; and exuberant, energetic creativity: these were the hallmarks of artistic youth for Diego, and he made them the anchoring motifs of his personal account of the Góngora tercentenary. In the "Crónica del centenario" that he published in the first two issues of *Lola* (December 1927 and January 1928), Unamunian distinctions between old age, false youth, and true youth structure Diego's reflections on the effort to vindicate and celebrate Góngora's work. An opposition between the youthful, even visionary spirit that fuels the project, and the youth-less character of all those that oppose or hinder it becomes clear within the first pages. After a description of the gathering of friends out of which the idea for the tercentenary had been born (one that loosely evokes the opening of F.T. Marinetti's account of the foundation of futurism), Diego lists the multitudinous forms they imagine their celebration might take: concerts, expositions, lectures, readings, "toda clase de manifestaciones juveniles en serio y en broma" ("every kind of youthful exercise, serious and lighthearted") ("Crónica" 1:2). When the question of whom to invite to participate in the celebration arises, youth immediately becomes a prerequisite. Diego writes that he and his colleagues agreed to limit their list to "artistas españoles y – espiritualmente – jóvenes" ("artists who were Spanish and – spiritually – young"), though they made exceptions for a critic, Miguel Artigas, and the Mexican (but "Spanish at heart") Alfonso Reyes. The rest of the invitees are largely those writers who by that time figured consistently in the roster of *la joven literatura* and its affiliates, as well as all the artists who had contributed work to the special tercentenary issue of *Litoral.*

In addition, from the beginning the pool of potential participants also included members of older generations, particularly Ramón del Valle-Inclán, Juan Ramón Jiménez, and Antonio Machado. Diego had alluded to these three figures as "maduros maestros" ("mature masters") for the younger generation in his poem "A Rafael Alberti," written in late 1926 and published in *Verso y Prosa* in early 1927. There he playfully references Valle-Inclán and Jiménez by metonymy, describing their facial hair: a flowing, silver beard and a dark, trimmed one. The stanza devoted to Machado takes a more melancholy turn:

> El otro, con su ausencia a cuestas, ciego
> va de armonía por sus soledades,
> con Dios hablando y, para el mundo, lego. (Diego, *OC* 1:590)
>
> (The other one, shouldering his absence, wanders
> blind with harmony through his solitudes,
> speaking with God, a layman to the world.)

These lines alude to the absence of Machado's wife Leonor, who had died in 1912 at the age of eighteen, as well as the metaphysical character that had deepened in the poet's writing since that event. At the same time, they inadvertently come close to describing the exiled Unamuno, at the time shouldering a different kind of absence. I have no interest in psychologizing these lines in order to argue for a subliminal reference to Don Miguel, but it is worth noting that Diego himself recognized Unamuno's important impact on Machado, his "primer discípulo" ("first disciple"). As he wrote years later, "cuando en los versos de un poeta reciente veáis proyectarse la sombra de Antonio Machado, debéis pensar que más allá de esa grave y nítida montaña se alzan, borrosas de luz de cielo, las cumbres desiguales y tormentosas de don Miguel" ("when you see the shadow of Antonio Machado in the verses of a contemporary poet, you should consider that beyond that grave and clear-cut mountain rise, hazy in the light of the heavens, the uneven and tempestuous peaks of Don Miguel") ("Presencia" 67). Unamuno, whom Diego does not mention in "A Rafael Alberti," does loom in the background of the "Crónica," both as one of the invitees to the tercentenary and as a point of reference for the fashioning of the tercentenary as a fundamentally youthful ordeal.

The anti-academic note that Morelli detects in "Á Rafael Alberti" (*Gerardo Diego* 19) finds full expression in Diego's "Crónica" as he describes the events that took place in Madrid for the official anniversary of Góngora's death, 24 May 1927. His narration of an *auto de fe* and subsequent burning of books draws on inquisitorial custom and its trace in Spanish literature, particularly the ransacking of Don Quijote's library in chapter six of Cervantes' novel. The heretics under scrutiny here, however, are those who have betrayed Góngora's creative spirit. The first objects to burn, Diego notes, are three effigies made by Moreno Villa that stand for "los tres enemigos de Góngora: El erudito topo, el catedrático marmota y el académico crustáceo" ("the three enemies of Góngora: The mole-like erudite, the marmot professor, and the crustacean academic") (1:7). Here already Unamuno's critical legacy surfaces. Such epithets echo the older writer's diatribes against unfeeling erudites with narrow vision in essays like "¡Adentro!," "Sobre la erudición y la crítica," or "Soledad" (the latter two included in the sixth volume of the *Ensayos*).[21] Unamuno was especially fond of the crustacean image, and uses it in "Soledad" ("Solitude") to distinguish the poet's open and flexible soul from the hardened shells of others: "Los más de los espíritus me parecen dermatoesqueléticos como crustáceos, con el hueso fuera y la carne dentro … el poeta es aquel a quien se le sale la carne de la costra, a quien le rezuma el alma" ("Most spirits seem exoskeletal to me, like crustaceans, with the bone on the outside and the flesh within … the poet is he whose flesh cannot be contained in the shell, whose soul overflows") (*E* 6:54–5). Poetry resists the limitations of ensconced categories and methodologies; it overflows its container and refuses to accept the hardening of the prescriptive systems that Unamuno called *ideocracias*. Such images of hard, exterior encasements in opposition to the fluidity of the poetic spirit, condensations of the understanding of intellectual history as aging that Unamuno had developed at the turn of the century, held great appeal for the young writers of the 1920s. It is worth noting, for example, that Federico García Lorca underlined the sentence quoted above and other references to "los crustáceos" in his copy of the *Ensayos*, and composed a poem on the blank pages following the essay.[22]

The condemnation of academic "crustaceans" and shortsighted erudites sets the criteria for the burning of books that Diego goes on to describe. All of the works condemned to the flames have in some way or another placed the scholarly tradition and the literary establishment before truly poetic interests, distancing themselves from Góngora's youthful spirit. Topping the list, but given special consideration and their own bonfire, are works by Góngora's contemporaries and rivals Francisco de Quevedo and Lope de Vega, along with Menéndez y Pelayo's *Historia de las ideas estéticas en España* (*History of Aesthetic Ideas in Spain*), a text by a revered critic judged to be unfortunately misguided in his view of Góngora. Destined to the much larger "Hoguera B" ("Bonfire B") are the less worthy opponents of Góngora, whom Diego presents as true traitors of poetic sensibility. Included are neoclassical tracts on poetics and histories of Spanish literature that shun or neglect Góngora, past editions of Góngora's work, all of the newsletters of the royal academies, all dictionaries and grammar guides, all issues of the high-profile literary newspaper *Los Lunes del Imparcial*, and a smattering of creative and critical works judged to have offended the spirit of the centenary. Notable among these is Ortega y Gasset's *Teoría de Andalucía* (*Theory of Andalusia*), which was likely received with skepticism by the great number of young poets who, like Góngora himself, hailed from southern Spain. Two other entries are of special interest. In a seeming about-face from his sentiments at the opening of the "Crónica," Diego condemns to the flames the complete works of Ramón del Valle-Inclán, vehemently demanding that they be "rociada con zotal" ("sprayed with disinfectant"). The last item on the list is the honorary issue that *La Gaceta Literaria*, edited by Giménez Caballero, had dedicated to Góngora.

The reason for Diego's censure of *La Gaceta Literaria*, as he explains, is that his "Crónica" was originally meant to appear in that publication, but was unexpectedly cut. When the honorary issue of the *Gaceta* appeared in June of 1927, Diego discovered the omission and vented his frustration in a letter to Dámaso Alonso, where he declared that if Giménez Caballero would not rectify his action, he believed it was time to "romper seriamente con él y con su *Gaceta*, retirarle públicamente toda colaboración y de publicar nosotros una '*Gaceta antiliteraria*'' ("cut all ties with him and with his *Gazette*, publically retract all collaboration and publish our own *Anti-literary Gazette*") (Morelli, *Gerardo Diego* 61). For Diego here, as for many modern writers from Verlaine to Unamuno and Jiménez, "literature" and the literary refers to a mundane profession while poetry is a transcendent calling. The implication in Diego's letter is that Giménez Caballero is more concerned with the existing establishment than with creativity and innovation. Indeed, as Andrés Soria Olmedo has observed, in his version of the homage Giménez Caballero "sided with the elders" (*Una densa polimorfía* 43, my translation). In his honorary issue he had run an advertisement for an erudite history of Spanish literature by Juan Hurtado and Ángel González Palencia (Diego includes it in the list of burned books in *Lola*), as well as a feature on Nicolás Urgoiti, owner of the powerful newspaper *El Sol*. What is more, the first page of the honorary issue featured several largely negative statements on Góngora by the members of what was by then known as the Generation of 1898 – Unamuno, Antonio Machado, Valle-Inclán, and Pío Baroja, along with Ortega y Gasset. The editor presented these statements as if they responded to a survey by *La Gaceta Literaria*, though in reality they were replies to the invitation sent by Diego and the other organizers of the tercentenary. To Diego's mind, Giménez Caballero's dubious editorial choices and "necesidad de llegar pronto a lo alto de la cucaña" ("need to be the first to the top") indicate his lack of youthfulness: they keep him both from feeling young ("sentirse joven") and from being fair to his young colleagues (Morelli, *Gerardo Diego* 61–2).

In the second issue of *Lola*, Diego continues airing his grievances against the *Gaceta*'s homage, declaring it "acomodaticio, pancista y de una seriedad impropia del aire juvenil que debía tener siempre *La Gaceta Literaria*, y más tratándose de honrar a un joven auténtico de 366 años" ("obsequious, opportunist, and displaying a seriousness alien to the youthful tone that *La Gaceta Literaria* should always have, and more so when it honors an authentic youth of 366 years of age") (2:2). The contrast between the chronologically-young-but-prematurely-old editor and a poet that is still young despite having been dead for three centuries could not be more striking. Giménez Caballero, bending to please the powerful rather than maintaining the subversive posture of youth, begins to look like one of the insecure tadpoles that Unamuno had ridiculed in his satiric account of *la charca nacional*. In his desire to associate himself with the authority of age, he commits treason against the timeless youth of art that Góngora captured, and which Diego sees living on in his work.

If Gecé's handling of the tercentenary aligned him with the enemies of Góngora and amounted to a betrayal of artistic youth in Diego's view, the behaviour of Valle-Inclán and Juan Ramón Jiménez in responding to the invitation to the tercentenary led the critic to portray them as hopelessly, grotesquely old. In Valle-Inclán's reply, printed with the others in *La Gaceta Literaria*, this writer had belligerently declared that he found Góngora insufferable and could find nothing good to say about him. Diego fired back in "Balance del gongorismo," condemning Valle-Inclán's outlook and his art as "definitivamente muerto y viejo" ("definitively dead and old") (Morelli, *Gerardo Diego* 203). While the young critic did not use the same words with Jiménez, this poet does not come off much better in the "Crónica." Diego's account of his refusal to participate paints Jiménez as arrogant, out of touch, and utterly lacking a sense of humour. As is well known, Jiménez chose to answer the invitation by composing an "Esquela contra" ("Notice of Dissent"), which he included in the first volume of the *Diario Poético* he was working on at the time. There he stated his disapproval of the character the tercentenary had assumed under Diego's direction, writing that Góngora required a critical eye that was "más apretado y severo" ("tighter and more exacting") ("Crónica" 2:3). It is quite evident that Jiménez's pride had been injured by not being put in charge. It is possible he was miffed that the younger artists had failed to recall that *he* had organized a survey about Góngora in *Helios* in 1903.[23] Despite the heated tone of his refusal, however, he adds an unexpected flourish when he signs the letter with the initials *K.Q.X.* In the "Crónica" the younger poet made fun of this incongruently playful touch at the end of such an aggressive letter, calling Jiménez "Kuan Qamón Ximénez." Before printing his own, parodical "Esquela pro," Diego asserted that a copy of the *Diario Poético* would retroactively join the pile of works to be burned "en holocausto a don Luis" ("in a sacrifice to Don Luis") (2:3).

In his "Crónica," Diego becomes the mouthpiece of a literary youth that claimed ownership of a new understanding of Góngora belonging to them alone, and more generally, of an aesthetic vision not shared by their older predecessors, nor by those whose youth Diego judged to be false. Yet, while he gives himself the authority to judge aesthetic youth in this text, the cultural symbolism of youth in the 1920s could also be used against him. To some on the outside, he and his fellow *gongorinos* could also represent a false youth – that of young people whose lack of political consciousness converted them into conformist supporters of the dictatorship. In July of 1927, a month after the appearance of the honorary issue of *La Gaceta Literaria*, a poet named Ernesto López-Parra published an article in Madrid's *El Liberal* where he argued that the instigators of the Góngora tercentenary were simply a group of bourgeois "señoritos" from the country: irresponsible, spoiled adolescents oblivious to concepts like civic duty. Though he had collaborated with Diego in *Ultra* and other journals of the avant-garde of the early 1920s, and although he has been viewed as following an artistic trajectory similar to that of the canonical members of the Generation of 1927, the author of this article clearly distances himself from the *gongorinos*. The reason for his frustration is not difficult to guess, since López-Parra was a fervent agitator against Primo's dictatorship, and was arrested for protesting against the regime a total of twenty-one times (Rojas 142). In his article, the difference between López-Parra and the Góngora enthusiasts comes down to the question of the kind of youth the latter represent. For López-Parra, they are "jóvenes de la minoría selecta" ("young men of the select minority") who approach literature as mere sport: "No sintieron nunca la emoción ciudadana ni otearon la responsabilidad de su destino ... Saturaron el Ateneo con sus perfumes caros, se desplazaron a los campos de fútbol y de golf, constituyeron peñas elegantes en los cafés" ("They never felt civic emotion nor considered the responsibility of their position ... They filled the Athenaeum with their expensive colognes, they went out to the soccer fields and the golf courses, they founded elegant clubs in the cafés") (Morelli, *Gerardo Diego* 220). Incorporating words and images that recall the sporting fields and elitist aspirations of the Residencia de Estudiantes, the article at the same time likens *la joven literatura* to one of the conservative Catholic youth organizations that existed in Primo's Spain. At one point, López-Parra invokes the moral authority of the exiled Unamuno in order to denounce the lack of social consciousness and political commitment of this group of young artists. As it happened, Unamuno was at this very time penning a similar critique of the political ignorance displayed in the Góngora tercentenary in the manuscript of *Cómo se hace una novela*.

While López-Parra may have accurately associated the members of *la joven literatura* with the kind of upper-class, minoritarian youth cultivated at the Residencia, his article was in large part the result of a misunderstanding. Behind this episode, once again, is Ernesto Giménez Caballero. Even as he excised Diego's "Crónica" from the Góngora issue of *La Gaceta Literaria*, Gecé *did* include a fictitious interview with his peer, to which he had given the provocative title "Gerardo Diego: poeta fascista." Interspersing lines from the opening poem of *Versos humanos* throughout, in this text Gecé constructed the argument that Diego's "vuelta a la estrofa" was in fact a turn to cultural traditionalism and totalitarian politics. It was this fabricated interview that caught the attention of López-Parra, who took Giménez Caballero at his word. Diego dispelled the confusion in a statement directed to López-Parra in the second issue of *Lola*, where he added that the organizers of the tercentenary were not all from the provinces, nor were they all Catholic. Despite his error, however, López-Parra's article casts illuminating scrutiny on the division between art and politics and the elitist ethos that defined the tercentenary and the work of *la joven literatura* for at least one observer. That López-Parra felt it appropriate to cite Unamuno's name to support his denunciation of the frivolity and irresponsibility of the Góngora tercentenary points to a conflict between two visions of youth in the Spain of Primo's dictatorship: a political one, in which university students and youth organizations challenged the dictator and his support by the Catholic church; and an aesthetic one that opposed poetic innovation to literary-critical convention and pedantry. The question of what constituted "true" youth was relevant to both arenas, and Unamuno was a key point of reference in both discussions. If he remained mostly in the background of the various creative and critical homages to Góngora in 1927, the following years would see Unamuno and his writing become more visibly present in the publications of *la joven literatura.*

Don Miguel and the *Jóvenes*

As the foregoing analysis has shown, Unamuno occupies an ambiguous position in the account the young Spanish writers of the 1920s give of their immediate predecessors. While they acknowledged and indeed appropriated his masterful example as a writer and a thinker, he also belonged to an older generation whose authority they sought to question, and from which they sought to distinguish themselves. Undoubtedly, this was also true for figures like Jiménez and Ortega y Gasset, whose complex relationships to *la joven literatura* have been more thoroughly examined. And yet, even as the youngsters rebelliously declare their independence from their elders, Unamuno enjoys a certain pride of place. In the second issue of *Lola*, Diego's frustration with Valle-Inclán leads to an illuminating statement. Seeking to discredit the force of the older writer's judgments, he writes, "Cada uno de nosotros pensamos y escribimos sin importarnos un rábano cuanto – en orden a un posible magisterio ideológico o estético – piensan y escriben Unamuno, Ortega y Gasset, Jiménez, y el propio magnífico Valle-Inclán" ("Each of us thinks and writes without worrying in the least about what – in order of a possible ideological or aesthetic influence – Unamuno, Ortega y Gasset, Jiménez, and the very fine Valle-Inclán himself think and write") ("Crónica" 2:2). Even as Diego denies the older thinkers' power over his peers, his ordering of names clearly privileges Unamuno. César Vallejo had employed a similar trope in the first issue of *Favorables París*

Poema, where he opened his article "Estado de la literatura española" ("The State of Spanish Literature") by asserting that "ni Unamuno, el más fuerte de los viejos escritores" ("not even Unamuno, the strongest of the old writers") could serve as a leader for the literary youth of Spain and Hispanic America (Vallejo 6). He also mentions Ortega in the opening paragraph, but only after dedicating several sentences to explaining why Unamuno cannot lead the young. Vallejo clearly judged Unamuno to be the most formidable of his predecessors, even as he argued against him. In the context of Diego's "Crónica del centenario," the privileging of Unamuno might suggest that this younger critic saw him as better able to retain the "spiritual" youth that serves as his guiding criterion in his assessment of the Góngora tercentenary. Be that as it may, from 1927 on several members of *la joven literatura* published Unamuno's writing and dedicated pieces to him, affirming implicitly – and at times explicitly – his enduring youthfulness even in old age.

In the "Crónica," Diego says relatively little about Unamuno's negative response to the invitation to participate in the tercentenary celebrations. Moreover, despite the Basque writer's notorious anti-*gongorismo*, none of his works are sent to the bonfire. Such deference stands in striking contrast to Diego's bitter attack on Valle-Inclán and the sarcasm that saturates his account of Jiménez's "Esquela contra." Perhaps this is because Unamuno's reply to the invitation lacked the antagonism and outright hostility of the others. So it would seem from Diego's statement that Unamuno "se excusó con nosotros de una manera digna y cortés, absolutamente respetable" ("excused himself in a dignified, courteous, absolutely respectable manner") ("Crónica" 2:2). The author of the "Crónica" gives the reader to understand that Unamuno's exile is part of what warrants this respect, as he alludes to the government censorship that makes further elaboration on this particular reply impossible. Laconic by necessity, Diego's words on this topic are among the most serious and un-ironic of his entire account of the tercentenary.

As Diego suggests, the tone of the letter that Unamuno wrote to the young *gongorinos* from Hendaye on 15 February 1927 is civil and reasoned, varying greatly from the heated words he had for the Góngora celebrations later in *Cómo se hace una novela*. In the first part of the letter Unamuno discusses his own relative ignorance regarding Góngora's work, and reiterates the distinction he had often made between Góngora the poet and the imitative poetic style, *gongorismo*. But it is in the long paragraph that comprises the second half of the letter that Unamuno expounds on the most fundamental reason for his abstention: his protest of the contemporary political situation in Spain. The passage has received far too little attention from critics, and so I cite it at length:

> Me he propuesto desde hace algún tiempo y en virtud de experiencias íntimas de mi destierro, limitar mi contribución a la obra de la cultura española ahí, en esa ex-España, a lo estrictamente necesario que me imponga la dura necesidad del pan de mi familia, a obra de esclavo. Tengan en cuenta, además, que mi vida universal y persecular está dolorosamente suspensa por mi vida local y cotidiana y que la repugnante realidad histórica concreta en que todos los españoles dignos de nuestra españolidad nos consumimos, me veda tomar parte en ciertas fiestas ... No tengo ojos para mirar el resplandor de Góngora – véalo o no bien ... Y presumo, acá en mis ensueños metafísicos, que el espíritu de Góngora me lo agradecerá más que otro tributo. No me es lícito celebrar a ningún espíritu de la España eterna mientras el ruin inespíritu de Primo de Rivera siga mandando y deshonrando el santo nombre de mi patria. (*Cartas del destierro* 206)

> (For a while now and in light of personal experiences in exile, I have decided to limit my contribution to the work of Spanish culture over there, in that ex-Spain, to the strictly necessary amount of slave labor that my family's basic need for bread demands of me. Bear in mind, also, that my universal and transhistorical life has been suspended in favor of my local and everyday life, and that the repugnant concrete historical reality in which all Spaniards worthy of our Spanishness are wasting away bars me from taking part in certain celebrations ... I do not have eyes to look at Góngora's radiance – whether I see it well or not ... And I venture to think, here in my metaphysical fantasies, that Góngora's spirit will appreciate it [my abstention] more than another tribute. I cannot celebrate a spirit of eternal Spain while the despicable non-spirit of Primo de Rivera continues to govern and dishonor the holy name of my homeland.)

The contrast between the eternal (*per-secular*, throughout the centuries) and the historical that had been central to Unamuno's thought for decades and that anchors the poetic philosophy of *Romancero del destierro* here provides the key to his understanding of Góngora and the rationale for his personal tribute to the seventeenth-century poet. Whether he has understood Góngora's work or not, he recognizes him as a part of an eternal Spain; that is, a Spain that does not grow old. The mourning period and vigil that he has sworn to keep while choosing to live in exile prevents him from taking part in the festivities, but does not dissolve the artistic bonds that transcend history and link him to Góngora – and to his young admirers, whom he addresses in the letter as "mis buenos amigos."

The general reaction to Unamuno's letter among the members of *la joven literatura* was one of comprehension and esteem. On 26 February Alberti made the first mention of it to Diego, in a postscript to a letter discussing other aspects of the tercentenary: "Se me ocurrió invitar a Unamuno. Te mando su magnífica y dolorosa negativa" ("It occured to me to invite Unamuno. I send you his magnificent and painful refusal") (Morelli, *Gerardo Diego* 76). The note indicates that it was Alberti who decided to send an invitation to Unamuno, thus including him in the list from which he is absent in Diego's poem "A Rafael Alberti." Moreover, it suggests that the exiled writer's response made a deep impression. (Was this one of the texts that contributed to the political awakening Alberti describes in his memoirs?) Upon receiving Unamuno's reply, Diego passed it on to José María Cossío, to whom Alberti had also sent a copy (Diego, *Epistolario* 159, 161). Cossío was well acquainted with Unamuno, having published *Rimas de dentro*, and having hosted him at his country house in the village of Tudanca in August of 1923, the year before the older writer's exile.[24] In fact, almost contemporaneously with receiving the copy of Unamuno's letter from Alberti, in the March 1927 issue of *Verso y Prosa*, Cossío published a series of documents that attest to their friendship and recall that visit. They were three dedications that Unamuno had written in copies of his works (the first volume of the *Ensayos* in the Residencia edition, *Del sentimiento trágico de la vida*, and *Rimas de dentro*) during his stay. Whether or not he had read Unamuno's letter when he sent this contribution to *Verso y Prosa*, Cossío's commemoration of a pre-exile encounter with Unamuno, four years after the fact, again speaks to the reverence in which the writer was held, even as it – like Diego's "Crónica" – carefully avoids a direct reference to his current political situation.

What was it that caused the change in tone between Unamuno's well-received letter from February and the angry words he wrote in *Cómo se hace una novela* in June? Though I have cited them in the introduction to this book, it is worth recalling them now:

> Y ahora en estos días mismos de principios de junio de 1927, cuando la tiranía pretoriana española se ensoece más y el rufián que la representa la vomita [*sic*], casi a diario, sobre el regazo de España las heces de su

> borracheras [*sic*], recibo un número de *La Gaceta Literaria* de Madrid que consagran a don Luis de Góngora y Argote y al gongorismo los jóvenes culteranos y cultos de la castrada intelectualidad española. (Unamuno, *Manual* 200)
>
> (And now in these first days of June, 1927, when the praetorian Spanish tyranny continues to degrade itself and the ruffian that represents it vomits the dregs of his drunkenness, almost daily, upon Spain's lap, I receive an issue of Madrid's *La Gaceta Literaria,* which the pretentiously learned youths of Spain's castrated intellectual class dedicate to Don Luis de Góngora y Argote and to *gongorismo.*)

La Gaceta Literaria is the fundamental and immediate cause of the outrage that Unamuno expresses so viciously here. In this passage, inserted into the manuscript as he was editing it,[25] he leaves little doubt that this publication's treatment of the Góngora tercentenary shaped his view of it. What he does not mention is that the letter he had written to the younger writers about Góngora appeared on the front page of that issue without his authorization and against his expressed wishes. A few months earlier Gecé had asked him to contribute to the *Gaceta,* but Unamuno refused, explaining, much as he had in response to Diego, Bergamín, et. al., that he would not subject his writing to Primo's censors (Unamuno, *Cartas del destierro* 219). Upon receiving the special Góngora issue, he wrote to Gecé once more: "No tienen ustedes, creo, derecho alguno a faltarme al respeto y hasta a ofenderme publicando una carta mía que les consta que no destiné a publicidad … Y, además, de esa carta se ha quitado el final, y eso es más grave aún" ("You all have no right, I believe, to disrespect and even offend me by publishing a letter of mine that you know I did not write for a public audience … And, moreover, the end of the letter has been left out, and that is even more serious") (223). Indeed, *La Gaceta Literaria* had only published the first paragraph of Unamuno's response, cutting the political commentary that was the heart of the letter. The partial publication may well have been due to concerns with censorship, as in the cases of the other journals that published texts relating to Unamuno around this time – the abrupt ending of the excerpt does suggest the work of a censor's rather than an editor's hand. Of course, the action was inexcusable from Unamuno's point of view. His use of the plural "ustedes" in his letter suggests that he did not distinguish Giménez Caballero's actions from those of the other young Góngora enthusiasts, as Diego did later, and emphatically, in his "Crónica." This treatment by *La Gaceta Literaria* inclines Unamuno to view the entire undertaking much as Diego viewed Gecé's approach to it, as obsequious and pandering. In *Como se hace una novela*, he continues in this vein, calling the homage "un tácito homenaje de servidumbre a la tiranía, un acto servil y en algunos, no en todos, ¡claro!, un acto de pordiosería" ("a tacit homage of servitude to tyranny, a servile and, in some – not in all, of course! – a beggarly act") (*Manual* 205).

Quiroga Plá expressed similar sentiments when he wrote to Unamuno in late June after seeing the special issue of *La Gaceta Literaria*. He comments that his father-in-law's "media carta" ("half letter") was good, but that according to what he had heard, the part that was left unpublished was even better (Martínez Nadal 45). For this younger writer, the whole ordeal confirmed a deepening negative impression of *La Gaceta Literaria*. In his letter to his father-in-law, Quiroga Plá shares Diego's view that the journal is the organ of false youth, an example of what Unamuno himself had recently called "jóvenes de vanguardia agazapados en una política de retaguardia" ("avant-garde youths stuck in a politics of the rearguard") (45). Quiroga Plá does not hesitate to assert that these "youths" are not truly young, observing that *La Gaceta Literaria* in fact seems much more interested in celebrating maturity. Still, he hastens to assure Unamuno that many members of the young generation have deep respect for him, and are even capable of articulating that respect intelligently. In this regard, he singles out in particular José Bergamín, whose intimate relationship and correspondence with Unamuno during these years are contrasted with those of Giménez Caballero in the following chapter.

The exiled writer's brief acknowledgment in *Cómo se hace una novela* that not all of those involved in the tercentenary were simply pandering to the State leaves open a possibility for further contact and exchange with at least some members of *la joven literatura*. Despite his harsh words, in the years following the tercentenary their affinities did continue to intensify. In the spring of 1928 Diego opened the fifth issue of *Carmen* with a letter Unamuno had sent to Bergamín, signed "Un poeta enigmático y solo" ("An enigmatic and solitary poet") – an allusion to the title of a previous piece by Bergamín, "Carmen: Enigma y soledad." Unamuno's letter reflects a certain approximation to the aesthetic ideas of the younger generation: "Quisiera escribir un tratado de geometría en verso y sin metáforas para hacer con geometría pura poesía pura, de inmaculada concepción" ("I would like to write a treatise on geometry in verse and without metaphors in order to make with pure geometry pure poetry, immaculately conceived") ("Carta" 2).[26] A reverential Manuel Altolaguirre paid a visit to Unamuno in Hendaye, just before the exiled writer's 1929 open letter to university students initiated a wave of enthusiasm among young people back in Spain. This excitement increased with the celebration of his homecoming in 1930. *La Gaceta Literaria* organized an honorary issue dedicated to Unamuno, reminiscent of the homage it had given Góngora in that it included comments and contributions from a great number of Spanish writers representing various generations.[27] Meanwhile Jorge Guillén, who was in Oxford at the time of Unamuno's return, wrote to him of the emotion that overcame him knowing that the writer could now resume his work in Spain: "Ahora sí que será usted, una vez más, el más joven, el menos 'pompier' de todos los españoles" ("Now you will be, once more, the youngest, the least 'pompier' of all Spaniards").[28]

In Guillén's letter, once again, the hallmark of youth is a lack of arrogance and pretentiousness. Youth devotes itself to its work, but does not take itself seriously. As Unamuno returns from exile, Guillén recognizes in him the same qualities that Gerardo Diego had seen in Góngora in 1926. Here is another moral example for the young Spanish writers, quite different from the one provided by Juan Ramón Jiménez, about which Christopher Maurer has written evocatively. When Guillén uses the word "pompier" it is difficult not to think of his relationship with Jiménez, which famously came to an end in 1933 with an argument that involved Unamuno's poetry. The story is well known to many: Guillén decided at the last minute to open the second issue of the journal *Los Cuatro Vientos* with a series of poems from Unamuno's unpublished *Cancionero*, demoting Jiménez, who had understood that his work would appear first, to the second slot. Jiménez insisted that he did not take issue with being published after Unamuno, but with his treatment by Guillén. Guillén argued that too much was being made of an editorial decision that he had the right to make. The rift deepened and remained, and several critics have attempted to sort it out.[29] Whatever his intent towards Jiménez, however, Guillén's decision to publish Unamuno's poems affirms the stature in public life and before the eyes of Spanish youth – literary and political – that Unamuno had gained while in exile.

All of the fifteen poems that appeared in *Los Cuatro Vientos* had been written in Hendaye. Two were published in the issue of *La Gaceta Literaria* dedicated to Unamuno's return in 1930, and one of these speaks especially to the paradox of aging and the passing of time. In it, Unamuno muses on the development of his own poetic language, playfully asking, "¿eres vejez de edad niña? / ¿eres niñez de edad vieja?" ("Are you the old age of childhood? / Are you the childhood of age?"). He then continues,

> ¿Vino viejo en odres nuevos?
> no; sino agua de ribera,
> su cauce en el valle verde
> canal que riega a la cepa.
> Voy a crear el pasado,
> mañana que fue no es muerta,
> vuelve mi río a la fuente,
> la creación es eterna. (Díaz de Castro 144)
>
> (Is this old wine in new wineskins?
> no; it's the water of a stream,
> the path it carves in the valley
> a canal to keep the vines green.
> I'm going to create the past,
> the tomorrow that was has not died,
> my river returns to its source,
> creation eternally thrives.)

These lines encapsulate the Unamuno that the poets of *la joven literatura* recognized as young, the one whose youth Manuel Altolaguirre would later describe as "vegetal." The poet rejects the idea that he is disguising himself, or simply putting on the trappings of the new in this phase of his career. His work is ongoing and forward-moving, not a stagnant substance to be poured into new containers. Yet it is also circular, part of an organic process of nourishment and growth. His river, unlike Jorge Manrique's, does not come to its end in the sea. When he closes the poem by specifying that his continual linguistic quest searches always for "la lengua / con que he de hablar a mi pueblo" ("the language / with which I will speak to my people"), the reader is reminded that for him *poiesis* is always a commerce of individual and community, the aesthetic and the social. It was this commerce, the deep interrelation of poetry and politics that the writer reaffirmed and rearticulated in compelling ways during his exile, that made him a point of reference for *la joven literatura,* just as his denunciation of Primo de Rivera won him the esteem and admiration of the youth protest movement. In the new political and literary landscape of the Second Spanish Republic, questions about the relationship between politics and aesthetics would be more present than ever for young writers and intellectuals in Spain.

Chapter Four

Hercules and Hermes: Versions of Artistic and Political Youth

In the two preceding chapters I have endeavoured to show how the glorification of youth in the modernist production of *la joven literatura* originated and flourished through a separation of art from political and social concerns, even as my analysis of Unamuno's reception among his successors suggests that his example challenged and nuanced that divide between art and life in ways that have been largely overlooked. My discussion in the previous chapter of Unamuno's role as a catalyst in the process of politicization undergone by many young writers in the late 1920s now leads to a more focused comparison of two of these writers: Ernesto Giménez Caballero and José Bergamín. Though in different ways, both of these men defended an interrelationship between art and politics for which they found support in ideas Unamuno had developed at the turn of the century. The notion of *intrahistoria*, as an unwritten history embodied by the Spanish people; the critique of reason and progress from the standpoint of faith and *poiesis*; and the idea that Spain was in need of cultural and political rejuvenation are all elements of the work of the early Unamuno that both Giménez Caballero and Bergamín found compelling in their own historical moment, between the First World War and their country's Civil War. In this chapter I argue that the treatment of youth developed by each writer during these years reflects an extended involvement with Unamuno's own use of this concept, even as it lays the groundwork for two very different readings of his work in the later twentieth century.

There has long existed a compelling case for a comparative study of Giménez Caballero and Bergamín. In the previous chapter I juxtaposed the two writers in discussing the essays on Góngora that each contributed to the journal *Verso y Prosa* for its honorary issue in June of 1927, but additional possible points of comparison abound. Indeed, the parallels between the work and lives of Giménez Caballero and Bergamín that arise under even passing examination make it surprising that no critic has yet carried out a thorough study of the two together.[1] Both were born in Madrid in the last years of the nineteenth century. In the 1920s, both displayed an avid interest in the new art of their time and its interpretation. They moved in the same intellectual circles, Giménez Caballero serving at the helm of *La Gaceta Literaria*, and Bergamín writing a number of essays about his close colleagues, the core members of *la joven literatura*. More specifically, both were creative artists best known during this decade for their imaginative literary criticism. Gecé's visual interpretations or "reviews" in poster form of newly published books earned him fame as a *cartelista* (he collected many of these images in his 1927 book *Carteles*), and as Nigel Dennis has noted, Bergamín's writing so illuminated the work of his friends that Gerardo Diego referred to him later as the "gusano de luz" ("firefly") of his generation (Dennis, *José Bergamín* 50). But perhaps what most assimilates Giménez Caballero and Bergamín to one another is their love of wordplay. In *Vida en claro*, José Moreno Villa calls attention to this common trait, describing it as a shared penchant for "malabarismo lingüístico" ("linguistic gymnastics") that likens both writers to Ramón Gómez de la Serna. In addition, however, Moreno Villa notes that they also display something not found in Gómez de la Serna: a tortured quality, "atormentamiento" (*Memoria* 146). While this quality in the writing of Giménez Caballero and Bergamín recalls other common influences like that of Nietzsche,[2] it can most certainly be traced to the paradoxes and contradictions, the agonic struggle of reason and non-reason, in the work of Miguel de Unamuno.

Of course, as those familiar with Giménez Caballero and Bergamín and their subsequent roles in the Spain of the 1930s (and beyond) will be quick to point out, there is one crucial difference between them: their political ideologies were widely divergent. Gecé followed what Enrique Selva has aptly dubbed a "vía estética" through the experimental art of the avant-garde to become the foremost ideologue of Spanish fascism. Meanwhile, Bergamín, deeply Catholic and just as deeply idiosyncratic, was a staunch supporter of the Second Republic and gravitated increasingly towards communism. This pairing of two charismatic writers succinctly illustrates the breadth of the political distances critics are wont to cite in discussing the cultural landscape of prewar Spain. What makes their case especially instructive is the parallel nature of their professional and intellectual trajectories from artistic expression to political engagement. While even early on the work of both writers defies the separation of art and politics assumed to reign throughout the 1920s in Spain, they also exemplify the process of politicization that took place in the years leading to the fall of Primo de Rivera and the creation of the Republic. It is tempting to read these shifts in Giménez Caballero and in Bergamín, respectively, according to Walter Benjamin's now-classic interpretation of right- and left-wing artistic practices during the period. Gecé's trajectory and writing, in particular, often conforms perfectly to Benjamin's description of the aestheticization of politics.[3] My primary interest here, however, lies in the way each of these writers respond to the concept of youth that already permeated Spanish cultural discourse when they began writing and only grew in prominence during the first decade of their careers. In this respect, the role Unamuno played in the developing ideas of each writer proves illuminating.

Both Bergamín and Giménez Caballero first established contact with Unamuno at the beginning of 1923. In the following years, Giménez Caballero became centrally involved in the Spanish avant-garde. After meeting Guillermo de Torre in 1925 and founding *La Gaceta Literaria* with him in 1927, Gecé had several years of prolific journalistic, critical, and creative production. At the same time, from his first exchanges with Unamuno, he was incorporating his predecessor's work into a burgeoning ultranationalist ideology. A trip to Mussolini's Rome in 1928 precipitated what he described as his "conversion" to fascism. Just after this experience he sent a postcard to Unamuno in which he wrote that he had discovered a new interpretation of the Basque writer's work. In the postcard, he speaks of planning an intellectual return to Unamuno ("una vuelta hacia Ud."), and elaborates, "Tenía Ud. razón. Hablo de su esencia antimoderna, de su fascismo" ("You were right. I'm talking about your antimodern essence, your fascism").[4] Gecé famously articulated his new understanding of his predecessor's work in 1929, with an article in *La Gaceta Literaria* titled "Carta a un compañero de la Joven España" ("Letter to a Member of Young Spain"). In it, he compared Unamuno to Curzio Malaparte and presented his own translation of Malaparte's writings under the blatantly Unamunian title *En torno al casticismo de Italia*. Giménez Caballero's subsequent writing fashioned the basis for later fascist and Falangist views of Unamuno as the dominant figure of the Generation of 1898. At the same time, these later texts, particularly *Genio de España* (1932), display a deepening ambivalence towards his predecessor that was the product of the many disagreements and conflicts that began to plague the relationship between Gecé and Unamuno already in 1927.[5]

Though Bergamín's relationship with Unamuno was by no means as contentious as that of Giménez Caballero, its chronology is remarkably similar. Unamuno became a cherished interlocutor and mentor for Bergamín from their first exchange of letters in 1923. They crossed paths at the Residencia before Unamuno's exile and wrote to each other throughout the older writer's absence from Spain, continuing to meet in person when Bergamín would visit Hendaye. In 1928, a few months after Giménez Caballero made his momentous trip to Rome, Bergamín travelled to Moscow. As in Gecé's case, the trip marked a political turn in Bergamín's work that manifested itself five years later when he founded the journal *Cruz y Raya* (1933–1936). His constant references to Unamuno in his writing indicate that his *maestro*'s thought was present to him at every stage of this process. As Bergamín moved from primarily literary to more broadly social concerns, with an approach always informed by his deeply held Catholic faith, Unamuno became for him a model of integrity, or "entereza." Much later, decades into his own exile from Spain, Bergamín wrote of the "íntima trinidad" ("intimate trinity") that he saw in all of Unamuno's life and work, commenting that his *maestro* could never separate "lo poético" from "lo religioso y lo político" (Dennis, *El epistolario* 205). The insistence on the interrelationship of artistic, political, and religious questions that had been and continued to be central to Unamuno's thought spoke to Bergamín's own paradoxical position in the Spain of the 1930s, as a Catholic defender of the Second Republic. In the prologue he wrote for a later facsimile edition of *Cruz y Raya*, Bergamín recalls how the publication, in presenting itself as both Catholic and Republican, alienated both potential constituencies (Bergamín, "Signo y diseño" ix). His spiritually motivated promotion of leftist politics in the journal's pages echoed Unamuno's early view of socialism as the "religion of humanity" – and met with similar incomprehension from intellectual and religious communities alike.

That Unamuno was a prominent point of reference in the work of two such ideologically opposed writers as Bergamín and Gecé not only attests, yet again, to his fundamental importance for their generation, but also provides a means to compare and contrast the roles that youth plays in their writing and cultural criticism. Both embrace the resistance to the teleology of development that youth represented within European modernism and in Unamuno's writing, but with markedly different results. Giménez Caballero reads Unamuno's call in *En torno al casticismo* for a "true youth" that might revive a stagnant Spain as the anticipation of a fascist vision of social order centred on an ideal akin to Mussolini's *giovinezza*. For Bergamín, by contrast, youthfulness resides in a creative animus akin to Unamuno's *pistis*, an ever-renewed contention between intellect and faith that he views as the core of poetic art. In his critical writing the poetic constitutes a realm of eternal youth that, while absolutely independent of the time-bound political and social world, continuously breaks in upon it, disrupting and challenging its logic of linear progress. In this, it recalls the *intrahistoria* of Unamuno's 1895 essays. In the late 1920s, these two distinct visions of youth coalesced around two figures from Greek mythology: Hercules and Hermes.[6] For Giménez Caballero, Hercules served as an emblem of strength, athleticism, power, heroism, and violence – a model of revolutionary force along the lines prescribed not only by fascism but also by the avant-garde. Bergamín, however, rejected the monumentalism of this muscular image in favour of the spry and mischievous young messenger of the gods, a divinity in constant motion and perpetual renovation, whom he dubbed "el recién nacido immortal" ("the immortal newborn").

Classical Mythology and the Spanish Avant-Garde

The figure of Hermes – the Greek god of boundaries and transitions, poetry, and athletics, among other things – has long been recognized as playing an important role in the imaginary of pre-Civil War Spanish literary criticism. In a contemporary review of Antonio de Obregón's novel *Hermes en la vía pública* (*Hermes on the Public Thoroughfare*, 1934), Benjamín Jarnés focused on the book's invocation of the deity as symbolic of a contrast between the prose fiction of the Spanish avant-garde and the conventional realist novel. The former, written under the sign of Hermes, was agile, light-footed, and effervescent; the latter, bound to mimetic representation and concrete reality, found its emblem in Prometheus, chained to his rock. According to Gustavo Pérez Firmat, Jarnés' opposition exemplifies the "pneumatic aesthetics" of Spanish vanguard prose in the late 1920s and early 1930s – a critical discourse that employed metaphors related to evaporation, gaseous states, and levitation in order to describe the new approach to prose writing embraced by young artists.[7] The foil to this disruptive aesthetics is the "arquitectonic" character of the novel in an earlier era, which seeks to construct a narrative edifice, reinforcing pre-existing generic conventions rather than challenging and deconstructing them. As a distillation of fundamental differences between "old" and "new" approaches to the Spanish novel, the contrast between Hermes and Prometheus is instructive. Still, there is more to be said about the way such classical references functioned in art and criticism more broadly, with reference to other genres like poetry and to the wider cultural context of interwar Europe. First of all, an understanding of Hermes' role in pre-Civil War Spanish literature is incomplete without an acknowledgment of Bergamín's essay "El pensamiento hermético de las artes," one of his key critical writings on the art of his generation, in which he elaborated at length on the similarities between the Greek god and modern poetics.[8] Second, Giménez Caballero's invocation of Hercules as an emblem of youth represents an interpretation of young art that departs from Bergamín's reading in important ways and, ultimately, posits a return to the concrete solidity and architectonic impulse that Pérez Firmat associated only with novels written before the 1920s.

Published the year after Bergamín's essay appeared in print and often characterized as the swan song of the apolitical aesthetics of the previous decade, Obregón's *Hermes en la vía pública* presents its protagonist as the incarnation of the values associated with the youth culture of the Gilded Age. His novel is also representative of the questioning of individual and narrative development that lies at the heart of modernism's reprisal of the traditional *Bildungsroman*. Carefree, playful, athletic, and above all young, the Hermes of this novel enjoys a life of ease and freedom supported by the cultural capital of his juvenility. In the opening pages of the book the narrator describes him as "un joven que cae de las nubes" ("a youth fallen from the clouds") (10), and the first chapters quickly associate him with sports, physicality, and money. As he moves through spaces of urban youth culture like dance halls and cabarets, he enjoys the returns on the "metálico de su juventud" ("currency of his youth") (37). These advantages facilitate the elements of "cold" modernism that Susan Larson has seen in the novel: Hermes' story skims over the surfaces of the modern city and avoids introspection (Larson, "Unreadable Bodies" 57). What is more, they free the protagonist from the obligation to make his life conform to a pre-ordained path. In a passage with clear metafictional implications, the narrator comments that Hermes "inventaba su propia vida, que ante él se desenrrollaba como un film increíble. Eso de inventar la propia vida se daba muy pocas veces en el mundo" ("invented his own life, which unfolded before him like a magnificent film. Being able to invent one's own life was a rare thing in the world") (36).

Hermes is an individualist and trailblazer who invents his life and its story rather than allowing them to follow a traditional trajectory based on coherent development. This resistance is felt on both structural and thematic levels in the novel. While a weak narrative thread does emerge in order to bring the story to a somewhat incongruous ending,[9] the book is comprised of fragmentary chapters that bear little causal connection to one another. In addition, the cynical view of bourgeois adult life that prevails in several parts of the novel (such as when Hermes marries the also-advantageously-young Adelaida in order to secure a business deal) displays a critique of dominant conceptions of maturity characteristic of many modernist novels. This critique, along with the novel's references to film and youth culture, harkens back to an earlier novel of the Spanish avant-garde, Antonio Espina's *Pájaro Pinto* (1927). Espina's novel is a fragmentary, montage-like work that also critiques the pairing of individual and narrative development, both through the unconventional selfhood of one of its main characters, Xelfa, and by supplanting traditional narrative structure with techniques borrowed from cinematography. *Pájaro Pinto* and *Hermes en la vía pública* are both radical modernist distortions of the *Bildungsroman* that render the genre nearly unrecognizable by combining their break from narrative conventions with aesthetic experimentation. In this sense, these two novels highlight an important paradox at the heart of the "Hermetic" aesthetics of Spanish vanguard prose: its highly anti-narrative quality. Indeed, as Pérez Firmat notes, contemporary critics most frequently described these experimental novels of the 1920s and early 1930s in terms of other genres. Calling them "poematic," "lyrical," or "essayistic," they highlighted a resistance to conventional narrative structures in these novels that corresponds to the broader suspicion of narrative and linear development throughout Spanish modernist production.

While emblembatic of the Spanish vanguard novel in its critique of traditional narrative(s of) development, *Hermes en la vía pública* was also viewed by Jarnés and other critics as representing an aesthetic moment that had ended by 1934. As the ideological conflict between fascism and communism grew on the global political stage, Spanish artists had begun to abandon the previous decade's values of dehumanization in favour of socially conscious writing. While the lack of political engagement or social awareness in Obregón's novel might have been praised a few years earlier, for many in Spain such a stance was no longer permissible. In his manifesto-like essay of 1930, "El nuevo romanticismo" ("The New Romanticism"), novelist José Díaz Fernández insisted that modern art must address the issues raised by contemporary politics. He made this argument especially forcefully in a section of the essay titled "La juventud y la política" ("Youth and Politics"), where he insisted on the social responsibility of the artist, and invoked the powers of Spanish youth much as Unamuno had in 1895:

> En el fondo de las provincias, perdida y anhelante en ciudades y pueblos oscuros, está una juventud que es espíritu vivo de la España que todos queremos. Juventud enemiga de la probreza, ansiosa de cultura, adversaria de la injusticia … A esa juventud hay que decirle que, en el fondo, lo que buscan quienes le aconsejan apoliticismo y abstención es la pasividad y la inercia para que las fuerzas tradicionales puedan permanecer en sus posiciones. (Díaz Fernández 360)

> (Deep in the provinces, lost and eager in forgotten cities and towns, there is a youth that is the living spirit of the Spain that we all want. A youth that despises poverty, longs for culture, and opposes injustice … This youth must be told that, on a fundamental level, what those who recommend apoliticism and abstention really seek is their passivity and inertia so that the traditional powers may remain in place.)

In stark contrast with the way Obregón would depict youth culture four years later, here Díaz Fernández resurrects a vision of regenerative youth that Unamuno had articulated at the turn of the century. In the context of the passage, however, the Unamuno that the essayist has in mind is not only the author of *En torno al casticismo*, but also the political dissident of the 1910s – a fact that becomes clear as he cites the concept of the "troglodita" that Unamuno developed during the First World War to describe Spanish conservatives.

In his rejection of apolitical aesthetics, Díaz Fernández criticizes the *gongorismo* of the previous years in much the same terms that Ernesto López-Parra had in 1927, especially denouncing the elements of Catholicism present in that commemoration and in the work of some of his contemporaries. He is particularly harsh in commenting on Bergamín, whose Catholicism appears as anathema to the leftist ideological leanings clearly held by the author of "El nuevo romanticismo." But the opening of the section of the essay dedicated to youth and politics focuses on another, greater adversary: the fascist who praises youth in order to retain control over it. This "fariseo," Díaz Fernández writes, "alude a una España joven, vital e impulsiva, y la quiere extraer exclusivamente de los campos deportivos, como si la vitalidad y el impulso fuesen cosa puramente física y no supusieran la existencia ineludible del resorte espiritual" ("alludes to a young Spain, lively and motivated, and tries to extract it exclusively from the playing fields, as if vitality and initiative were purely physical things and did not imply the undeniable existence of a spiritual source") (359). Fascism attempts to reduce youth to mere physical strength, but in this it is mistaken. Again articulating a vision contrary to that espoused by Obregón in *Hermes en la vía pública,* Díaz Fernández insists that "spiritual" qualities – here understood in a general sense as those attributes of the human being that are not physical, particularly moral conviction and creativity – are essential to the nature of youth.

A few lines below, Díaz Fernández's argument leads him to remark that "el hércules de feria es una fuerza intrascendente" ("the fairground Hercules is an intranscendent force") (359). The statement is made in passing: in order to flesh out the distinction between brute strength admired by those of fascist leanings and the spirituality that must infuse the politically engaged art of Spanish youth, the essayist employs the metaphor of a strongman at a town fair, colloquially referred to as a "Hercules." Nevertheless, the appearance of the name of this mythological hero in this context helps to further clarify the range of aesthetic and political postures present in the cultural realm of the late 1920s and early 1930s. By the time Díaz Fernández wrote "El nuevo romanticismo," Giménez Caballero had already made the figure of Hercules the centerpiece of a collection of essays entitled *Hércules jugando a los dados* (*Hercules Playing Dice,* 1928), which he published in the midst of his increasingly public affirmation of fascist ideology. As Nil Santiáñez has argued, the work of Spanish fascist writers like Giménez Caballero was fundamentally concerned with a particular kind of physicality: the topographical ordering and production of space. Among these writers, the "concrete" and "architectonic" elements that Pérez Firmat associates with the literature of a period prior to and rejected by the vanguard moment reappear under a new guise. Though, like the "Hermetic" novel defined by Jarnés, Herculean art also destroys the "old" models of mimetic aesthetics, it does so in order to erect new ideological edifices of its own construction. Whereas the tendency towards disruption, dissolution, fluidity, and effervescence that Jarnés identified in the work of his contemporaries and that Díaz Fernández linked to social justice and spirituality recalls Unamuno's allergy to processes of solidification as harbingers of old age, a writer like Giménez Caballero was capable of taking the culturally charged concept of youth and making it the basis of a new *ideocracia*. Analysed together, the cases of Bergamín and Giménez Caballero indicate that the subversive energy of young art that Jarnés contrasted with the conventions of the old, "Promethean" novel could be and was channeled in divergent political and artistic directions: that of what Santiáñez calls a fascist "will-to-architecture," or the spiritual vision that appears in Bergamín's writing and, both through and despite his Catholicism, ultimately approaches Díaz Fernández's concept of politically engaged young art.

In order to further clarify the differences between Bergamín's "Hermetic" theory of modern art and Gecé's "Herculean" one, a distinction between modernism and the avant-garde is useful. In scholarship on early twentieth-century Spanish writing and especially in the case of the so-called Generation of 1927, there has been some debate about the appropriate application of these categories to groups and individual artists. While a scholar like C. Christopher Soufas, who advocates for the inclusion of Spanish literary production of this period under the broad rubric of European modernism, prefers to use this term as a general descriptor, others (particularly Anderson in *El Veintisiete*) argue that there are good historical and theoretical reasons to distinguish between avant-garde and modernist tendencies in the practice of particular Spanish artists from this time. To be sure, as Andrew Hewitt has pointed out in *Fascist Modernism*, the word *modernism* serves as a convenient platform for comparison, but should not erase discernible differences between the modernist critique of modernity and/or modernization on the one hand, and on the other, the avant-garde's conception of itself as the culmination of that critique. This is particularly important to bear in mind when the distinction appears in the discourse of the writers themselves, as is the case in the Spain of the 1920s and early 1930s. Anxiety about the implications of the term "avant-garde" appear in "El nuevo romanticismo," where Díaz Fernández prefers to speak of "literatura de avanzada" (Díaz Fernández 355), as well as in Bergamín's writing, as we shall see.

According to Hewitt, who reads fascist cultural production in relation to Peter Bürger's interpretation of the avant-garde as the ultimate reintegration of modern aesthetics and everyday life, the avant-garde is a modernism "that is somehow 'completed'" (45) – that is, we might say, fully mature. With this maturity comes the annihilation of the open-ended temporality characteristic of modernist art. The avant-garde replaces sequentiality with simultaneity, exchanges narrative for monumentality, and insists "upon the reality of the text rather than upon the textuality of the real" (14). In other words, the avant-garde generates texts that perform and produce reality, and understand that reality in terms of spatial relations (the page as map) rather than according to temporal or historical succession. The break with the historical past, while at face value a rebellious gesture against all things "old," also renders the term meaningless in any chronological sense. The same can be said, of course, of the word "young." Herein lies the link that Renato Poggioli pointed to in his own theory of the avant-garde, between Decadent aestheticism and the avant-garde's idolization of futurity, the continuity between a longing for dissolution or "return to barbarism" and the effort to "transform the catastrophe into a miracle" (Poggioli 76, 66). If the avant-garde represents the last stage or "full unfolding" of the historical development of modern art, its celebration of youth must be merely nominal, and abstract. It values youth as an emblem of (masculine) strength or power rather than for its potentially subversive position within a process of becoming. Especially in its fascist manifestation, the avant-garde takes the values of aestheticism and imposes them on social and political life, crossing a line drawn in the *fin-de-siècle* and creating a phenomenon that Hewitt calls "a decadent decadence: the decay of decadence in its aesthetic form" (71). The stasis that results when historical vision cedes to aesthetic vision replicates the social paralysis that Unamuno and his contemporaries lamented in late nineteenth-century Spain. It is decadence or senility under the guise of youth.

Santiáñez has shown that the writing of Spanish fascism is intimately connected to the production of space, especially in the work of Giménez Caballero, one of its seminal authors. The "cartographic gaze" and "will-to-architecture" that Santiáñez identifies in Gecé's writing endeavour to make the modernist break with linear temporality the basis of a new social reality, one that exchanges political deliberation and historical hermeneutics for an overarching aesthetic vision. In this, the category of the poetic acquires a new meaning. As Santiáñez observes, fascism "is a performative speech act of sorts that, like poetry, brings into existence a space-time of its own" (26). Like a lyric poem, fascist writing offers not a plot but a series of images or observations whose interrelationship is driven more by linguistic links and resonances than by logic. By speaking in terms of the poetic,[10] writers like Giménez Caballero account for national character and national history without history, and eschew rational argument in favour of sheer "illocutionary force" (49). This rhetorical posture also allows for a particular treatment of youth. As the fascist aesthetic spatializes the time of historical and national becoming, it extracts this life stage from the process of development and makes it occupy the monumental centre of its map. Youth, as a heroic – and, once again, overwhelmingly masculine – icon, presides over the landscape of fascist ideology like a towering statue of Hercules.

By contrast with Giménez Caballero's avant-garde and fascist aesthetics,[11] the view of art that develops in Bergamín's writing from early on is more properly described as modernist. Like Baudelaire, Bergamín conceives of the modernity of art as something at once intensely rooted in its own historical moment and capable of transcending history. Thus artistic creation is in constant motion, ever renewing itself like Hermes in order to engage adequately with both its present and the transhistorical – and for Bergamín, eternal – demands of *poiesis*. Rather than occupying a fixed position of authority in the ideological landscape of fascism or the avant-garde, Bergamín's hermetic youth displays the agility and dexterity to evade all structures imposed on it. In "El pensamiento hermético de las artes" he does compare poetry to architecture and mathematics, disciplines he describes as "ciencias universales de la construcción" ("universal sciences of construction") (61); nevertheless, in Bergamín's view the best works of art build rational edifices in order to defy them. If fascist art in Spain seeks to fix its coordinates within what Santiáñez calls "absolute space" and uses the category of the poetic as the cement that seals its structure like an impenetrable fortress, Bergamín's hermetic art builds structures so that its ineffable, poetic, youthful quality may escape from them, vindicating the freedom of the imagination.

This form of modernist youth also resists its confinement to rhetorical language in the cultural and political spheres. In the early 1930s, as Spanish fascists increasingly appropriated the language of youth for their own ends, Bergamín began to abandon it. In this, his attitude echoes that of Unamuno. Recently Sandro Borzoni has demonstrated that fascism's ability to attract Spanish young people to its cause in the years before the Civil War led the older writer to become increasingly disillusioned with youth. Much the same can be said of Bergamín, who largely deserts the vocabulary of juvenility in the years preceding the Civil War. In response to the appropriation of the language of youth by ultranationalist rhetoric, he focuses on the eternal, immortal quality that ties youth to poetic creation in modernist art. Eschewing the Decadent or avant-garde vision of art as subject to development and decay, he promotes its immortality, its belonging to an eternal realm represented by Hermes, the guide to the afterlife.

Two First Books, Two Reviews

As I have indicated above, both Giménez Caballero and Bergamín established contact with Unamuno in early 1923. In the former case, the catalyst for the correspondence between the elder and younger writer was the publication of Giménez Caballero's first book, *Notas marruecas de un soldado* (*A Soldier's Moroccan Notes*).[12] A compendium of observations written about the author's service in Morocco during 1921 and 1922, just after Spain's embarrassing defeat at the Battle of Annual, the book's satirical portrayal of the mishandled military endeavours in North Africa immediately struck a chord with political progressives who were critical of the campaign – Unamuno prominent among them. In fact, it was Unamuno who initiated correspondence with Giménez Caballero when he wrote to congratulate him on the book. In his reply dated 18 February, Giménez Caballero urges his "maestro" to be equally gracious "con cuantos muchachos se le acerquen" ("with all of the youngsters who approach you"), noting how rare such enthusiasm for a young writer's work is in the Spanish literary world.[13] Later in the year, Unamuno had an occasion to continue his support. Accused of disrespecting the army and therefore violating the Ley de Jurisdicciones, *Notas marruecas de un soldado* was pulled from the shelves just weeks after its appearance (though it had already sold in large numbers), and Giménez Caballero was called to court and prosecuted. A critic of the Ley de Jurisdicciones since its institution in 1906, Unamuno was quick to sympathize with the plight of the young author, and made *Notas marruecas de un soldado* the subject of an article that appeared in *España* on 7 April with the title "Cola de humo" ("Trail of Smoke").[14] There he described Giménez Caballero favourably, as "una muestra de la mocedad española que está pasando por esa terrible escuela de la campaña de Marruecos" ("a representative of the Spanish youth that is passing through the terrible school of the Moroccan campaign") (1–2). Viewing the soldiers as yet another sector of young people underserved by the Spanish State, Unamuno argued as he had in previous years that their voices and their critiques of their elders must be heard.

While the politics surrounding the conflict in Morocco provides the context for the beginning of the relationship between Unamuno and Giménez Caballero, Bergamín's first interactions with the admired older writer were predominantly literary. At the beginning of 1923 Bergamín had been appointed editor of the well-known literary supplement *Los Lunes de El Imparcial*, and wrote to Unamuno to ask him to be a regular contributor to the periodical. In the letter he expressed regret that he had thus far only met the older writer in passing, adding that he hoped that would change. As his appointment to the position at *El Imparcial* suggests, Bergamín was well connected in Madrid's literary world. He had been a regular attender of Gómez de la Serna's *tertulia* in the Café Pombo since its founding in the 1910s, and by the early 1920s he was frequenting the Residencia de Estudiantes.[15] He knew Unamuno's work well, having, as he wrote in a later essay, "devoured" it along with writings by Nietzsche and Kierkegaard during his adolescence (Bergamín, *Detrás de la cruz* 60–1). While his tenure at *El Imparcial* only lasted a few months, his intellectual affinity and eventual friendship with Unamuno would be life-long. This relationship began to deepen later in 1923, when Bergamín published his own first book, a collection of aphorisms titled *El cohete y la estrella* (*The Rocket and the Star*). As in the case of *Notas marruecas de un soldado*, Unamuno responded to this work by a new, young writer with encouraging words for the author and a published commentary. His reflections on *El cohete y la estrella* appeared in *Nuevo Mundo* on 7 March 1924, just weeks after his exile to Fuerteventura.

Youth frames the ideas and observations put forth in both *Notas marruecas de un soldado* and *El cohete y la estrella*, if in different ways. As Unamuno noted, Giménez Caballero presents himself in his book as speaking for an entire generation of young men who lived through and learned from the campaign in Morocco. *Notas marruecas* opens and closes with elegies for sacrificed youth that recall laments for the "lost generation" of the First World War. The first section of the book, "Notas del campamento" ("Notes from the Encampment"), includes profiles of several young men who have died in Spain's conflict, beginning with a symbolic unknown soldier. This "soldado desconocido" is described as one who carries on his shoulders "la desgraciada carga de nuestra política internacional" ("the disgraceful weight of our international politics") (Giménez Caballero, *Notas* 29). A modern-day Atlas, he is forced to bear the burden of his country's unwieldy and precarious standing in the world. The subsection that closes "Notas del campamento," titled "Nota funeral" ("Funereal Note"), commemorates three of Giménez Caballero's deceased comrades from the Rif. There is Fernández, oldest child of a working-class family that had put all of their hopes in him; and Santiago, a well-to-do "señorito" from a landowning family in the provinces who quickly became disenchanted with the purportedly heroic life of the soldier. The narrator saves his most lyrical evocation for Pepe Díaz, a young, robust, and pure-hearted Andalusian whose life is marked by innocent love and familial tragedy. Cruelly orphaned, he had dedicated himself to a girl back home in Andalusia, whom he was planning to marry upon his return. Like Don Quijote, he aspired to perform heroic feats in Morocco out of love for his Dulcinea. Giménez Caballero highlights the injustice of the soldier's fate: "Pepe Díaz fue muerto en la primavera y por un motivo romántico. Su memoria nos ha quedado envuelta en una aureola luminosa de juventud, de simpatía y de ímpetu" ("Pepe Díaz died in the springtime, and for love. His memory remains with us surrounded by a glowing halo of youth, amiability, and vigor") (*Notas marruecas* 35). Struck down in the springtime of his life, Pepe Díaz appears as an icon of youth akin to Rupert Brooke a few years before.

In contrast to the nobility of the young fallen that the narrator describes, the older and more powerful generals and commanders in Morocco are lazy and corrupt. Giménez Caballero's sardonic portrayal of General José Millán-Astray in the subsection "Legionarios" received special attention from Unamuno, who already harbored a great dislike for this general (with whom he would have a fateful and famous encounter years later, during the early months of the Spanish Civil War).[16] In the concluding subsection of *Notas marruecas*, "Nota final en Madrid" ("Final Note in Madrid"), frustration with the incompetence of the leaders arises alongside the author's elegiac glorification of youth. Once again scorning the conflict "que tanta vida y tanto porvenir ha segado" ("that has cut short so much life and so much future") (185), he implores his peers not to bow before those who may outrank them in age, but by no means exceed them in talent or intelligence: "No permitamos más, que algunos ineptos con galones y estrellas imperen sobre nuestra juventud más delicada y más culta" ("Let us no longer allow a few inept men with decorations and stars to command our most refined and learned youth") (186). Here it is important to remember that Giménez Caballero speaks not only as a representative of a generational consciousness shaped by war, but also as a *soldado de cuota*, one of the advantaged young men with the financial resources to shorten their military service and secure administrative positions that kept them from combat. *Notas marruecas* reflects the status of its author in that it at no point describes actual fighting, a fact that would seem to undermine the Mussolini-like *trincerocrazia* that infuses Giménez Caballero's closing words. Nevertheless, his privileged position does allow him to launch an attack on the administration of the Spanish government and the army under the Bourbon monarchy, clearly defined in terms of a generational conflict between incompetent elders and a bold and heroic youth.

In the case of *El cohete y la estrella*, the rebellion of youth against the established order also emerges as a central theme of Bergamín's writing, though he approaches this topic in a much more abstract, philosophical, and literary key than Giménez Caballero does. The juxtaposition of a rocket and a star in the book's title emblematizes a contrast between ephemerality and permanence, impetuousness and impassivity that runs through many of the aphorisms it includes. Bergamín suggests that the aphorism itself is a rocket, its limited brilliance blazing for a moment before the unmoved night sky. Nigel Dennis and other critics have read this opposition of rocket and star as representing the distance between transient human endeavours and the enigmatic, unchanging authority of eternal or divine truth. I do not wish to deny this reading, which highlights the theological charge that suffuses all of Bergamín's writing. The opposition of earthly time and human history to the transcendent reality of Christianity is present throughout his work. However, the spontaneous blast of the rocket and the silence of the star may also be understood as reflections of qualities that Bergamín considered essential to youth and age. The rocket's eruption of light, sound, and motion – what Bergamín calls "algarabía y alboroto" ("clamor and commotion") in the first aphorism of the collection (*El cohete* 17) – is an ideal illustration of the energy youth is capable of discharging, freely and unselfconsciously, in the face of all-knowing order and authority. Before the ironic distance of the firmament, as before what Walter Benjamin called the impenetrable "mask" of the adult, the small and earthbound rocket nevertheless has the audacity to fling itself into the sky and interrogate the stars.

Related to this thematic element is Bergamín's own relative youth at the time he published *El cohete y la estrella*, a fact noted by various critics and reviewers. In the sketch of Bergamín that he provided as a prologue to the book, Juan Ramón Jiménez describes its author as just emerging from adolescence, having finally had the last growth spurt ("estirón") that gave his lanky frame the stature to reach the lofty realm of new ideas (8). For Antonio Espina, Bergamín is "un escritor de talento, *pero* joven y moderno" ("a write of talent, *but* young and modern," original emphasis) (Espina 126). The implication is that the last two traits do not mitigate, but in fact augment the writer's abilities, making them superior to established literary talent. To be sure, Espina does view some of Bergamín's pronouncements as arbitrary and puerile – particularly those dealing with older literary and intellectual figures like Pío Baroja and José Ortega y Gasset, whom the aphorist calls "viejo como el mundo" ("old as the hills") (*El cohete* 69–70). Dennis has similarly dismissed these aphorisms, reading them from the standpoint of later editions where they have been removed (*José Bergamín* 26–8). Nevertheless, these impulsive and potentially off-target statements, these "stray rockets," reflect the same rebellious spirit that seeks to overturn generational hierarchies elsewhere in the collection. In one aphorism, for example, Bergamín revisits the Wordsworthian adage on the child as the father of the man as he writes, "la verdadera enseñanza de la vida no la dan los padres a los hijos, sino los hijos a los padres" ("life's true lessons are not given by parents to their children, but by children to their parents") (*El cohete* 19). Elsewhere, he subverts the traditional view of the relationship between masters and disciples: "No hagáis lo que yo hago, pero menos aún lo que yo digo – dice el buen maestro" ("Do not do what I do, but much less what I say – says the good teacher") (23). Behind both of these aphorisms is a resistance to the kind of age that seeks to impress its authority on others and demands respect with the humorless seriousness that, as noted in the previous chapter, Gerardo Diego also criticized in some of his elders, including Ortega. It bears remembering here, too, that *El cohete y la estrella* was written in Madrid on the cusp of the surge in youth organization and student protests that occurred soon after Primo de Rivera's rise to power. As Bergamín later acknowledged, there is an important historical parallel between his use of the intellectually disruptive form of the aphorism and the political disruption led by young people during these years.[17]

Unamuno's response to *El cohete y la estrella* seems to have encouraged the young aphorist to think along these lines. The fact that the older writer was already in exile when his review of Bergamín's first book appeared surely accentuated the political overtones of his reflections. More than critical judgments, his comments are collaborations with the book's author and riffs on a few select aphorisms. Unamuno begins the piece by considering one of the most politically charged statements in the collection: "Existir es pensar, y pensar es comprometerse" ("To exist is to think, and to think is to take a side") (*El cohete* 33). Even before Primo sent him to Fuerteventura, these words led Unamuno to remind his readers that thinking often brings harsh consequences. He had experienced these consequences first hand, in the loss of his rectorship in 1914 (which had, in fact, been carried out by Bergamín's father), and in more recent legal battles with censors in Valencia. Unamuno adds to the aphorism with a Calderonian reflection: "Y, a las veces, caer bajo el Código. Porque el delito mayor del hombre es haber pensado" ("And, at times, to be condemned by the law. Because man's greatest crime is to have thought") ("Comentario"). The second aphorism that catches Unamuno's attention is one that he interprets along the lines of his own lifelong struggle with faith. Where Bergamín writes, "tener sed y beber agua es la perfección de la sensualidad, rara vez conseguida. Unas veces se bebe agua y otras veces se tiene sed" ("to be thirsty and drink water is the perfection of sensuality, almost never achieved. At some times one drinks water and at others one is thirsty"), Unamuno adds, "y otras se bebe uno su sed" ("and at others one drinks his thirst"). To drink one's thirst, to subsist on the mere desire for the future alleviation of a present discomfort, is a concise summary of the understanding of faith in the face of doubt that had preoccupied the older writer for decades – the struggle or *agonía* about which he would soon write again in *La agonía del cristianismo*. In the years of separation from Spain that lay before him, exile would add a new experiential dimension to the longing that Unamuno so eloquently described in his response to Bergamín.

The correspondence between these two men includes evidence that Bergamín began to think more concertedly about the social dimensions and ramifications of his intellectual work during Primo de Rivera's dictatorship. In a letter from 30 August 1924, he acknowledges his personal debt to Unamuno, remarking on how having contact with him has revitalized particular areas of his thought and emotional life that he thought he had lost "al salir de la adolescencia" ("upon leaving adolescence") (Dennis, *El epistolario* 44). His relationship with Unamuno has been a source of rejuvenation, and beyond this, he writes that Unamuno has helped him understand "el sentido de lo popular" ("the meaning of the popular"), to recognize the humanity of the Spanish people and not to view them as amorphous masses. For Bergamín, this sense of shared humanity learned from Unamuno casts the falsity, vice ("vicio"), and hypocrisy ("charlatanería") of Primo de Rivera's regime into sharp relief (92). He writes to Unamuno that the current regime is an obstacle to the ideals and desires of young people in Spain, adding that "cuando vayamos a quitarle, se deshará él mismo, ya putrefacto" ("when we go to remove it, it will fall on its own, already rotten")

(92). Using the term that his peers would soon employ as shorthand for the philistine, old culture of the bourgeoisie, Bergamín supports Unamuno's view of the dictatorship as an extension and exacerbation of the decadence of the Restoration.

Giménez Caballero's attitude towards Primo's dictatorship was different from those of Bergamín and Unamuno. The publication and prohibition of *Notas marruecas de un soldado* and Giménez Caballero's subsequent prosecution under the Ley de Jurisdicciones all took place before Primo came to power, and a few days after the coup, the new dictator dropped the charges against him. Giménez Caballero was able to return to Strasbourg, where he had been working as a lecturer in Spanish literature at the university before serving in Morocco. In his correspondence with Unamuno he poked fun at the Spanish military for the inconsistency of this sudden about-face, though he was by no means as critical of Primo as the exiled writer was. On the contrary, with time he found that the dictator's emphasis on Catholic traditionalism and national unity coincided with his own views. Indeed, Primo sympathized with the critique of the Restoration goverment put forth in *Notas marruecas de un soldado*, and especially with the nationalist call for the unification of Spain that emerges in the final pages of the book.[18]

When Giménez Caballero returned to Strasbourg he arrived with a new set of questions about Spain's relationship to Europe and a critical vision newly attuned to the differences between his homeland and its neighbours to the north. In the letter to Unamuno that he wrote upon his arrival in Strasbourg, dated 26 September 1923, he describes the ironic distance with which he now views the entrenched idea that Spaniards needed to turn to Europe to find the secret ingredient for their own country's regeneration – the yeast that could be introduced into Spanish civilization and make it rise. Noting the contrast between his homeland and the carefully ordered and regulated culture of the Alsatian city at the centre of Europe, he writes: "Este orden y este equilibrio siempre serán para nosotros, don Miguel, buenos iberos, queramos o no, una superstición, una ilusión" ("For good Iberians like us, Don Miguel, this order and balance will always, like it or not, be a superstition, an illusion").[19] Perhaps, he suggests, the idea that Spain will find its "fermento," its leavening agent, in Europe is also an illusion. Luckily, he continues, "creo que mi generación representa ya el estadio de sonreirse del 'fermento' sin dejar de rendirle tributo" ("I think that my generation has now reached the point of being able to smile at this 'yeast' while still respecting it"). He then tells Unamuno that he has expressed these thoughts in a second book that he has written but not published, a work he elsewhere calls *El fermento*. In his letter, Giménez Caballero seems to be testing his ideas to see what reception they receive, fully aware that he is criticizing an idea (the importance of Spain's "Europeanization") that previous generations had promoted, and that Unamuno had engaged often, if in a contrarian manner. Indeed, in *El fermento*, now lost, the young writer may have attempted to reconcile the call for openness to the rest of the continent found at the end of a text like *En torno al casticismo* with the critique of the notion of "Europe" Unamuno had expressed in his later essay "Sobre la europeización" ("On Europeanization"), a text that was particularly well received and studied by Italian and Spanish fascists (Borzoni 292–5). When Giménez Caballero mentions later in the letter that his limited library at the University of Strasbourg contains the complete Residencia edition of Unamuno's *Ensayos*, it seems likely that he was consulting these essays as he worked through his predecessor's ideas and formulated his own. Through these readings, the conflation of "Sobre la europeización" and *En torno al casticismo* that would appear in his "Carta a un compañero de la Joven España" in 1929 was likely already coming together.

Behind Giménez Caballero's disillusionment with the idea of Europe, with its order and balance, lies a rejection of the values of rationality and "science" that Spanish intellectuals from the founders of the Institución Libre de Enseñanza to Ortega y Gasset had associated with the more northern parts of the continent. If the conflict in Morocco brought Giménez Caballero into contact with Unamuno, it was the older writer's own critique of these values that held his attention. Unamuno's defence of the irrational appealed to Giménez Caballero politically and aesthetically, as a marker of the difference between Spain and Europe, and as a mode of thought that proffered flexibility in the artistic use of language. His taste for irrationality and experimentation prepared him to meet the poet Guillermo de Torre in 1925 and be swept into the cyclone of the avant-garde – a cyclone that he himself kept in motion in subsequent years.[20] Bergamín also questioned the hegemony of the rational, but did so from a more theological or existential standpoint, taking Unamuno's concept of *agonía* as a model for intellectual engagement with the most enigmatic aspects of human experience. While Bergamín's and Giménez Caballero's first published works were different generically, stylistically, and thematically, each one initiated a reflection by its author on what it meant to be young, politically or aesthetically, in 1920s Spain. As they engaged with Unamuno's ideas on the topic, *Notas marruecas de un soldado* and *El cohete y la estrella* prepared the way for two different visions of youth, respectively: youth as monument and youth as continual subversion.

The Herculean Cult of Youth

In the final pages of the issue of *La Gaceta Literaria* dedicated to the Góngora tercentenary in 1927, Giménez Caballero offered a personal interpretation of the cultural significance of *gongorismo*. His remarks give an indication of his views on the relationship between art and history, and youth as an actor in both, that would become increasingly central to his thought in the following years. "Pespuntes históricos sobre el núcleo gongorino actual" ("Historical Backstitches on Today's Gongorine Group") sketches the history of Spanish literary culture by pointing to a series of past moments taken to represent the motto "cultura contra barbarie" ("culture against barbarism"). Gecé argues that, from the Renaissance to the modern day, passing through the Generation of 1898, the founding of the Junta para Ampliación de Estudios, and José Moreno Villa's *El pasajero*, Spanish intellectuals have prioritized the development of culture, viewing it as a civilizing force to be imported from elsewhere in Europe. The author points out that this emphasis on culture has sponsored the vindication of Góngora in the 1920s and further argues that the purist aesthetic stance assumed by the participants in this project has neutralized it politically and allowed it to thrive in the midst of Primo de Rivera's regime. Dictators, Giménez Caballero quips, respect pure literature.

With this statement, Gecé begins to express his dissent from the Gongorine core. After centuries of obsession with culture, with ostentation, and with the autonomous world of art, he asserts, Spain – particularly young Spain – is ready for a new barbarism: "En ciertos espíritus jóvenes de última hora se inicia un cansancio, una asfixia. Y preparan un esfuerzo para romper la deliciosa cárcel de oro, que impide sentir los lejanos clarines de un alba, de otra barbarie, de otra vez la vida que vuelve, buscando estructuras y postulando formas" ("Some of the most recent young spirits are beginning to show signs of frustration, of suffocation. And they are preparing an effort to break the beautiful gilded cage that keeps one from hearing the far-off bugles of a dawn, of another barbarism, of life returning once more, searching for structures and proposing shapes it might take") ("Pespuntes" 7). The visionary tone of these words, the military imagery of bugles at dawn, the emphasis on rupture with the historical tradition, and the call to break art out of its golden cage are all thoroughly avant-garde traits, as is Giménez Caballero's reference to youth. At the same time, his specification "de última hora" ("most recent") reiterates an idea used by many of the proponents of what he calls "culture" – the concept of a younger youth, the "juventud más joven" sung by Antonio Machado in "Una España joven." The difference between Machado's liberal vision of youth as the emblem of incremental national progress and Giménez Caballero's view is that his youngest youth represents a totalizing conclusion of an old order and the inauguration of a new one. He writes that this new generation lives in an epoch "de final y de crisis" ("of ending and of crisis").

Having announced the emergence of a younger youth, the editor of *La Gaceta Literaria* proceeded in the next years to focus the journal's attention on all things young: the young writers of Spain, their political leanings, their artistic interests, and their relationships to the generations that had gone before them. From the end of 1927 through early 1928 the publication ran instalments of a segment titled "Encuesta a la juventud española" ("Survey of Spanish Youth") that asked a number of the country's burgeoning intellectuals about their view of the proper relationship between literature and politics. Later that year Gecé inaugurated a series titled "Itinerarios jóvenes de España" ("Spain's Young Itineraries"), which set out to showcase Spain's newest artists. It ran from October 1928 to January 1929.[21] In the first instalment, Gecé describes the series as a "mapa juvenil español" ("map of Spanish youth") and as a set of train tracks ("rieles"). His wish is that these articles will provide orientation for the critic and reader who (he remarks somewhat condescendingly) does not possess "puntos de latitud y longitud para las situaciones aurorales" ("points of latitude and longitude for situations that are just dawning") ("Itinerarios" 7). Clearly, what Santiáñez has called Giménez Caballero's "cartographic gaze" is at work here. As he likens the series to a map complete with routes already marked out on it, he seeks to exert control over the public's understanding of the most recent developments in Spanish art.

In 1929, *La Gaceta Literaria* filled out its map of the contemporary literary and artistic scene by placing Spain's young writers in relationship to their older predecessors, much as Gecé had in his *cartel* "Universo de la literatura española contemporánea" ("Universe of Contemporary Spanish Literature"). A survey that asked the older generation "¿Cómo ven la nueva juventud española?" ("How Do You View the New Spanish Youth?") gathered responses from established intellectuals including Eugenio D'Ors, Andrenio (Eduardo Gómez de Baquero), Manuel García Morente, Gregorio Marañón, Manuel de Falla, Nicolás María de Urgoiti, and Antonio Machado. (As noted in the last chapter, Unamuno's exile and refusal to publish work in Primo's Spain kept him from contributing to *La Gaceta Literaria*.) Their commentary on the young writers ranges from indifference (Marañón) to enthusiasm (Falla), to the attitude of reserved support offered by Machado. This poet, while viewing the youth of the day as well-intentioned, nevertheless urges the younger writers to take more interest in the concerns and needs of the Spanish people. Perhaps because he was critical of the distance between purist art and social life that had prevailed in Spanish letters during the decade, Machado was willing to affirm the militancy with which Gecé pursued the question of art's relationship to politics. He closes his remarks with this salutation: "A usted, amigo Caballero, gran estandarte, cartelista y jaleador de un *ejército de jóvenes*, mi saludo militar y un cordial apretón de maños" ("To you, my friend Caballero, a great standard bearer, poster artist, and stimulator of an *army of young people*, my military salute and a heartfelt handshake") ("¿Cómo ven," my emphasis). Machado's words, published on the first day of March, reinforced the image of Gecé that the writer himself had put forth in the previous issue of *La Gaceta Literaria*, with his "Carta a un compañero de la Joven España."

In the months leading up to Gecé's confession of fascist faith in his "Carta" – a confirmation of the conversion experience he had undergone in Rome – he wrote and published *Hércules jugando a los dados*. Appearing after others of his avant-garde works like *Yo, inspector de alcantarillas* and *Los toros, las castañuelas y la Virgen*, this book represents the culmination of the writer's efforts to map or spatialize youth. Through a series of reflections on various aspects of contemporary youth culture that focus especially on sport and games though also touch on cinema, he converts the idea of youth into the cornerstone of a fascist understanding of modernity, presenting it as the defining quality of a new hegemonic elite. In this text, the utopia that youth represented for modernists like José Moreno Villa, who consistently understood it as conditioned by its impermanance, is converted into the basis of an ideological project. Adolescence, once idealized for its changefulness and flexibility, becomes a static icon, the totalizing emblem of several values glorified in connection with youth since the period of the First World

War – masculinity, heroism, military discipline, and strength. Also present is the idea of a new aristocracy that had been promoted by Ortega y Gasset and at the Residencia de Estudiantes. While Gecé adds to this list of traits a Futurist's love of speed and cutting-edge, fast-moving technology, the vision that he in reality puts forth in *Hércules jugando a los dados* is one of stasis. After hammering a series of markers or signposts into what might be called, following Santiáñez, his "topography of youth," the author proceeds to draw arbitrary associations among them, connecting them like a spider weaving a web.

In this process of mapping and construction, Gecé draws not only on the novelties of the contemporary age (soccer, airplanes, racecars) but also on the mythical past and a category that he refers to as the "primitive." He argues that there is a deep connection between customs of ancient civilizations and the "magic" of modern pastimes and technologies. As Robert Davidson has pointed out, behind this new enchantment of modernity lies a reactionary sociopolitical agenda. Gecé's emphasis on the contemporary age's "vuelta al totemismo" ("return to totemism") amounts to an effort to incorporate the working class – particularly Spain's still large agrarian population – into a fascist social order. According to Davidson, *Hércules jugando a los dados* anticipates its author's later, more explicitly ideological work as it promotes a form of class reconciliation in which traditional popular culture is assigned a position at the base of a vertical, totalitarian social framework. This structure is topped by the figure of Hercules, a symbol of strength, vitality, and youth. When Gecé describes Hercules as a "castizo campesino" ("pure-blooded peasant") (89) and "héroe de vaqueros y segadores" ("hero of cattle hearders and reapers") (90), his populist rhetoric marshalls Unamunian *intrahistoria* in support of his totemic vision. This invocation of peasants and rural workers as the foundation of a regenerated Spain also foreshadows Gecé's rhetoric in the "Carta a un compañero," where the writer's argument for a fascist rejuvenation of Spain takes *En torno al casticismo* as its urtext.

In the opening chapter of *Hércules jugando a los dados*, Giménez Caballero presents contemporary youth – made up of the followers of Hercules – much in the way it had been depicted in Spain in the 1910s, with the turn to classical culture that coincided with the military conflict of the First World War. He asserts that this youth has nothing to do with the values of the nineteenth century, represented by Anatole France, whom he calls a "viejo cristiano tumefacto" ("old overstuffed

Christian") (*Hércules* 5). Hercules, an incarnation of Nietzsche's *Übermensch*, leads a new generation of powerful young men whose bodies recall the athletes of ancient Greece most especially in their nakedness: Herculean youth is a "juventud gimnosdérmica," a youth of bared skin (5). Like the ephebe that the Residencia de Estudiantes had made its emblem, the young body that Gecé imagines represents the action, movement, and power of humanity at its raw physical prime, suggesting that it will serve as the engine for society's future progress. Later in the book, however, the nudity of the strong young body is subtly replaced with the armor of modern technology. In chapter four, "Los cascos mágicos" ("The Magic Helmets"), Gecé declares that the icon of modernity is now not the naked adolescent, but a hybrid of human and machine, a man encased in and fused with a protective shell. He focuses particularly on four kinds of headgear that exemplify modern man's ability to defeat the dangers of the classical elements, water, air, earth, and fire. The diving bell represents the triumph over water, while the aviator's cap and goggles signal the conquering of the air. The racecar driver's helmet allows him to overpower the earth in his car, and the helmet of the soldier – specifically, a soldier of the First World War, fighting in the Battle of Ypres – defies the power of fire. As Davidson has observed, the wearers of these different helmets become superhuman cyborgs and the objects of a new spiritual fervor; according to Gecé, they represent society's return to a totemic structure, serving as its objects of superstitious adoration. Thus the appeal of youth no longer stems from mere muscular agility, but also, and more, from the modern accoutrements provided by technology. As Gecé elevates the de-humanization of modern sport, youth must become less a stage in human development than a symbol, a talisman cut off from temporality, and from history, as its meaning is now tied to innovations that belong wholly to the present. Over the course of this chapter, the symbolism of youth changes in character, from temporal to material. The beauty, strength, and flexibility evoked by a statue of a Greek ephebe cede in importance before the hard materiality of the stone from which it is made.

When Gecé declares at the end of "Los cascos mágicos" that the human head has become "un conglomerado de cuero, duraluminio y mica" ("a conglomerate of leather, aluminum alloy, and mica") (33), his imagery of immobilization echoes the Unamuno of *En torno al casticismo* and "La ideocracia." Of course, in those essays the older writer was denouncing, not celebrating, the formation of shells and hardened exteriors, for he saw them as signs of the decay and senility of Spanish society. In *Hércules jugando a los dados*, Gecé takes the concept that Unamuno had seen as the antidote to this process of solidification – youth – and makes it the cornerstone of a new *ideocracia*. This is also a form of decay: the decay of a notion of youth as a decisive period in a time-bound process of development. When transferred from the temporal to the spatial, youth loses its critical ability to oppose the *télos* of development and the authority of the adult. The biological metaphor upon which the modernist discourse of youth is based is hollowed out and becomes an empty signifier: it may mean whatever an author wants it to mean.

Giménez Caballero's depiction of Herculean youth enacts this subtle transformation, as it puts forth a glorification of speed that congeals all movement and promotes the aestheticization of public life that Hewitt characterizes as fascist modernism's ultimate realization of decadence. The transformation of the athlete's naked body into an armored cyborg is one example of this process. Another appears in the chapter "Las sirenas" ("Sirens"), where Gecé contrasts his totemic vision with the social order of nineteenth-century liberalism. At the end of the preceding chapter, he encourages the "espíritu joven" of the early twentieth century to reject "la moral acartonada de los viejos Estados" ("the withered morality of the old States") (66). Then in "Las sirenas" he explains his rejection of this old order by way of an extended comparison between the sirens of classical mythology and modern industry. Basing his account primarily on the story of Orpheus and the sirens in Apollonius' *Argonautica*, he likens the sounds of the factories that proliferated in nineteenth-century Europe to the mythical creatures' song, equating capitalist production with a numbing, controlling, hypnotic music. According to Gecé, the sexual appeal and sweetness that Homer associated with the sirens was imprecise; in reality, they had always simply been emitters of an inexorable, authoritarian voice, the song of "el látigo del Cómitre" ("the whip of the Overseer") or the "silbato irrebatible del Capataz" ("irrefutable whistle of the Foreman") that sought to drive humanity to a tragic fate (71). In Gecé's analysis, it was communism that first provided a means of drowning out the sound of capitalism's sirens. He writes that Russia discovered the "orphic" solution of singing a louder and more beautiful song to drown out the sirens of the factories. He does not analyse communism's reordering of socio-economic relations, preferring to describe the political alternative that it offered in the purely aesthetic terms of the classical analogy, as "la armonía de las estridencias" ("the harmony of stridencies") and "la disciplina melódica de las furias" ("the melodic discipline of the Furies") (71). Somehow this merely acoustic tactic magically vanquishes the sirens, transforming the curse ("imprecación") of dismal labour that they represent into symphonic rejoicing ("gozo y sinfonía") (72). As it turns out, the interruption of their soporific song is simply the imposition of another music. "Las sirenas" thus reads like a perfect illustration of the Benjaminian account of the aestheticization of politics, as the "orphic" song of totalitarianism presents the masses with a means of expressing themselves while stopping short of changing any material relations. Indeed, the song functions like the helmets Gecé describes earlier in *Hércules*: as an attractive veneer that at once covers and immobilizes social life, sublimating class difference as order and harmony.

In the closing pages of the book, Gecé argues that the aestheticization of political life he describes in "Las sirenas" will inspire and attract the attention of young people. He heralds the "renacimieto de las tiranías" ("renaissance of the tyrannies") as a poetic phenomenon (93), and uses the elliptical, associative language that characterizes his writing throughout *Hércules* to support this view. The language of age and youth re-emerges forcefully:

> Por ser interpretado – ¡ah, viejos gerontes! – , hasta ahora, como exclusivo fenómeno político – mucha juventud se ha sentido ajena e indiferente. (Sobre todo, en lugares donde ha venido siendo – de hecho – una gerontarquía, un anticesarismo. Y se ha confundido el militarismo y la burocracia – es decir: lo siglo XIX – con el militantismo y la Aventura: es decir, lo siglo XX.)
>
> Pero ya es momento de desgarrar la magnífica entraña de las tiranías hasta su mismo fondo. Hasta su poema.
>
> Las tiranías no habrían podido nacer – renacer – si el mundo no hubiese tornado a una infancia casi selvática. (93)
>
> (Because until now it has been interpreted – oh, old geronts! – as an exclusively political phenomenon – many young people have felt distanced and indifferent. [Above all, in places where it has become – in fact – a gerontarchy, an anticeasarism. And militarism and bureaucracy – that is to say: the things of the nineteenth century – have been confused with militantism and Adventure: that is, the things of the twentieth century.]
>
> But now is the time to rip the magnificent guts of the tyrannies open, down to their base. To their poem.

These tyrannies would not have been born – reborn – if the world had not returned to an almost jungle-like childhood.)

Though the return to a forest- or jungle-like state mentioned here recalls Moreno Villa's conception of adolescence, the childhood Gecé has in mind is one of uncritical amazement, an innocence that submits easily to the enchantment and spectacle of power. The writer himself relies on this innocence in his reader as he stuns him or her with a barrage of forced linguistic links. The equation of *gerontarquía* with *anticesarismo* and the hair-splitting distinction between *militarismo* and *militantismo* advance the writer's argument more by linguistics than by logic. As Anderson points out, in *Hércules jugando a los dados* Gecé relies on a Surrealist treatment of metaphor in order to create "a sleek, self-confident, and often fast-moving package that discourages careful and pondered critical scrutiny" (*Ernesto Giménez* 160). In doing so, he establishes and solidifies an unexpected connection between youth and authoritarianism, insisting that monarchy is the only possible form of government for the kind of populace that he describes as a "juventud humana" (*Hércules* 94).

While fast-paced, however, this language is also immobilizing. Gecé's text seems to screech to a halt as the book comes to its end. Composed of sentence fragments that lack action verbs and clear antecedents, it layers images and associations on top of one another as if they were bricks. Chronological markers seem to be set up, but this only serves to confuse all sense of temporal progression. Rather than calling for and describing action, the discourse builds a rhetorical container for action left unspecified:

> En las avanzadas de la novísima humanidad, que ya no entiende de burgueses ni de proletarios, sino de regidores y regidos, de proas y masas.
> Antes de que esta humanidad torne a hacerse vieja.
> Torne a la gerontocracia.
> Torne a los sistemas mecánicos y antiheroicos.
> Torne al terror del individuo – o de la minoría de individuos – en absoluta libertad. Antes de que esta joven y atlética humanidad se adulte y adultere. (95)

> (On the avant-garde of the newest humanity, which no longer thinks in terms of bourgeois and proletarians, but of rulers and ruled, of figureheads and masses.

Before this humanity becomes old again.
Returns to gerontocracy.
Returns to mechanical and antiheroic systems.
Returns to the terror of the individual – or the minority of individuals – in absolute liberty. Before this young and athletic humanity becomes adult and adulterates itself.)

A superlatively new avant-garde that "no longer" thinks in the terms of the "old" liberal world is also somehow anterior to that world, for it anticipates a return to these old ways. In this chronological limbo, Gecé seems to advocate for the freezing of time, the preservation of the youthful moment of the present in the idyllic garden or Never-Land that totalitarianism guarantees. Like many of his contemporaries in Spain and Europe, this author rejects the pull towards adulthood, equating it with the corruption or decadence of youthful ideals. But at the same time, he seeks to monumentalize the present youth, defining it and fixing it in place within his conceptual landscape. The series of nouns with which the book ends reads like a succession of nails driven into this figure, holding it to a single set of ideological coordinates. The triad of "Lo antijoven. Lo antidivino. Lo antiheraclida" ("The antiyoung. The antidivine. The antiherculean") is set in opposition to all that Hercules may symbolize: "¡Hércules! Jugando a los dados. Juego y Fuerza. Suntuosidad vital. (Dominio.) Serendidad. / Cinema. Realeza natural. Atletismo. Cornete de dados" (Hercules! Playing dice. Play and Strength. Opulent vitality. [Dominion.] Serenity. / Film. Natural Royalty. Athleticism: Dice cup") (95). As Giménez Caballero constructs an immobile rhetorical structure and labels it "youth," he betrays a characteristic that many of his contemporaries, Unamuno especially, considered central to this concept: constant changefulness or protean plasticity. His references to speed, agility, and generation are all in service of rigid order and ideological stasis.

This betrayal of an Unamunian understanding of youth continues in Gecé's "Carta a un compañero," where he casts *En torno al casticismo* as a proto-fascist text. Largely ignoring the critique of nationalism that runs throughout the 1895 work, Gecé redirects its invocation of "jóvenes ideales cosmopolitas" towards a youth that will build Spain up in opposition to Europe. Clearly framed as "a fascist call to youth" (Areilza 38), the "Carta a un compañero" builds directly on the rhetoric of *Hércules jugando a los dados*. It opens with a quotation from a letter that Gecé says he has received from a young man. Suspiciously similar to Gecé himself (the phrase "como yo" ["like me"] echoes as a refrain throughout the first paragraphs), the author of the letter has been inspired and energized by reading about Italian fascism, and he writes to ask the editor of *La Gaceta Literaria* if this political movement can be brought to Spain. These words provide Giménez Caballero with the perfect prologue to the announcement of the publication of his *En torno al casticismo de Italia*, a selection and translation of writings by Curzio Malaparte. Framing his book as just what the young generation is looking for, he rushes to explain that he has undertaken this project precisely because he sees similarities between Malaparte's critique of "Europe" and an element in Spanish culture that he traces to Unamuno. Declaring, "ya vio este fascismo Unamuno" ("Unamuno already perceived this fascism"), he cites two passages from the second chapter of *En torno al casticismo* that describe the historic unification of the Iberian Peninsula. In one of them, Unamuno employs the word "haz" ("sheaf" or "bundle," the Spanish equivalent of the Italian *fascio*) as he describes the convergence of the Iberian kingdoms. Lifted from their original context, the quotations appear to support Giménez Caballero's ultranationalist argument perfectly. What remains unacknowledged, however, is that in this section of *En torno al casticismo* Unamuno describes the process of national unification as the loss of Spain's youth, and the inauguration of several centuries of aging, decay, and general malaise (*E* 1:67).

Giménez Caballero attempts to discover in Unamuno's 1895 text an anti-European sentiment that the writer, in reality, did not adopt until years after writing *En torno al casticismo* (Selva 120). Gecé fails to perceive the critiques of Spanish nationalism that are present in a work written while Unamuno was still a member of the Socialist party. Or perhaps he does perceive them, and chooses to interpret them as irresolution. At one point he declares, "el mérito de Malaparte en Italia ha consistido en señalar, sin vacilaciones, una vía de conducta que en España ya había señalado Unamuno, con vacilación" ("Malaparte's achievement in Italy has been to point out, without vacillation, a path of conduct that Unamuno had already pointed out, with vacillation") (Giménez Caballero, "Carta" 5). This comment highlights the interpretive violence that Gecé must carry out in order to make the nuanced text of *En torno al casticismo* fit into his fascist vision. Unamuno's original search for Spain's "tradición eterna" had implied a questioning of the old concept of *casticismo*, a revision of the values that had characterized Spain for four centuries and brought it to its modern senility. In

"Carta a un compañero," Giménez Caballero also calls for a break with the country's past and a return to new youth; yet the past that he views as worn out and corrupt is one he also views as "irresoluta" ("indecisive"). The youth he champions aligns itself once again with the political and religious ideology based on the union of Church and State that Unamuno condemned as "la vieja fórmula unitaria castellana" ("the old Castilian unitarian formula") (*E* 6:151). In the closing paragraphs of his piece, Giménez Caballero seems to echo the last lines of *En torno al casticismo*, as he calls out to "los jóvenes espíritus de nuestro país para preparar el resurgimiento hispánico" ("the young spirits of our country to prepare the Hispanic resurgence") (5). Yet a notable difference presents itself: while the Unamuno of 1895 claimed that the only possible regeneration would come through openness to European influences ("europeizándonos para hacer España") and spoke of ideal youth as cosmopolitan, Gecé imagines a youth that will build an "España contra Europa" ("Carta" 1).

The printing of the "Carta a un compañero" marked the beginning of the decline of *La Gaceta Literaria*. After this article appeared, Gecé's political and ideological allegiances caused many contributors to cut ties with the publication. Antonio Espina, for example, retracted his long-time support immediately after the appearance of the "Carta." Gecé was eventually left to write the last six issues of the publication entirely by himself, giving it the histrionic new title *El Robinson literario de España* (*Spain's Literary Robinson Crusoe*). This sense of isolation and abandonment carries over into later works, particularly his 1932 book *Genio de España. Exaltaciones a una resurrección nacional. Y del mundo* (*Genius of Spain. Exaltations towards a Resurrection of the Nation. And the World*). In *Genio de España*, Giménez Caballero proclaims himself to be a new prophet for Spain and the only true inheritor of a tradition founded in 1898. In the first part of the book, "Los nietos del 98 (Notas a Unamuno)," he identifies his own generation as the grandchildren of "98." Still, he insists that he is the only member of the generation willing to accept this heritage: "Me consta que a muy pocos, por no decir ninguno, de esos 'nietos automáticos del 98' les interesa asumir tal nietez. (Ninguno, excepto yo)" ("It seems that very few, perhaps none, of these 'automatic grandsons of 98' are interested in taking on the role of grandchild. [None, except me]) (*Genio* 17).

Much like Gerardo Diego in his compilation of a poetic lineage in *Poesía española*, Giménez Caballero strove to establish a genealogy that linked him to Unamuno, and he is among those of the younger generation who most called attention to the *maestro*'s legacy. In 1930, when the older writer returned from exile, Gecé was quick to organize the honorary issue of *La Gaceta Literaria*, which he described in its pages as a congregation of almost all of the Spanish literary world, both those of the older generation and the young ("Colofón" 20). While with that honorary issue he sought to gather a range of comments on an important political moment and a significant public figure, Gecé also appropriated Unamuno's ideas for his own ends. While Diego presents himself as Don Miguel's advocate in his critical writing about the older writer, Giménez Caballero expresses a mixture of excitement about Unamuno and frustration with the ambiguities of his thought. In "Carta a un compañero" and in *Genio de España*, he adapts the older writer's early ideas to his own ultranationalist agenda with intellectual violence, and in the end comes close to declaring himself more Unamunian than Unamuno. Perhaps this is why he begrudges José Bergamín's closeness to the *maestro* in one passage from the beginning of *Genio de España*: "Aun recuerdo el primer artículo de José Bergamín publicado en la 'Gaceta Literaria' … titulado 'La literatura difunta', que empezaba así: 'Dijo 'noventa y ocho', y al decirlo, su voz doblaba a muerto, lánguidamente, como una campana.' (¡Y Bergamín era de los que iban más a comer y jugar a casa del 'abuelito'!)" ("I still remember the first article that José Bergamín published in the 'Gaceta Literaria' … titled 'Deceased Literature,' which began like this: 'He said 'ninety-eight,' and in saying it, his voice rang out dead, languidly, like a bell.' [And Bergamín was among those who went most often to eat and play at 'grandfather's' house!"]) (17).

Hermes between History and Eternity

As Giménez Caballero's words suggest, of all the young writers of the 1920s Bergamín is the most recognized as a disciple of Unamuno. Citations of and references to his predecessor's work run throughout his writing. For example, Bergamín's second book of aphorisms, *La cabeza a pájaros* (*Head in the Clouds*, 1934), bears a dedication to Unamuno that describes him as a "místico sembrador de vientos espirituales" ("mystical sower of spiritual winds"). The correspondence these two writers maintained between 1923 and 1936 documents an intellectual exchange that continued to develop throughout the years in which *la joven literatura* was coming to prominence within Spain, an exchange that shaped the younger writer's approach to the art of his peers and his theory of art in general. The information it provides is partial, to be sure – not only because many of Bergamín's papers were lost when his apartment was ransacked after he left Spain at the end of the Civil War, but also because the visits he paid to the exiled Unamuno in Hendaye have left no written record, and because in the 1920s the extremely active Bergamín planned out many projects that never came to full fruition. Nevertheless, the letters offer a number of indications about how Bergamín read Unamuno, and how his spirit was "sown" with insights gleaned from his predecessor.

A recurring theme in the letters is the relationship between history and eternity, which emerges as a question of particular importance for Bergamín's evolving thoughts on artistic creation and on political action. This interest appears very early on in the correspondence. In the letter Bergamín wrote to thank Unamuno for committing to review *El cohete y la estrella*, dated 18 February 1924, he also commented on an article that the elder writer had just published – one whose argument spoke to the contrast between the ephemeral rocket and the everlasting star that Bergamín had set up in his first book. In the article, "El tiempo material" ("Material Time"), Unamuno had written,

> Hay un modo de sentir la historia, y de hacerla, desde la eternidad. Que no es precisamente desde el porvenir y mirando al porvenir, no. Un político de eternidad no mira al porvenir, sino a la eternidad; no le importa tanto el resultado futuro de un acto cuanto su valor absoluto, material, ahora. Y a este valor absoluto, material, de instante eterno, de eternidad instantánea y pasajera, le llamamos Justicia. ("El tiempo" 2)

> (There is a way of feeling history, and of making it, from eternity. Which is not exactly from the future and looking to the future, no. A politician of eternity does not look to the future, but rather to eternity; he does not care so much about the future result of an act as about its absolute, material value now. And this absolute, material value, that of an eternal instant, of instantaneous and passing eternity, is what we call Justice.)

Eternity is imagined as a vantage point, a place from which to view and read the present. The theological dimension in this view of time as subject to an eternal gaze recalls Bergamín's *estrella*, but here Unamuno suggests that it is possible to take on that perspective for oneself as one acts in history, and to be guided by a transcendent sense of justice not unlike the one Díaz Fernández would invoke a few years later in

El nuevo romanticismo. While bringing justice "down to earth," however, such a vision also creates a painful distance between the self and the historical moment in which one lives. This is the lesson that Bergamín seems to have gleaned from the exiled Unamuno in a letter from April 1926, where he writes, "desde que leí – le leí – en 'La agonía del cristianismo' me parece entender mejor – entenderle o entenderme mejor – en esta tendencia que me separa, dolorosamente, del escenario histórico" ("ever since I read – and read you in – 'The Agony of Christianity' I seem to understand better – to understand you or understand myself better – in this inclination that distances me, painfully, from the historical arena") (*El epistolario* 68). For Bergamín, as for his predecessor, spiritual matters are at odds or in tension with the temporal-spatial setting of current events and politics. This need not imply, however, that these matters and the artistic work that they inspire have no bearing on history. The separation from contemporary events that Bergamín feels so keenly simply allows him to view these events through a different lens. When he founded *Cruz y Raya* later on, Bergamín endeavoured to make the journal reflect just this kind of eternal perspective on the contemporary moment, particularly in the section of the publication that he titled "Cristal del tiempo" ("Lens of Time").

The fact that Bergamín wrote to Unamuno about this separation from history already in 1926, one year before he would be centrally involved in the historical and poetic affair of the Góngora tercentenary, suggests that Unamuno's historical vision was present not only in Bergamín's philosophical or religious thought at this time, but also in the theory of contemporary art that he soon began to develop. According to the account Unamuno gives in *La agonía del cristianismo*, passion and reason contend with one another within the life of Christian faith, and Bergamín came to define art in a similar fashion, as an endeavour in which inspiration and intellect exist in perpetual, productive strife. This idea is central to his argument in "El pensamiento hermético de las artes." Though this essay appeared in print in the inaugural issue of *Cruz y Raya* in 1933, Bergamín first delivered it as a lecture at Madrid's Museo de Arte Contemporáneo in the fall of 1927, in the midst of the Góngora tercentenary. From its opening paragraphs, the essay identifies the spirit of the new art celebrated in that year with the "pensamiento poéticamente puro o recién nacido inmortal a que los griegos llamaron Hermes" ("poetically pure or newborn, immortal thought that the Greeks called Hermes") (Bergamín, "El pensamiento" 45). In this description, the word "Hermes" names a category of thought that can also be described as poetic and immortal – a kind of thought bound neither by strict logic nor by time. Here Bergamín draws on Greek mythology in order to flesh out an understanding of his contemporary, modern culture, much as Giménez Caballero would in *Hércules*. Unlike Gecé, however, Bergamín restrains his analysis to the realm of art, focusing especially on the literary production of his own peers. Taking advantage of the association with obscurity and difficulty implied in the term "hermetic," Bergamín fashions his Hermes as a representative of creative struggle: between reason and imagination, and also between the present and the eternal. As a diety that moves freely between the spheres of the mortal and the divine, Hermes is a symbol of continual rebirth, ever-renewed youth. In this, Bergamín's version of the divinity differs significantly from the Hermes that Antonio Obregón would create in 1934: rather than the intensely present-focused incarnation of modern youth culture in *Hermes en la vía pública*, Bergamín's Hermes stands as a symbol of art's ability to transcend the present by way of the present – to make youth open up on eternity.

The emphasis on poetic purity that appears in Bergamín's definition of Hermetic thought reflects the inclinations of the decade – particularly the influence of Juan Ramón Jiménez, a great mentor to Bergamín during the first years of the 1920s and an advocate for the stripping-down of poetry, the removal of the excessive ornamentation especially associated with *modernismo* in Spain. The conscious distancing from Decadent aesthetic practice in Spanish poets following Jiménez leads Bergamín, in the first pages of the essay, to a rejection of aestheticism that contrasts sharply with Giménez Caballero's exaltation of "orphic music" in *Hércules jugando a los dados*. In fact, Bergamín also makes reference to Orpheus, casting this deity as the foil to Hermes. He writes that the difference between these two figures is that between "el que vuelve del infierno huyendo de una sombra" ("he who returns from hell fleeing a ghost") and "el que nos guía para ir a él, laberínticamente, buscando una sombra perdida" ("he who guides us so that we can go there, in a labrynthine manner, searching for a ghost we have lost") (44). Orpheus' unsuccessful descent to the underworld represents subliminal, irrational impulses that lack the analytical rigor, precision, and depth of Hermetic art. Here and throughout the essay, the author has little patience for the aestheticism that Giménez Caballero sees as Orpheus' appeal; for Bergamín, the value of artistic creation lies in its intellectual dimension, its sophisticated effort to penetrate the enigmas of human experience by means of the productive strife of reason and imagination.

The central enigma in the artistic endeavour as Bergamín depicts it in this essay is, once again, the question of the relationship between the temporal and the eternal, between time-bound, physical nature and transcendent, elusive spirit. The essayist posits that an ideal kind of knowledge would be simultaneously "natural" and "spiritual," a synthesis of temporal and eternal perspectives that seems to have been possible only in a much earlier, antediluvian age. Here he confronts the problem of the aging of history. Bergamín writes that the "new" arts of his day find themselves, chronologically speaking, in "el momento más viejo del mundo, que es el nuestro, el que ahora vivimos" ("the world's oldest time, which is our own, the one we live in now") (44). It seems that modernity may be too old to remember an epistemological condition that combined the natural and spiritual, temporal and eternal forms of reason. Such a reflection on history stands out especially in the printed version of the essay in *Cruz y Raya*, where it appeared directly after an essay on Hegel by the philosopher Xavier Zubiri. Zubiri described the German thinker as encapsulating the "madurez intelectual" ("intellectual maturity") of Europe and insisted that all contemporary philosophy must begin as a conversation with Hegel (Zubiri 13–14). In "El pensamiento hermético de las artes" Bergamín, like Kierkegaard, Nietzsche, or Unamuno before him, carries out an implicit dialogue with Hegel as he questions the desirability of modernity's maturity. If the modern age is defined, according to Hegel, by the progressive prosification of understanding, the triumph and full revelation of systematic reason, Bergamín defends the notion of a poetic form of reason, one that exists – and has always existed, and will continue to exist – in the realm of art. The arts of the early twentieth century, then, as they combine their temporal, historical position and their "hermetic" capacity for continual rebirth, are paradoxically both old and young, oscillating between the age of history and the infancy rediscovered in artistic creation. In this way, they occupy a state of perpetual adolescence.

Notably, however, Bergamín does not use the term adolescence in this essay. In fact, the only time he uses even the word "joven" is to object to its use by other critics, who, he argues, commit the fallacy of analysing art according to a criterion that he calls alternatively "historicista" and "vitalista." Like his contemporaries the Russian Formalists, Bergamín critiques an approach to art that bases its interpretation on the life of its author or the historical moment in which it was created. In his view, the critical effort to anchor art within history has the effect of limiting it to its temporal dimension and saddling it with the mortality of the human beings who have created it. The historicist approach, he asserts, "opera siempre sobre cadáveres" ("always operates on cadavers") (46). Its imposition of a historical framework reifies art, locking its interpretation within one particular meaning that resists movement and change. For this reason, the trend of referring to works of art in terms of youth and age, so prevalent in the critical discourse of the 1920s, is misleading and in fact detrimental to criticism:

> Cuando se habla de arte nuevo o antiguo, reaccionario o de vanguardia, se afirma, aunque se ignore, tácitamente, su determinación vital histórica: y a un criterio de valoración racional, el único posible, se sustituye un pretendido criterio de valoración histórico, vitalista o imposible. Así, se dice, por ejemplo: esto es joven o viejo, esto es trasnochado o moderno. (46–7)

> (When one speaks of art as new or old, reactionary or avant-garde, one tacitly, even if unconsciously, affirms its vital determination within history: and the only valid criterion, one of rational evaluation, is exchanged for a supposed criterion of evaluation that is historical, vitalist, and impossible. In this way one says, for example: this is young or old, this is outdated or modern.)

In Bergamín's view, the error of the avant-garde is its whole-hearted embrace of this "vitalist" perspective on art, its eager declaration of historical novelty or youth. Again his understanding of aesthetics diverges from that of Gecé: while the burgeoning fascist writer is drawn to the avant-garde primarily *because of* its rhetoric of rupture and youth, Bergamín shows deep scepticism towards this language.

This allergy to the terminology of the avant-garde appeared later in Bergamín's 1929 article "Literatura y brújula" ("Literature and Compass"), a piece dedicated to the poetry of Pedro Salinas that begins with a general reflection on the phenomenon of *la joven literatura,* tracing its origins to the 1924 issue of *Intentions* and offering an extensive roster of its members (which in fact includes Giménez Caballero). In this article, Bergamín acknowledges that the group is commonly referred to as "*joven* o *nueva literatura,*" but also, "más confusamente (y bastante estúpidamente)" ("more confusingly [and quite stupidly]") as "*vanguardismo*" (original emphasis). A few paragraphs later he characterizes the Spanish *ultraístas* as "pueriles 'boy-scoots' [*sic*] literarios" ("puerile literary boy scouts"), playing on the link between militarism and the avant-garde in order to suggest that its tactics are unthinking, unoriginal, and childish. Given this view of self-proclaimed avant-garde movements and their "historicist" understanding of art, it is not too difficult to understand why Bergamín would have referred to the Generation of 1898 as "literatura difunta" in the article that Giménez Caballero cites in *Genio de España*. After all, what could be more historicist than to name a group of writers for a given year?

Bergamín's instinctive rejection of developmental language applied to art reacts to and illuminates the contradictory nature of fascist modernism, whose vitalist rhetoric works like a mask to disguise a fundamentally decadent vision of a world and a politics subjugated to (and by) aesthetics. In a sense, of course, decadence and vitalism are one and the same thing, for the human body from which they draw their metaphorical meaning is irremediably mortal. In Bergamín's view, however, poetry is something different: an inspired and intellectual construction that defies the passage of time. In this it resembles architecture and mathematics – like a building, it is inorganic; like mathematics, it is abstract, set apart from historical events. But Bergamín does not take this resemblance to mean that poetic art lends itself to static or unchanging thought. The poetic artefact serves as a solid structure that challenges and encourages cognitive activity, like an obstacle course. In his words, "la obra poética, *artefacto* imaginativo, es una cerradura que pone la razón al pensamiento: y el pensamiento escapa, divinamente, como Hermes, por el ojo de la llave de la cerradura que quería impedirlo" ("the poetic work, imaginative *artifact*, is a lock that reason puts on thought: and thought escapes, divinely, like Hermes, through the keyhole in the lock that attempted to impede it") (65, original emphasis). Unlike Giménez Caballero's Herculean aesthetic, whose frantically spun associative web ultimately paralyses critical analysis, Bergamín's Hermetic thought defies the limitations placed on it even by reason. Or better, it uses reason to catapult itself beyond its immediate historical moment. As Gonzalo Penalva has put it, for Bergamín the purpose of art is to eternalize the present, to extract that moment from history and "win it" for eternity ("El clavo" 73).

The year that followed the first delivery of "El pensamiento hermético de las artes" was one of especially rich critical activity for Bergamín. At the end of 1927 he participated in the final celebrations of the Góngora tercentenary in Seville, giving a second important lecture on contemporary poetics, "Notas para unos prolegómenos a toda poética del porvenir que se presente como arte" ("Notes for an Introduction to Any Future Poetics that Presents Itself as Art"). His theory of hermetic art continued to infuse his creative and critical writing, appearing in the series of aphorisms he published in January 1928 in *Carmen* under the title "Carmen: Enigma y soledad." Among these aphorisms he included a reiteration and condensation of his theory of "Hermetic" art: "La poesía es hermética, como el dios griego: recién nacida inmortal" ("Poetry is hermetic, like the Greek god: an immortal newborn"). Working with this conceptualization of poetry, he also made plans to write about the work of several of his Spanish contemporaries – not only the young writers who were his peers, but also his *maestro*, Unamuno. Bergamín in fact considered Unamuno's work to be representative of what he had come to call Hermetic art, as he indicates in a letter from March of 1928 where he describes a poem the older writer had sent him as "puro y nuevo, novísimo, como acabado de nacer" ("pure and new, very new, as if it had just been born") (Dennis, *El epistolario* 75). Later in the letter he tells the exiled Unamuno that he wants to speak with him about "un propósito que tengo hace tiempo de hacer un libro antología de Ud. Y una biografía y crítica fervorosa" ("an idea I have had for a while to prepare an anthology of your work. And a biography and fervent critical analysis") (85). Notably, even as he began to imagine this book about Unamuno and his work, Bergamín was also planning to compose a series of essays to be titled *Límites de una nueva literatura* (*The Scope of a New Literature*), conceived as an introduction of sorts to the work of his young peers.

Bergamín details his ideas for this latter collection in a series of letters to the bookseller León Sánchez Cuesta sent in September 1928.[22] Apart from the interest these letters hold as blueprints for a critical project that would have provided a singular contemporary vision of the writers of *la joven literatura* (had it come to fruition), they are valuable for the wider picture that they provide of Bergamín's thought and activities during these months. They were written, in fact, upon Bergamín's return from the newly formed U.S.S.R., which he visited as part of the honeymoon trip he took with his new wife, Rosario Arniches (the couple wed on 2 July 1928). Though Bergamín's trip did not precipitate a dramatic and instantaneous political conversion as Gecé's pilgrimage to Rome had, upon returning he wrote to Sánchez Cuesta of the experience as something that required his deep and careful reflection: "En poco tiempo, tantas cosas exigen un examen de conciencia para valorar y estimar todo" ("In a short time, so many things call for a soul-searching evaluation and estimation of everything").[23] In the following years, Bergamín's thoughts on poetry developed as part and parcel of a political vision that sympathized increasingly with communism – a communism understood in consonance with the writer's Catholicism, and with his opposition to fascism. In his willingness to cross cultural boundaries in order to view leftist politics as coherent with Christian values, he replicated the social heterodoxy that had led Unamuno to align Marxism with religion in the 1890s. Though these sympathies towards communism did not fully develop until the mid-1930s, after the Asturian mining crisis in 1934 and the International Writers Conference in Defence of Culture held in Paris in 1935, already in 1928 the future president of Spain's Alliance of Anti-fascist Intellectuals was relating his aesthetic ideas to broader social and cultural questions.[24] Upon returning from his trip, Bergamín started to formalize his thoughts on Russia and the alternative that it presented to Western Europe with the article "Rusia capital," which appeared in *La Gaceta Literaria* that November. Through a play on a number of words borrowed from the language of economics – *capital* (assets or, etymologically, an adjective pertaining to the head), *inversión* (investment or reversal), *interés* (interest in financial and aesthetic senses), and *especular* (to speculate or, literalizing, "to spectacle") – Bergamín imagined Russia as a phantasmagoria where European images and values are turned on their heads, extracted from their mundane realms of significance, and endowed with new transcendent meaning. Undoubtedly fetishizing modern Russia, Bergamín comprehends its turn to communism as a breaking-in of an eternal perspective on historical events, an impulse "que quisiera echarnos de todo, hasta del mundo, de este mundo a otro desde el que le pudiéramos contemplar" ("that attempts to throw us out of everything, even out of the world, out of this world to another from which we can contemplate it"). What Bergamín sees in 1920s Russia is an example of justice, as Unamuno had defined it in "El tiempo material": the application of an eternal perspective to historical events.

Though Bergamín's ideas remain abstract in this first article, they would become more concrete in the years of the Second Spanish Republic, when ideological conflicts at home made his thought more focused. In particular, the "sentido de lo popular" that Bergamín wrote of to Unamuno in 1924 was taking on a more defined shape in his thought, and it turned out to have quite a bit in common with the concept of art he had put forth in "El pensamiento hermético de las artes." A lecture he read at the Residencia de Señoritas in 1930 and published in 1933, to which he gave the Wildean title "La decadencia del analfabetismo" ("The Decadence of Illiteracy"), brings the critic's ideas about poetic art and eternity to bear on popular culture and the Spanish people or *pueblo*. In doing so, the essay also articulates a critique of progress and (or as) maturation. "La decadencia del analfabetismo" is an impassioned defence of "la razón poética" ("poetic reason"), a form of knowledge that Bergamín describes as innate in children but that begins to fade when a child learns to read and write. He links this poetic reason to pure play, and to the constant movement and agility that he had earlier associated with Hermes, the child god. Over the course of the essay, it becomes clear that what Bergamín calls *analfabetismo* here is very close to what he had previously called *hermetismo*. In fact, he uses the terms as synonyms on multiple occasions. Still, the new focus on illiteracy – a topic of immediate social importance in early twentieth-century Spain, where a large part of the population, especially in rural communities, could not read – marks a shift away from a lingering elitism in the concept of hermetic or esoteric art, and towards a common, popular cultural heritage.

"La decadencia del analfabetismo" certainly reflects the growing presence of social concerns in Bergamín's work, but it does not present a straightforward political message. Indeed, when it appeared in print the essay's apparent praise of illiteracy was received with indignation by leftist intellectual Antonio Sánchez Barbudo, who saw it as undermining educational initiatives like the Republic's Misiones Pedagógicas (Arana Palacios 39). But Bergamín's aim was not to glorify anti-intellectualism. His essay celebrates the childlike, poetic quality preserved in the *pueblo analfabeto* in order to reveal a kind of strength present in the supposed "underdevelopment" of the Spanish people. In particular, he contrasts the playful flexibility and creativity of such "illiteracy" – whether exemplified by children or by the emotive richness of the Andalusian *cante jondo* – with the immobility of the bourgeois, capitalist, professionalized, "literal" world. Playing on the idiomatic phrase "al pie de la letra" ("to the letter"; literally, "to the foot of the letter"), he writes that the modern world of letters has feet that are made of lead: "No bailan, no corren ni saltan, avanzan lentamente" ("They do not dance, nor do they run or jump; they advance slowly") (Bergamín, *La decadencia* 14–15). He continues, "de estos pies literales hizo el hombre de letras su pedestal intelectualista: amontonó sus estiletes para subirse encima, y permanecer en lo alto inmóvil" ("the man of letters made his intellectualist pedestal from these literal feet: he piled up his pens so he could stand on top of them and stay there on high, unmoving") (16). In this image of the man of letters who builds a pedestal for himself and becomes a statue, Bergamín reiterates the critique of stagnation of Spanish literary culture that Unamuno denounced as cultural old age at the turn of the century.

In his analysis of contemporary literary culture, Bergamín denounces precisely the totemization that Giménez Caballero celebrates. Like Unamuno in *En torno al casticismo*, the author of "La decadencia del analfabetismo" associates decadence with immobilization, with the hardening of thought into set patterns dictated by the literary establishment. The end of the essay emphasizes the need for revitalization of Spanish culture that again strongly recalls Unamuno's brand of regenerationism at the turn of the century; what Bergamín calls Spain's "analfabetismo espiritual permanente" ("permanent spiritual illiteracy") is very close to what his predecessor had called *intrahistoria* in 1895. While his writing echoes the same essay that Giménez Caballero had cast as the urtext of Spanish fascism, however, he departs from Gecé's reading of that text in at least one significant way. While Giménez Caballero draws on and exploits the language of youth present in Unamuno's essays and in the cultural discourse of the 1920s, Bergamín abandons this vocabulary, opting instead for the language of childhood, eternal rebirth, and poetic reason that he crafted a few years earlier in writing about "Hermetic" art.

The End, or Endlessness, of Art

In a time and society where youthfulness carries a great deal of cultural capital, what does it mean to tie youth to politics, or to art? In many ways, what is at stake in the artistic production and critical reflection of both Giménez Caballero and Bergamín in the 1920s and early 1930s is the question of whether art itself ever reaches maturity, whether it ever becomes fully developed. A survey of Giménez Caballero's work during these years suggests that for him, avant-garde aesthetics did represent a culmination of art's function in society, despite the fact that he (like many) chose to describe the avant-garde in the Messianic terms of a new dawn or a new youth. The subjugation of everyday life (and even rational argument) to aestheticism, the ultimate triumph or decay of art for art's own sake made possible by the avant-garde, appealed to the totalitarian leaning of his burgeoning fascism. At the same time, it rendered artistic innovation impossible, for it bound the artistic endeavour to a historical narrative of development that had to come to an end. As Bergamín might have put it, Gecé's avant-gardism made art mortal.

By 1930, Giménez Caballero had concluded that the artistic avant-garde had, in fact, grown old and reached its end. That year, in response to a survey titled "¿Qué es la vanguardia?" ("What is the avant-garde?"), organized by Miguel Pérez Ferrero and published in *La Gaceta Literaria*, Giménez Caballero wrote that the artistic vanguard no longer existed in Spain. He went on to remark that "sólo queda el sector específicamente político, donde la vanguardia (audacia, juventud, subversión) puede aún actuar" ("the only remaining sector in which the avant-garde [audacity, youth, subversion] may still act is the specifically political one") (Pérez Ferrero 1). The powers of art had been exhausted; politics was now the only realm in which youth could thrive. In this brief text, Gecé continues to use the language of youth and maturity as a kind of scare tactic, as he warns young Spaniards, "¡alerta a todas las madureces emplastadas!" ("beware of all phony maturities!") (1). At the same time, however, he appears to leave behind the world of artistic production in which he mastered this vocabulary.

Giménez Caballero's dismissal of the artistic avant-garde in this survey reflects the general shift that took place in his work the 1930s, as he wrote *Genio de España*, *La nueva catolicidad* (*The New Catholicity*, 1933), and *Arte y Estado* (*Art and the State*, 1935) – all books that deserted the more experimental aspects of his earlier writing in order to self-consciously lay the ideological groundwork for Spanish fascism.[25] With *Genio de España* in particular, Gecé was also building on the interpretation of Unamuno's work that he had begun in his "Carta a un compañero de la Joven España." It is a reading that ties Unamuno closely to 1898, reducing his vast thought and activity to a single year and a limited set of concerns – most prominently, existential angst in the wake of imperial loss. In the section quoted earlier, "Los nietos del 98 (Notas a Unamuno)," he converts the year 1898 into a paradigm, retracing and reinterpreting Spanish history as a succession of thirteen "98"s – i.e., moments of imperial loss for Spain. He begins with the relinquishment of the Netherlands in 1648, and identifies other "98" moments in the independence of Hispanic American nations between 1810 and 1825 ("Un 98 de quince años"), the actual events of 1898, and the Battle of Annual in 1921. This history of loss culminates, for Gecé, in his present day, with the Second Republic.

In this retracing of history, *Genio de España* cements its association of Unamuno with 1898 (and all that year symbolizes for Giménez Caballero) not only through explicit reference, but also through a replication of the historical-critical approach and the tropes that the older writer had used in *En torno al casticismo*. Especially striking is the reappearance of a language of excavation. In the closing lines of "De mística y humanismo," Unamuno suggested that scratching below the surface of Restoration Spain would reveal a persisting Inquisitorial repression and "la vieja *morgue castillane*" ("the old Spanish arrogance") (*E* 1:185). This is echoed in Gecé's account of the Spain of the Second Republic when he writes, "si se cortara una sección de esta República – como se secciona una materia para someterla a análisis químico – nos encontraríamos una contextura de vieja, lenta formación" ("if we were to cut a section of this Republic – as one sections a substance in order subject it to chemical analysis – we would find an old composition formed slowly over time") (*Genio* 62). Gecé preserves the rhetoric of undesirable old age, but abandons the liberal aims that had led Unamuno to his excavation of Spanish culture almost forty years earlier. The "resurrection" that he proposes for Spain in this book is not the same as the rejuvenation that Unamuno had called for, because instead of anti-traditionalist rupture, critique, and creative exchange with Europe, *Genio de España* prescribes the construction of a monumental State.

While Giménez Caballero portrayed the new Spanish Republic as a product of age, Bergamín experienced it as a time of unprecedented youthfulness for Spain. Looking back on the early 1930s in an essay about the origins of *Cruz y Raya* decades later, he recalled the energy and excitement, and "acento juvenil" ("youthful accent") that had characterized these years for him ("Signo" viii). Still, he continued to be skeptical of the rhetoric of youth that pervaded Spanish and European culture, especially as it was being used by right-wing and fascist groups. At this time Unamuno also began to express disillusionment with political youth organizations, on both extremes of the ideological spectrum. Commenting on this disillusionment, Borzoni goes so far as to speak of Unamuno's loss of faith in the young, whom he had previously championed as the defeaters of Primo de Rivera, those who had made the Second Republic possible (Borzoni 255–7). Always quick to condemn what he deemed false or inauthentic youth, the now-reinstated rector of the Universidad de Salamanca wrote articles criticizing Mussolini's *giovinezza* and the similar forms of political collectivization, whether fascist or communist, that were attracting young people in Spain.[26] In the (fittingly titled) 1935 article "Otra vez con la juventud" ("On Youth Once More"), he denounced the self-styled youth groups of both the right and the left, insisting as ever that the young people that mattered to him were "los verdaderos jóvenes de espíritu y no de edad tan sólo" ("the truly young in spirit and not just in age"), the individual youths who existed apart from the collectivized masses (*OCE* 8:1229). While Borzoni is right to point out Unamuno's disillusionment with the politicized organizations that used (or abused) the language of youth to further their cause, the writer's words in this article indicate that he retained his faith in a kind of youthfulness that transcended temporality and history. This is the same concept of youth that he associated with *pistis*, with poetic creativity, and even with socialism in the early years of the century – and it is the youth that Bergamín reconceptualized in terms of Hermetic art and "illiterate" poetic reason in the late 1920s and early 1930s.

In a brief piece that appeared in *Cruz y Raya* in September of 1933, "Unas palabras al oído" ("Some Words Whispered in the Ear"), Bergamín articulates his rejection of the discourse of youth and age as employed by his political rivals, precisely through a discussion of Unamuno and his work. The essay begins as a review of Unamuno's recently published *San Manuel Bueno, mártir y tres historias más*, but quickly strays from this topic in order to consider the figure of Unamuno himself, in his old age. Bergamín describes this period of his predecessor's life as a crystalline winter, subtly evoking Unamuno's white hair: "Invierno puro o depurado, depurador, claro, nítido" ("A pure or purified or purifying winter, bright and clear") (Dennis, *El epistolario* 140). He contrasts the refined and refining character of Don Miguel's old voice with a kind of youth that he describes as erroneous and pathological:

> ¡Qué joven está D. Miguel! – solemos oír decir nosotros. No, ¡qué viejo! ¡Qué estupendo viejo! Mientras tanto se exaltan, estúpidamente, equívocos mitos juveniles, esta excelsa vejez humana, la que no se empaña, tristemente, por la turbulencia de una sangre reverdecida en moho de juventud, en virulento sarpullido juvenil, es ejemplo que alcanza más que nunca y que todo, la sublime enseñanza de lo eterno. (140)
>
> ("How young Don Miguel is!" we often hear people say. No, how old! What a wonderful old man! At a time when so much praise is given, stupidly, to dubious myths of youthfulness, this excellent, human old age, untarnished by the sad turbulence of blood tinted green with the mold of

youth, with a virulent, juvenile rash, is an example that communicates, more than ever and more than anything, the sublime teaching of eternity.)

Bergamín subverts the common associations of old age and youth found in contemporary political and cultural discourse, casting youth as diseased and moldy, while age – at least Unamuno's – remains unblemished. Moreover, the humane vision of this old age is eternal, not bound by history. As such, it is also "una especie de juventud divina" ("a kind of divine youth") (140). In its divinity, its eternity, it does not lose the transitional, protean quality that defines adolescence within the span of human life. Indeed, it is precisely this quality that defines the old age or youth that Unamuno embodies for Bergamín. It is development redeemed from temporality, oriented towards a goal outside of time, a death that Bergamín's Catholicism leads him to understand as rebirth. The mission of youth, he reflects, is to grow up – but to grow towards an alternative form of maturity:

> Cuando tanto se habla de los jóvenes, de no sé qué misiones juveniles, de no sé qué razones de la juventud, con o sin adecuado acompañamiento de musiquillas ratoneras o ratoniles a la italiana, hay quien piensa al oírlo que los jóvenes de esa juventud no tienen más misión, más razón de ser, que una: la de dejar de serlo. Oír a Unamuno es ir aprendiendo a dejar, en plena juventud, de ser o parecer joven falsamente; de ese modo, o de tantos otros falsos modos parecidos. Ser joven, cuando de veras se es, es aprender a dejar de serlo; porque es apurar la juventud, en el tiempo, depurándola, para llegar hasta la muerte: hasta una vejez como ésta que Unamuno, por su voz, su palabra, su vida, nos enseña. (141)
>
> (When so much is said about youth, about I-don't-know-what youthful missions, about I-don't-know-what arguments of the young, with or without the usual accompaniment of badly tuned Italian marches, some of us respond by reflecting that the young people of that youth have no other mission, no other *raison d'être*, than this: to stop being young. To hear Unamuno is to start to learn, while one is still young, how to stop being or seeming young in a false way; in the aforementioned way, or in many similarly false ways. To be young, when one is truly young, is to learn to grow up; because being young is pushing youth forward in time, purifying it, in order to arrive at death: at an old age like the one Unamuno demonstrates for us, through his voice, his word, his life.)

To be truly young, one must cease to be so: that is, cease to ascribe authority or value to temporal categories of age and search out eternal – intellectual, spiritual, divine, "Hermetic" – values by which to live and understand the world. While for Giménez Caballero these values are static, representable in maps or buildings, for Bergamín they are ever changing, ever adapting to meet new demands presented by the intellect's struggle with "poetic reason"; increasingly, this includes the demands of social justice, the moral imperative to fight the oppression of fascism. Compared with the fascist (and later Falangist) hermeneutic applied to Unamuno's work in Giménez Caballero's wake, Bergamín's relationship with his predecessor illuminates another reading of Don Miguel and his literary production. It is a reading that emphasizes the centrality of poetry and *poiesis* in his work, and its role in Unamuno's thoroughly integrated artistic, spiritual, and political self. Furthermore, the Bergaminian view of Unamuno offers an important closing perspective, for this book, on youth – youth not as mere national regeneration, but as a stage of transition and creation that art alone can preserve against the passing of time. Just a few short years before the end of Unamuno's life, and before the outbreak of a civil war that would put an end to Spanish culture's widespread glorification of youth during the early twentieth century, Bergamín affirms that the kind of youth his predecessor champions and represents is one that defies chronology, rational progress, and *Bildung*. This youth, found in art and also embedded in political action, achieves immortality because it orients itself not towards maturity or the final culmination of a historical process, but towards justice.

Supervivencia

In the eyes of some, the inauguration of the Second Republic in 1931 marked a coming of age for Spain and Spanish politics, and put an end to the dominance of youth that had characterized the culture of the 1920s. According to Anthony Geist, at this point in time the members of *la joven literatura* were conscious "of having reached cultural maturity" and of the need to engage more directly with the world beyond the boundaries that had cordoned art off from society in the previous decade (*La poética* 9). In May of 1931, Francisco Ayala expressed a similar sentiment, giving voice to his own sense that Spanish art was reaching the end of an era. In the new decade and in the midst of a new political reality, he observed how the literary world was passing from adolescent, playful exuberance to an unfamiliar, adult responsibility: "Toda una promoción literaria ha encontrado, de pronto, su adultez. Ha tirado los juguetes, y ahora se siente desconcertada porque, en cierto modo, había hecho profesión de la edad infantil" ("An entire literary cohort has suddenly entered adulthood. It has thrown out its toys, and now feels perplexed, for in a certain way it had made a profession of being young"). As they faced this new stage of their artistic lives, Ayala and his peers perhaps experienced some of the reluctance and dread that Unamuno had before his fortieth birthday in 1904. How would they proceed into maturity, after making youth such a central component of their art and their identities? How would they retain aesthetic and intellectual youth in the face of the irremediable passage of time?

As I have shown in the last chapter, José Bergamín framed this question in terms of how the artist might continue the struggle against the progressive "literalization" of the modern world, how to preserve "poetic reason" against modernity's tendency towards the prosaic, and he saw Unamuno as the model to follow in this struggle. On 23 July 1931, a text bearing Bergamín's distinctive style and signed by him and many members of his generation appeared on the front page of the Madrid newspaper *El Sol*. This short, manifesto-like article declared that, regardless of whoever might be appointed as the official president of the new government, Don Miguel already held the position in these young artists' estimation: he was the cultural president of the Republic, by way of "razón poética" if not in political fact. After affirming that Unamuno had been the "creador verbal" ("verbal creator") of Republican Spain, the statement concluded with a call for the provisional government to support the preparation and publication of his complete works. This editorial impulse to collect the writings that Unamuno had been producing since the end of the previous century indicates that his own work, as well, was by then entering into a period of perceived fulfilment and maturity.[1] Though his relationship with the Republican government would soon become strained as he critiqued what he viewed as its excesses, by this time he had clearly achieved a level of prestige that placed him among the most important Spanish intellectuals of the century.

When Gerardo Diego published his carefully curated anthology of contemporary Spanish poetry in 1932, he reinforced the cultural weight of this prestige. As the poet whose work opened the collection,[2] Unamuno stood out as something like the patriarch of the twentieth-century lyrical tradition that Diego sought to highlight and canonize. Still, although he was the oldest poet included in this first edition of the anthology, contemporary reviewers repeatedly stressed his youthfulness and the unity of his poetic sensibility with that of the younger writers. A critic from Santander wrote of the "permanente juventud" that characterized both Unamuno's and Machado's work, and therefore justified their presence in the anthology, while a reviewer in Buenos Aires' *La Nación* observed that poets as different in age as Unamuno and Cernuda nevertheless oriented their work "hacia un fin igual" ("toward the same end") (Morelli, *Historia* 268, 321). This common "end" was clearly understood as poetic, not chronological; the critic specified that he was speaking of "la poesía intemporal donde no cuenta la aritmética de los calendarios" ("atemporal poetry in which the arithmetic of calendars does not count") (320). Poetry's ability to defy and transcend the passage of time unified all of the writers, otherwise separated by age and experience, that Diego gathered in his book.

If the beginning of the 1930s represented an initial passage into adulthood, the end of youthful illusions, and the onset of seriousness and social responsibility for *la joven literatura*, this gravity and sense of moral responsibility intensified with the outbreak of the Civil War. In this phase Unamuno could not lead the way as he had in the past. He died six months after the start of the conflict, on 31 December 1936, while under an unofficial house arrest imposed by the forces of the Nationalist uprising. His incorporation into Falangist cultural history began immediately following his death, and proceded to shape the image of the writer that would prevail in Spain throughout the Francoist period. Yet Unamuno did not cease to be an example for the members of *la joven literatura*, and especially for those who went into exile during and after the war. The Basque poet's presence in their thoughts is apparent in the various essays and memoirs written from exile that have been cited in this book. As the community that Bergamín dubbed "La España peregrina" ("Spain in Pilgrimage") spread out into the diaspora, they especially recalled the Unamuno who had himself lived in exile in Fuerteventura and Hendaye, and the one who had striven to support – and critique – the Republic after his return. Bergamín kept the memory of the most recent Unamuno alive through Editorial Séneca, the publishing house that he founded in Mexico in 1939, where he produced two collections of Unamuno's articles from the years of the Republic.[3] In Cuba, María Zambrano gathered and wrote down her thoughts about Unamuno's place in twentieth-century European thought. And back in Mexico, Moreno Villa recorded his memories of Don Miguel in his autobiography, in various articles on poetry, and in his memories of the Spanish intellectual world that had existed prior to the war.

Yet another writer of the Republican exile and former member of *la joven literatura* who recalled Unamuno in the postwar years was Manuel Altolaguirre. Altolaguirre had first met Unamuno during the older writer's exile, when he made his literary pilgrimage to Hendaye in 1929. This solidified a poetic relationship that, like the others mentioned above, would extend beyond Unamuno's lifetime. The following years took Altolaguirre briefly to England, where he founded the journal *1616*, dedicated to English and Spanish literature in translation, and then back to Spain, to champion the cause of socially-motivated, "impure" poetry with Pablo Neruda in *Caballo Verde para la Poesía*. After the Civil War, he carried with him into exile his passions for publishing and for creating dialogue across national boundaries. In Cuba, he founded a new series of publications, including the diminutively-sized weekly *La Verónica* (1942). The pages of this (truly) little magazine featured multiple poems by Unamuno, printed alongside those of former members of *la joven literatura*. Significantly, the first issue of *La Verónica* opened with "Si caigo aquí" from *Romancero del destierro* – a choice that, as James Valender observes, "confirms the importance that [Unamuno's] book had for Altolaguirre, as for other poets of exile who would have found projected in this poem a concern and an experience very similar to their own" (*El impresor* 39, my translation). The verses that Unamuno had written in Paris while recalling the lost boy-poet of the First World War, Rupert Brooke, now spoke to a Caribbean audience of the longing the exiled Spaniards felt for the land of their youth.

The work of preserving the Spanish literary tradition in the diaspora that Altolaguirre and his colleagues in exile undertook was an act of translation, in an etymological sense: a carrying-over of their culture, across national borders and across the sea. In travelling to the Americas, as many of them did, they also carried this tradition and their personal histories from the Old World of Europe to societies that were perceived as "younger." Exile, in more violent and concrete ways than their experience of adolescence, interrupted the trajectory of these writers' lives and introduced them into a strange and uncertain temporality. If the Spanish Silver Age had been dominated by a celebration of youth and a suspicion of adulthood and *Bildung*, exile did away with the question of development altogether. It put a definitive end to the period of youth that Ayala associated with the 1920s, and yet the insecurity and unfamiliarity of exile could not be called maturity. For Moreno Villa, for example, exile affirmed and crystallized the in-between-ness, the "interinidad" that he saw as the sign under which his life had unfolded.

In a short text from 1957 that remained unpublished during his life, Altolaguirre surveyed the history of his generation since the Civil War and defined the lifespan of the artist in terms of an opposition not between youth and age, but between youth and survival, "juventud y supervivencia." For the author of this text, youth is the stage of life – or better, the state of mind – in which poetic creation happens. The time that comes after this period of production and generation is simple subsistence, the afterlife of artistic youth. In Altolaguirre's retrospective view, the breaking-up of his own literary circle of friends, due to war, exile, aging, and death, is what marks the passage from youth to survival. Federico García Lorca, Miguel Hernández, Moreno Villa (who died in 1955), and others continue in their *supervivencia* beyond the grave. Altolaguirre writes of Moreno Villa that "sus versos nos llevan hacia su persona y estos sorprendentes encuentros con el poeta nos hacen dudar de su muerte" ("his verses lead us to his person and these surprising encounters with the poet make us question the reality of his death") (88). Though Altolaguirre does not mention any older poets in this brief piece, the way he describes the persistence of youth in literature there does recall the essay he wrote on Unamuno almost two decades earlier. As he argued there, Unamuno's kind of youth was more "vegetal" than human, one that bloomed perennially rather than passing with a certain phase of history, and after his death it was up to the living to make sure it would continue to flower (Altolaguirre 136). If political circumstances had forced the poets of the Republican exile out of artistic youth and into a mode of subsistence, in their new reality it was their task to ensure the survival of those lost to death. In a sense, then, the writers of *la joven literatura* – both those who went into exile and those who stayed in Spain – were responsible for the afterlife of Unamuno's work, its survival outside the immediate time and place of its production. This was a task of particular importance in the case of a writer who had so often compared literary legacy to immortality, and who had foreseen the role his future readers would play in keeping his work alive in compositions he addressed to young people, like "Mi confesión" or "Cuando yo sea viejo." It is possible to see these younger writers as facilitating the afterlife of their predecessor's work in a Benjaminian sense, as a fulfilment of and testament to that work's "translatability" – even though they did not do the work of translating Unamuno to other languages themselves. Indeed, Benjamin's description of a work of art continually "flowering" in new versions and interpretations (*Illuminations* 72) recalls the perennial youthfulness that Altolaguirre saw in Unamuno and his writing.

Interpretations of Unamuno's work were various already during his lifetime, spanning wide political divides and often departing from the canonical image of the older writer that we know today, consolidated through an approach to early twentieth-century Spanish literature based on the framework of the literary generation. From Bergamín's Catholic-and-Republican appreciation for Unamuno's "entereza" to Giménez Caballero's fascist reading of *En torno al casticismo,* to the primarily poetic (but not completely apolitical) surveys of his significance by Moreno Villa and Gerardo Diego, youth in Unamuno's writing bridges the historiographical gap between their generations in diverse ways. It is undeniable that generational consciousness, the awareness of belonging to a group based on biological age, is foundational for this period. Yet too often critics have failed to recognize this generational consciousness as a function of a changing understanding of adolescence and youth, a shift that left an indelible mark on modernist literary production, especially in a country that had long been aware of its relative "immaturity" compared to other parts of Europe. In the end, Spanish modernism's reimagining of adolescence signalled more than a passing "time of youth," to use Ortega's phrase: it defined a poetics, a way of writing and a way of life that strives to hold modernity's dominant models of maturity at bay.

Of course, this critique of a maturity long associated with the greater scientific and technological development of "Europe" facilitated an ultranationalist notion of Spanish identity that not only appropriated the early twentieth century's exaltation of youth in the years prior to the Spanish Civil War, but also limited and controlled Unamuno's reception in Spain in the postwar period. Censorship during Franco's regime suppressed significant aspects of his work, particularly from the period of his exile and his critique of Primo de Rivera. The revered icon of Spain's student protest movement was obscured by the "caudillo" of the Generation of 1898. To be sure, works like *En torno al casticismo* and *Del sentimiento trágico de la vida* continued to be read, and the poet born in the Basque Country continued to inspire later generations of Spanish poets, particularly those writing in a religious vein. But the youthful Unamuno, the Unamuno who wrote about and for youth and took an interest in it on a political and an aesthetic level, was largely forgotten. In more recent years, discoveries of previously unpublished texts like *Nuevo mundo* and "Mi confesión" have made the Unamunian treatment of youth more visible. This study has endeavoured to further elucidate this aspect of Unamuno's work, and demonstrate that it was a foundational element not only in his writing but also for Spanish literature of the modernist period in general. It is my hope that the reflections presented here will lay the groundwork for further study of tropes of youth and age in the literary and cultural production of modernist-era Spain, ever in dialogue with a broader European and global reality.

It is true in some ways that the end of the Silver Age brought with it the waning of a modernist aesthetics of youth in Spanish culture – or at least a profound transformation of that youth, by way of the experience of exile or that of dictatorship. Yet, of course, in later decades youth's presence in politics, social change, popular culture, and society at large would not fade. Adolescents have retained the role of protagonists assigned to them by turn-of-the-century thinkers like G. Stanley Hall throughout the twentieth century, and indeed, into the twenty-first. As Western culture passed into a process of juvenilization or juvenescence after the Second World War, Spain participated, if not as directly in the protest culture of the 1960s, certainly in the commercialization of youth and the generation of popular culture intended for young audiences. As a nation, it experienced a new set of growing pains in the transition from dictatorship to democracy. In recent years, critics have begun to look again at the narrative of formation that framed that period, and question the ways that this coming-of-age tale has been told.[4] The beginning of the twenty-first century in Spain, in fact, has often echoed the beginning of the twentieth, as economic and political crises position the nation (and its young people) before an uncertain future, and calls for renovation and rejuvenation are heard again. I do not desire to read this recent history, from Franco to democracy to the present, teleologically – indeed, it would be extremely difficult to do so. It is a history much better understood, perhaps, in terms of genealogy, or archaeology. As part of that much larger endeavour, the excavation of literary and critical history undertaken in these pages has sought to perpetuate the *supervivencia* of Spanish modernism's poetics of youth, in Unamuno and in some of the young people he once imagined reading him, in a future "then": "los jóvenes de entonces."

Notes

Introduction

1 I find most English translations of this title inadequate. The French title, *L'Essence de l'Espagne*, translates to some extent the emphasis on autochthony in the Spanish "casticismo," but ignores completely the prepositional phrase that precedes it, "en torno de" – "of" or, literally, "around" – that indicates the analytical nature of the author's approach to the topic addressed. Martin Nozick's English version, *On Authentic Tradition*, is more accurate, though it still softens the highly critical view of *casticismo* – the cult of *lo castizo* – that Unamuno puts forth. The concept of *lo castizo* is difficult to translate in itself, with its references to purity of blood, but also to purity or authenticity of customs and traditions within the cultural, not strictly biological, realm. That the term and what it stands for – that is, the concept that Unamuno seeks to critique in his essay – had traditionally been associated solely with the central region of Castile is a point that the author stresses in the first chapters of the work, hence the absence of the word *España* in the title Unamuno gave the essays when they were collected and reprinted in 1902.

2 On Benjamin and youth, see Wohlfarth.

3 It is likely that Unamuno knew Yeats' poem, which dates from 1891, and was included in his *Poems* (1895, rpt. 1899). This book figures in Unamuno's library (Valdés and Valdés 262).

4 As Bénédicte Vauthier indicates in her edition of *Cómo se hace una novela* (2005), Unamuno added the passage in which this quotation appears in 1927 while retranslating the work from the first French version, itself translated by Jean Cassou in 1926 (the original Spanish text, composed in 1924–1925, was lost). The sentences I quote appeared in the edition

published by Editorial Alba in Buenos Aires in 1927, but were deleted by censors in the Spanish edition of Unamuno's *Obras completas* edited by Manuel García Blanco and published by Afrodisio Aguado in 1958. Parts of it remained censored in the Escelicer edition that commenced in 1961. On the history and versions of the text, see Vauthier's editorial commentary (Unamuno, *Manual* 137–48).

5 In the collection *Ecos de la generación de 98 en la de 27*, both Carlos Blanco Aguinaga and Ricardo Senabre feel obligated to cite these lines from *Cómo se hace una novela* as they attempt to draw connections between Unamuno and the later writers (Enciso Recio 58–61, 82–4). For further consideration of Unamuno's critique of the tercentenary, see Enjuto Rangel.

6 As Jed Esty summarizes, modernist novels of formation "rework narrative time via youthful protagonists who conspicuously *do not grow up*" (2). See also Spacks (chapter 9), Neubauer, Moretti, and Mao. In his book, Mao responds to interpretations of the history of the *Bildungsroman* by Moretti (see especially 257–8) and Spacks (236–7) that view the novel of formation of the modernist period as arresting development, exchanging movement for stasis. Spacks's emphasis on the idea of adolescents as "trailblazers," however, indicates more of a forging of new paths than simple stagnation. On adolescence as a productive stasis, a site "of many potentials, including maturity," see Driscoll (49). For an analysis of the phenomenon as it relates to twentieth-century poetry in English, see Burt, and in relation to the politics and poetics of Rimbaud and Lautréamont, see Ross (21–8).

7 See Costa, *Oligarquía* 679–80. On Costa's view of Spain's "minoría de edad," see Menéndez Alzamora 26–7.

8 Often attributed to Alexandre Dumas, this phrase was still quoted in W.Z. Ripley's 1899 anthropological study *The Races of Europe* (272).

9 While Philippe Ariès' view that the qualitative differentiation between childhood and adulthood as a strictly modern phenomenon has been discredited, many recent studies do confirm his association of the modern idea of adolescence with nineteenth-century social developments. See Gillis chapters 1 and 2, Feixa 34–41, Savage xvii-xviii, and the contributions to *A History of Young People in the West* (vol. 2, Levi and Schmitt, eds.) by Sabina Loriga, Michelle Perrot, Jean-Claude Caron, and Sergio Luzzato.

10 The title of a pamphlet from 1912 describing their activities – *Los Exploradores de España (Boy-Scouts Españoles)* – makes clear that the Exploradores were modelled on the British organization. The content of the pamphlet, written by Arturo Cuyás Armengol, confirms that the name of the Spanish iteration was chosen in connection to the glories of the imperial past. Cuyás writes that troop leaders should tell the scouts "relaciones de episodios

históricos referentes a los esfuerzos varoniles, a la valentía y arrojo, a la tenacidad y perseverancia de los descubridores y exploradores españoles: Colón, Hernán Cortés, Pizarro, Magallanes [. . .]" ("stories of historical episodes relating to the manly efforts, the bravery and fearlessness, the tenacity and perseverance of the Spanish discoverers and explorers: Columbus, Hernán Cortés, Pizarro, Magallanes [. . .]) (15). The following year, Cuyás authored a didactic book for adolescents titled *Hace falta un muchacho* (*Boy Needed*).

11 For a comparison of Pérez de Ayala's *A.M.D.G.* and Joyce's *Portrait*, both novels that center on the experience of young boys in Jesuit schools, see Schork.

12 See Celma Valero 11–15 and Thion Soriano-Mollá, "La Gente Nueva" and "Gente nueva versus Gente vieja."

13 In setting up this opposition, Ricoeur follows Karl Mannheim, whose own *Ideology and Utopia* was published during the period under examination in this book, in 1929. His main divergence from Mannheim is that for Ricoeur, ideology and utopia are modes of social imagination that not only critique, but also constitute social reality: "the presupposition here is precisely that of a social imagination, of a cultural imagination, operating in both constructive and destructive ways, as both confirmation and contestation of the present situation" (Ricoeur 3).

14 Michael D. Thomas has identified this use of the *Bildungsroman* in the postwar novels of Ramón Sender, Miguel Delibes, Carmen Laforet, Ana María Matute, and Carmen Martín Gaite. On female adolescence and development in Spanish literature of the postwar period and later twentieth century, see Rodríguez.

15 See Zambrano, *La tumba de Antígona* (Cátedra, 2012). On Antigone and female development, see Hirsch, "Spiritual *Bildung*: The Beautiful Soul as Paradigm," pages 23–48 in Abel, Hirsch, and Langland.

16 See Jed Rasula's catalogue of modernist uses of the word "new," and Michael North's response and investigation into the word's meaning in *Novelty* (6–7, 36–59).

17 For the correspondence between Unamuno and Candamo, see Blázquez González (on *Arte Joven* in particular, see 324–37). The first issue of *Arte Joven* was designated "número preliminar," with the second becoming "número 1," etc. Unamuno's poems first appear in number 1 and are reprinted in number 2. For more about the journal and Unamuno's interaction with it, see Herrera, Flores Arroyuelo, and Franz.

18 On the role of *poiesis* in Unamuno's literary theoretical thought, see Álvarez Castro, *La palabra y el ser* 75–81. The word *poíesis* appears as the title on the

first page of the complete manuscript of *Poesías*, held at the Casa Museo Unamuno, CMU 74/11.

19 See Ortega, "Unamuno y Europa, fábula" (*OCT* 1:128–32) and Unamuno, "Sobre la europeización (arbitrariedades)" (1906) and "Sobre la tumba de Costa" (1911) (*E* 7:157–219). For the background to this public dispute, see the personal correspondence between the two thinkers from 1904 to 1908, in Robles, *Epistolario completo Ortega-Unamuno*.

20 Studies on Jiménez and the younger writers include Dennis, *Perfume and Poison*; Cano Ballesta, "Poetas celestes, poetas demoníacos"; Maurer, "Más allá de Eco y Narciso"; Ciplijauskaité, "Apostilla a una polémica"; and Nahorro-Calderón. On Ortega's relationship to the group, see Silver, Cate-Arriès, and Wahnón. For an example of anecdotes about Unamuno's presence at the Residencia de Estudiantes, see Onieva. A handful of studies on Unamuno's relationships with or influence on individual members of the Generation of 1927 do exist, including Dennis, *El epistolario* (correspondence between Unamuno and José Bergamín); Pao (on Benjamín Jarnés); Sotelo Vázquez, "Miguel de Unamuno y la génesis del *Romancero gitano*" and "Pedro Salinas"; and Teruel Benavente (on Unamuno and Cernuda). In scholarship on Spanish narrative of the 1920s, there has been some critical debate regarding the degree of Unamuno's importance for the prose writers of the avant-garde. See Pérez Firmat 29, Spires x-xiv, and del Pino 45–6. Álvarez Castro ("Nivola y metaficción") argues for an Unamunian legacy in Spanish vanguard narrative in the subversion of realist conventions.

21 The refutation of the generational model has a history that is several decades long, beginning at least as early as 1968, when Ricardo Gullón decried "the error of particularizing the general" (my translation) that he saw in its presentation of each generation as a singularly Spanish phenomenon, which separated Spanish works from the broader context of Western or European literature. For subsequent appraisals and critiques of the generational model as it applies to Spanish literature and its generations of 1898 and 1927, see Fox, "La generación de 1898"; Gambarte; Anderson, *El Veintisiete*; and Soufas, *The Subject in Question*, introduction and chapter 1.

22 The concept of the Generation of 1898 originated in a series of essays written by the novelist Azorín for the newspaper *ABC* in 1913. However, it received much of the theoretical framework that defined it for the rest of the century in critical studies like Pedro Salinas' "El concepto de 'generación literaria' aplicado a la de 98" (1935); Hans Jeschke's *Die generation von 1898 in Spanien* (1934), which excludes Unamuno because the author considers him too old; and Pedro Laín Entralgo's *La generación del 98* (1948). Salinas,

Jeschke, and Laín Entralgo relied on the generational theory of German critic Julius Petersen in their studies, but it was not until Guillermo Díaz-Plaja's *Modernismo frente a noventa y ocho* (1951) that Unamuno was overtly identified as the group's leader ("caudillo" or, in Petersen's German, "Führer"). On the ultranationalist origins of Petersen's theory and its uses in Franco-era literary criticism, see Soufas 28–36.

23 In *Modernismo frente a noventa y ocho*, Díaz-Plaja actually refers to the two tendencies as "not one, but two generations" (107). Throughout this book, I use the Spanish term *modernismo*, in italics, to refer to this movement. Modernism, unitalicized, should be understood as the worldwide tendency in arts and letters dating from the mid-nineteenth century in Europe, an expanding field of study that, if in the past associated solely with northern European and Anglo-American literatures, increasingly includes Spain and other "peripheral" European nations as well as non-Western literatures. On modernism's changing disciplinary boundaries, see *Modernism* (Eysteinsson and Liska, eds.) and *The Cambridge Companion to European Modernism* (Lewis, ed.).

24 Again, see Ramsden and Shaw, and more recently, Labanyi ("Nation, Narration, Naturalization"; *Myth and History* 35–57). A key example of a critique of the veneration of the Generation of 1898 by literary critics during Franco's dictatorship is Juan Goytisolo's essay "La herencia del noventa y ocho o la literatura considerada como una promoción social," included in *El furgón de cola* (Paris: Editions Ruedo Ibérico, 1967).

25 In *La generación poética de 1927* (1966), editors Joaquín González Muela and Manuel Rozas play down the influence of Unamuno and Machado while stressing the importance of Jiménez – "a poet who had, like Góngora, dedicated his life to the 'useless' worship of Beauty" (15). Similarly, in *El grupo poético de 1927* (1976) Ángel González argues that Unamuno's works were discredited by the *jóvenes* as "impure for their ethical, sentimental, religious, biographical, or political 'contaminations'" (29). Antonio Blanch's scholarly study *La poesía pura española* (1976) underscores Jiménez's role in the development of the poetics of *la joven literatura*, but takes pains to point out the disparities between their "dehumanized" art – which he links to French *poésie pure* – and that of Unamuno and Machado.

26 In "Una generación poética (1920-1936)," Alonso divides the history of the group into two halves, distinguished by the appearance of "the demon of politics" (*OC* 4:670). This split is maintained in the periodization that informs Blanch's study (1922–1928) as well as Juan Cano Ballesta's *La poesía española entre pureza y revolución (1930-36)* (1972), and in general terms, continues to structure historical accounts of the Generation of 1927 today.

27 Ana Urrutia Jordana observes in her study of the poetry of Unamuno's exile, "not only were Don Miguel's political leanings falsified at the end of his life, adding to the confusion surrounding such an indeed confusing figure for the rest of the population, but the death and assassination of other poets during the Civil War (Machado, Lorca), far from promoting praise for Don Miguel, buried his memory for good … moreover, he was left without advocates for his poetic work" (15–16, my translation). To be sure, Unamuno's early support for the Nationalist uprising in 1936 did cost him dearly in the eyes of some. Ramón Sender, for example, makes a point of mentioning the older writer's failure to denounce the rebel forces as part of his highly critical assessment of his work and legacy in the essay "Unamuno, sombra fingida."

28 Coke-Enguídanos and Cruz Mendizábal are among the few who have reflected on Unamuno's early essays, providing article-length analyses of the relationship between poetry and the essay and the "poetic" character of Unamuno's essayism. With regard to criticism on Unamuno's poetry, Manuel García Blanco's meticulous *Don Miguel de Unamuno y sus poesías* (1954) compiled a great deal of useful information and laid the foundations for much later work. For further studies see Ynduráin; Álvar; Zardoya; and Blasco, Celma, and Rodríguez.

1 Unamuno's Poetics of Youth

1 Geoffrey Ribbans ("Unamuno y 'los jóvenes' en 1904") documented other references to the fateful birthday, made by Unamuno in interviews with Enrique Gómez Carrillo in the months leading up to it. Ribbans underscores Unamuno's desire to become a leader of young people, but pays less attention to Unamuno's own anxieties about aging.

2 As Villar Ezcurra explains in the introductory note that preceeds her critical edition of the text (9n), the manuscript was found in the Casa Museo Unamuno, among Unamuno's papers for *Tratado de amor de Dios*, itself an early version of what would become *Del sentimiento trágico de la vida*. *Mi confesión* includes several ideas, and at times entire passages, that appear in this later work. Unamuno mentions the text in a letter to his young correspondent Candamo as "un libro, regularmente extenso, que titularé 'A la juventud hispana'" ("a book of regular length, which I will title 'To Hispanic Youth'") (Blázquez González 360). Though the manuscript comprises only the first pages of the work, Unamuno planned it as a collection of essays all intended for an audience of young people, in Spain and

Spanish America. In his letter to Candamo, he describes the book as a series of interlinked essays dedicated to various topics that he was writing on at the time: literary fame or what he called *erostratismo*, patriotism, science, and religion in Spain. What was to link them was the fact that they were written for a young audience.

3 In this regard, critics have pointed especially to the influence of thinkers like Johann Gottfried Herder and Hippolyte Taine. On *En torno al casticismo* see Serrano; Cerezo Galán, *Las máscaras* 104–25; and Rabaté, *Guerra de ideas* 50-121, introduction to *En torno al casticismo*, and *Crise intellectuelle et politique* (ed.).

4 Here I see a deeper connection between *En torno al casticismo* and Unamuno's novelistic work than Longhurst admits when he states that the philosophical work simply reflects nineteenth-century ideas while the novels anticipate a new, twentieth-century aesthetic (36).

5 On this exchange see García Blanco, "Clarín"; Ramos-Gascón; and Lissourges. Roberta Johnson gives a good summary of the relationship between Unamuno and Clarín and the generational dynamics that defined it (24–6).

6 For an extensive comparative consideration of the modernist novel in Spain and elsewhere in Europe, see Longhurst. On the role of the *nivola* in the development of Unamuno's narrative work, see Vauthier.

7 See the essay "Tres poetas metafísicos" (Cernuda 761–76).

8 The phrase Unamuno quotes comes from Nicolás Salmerón, a leading Krausist and one of the presidents of the First Spanish Republic.

9 On the impact of these readings on Unamuno's theology and understanding of religion, see Orringer, *Unamuno y los protestantes liberales*. Of particular relevance to the historical account given in "¡Pistis y no gnosis!" and "La fe" is the fifth chapter of Orringer's study, "Historia de la religión: de sus orígenes al catolicismo" (155–80).

10 See Ricoeur 21–8. Ricoeur notes that Marx reduces Hegel's concept of mind or spirit, making it signify something wholly alterior to material experience. Unamuno clearly had a more nuanced understanding of Hegel's concept of the idea, as he shows when he writes, "al afirmar con profundo realismo Hegel que es todo idea, redujo a su verdadera proporción a las llamadas por antonomasia ideas" ("when Hegel affirmed with profound realism that everything is an idea, he brought what we commonly call ideas down to their true scale") (*E* 2:202).

11 Marshall Berman has paid great attention to the images Marx employs in *The Communist Manifesto*, above all the image of dissolution encapsulated in the cited phrase, which Berman uses as the title of his book and views

as a vital illustration of the modernists' understanding of their historical moment. On the idea of development that Marx draws from German romanticism, see Berman 96.

12 The bibliography on Unamuno's socialism is extensive. For a summary of his involvement with the movement between 1891 and 1900, including his religious reading of it, see Ribas, "Unamuno y el Marxismo." Carlos Blanco Aguinaga demonstrated early on ("El socialismo de Unamuno"; "De nuevo") that in the political writings contemporary with the composition of *En torno al casticismo*, particularly those published in the anarchist journal *Ciencia social* in 1896, Unamuno shows familiarity with a number of Marxist concepts. Rafael Pérez de la Dehesa recognized socialism as playing an important role in the development of Unamuno's political thought, and catalogued some of his contributions to socialist publications like Bilbao's *La Lucha de Clases*. Manuel María Urrutia has fleshed out this picture in his own study of Unamuno's political evolution, as have more recent studies of the writer's contributions to *La Lucha de Clases*, which suggest that he published upwards of 350 articles in the periodical, the vast majority between 1894 and 1897 (see Robles, "La colaboración de Unamuno"). On Unamuno's approximation to, relations with, and eventual break from the Socialist Party, see the correspondence collected in María Dolores Gómez Molleda, *El socialismo español y los intelectuales*. For further bibliography, see Nuñez and Ribas 62–3.

13 As Ribas points out, though Unamuno's intense collaboration in *La Lucha de Clases* between 1894 and 1897 fell off drastically after he left the party, he did continue to contribute to the annual celebration of the May 1 worker's holiday upon request. "Socialismo y juventud" was published 11 May 1907, following another article by Unamuno that had appeared in the previous issue on May 1.

14 The first line of the poem reads "Cuando de juventud y de frescura ..." Like "Cuando yo sea viejo," this poem aligns the youth of future readers, invoked with an epigraph from Walt Whitman's *Poets to Come*, with the youth of poetry itself. In fact, the second-person interlocutor, at first singular and then plural, to whom it is addressed remains unidentified – it might be the future poets referenced in the epigraph, or the poet's own poems. Such thematic similarities with "Cuando yo sea viejo" suggest that the two poems were composed around the same time.

15 This comment seems to respond to urban planning debates that took place in the late nineteenth century regarding the expansion of Barcelona, in which architects (still affiliated with the upper clases) and engineers (symbols of the industrial revolution and the burgeoning bourgeoisie)

clashed over form-versus-function questions. On this history, see Aibar and Bijker.

16 With this reference to the coda to "The Work of Art in the Age of Mechanical Reproduction," I in no way suggest a link between Catalan nationalism and fascism. Rather, I cite Benjamin's phrase in order to underscore Unamuno's sensitivity to any and all situations in which the aesthetic or the spectacular becomes an instrument of creating consent.

17 Meyer's two-volume work, which Unamuno owned and annotated (Valdés and Valdés 162), clearly informs the Spaniard's ideas in this essay. In the book, Meyer outlines the arrangement of atoms in both "static" and "dynamic" conception, describes reactions caused by shaking (*ébranlement – sacudida* in Spanish), heat, light, and electricity. Of special importance for Unamuno's concept of *metarritmisis* is Meyer's assertion that atoms are in constant vibration ("toujours animés d'un mouvement rapide"), and thus have a kind of unique rhythm appreciable also in the molecules they form (1:326, 2:198–9).

18 On this subject, see Unamuno's 1900 essay "Contra 'los jóvenes'" (*OCE* 7:1261–3).

19 While Unamuno's ideas on culture often have a pan-Hispanic frame of reference (as in *Mi confesión*), in the case of *modernismo* (particularly in essays like "Los melenudos" [1901] and "El modernismo" [1907]) he reacts most directly to the movement's manifestation in Spain, and especially in Madrid, which flourished after Rubén Darío's first visit to the country in 1898. Sotelo Vázquez offers an interesting point of contrast in his analysis of Unamuno's reaction, a few years earlier, to Catalan *modernisme*, concluding that the writer welcomed "the dose of strangeness and extravagance that Barcelonese *modernisme* brought with it because he saw it as a regenerative alternative to the immobility and stupidity that presided over the cultural inaction in other parts of Spain" ("El primer Unamuno" 80, my translation). In a letter from February of 1896, which Sotelo Vázquez publishes in his article, Unamuno affirms, "es preferible ese hormigueo de extravagancias de la juventud de allí, con su snobismo y sus modernisterías todas, al tremendo empantanamiento de Madrid" ("this swarm of extravagances in their young people, with all of its snobbery and modernistries, is preferable to the terrible stagnation of Madrid") (85). As in the political realm, here the periphery of the Iberian Peninsula offers life and rejuvenation to the decrepit center.

With regard to Unamuno's critique of *modernismo*, scholarly commenters tend to fall into two groups: those who identify Unamuno as an *antimodernista*, due to his association with the Generation of 1898 and its philosophical and sociological preoccupations (Díaz-Plaja, Dobón, Meier); and those who point out fundamental commonalities between his work and that of the *modernistas*, usually drawing on a broader definition of modernism in the European context (*inter alia*: Jiménez, Gullón, Blasco). On *antimodernista* rhetoric in the criticism of the time, see Litvak.

20 After describing the "charca" in the essay Unamuno moves to the image of a traditional processional march in Spain, wherein a *dulzainero* attempts to improvise within the confines of the drummer's authoritative beat.

21 Marta Palenque has prepared a facsimile edition of the anthology, which was originally published in Madrid by the Librería Pueyo. On Unamuno's reaction to Carrere's collection and his poem, see her introduction, pages xxvi-xxvii. It is possible that Unamuno composed the text of "A la corte de los poetas" or some version thereof at an earlier date and added the title as he prepared the manuscript of *Poesías* – or, that he composed it in a direct response to Carrere's book.

22 The poems of this opening section are "¡Id con Dios!," "Credo poético," "Denso, denso," "Cuando yo sea viejo," and "Para después de mi muerte." María Pilar Celma writes of this opening section, "the first six poems appear as a unit, whose theme centers on poetry – how it ought to be, its persistence after death, the work's idependence from the author and, lastly, what the poetry being written in that moment is really like" (Blasco, Celma, and González 194–5, my translation).

23 Biruté Ciplijauskaité has drawn a similar comparison between Unamuno's stance and Mallarmé's condemnation of *vers officiel* ("Los valores fónicos" 35). On Unamuno y Verlaine, see Unamuno Pérez 90-2.

24 See Meier 138. For more on Unamuno's relationship to French culture, see Unamuno Pérez, who judges that, in spite of "his aversion to the French spirit," "he does not disdain nor ignore the importance of French culture" (36, my translation). One of the Basque writer's repeated complaints about the *modernistas* is that for them all literary culture is filtered through France: the classical and mythological references that they use have come to them in French translation. Thus while possibly revealing insecurity about France's cultural hegemony, it also displays a frustration with the *modernistas'* willingness to rely on translations rather than consult a direct source.

25 See the review published by Adolfo Rubio in *Nuestro Tiempo*, and Ribbans' reprint and commentary of another, anonymous contemporary response to the collection (Ribbans "'Indigesto, mezquino'"). In later analyses, Gerardo Diego and Luis Cernuda also comment on the clumsy and unrefined character of Unamuno's early verse as part of the critical reception of his poetry in the 1920s that I discuss in chapter 3.

26 Most recently, Cristina Flores Moreno has written on the influence of S.T. Coleridge in *Poesías*. See also Elizalde.

2 The Heroic Age

1 Francisco J. Romero Salvadó indicates the similarities in the war's effect on Spain to the changes experienced by other European nations in *Spain, 1914–1918*, one of very few studies dedicated solely to Spanish history during the First World War. Others include Ron Carden's *German Policy Toward Neutral Spain, 1914–1918*, and Fernando García Sanz's recent study of Spain's covert involvements in the conflict, *España en la Gran Guerra. Espías, diplomáticos y traficantes* (Galaxia Gutemberg, 2014). On this period in Spanish cultural history, see Fernando Díaz-Plaja, *Francófilos y germanófilos* and Mainer, *Literatura y pequeña burguesía* 121–70.

2 On the political debates that arose in Spain during the First World War as prefiguration of the ideological divides of the Spanish Civil War, see Krauel, "Visión parcial."

3 Romero Salvadó observes that the debate surrounding neutrality "revealed a deep pre-existing spiritual division within the Spanish people which the war did not create but only exacerbated" (9). On this debate see also Díaz-Plaja, *Francófilos* 13–23; García Sanz 38–45; and Menéndez Alzamora 269–81.

4 On the prelude to and circumstances surrounding Unamuno's dismissal from the rectorship, see the section of the Rabaté biography titled "Crónica de una destitución anunciada," especially pages 327–41.

5 The participation of Giner de los Ríos and other professors philosophically aligned with Krausism in the "cuestión universitaria" of the 1860s and 1870s set the stage for the institution's founding in 1876, which came about in response to renewed restrictions imposed by the government of the Bourbon Restoration and its sanctioning of professors who refused to abide by them (Giner was stripped of his professorship at Madrid's Universidad Central). On this episode, see Cacho Viu, *La Institución Libre*, vol. 1, chapters VII and X; Jiménez Fraud, *Historia* 354–74; and Capellán de Miguel 236–51.

6 Article 15 of the statutes was reproduced at the head of the first and every subsequent issue of the *Boletín de la Institución Libre de Enseñanza* (*BILE*), a fact which indicates the special importance assigned to the statement.

7 On this trip, see Chica 91–4; Jongh; and Robles, "Unamuno en Málaga."

8 Jiménez Fraud writes to Unamuno of the dispersal ("desbandada") of the group, and speculates, "¿Queda un lazo entre nosotros? Yo creo que sí.

Quizá sea este el mejor (si no el único) fruto" ("Does a bond among us remain? I believe so. Perhaps this is the best [if not the only] fruit") (Jiménez Fraud, *Residentes* 131). On the camraderie among the young men from Málaga, see Chica; Pérez de Ayala, "José Moreno Villa" 156–7.

9 In a review of Unamuno's visit – Moreno Villa's first known publication, accompanied by the future painter's first published sketches – he wrote, "espolea el espíritu, lo maltrata, lo vuelve a la vida (que antes dormía)" ("he prods the spirit, he batters it, he brings it to life [for until now it was sleeping]" *Memoria* 245). Several years later in 1913, Moreno Villa employed the term again in a letter to Unamuno where, calling himself "uno de aquellos mozos de Málaga, del año 6" ("one of those kids from Málaga, in 1906"), he confessed, "usted fue en mi edad moza, uno de los que espolearon mi alma con más fuerza" ("in my early years, you were one of those who most stimulated my soul") (Robles, "Doce cartas" 63–4).

10 The manuscript of *Niebla* was written in 1907, though not published until 1914. On this history, see Mario J. Valdés' critical introduction to the novel, pages 47–58.

11 For an extensive consideration of the origins, arguments, and reception of this speech, see Pedro Cerezo Galán's introduction to his edition of this text and others of Ortega's related writings.

12 McFarland further notes that numerous articles dedicated to the topic of physical education appeared in the *BILE*. On the *institucionista* approach to physical education, see Jiménez-Landi 2:130, 680-3, and 3:77–85; Capellán de Miguel 246–7.

13 J.B. Trend, in his *A Picture of Modern Spain* (1921), singled out the youth of the institution's leadership as one of its greatest assets, one in which it surpassed the English schools it had been modeled after: "I do not know what the average age may be of the heads of houses at Oxford or Cambridge, but it must be over forty. The head of the Residencia on the contrary is considerably younger than that; indeed, he is one of the youngest members of the council, and the gain to the college in having its youth and vigour concentrated in the mastership is incalculable" (Trend 34–5).

14 Tennis, hockey, hiking, soccer, skiing, and track and field were among the sports practiced by the *residentes*. On athletics at the Residencia, see Sáenz de la Calzada 120-6, Pérez-Villanueva 533–52.

15 In the preface to *Adolescence*, Hall asserted that youth had been "better understood" in ancient Greece and Rome than it was in modern Western society (xviii). In a similar vein, Massis and de Tarde had claimed that "les jeunes gens d'aujourd'hui sont plus attachés que leurs aînés à la

culture classique" ("the young people of today are more interested in classical culture than their elders") (96). Also relevant here is the return to classical culture emphasized in various Mediterranean national and artistic movements during the early twentieth century, whose manifestations included *romanità* in Italy and, in greater geographical proximity to the Residencia, Catalan Noucentisme (see d'Ors, *El Noucentisme* 187–215).

16 CMU 21, 36, document 8.

17 Onís grew up in Salamanca, met Unamuno at a very young age, and studied under him at the university, where in 1904 he founded a student periodical entitled *Gente Joven* (a possible parody of the concurrently published *Gente Vieja*), which cited Unamuno as its inspiration and guide (see Onís, "El magisterio de Unamuno" 1–2). Zulueta's correspondence with Unamuno began in 1903, when the older writer wrote him in appreciation of an article he had published. Zulueta responded by asking the rector in Salamanca for advice about his studies, noting that he wished to travel to another part of Europe to resolve what he calls "unas ciertas desaventuras de joven Werther" ("a few young-Werther-type misfortunes") (Zulueta, *Cartas* 20).

18 On the funding of the JAE and the Residencia, see Pérez Villanueva 62–70.

19 While John Crispin concludes that Jiménez Fraud had handled the relationship with "Senecan equaminity" (36), Alison Sinclair has argued that the king's visits were used to heighten the Residencia's cultural prestige, particularly in its journal *Residencia*, which began appearing in 1926.

20 See Giner, "Aspectos del anarquismo." In the article, Giner cites Unamuno's essay "Renovación," which had appeared in *Vida Nueva* on 31 July 1898.

21 To be sure, Unamuno had cultivated this likeness through his reflections on the figure of Don Quijote, in his *Vida de Don Quijote y Sancho* (1905). See Roberts 104–10.

22 See Cirre 47–54, López Frías 85–90, and Romojaro 24–7.

23 From "[Mi segundo libro fue titulado 'El pasajero' 1914 por una preocupación]," unpublished notes held in the Fondo José Moreno Villa, Centro de Documentación, Residencia de Estudiantes (JMV/5/55/1).

24 I have not been able to locate this article by Pérez de Ayala.

25 In "La imagen poética de don Luis de Góngora," Lorca details the difficulties of this endeavor: "¿cómo mantener una tensión lírica pura durante largos escuadrones de versos? ¿Y cómo hacerlo sin narración? Si le daba a la narración, a la anécdota, toda su importancia, se le convertía en épico al menor descuido. Y si no narraba nada, el poema se rompía por mil partes

sin unidad ni sentido" ("How to maintain a pure lyric tension throughout such long squadrons of lines? And how to do so without narrating? If he gave narration, the story, all of its importance, the work would turn into an epic the moment his attention wavered. And if he did not narrate anything, the poem would break into a thousand pieces with no unity or sense") (García Lorca, *OC* 3:73). These questions are very similar to the ones Moreno Villa says he asked of himself. His distaste for the epic may also have been coloured by Ortega y Gasset's denigration of the genre as decidedly un-modern in *Meditaciones del Quijote* (*OCT* 1:799–800).

26 Unamuno began *El Cristo de Velázquez* in 1913, and it was published in 1920. On this work's uniqueness, given the rarity of the long poem in early twentieth-century Spanish poetry, see Maurer, "*El Cristo de Velázquez*" 22–8. For Moreno Villa's account in *Vida en claro*, see *Memoria* 94.

27 For the original sonnet, see *OCE* 6:880. "En horas de insomnio" appeared in *Los Lunes de El Imparcial* in 1911 but was never collected in any of Unamuno's books of poetry. For more information see García Blanco, *Don Miguel* 179–81. The other epigraph to "En la selva fervorosa" is taken from Goethe's diaries, likely reflecting the reading Moreno Villa did while living in Germany.

28 In a letter to Unamuno dated 27 June 1914, Moreno Villa comments on the differences between depictions of Saint George and Saint Michael, which Unamuno apparently confused in a previous letter, now lost. Moreno Villa recalls the image of Saint Michael in Salamanca's Catedral Vieja, and mentions a photograph he made of it during his visit in November of 1913. The photograph is preserved along with Moreno Villa's letters in the Casa Museo Unamuno in Salamanca.

29 See "Mensaje a Moreno Villa" in *Leyenda (1896–1956)*, pages 518–19. Originally published as "A José Moreno Villa" in *Los Lunes de El Imparcial*, 2 November 1914, page 3.

30 Ribagorda states that Moreno Villa remained in charge of editing the *Ensayos* throughout the three years they were printed ("Las publicaciones" 57), but he bases his assumption on a misreading of one of the younger writer's letters to Unamuno. The letter, from December of 1919, inquires not about one of the essays published by the Residencia, but rather about a series of poems that Unamuno had sent to be included in a journal Moreno Villa was hoping to found with Enrique Díez Canedo and Alfonso Reyes (Robles, "Doce cartas" 66–7). This project was not brought to fruition, though when the trio began to publish their "Cuadernos literarios" series in the early 1920s they turned to Unamuno again. On this collaborative project, see Bockus Aponte 55–8.

31 On these journals, see Celma Valero 28–36 and 70-2.

32 For a complete list of Unamuno's contributions to *España*, see Urrutia, "Miguel de Unamuno y la revista *España*." Enrique Díez-Canedo reviewed the *Ensayos* for the journal in the issue dated 15 February 1917.

33 Juan Pérez de Ayala's edition of Moreno Villa's *Poesías completas* reproduces the poem as it appeared in *Evoluciones*, making no note of the original publication of the poem, nor of the historical context in which it appeared.

34 In the sheet included with the original edition of *Luchas de 'Pena' y 'Alegría'* that lists errata, not accounted for in *Poesías completas*, Moreno Villa corrects the printed "más" (more) with "mas" (but).

35 See, for example, Emilia Pardo Bazán's lecture *El porvenir de la literatura después de la Guerra* (*The Future of Literature After the War*), published by the Residencia in 1917.

3 "Un joven auténtico de 366 años"

1 On Unamuno's relationship with Crawford Flitch, see García Blanco, "Un hispanista británico" and Kerrigan xxiv-xxv.

2 In his acceptance, collected in the volume *Hommage à Rupert Brooke* organized by Paul Vanderborght and published in Brussels in 1931, Unamuno writes, "Je connais depuis tout un temps *1914 and other poems* de Rupert Brooke et, dans ce livre, le merveilleux sonnet: *If I should die, think only this of me* … Cette voix d'un jeune homme qui m'enchante de rêve au seuil de ma vieillesse! … Lorsque j'écrivais, dans mon exil, à Paris, un poème qui commençait par ces mots: <<*Si caigo aquí, sobre esta tierra verde*>> … comme je me souvenais de Rupert Brooke!" ("I have known Rupert Brooke's *1914 and Other Poems* for a long while, and within that book, the marvelous sonnet: *If I should die, think only this of me* … That young man's voice that enchants me with dreams at the threshold of my old age! … In my exile in Paris, while I wrote a poem that began with the words: '*If I should fall here, on this green earth*' … oh how I remembered Rupert Brooke!") (Vanderborght 191). Unamuno's connection to the Comité was the result of a trip to Belgium he had taken early in his exile, in August of 1924, where a group led by Vanderborght held a banquet in his honor. On Unamuno's Belgian connections see Verbeke.

3 Gabriele Morelli has called Diego the "miglior fabbro" of the Generation of 1927. On this writer's central role in the fashioning of the Generation of 1927 and the rationale behind his choices in *Poesía española. Antología*, see Morelli, *Historia* and Anderson, *El Veintisiete* 81–7 and 340-1.

4 González Calleja summarizes the origins of the student protest movement during the dictatorship and the history of the ULE and the FUE (99–110). See also González Calleja and Souto Kustrín, López-Rey.

5 On this issue of *Intentions*, see De Paepe, "Aquella intentona" and "Lorca y *La Jeune littérature.*"

6 In yet another letter, which Unamuno subsequently wrote to Spanish parents, it is clear that he saw the student protesters of the 1920s as embodying and enacting the kind of youth he had envisioned for Spain at the beginning of the century. He writes that these young men and women have executed an admirable "patriótica protesta" ("patriotic protest") and praises them again for not becoming "reclutas mecanizados" ("mechanized recruits") or "*bueyes cautos*" ("bullied cows," Unamuno's play on the English "boy scouts") (*Cartas del destierro* 302, 303). Particularly striking is his characterization of this youth as "en el más hondo sentido socialista" ("socialist in the deepest sense"): to him, these young people represent the kind of socialism that had inspired him at the turn of the century, based on generosity and solidarity with the working class, not on political partisanship or dogma.

7 Here I follow Juan Cano Ballesta's account of Jiménez's activity during this period (*La poesía pura* 63–7). On Jiménez's rifts with the members of the younger generation, see Cano Ballesta, "Poetas celestes"; Dennis, *Perfume and Poison* 46–56; Maurer, "Más allá de Eco y Narciso"; Cliplijauskaité, "Apostilla a una polémica."

8 See Álvarez Castro, "Miguel de Unamuno, ¿poeta vanguardista?"

9 Henri Brémond's *La Poésie pure*, published in 1926, excited a debate that extended from France to Spain. On the relationships between French and Spanish "pure poetry," see Blanch, chapters 6–8.

10 While Nigel Dennis saw this rephrasing as a largely inconsequential rhetorical flourish on Bergamín's part (*José Bergamín* 57), I would argue that the revision is highly significant. It reflects the author's insistence not only on art's humanity, but also on its capacity for transcendence – something that Ortega had denied in "La deshumanización del arte." Bergamín's term *desvivirse* rehumanizes, and even personifies modern art as capable of intense passion, while at the same time it suggests that this passion pushes it beyond the here-and-now to the eternal, evoking a religious sentiment like that expressed in Teresa de Ávila's "muero porque no muero" ("I die because I do not die"). I discuss the conflation of religion and politics with art in Bergamín's work in the next chapter.

11 All of these works are included in Diego's library, held at the Fundación Gerardo Diego in Santander, and bear markings and annotations. Of the

Ensayos, the library includes volumes three through seven of the Residencia de Estudiantes edition.

12 In this combativeness, Unamuno's approach to art clearly differs from Juan Ramón Jiménez's concept of "ética estética" (see Blasco, *La poética* 211–13). Later Diego would clarify his view of the relative influences of each of these three poets, writing of Jiménez, "su influencia es principalmente estética y técnica. La de Unamuno, metafísica y moral. La de Antonio Machado, metafísica y técnica" ("his influence is principally aesthetic and technical. That of Unamuno, metaphysical and moral. That of Antonio Machado, metaphysical and technical") ("Presencia" 67).

13 Diego's allergy to bringing questions of politics to bear on literature is apparent in his response to a survey on the topic in *La Gaceta Literaria* in 1927, and later on he would refuse to take sides in the debate over "pure" and "impure" poetry that arose between Juan Ramón Jiménez and Pablo Neruda in the 1930s (Gómez-Santos 39). A firm Catholic, he tacitly supported the Nationalist forces during the Civil War and remained in Spain during Franco's dictatorship.

14 *Versos humanos* won Spain's Premio Nacional de Literatura in 1925, sharing the award with Alberti's *Marinero en tierra*.

15 See José María de Cossío's mention of this trip in "Tres dedicatorias," *Verso y Prosa* 3 (March 1927): 3.

16 Following Unamuno himself, Zardoya preferred this concept of "humanation" to "humanization," which would be the mere converse of Ortegan *deshumanización*. See Zardoya, "La 'Humanación' en la poesía de Unamuno."

17 For one approach to the role of faith in Diego's poetry, see Pérez Gutiérrez, "La fe y lo religioso." While this survey is instructive, I believe that the case of poems like "El ciprés de Silos" ought to nuance Pérez Gutiérrez's view of Diego's poetic treatment of religion as wholly opposed to ("en las antípodas de") Unamuno's (165).

18 Here it is worth remembering that Unamuno was about to begin work on *La agonía del cristianismo*. It originally appeared in French as *L'agonie du cristianisme*, translated by Jean Cassou.

19 It should be noted that Ortega had actually highlighted the unserious, ludic character of contemporary art both in *El tema de nuestro tiempo* and in "La deshumanización del arte." See Anderson, *Ernesto Giménez* 138–40.

20 Interestingly, in the 1927 version of the text that appeared in *Verso y Prosa*, from which I quote here, and in the 1929 edition of the book *Julepe de menta* in which it was collected, Gecé's past love interest is distinctively androgynous. Despite the mention of "la musa gongorina" that I quote, the rest

of the references to Góngora omit the mention of the muse and use masculine pronouns, even as the poet is imagined wearing rouge and dancing for men. This androgyny is consonant with 1920s youth culture broadly, if one considers the fluid gender norms embraced by social groups like the Bright Young Things in Britain. By contrast, however, the text of the article in the 1981 edition of *Julepe de menta* consistently refers to a feminine muse.

21 To be sure, especially in the opposition of poetry and criticism, Unamuno was also drawing on a preexisting tradition perceivable, for example, in Gustavo Adolfo Bécquer's *Cartas literarias a una mujer*.

22 The poem "Todo será el corazón" was published and the annotations documented by Manuel Fernández-Montesinos in the newspaper *Ideal* (Granada; 29 May 1986), which I have not been able to consult. For the poem, see García Lorca, *Poesía inédita* 580-2.

23 On this possibility, see Dennis, *Perfume and Poison* 118–19.

24 On Cossío's role within the so-called Generation of 1927, and for information on his interactions with Unamuno and esteem for his poetry, see San José Lera.

25 As noted in the introduction, Unamuno was retranslating the text from Jean Cassou's French version, since the original had been lost.

26 Such lines might support Álvarez Castro's argument ("Miguel de Unamuno, ¿poeta vanguardista?") that Unamuno's late poetry approximates the avant-garde, although this depends on what one means by "avant-garde." The deepening in the older writer's understanding of contemporary poetic trends occurred as some lyricists of *la joven literatura* sought to distance themselves from what they, at least, understood to be "la vanguardia." Quiroga Plá, a consistent critic of *La Gaceta Literaria* from 1927 on, differentiated the work of the supposedly young vanguardists from "poesía joven – eso es, de siempre" ("young poetry – that is, enduring poetry") (Martínez Nadal 83). Whether the writing of the so-called Generation of 1927 can be called avant-garde in the language of present-day criticism is a question taken up by Anderson (*El Veintisiete* 280-316) and Soufas (introduction and chapter 2), both of whom – but for different reasons – prefer the term "modernist."

27 From among the artists of *la joven literatura*, Rafael Alberti and Pedro Salinas contributed creative pieces, Melchor Fernández Almagro sent an article on Unamuno's dramatic work *Fedra*, and Antonio Marichalar and Benjamín Jarnés also wrote short reflections. Quiroga Plá declined to participate in the "gimenezcaballeresco" homage, joining others who had by then cut ties with Gecé's increasingly right-wing publication.

28 CMU, Caja 23/63. The letter has been reproduced in Ricardo Senabre's study, "98 y 27: Acciones y reacciones" (Enciso Recio 90).
29 See the special treatment of the debate in *Índice* ("La polémica J.R.J./J.G.") and among others, Maurer, "Más allá de Eco y Narciso"; Ciplijauskaité, "Apostilla a una polémica"; and Sody.

4 Hercules and Hermes

1 Anderson acknowledges that the comparison might "prove illuminating," but does not pursue it (*Ernesto Giménez* 161). Nigel Dennis also wrote extensively on both figures, but did not carry out an explicitly comparative study. See, among other publications, his *José Bergamín: A Critical Introduction*, and the introduction to his critical edition of Giménez Caballero's *Visitas literarias de España*. Throughout this chapter I refer to Dennis' invaluable edition of the correspondence between Bergamín and Unamuno, *El epistolario. José Bergamín. Miguel de Unamuno (1923–1935).*
2 For information on Bergamín's and Giménez Caballero's respective readings of Nietzsche, see Sobejano 646–9, 651–4.
3 Miguel Corella Lacasa has analyzed the arc of Gecé's production in terms of Benjaminian aestheticization.
4 CMU 21, 35, document 9.
5 Here I refer not only to the conflict over Gecé's printing of Unamuno's letter in the Góngora issue of *La Gaceta Literaria*, but also to the more critical view Unamuno took of the younger writer's work. Borzoni highlights one particular episode in which Unamuno voiced his disapproval of a comparison between Primo de Rivera and Teresa de Ávila that Giménez Caballero made in *Los toros, las castañuelas y la Virgen* (Borzoni 268).
6 I recognize the inconsistency of using one Roman and one Greek name in referring to these two figures (Heracles/Hercules and Hermes/Mercury), but do so in order to preserve proximity in English to the terminology chosen by the writers themselves.
7 Pérez Firmat documents numerous examples of the pneumatic "isotopy," culminating with Jarnés' distinction (40-50). Strikingly, despite the obvious resonance of Unamuno's *Niebla* in this context, Peréz Firmat is reluctant to acknowledge a direct connection between the *nivola* and the vanguard prose that interests him.
8 On "El pensamiento hermético de las artes," see Dennis, *José Bergamín* 54–8.
9 As Susan Larson has written, with particular attention to the novel's treatment of gender, "*Hermes* can be compared to a vigorously shaken snow globe whose fluffy, delicate sedimentations are briefly and violently

unsettled for a time before they return to their tightly enclosed and familiar pattern" ("Unreadable Bodies" 67).

10 Santiáñez cites José Antonio Primo de Rivera's speech of 29 October 1933, delivered in Madrid's Teatro de la Comedia, to illustrate the role of poetry in the Spanish fascist imaginary (25–6).

11 Anderson stresses in his book on Giménez Caballero that the two phases into which the writer's life are usually divided in reality reflect different manifestations of a single set of interests.

12 On *Notas marruecas de un soldado* see, among others, Foard 45–60, Selva 39–51, and Santiánez 76–83.

13 CMU 21, 35, Document 1. The full correspondence between Unamuno and Giménez Caballero has been documented in Borzoni's doctoral thesis on the complex relationship between Unamuno and totalitarian ideologies, "Fajismo y fascismos," pages 258–86.

14 See also "Peliculerías," originally published in *El Mercantil Valenciano* on 18 February 1923, and collected in Unamuno, *Artículos desconocidos* 488–9.

15 See Dennis, *El epistolario* 45n1. Multiple references to the Residencia appear in Bergamín's letters to Unamuno, indicating that it was often the setting of their encounters in the first year of their acquaintance, before the older writer's exile.

16 Moreover, Unamuno was highly critical of the Spanish Legion or Tercio that Millán-Astray had created. On Unamuno's disdain for Millán-Astray and the Tercio, see Borzoni 91–5.

17 In the prologue to the 1942 edition of his collected aphorisms, Bergamín remembers his participation in the "algaradas estudiantiles" ("student uprisings") of his youth, and likens this form of social disruption to the intellectually disruptive work of the aphorism (*Caballito* 9).

18 On Primo's response to *Notas marruecas de un soldado*, see Foard 60.

19 CMU 21, 35, document 5.

20 Anderson cites this encounter with de Torre and the avant-garde as one that opened up "a whole new way of looking at the problem" of regeneration that preoccupied Giménez Caballero in the early 1920s: one that was literary rather than solely political (*Ernesto Giménez* 258–9). To the extent that Unamuno was also recognized as a predecessor by the avant-gardists (Guillermo de Torre speaks of Don Miguel as a prodigious "islote," a solitary and uncompromising individualist, in his *Literaturas europeas de vanguardia*, which Giménez Caballero read with great interest), the impression that he had already made on the young *madrileño* facilitated this new development in his thought.

21 The first piece, on Guillermo de Torre, was followed by articles dedicated to Benjamín Jarnés; Federico García Lorca; Sebastià Gasch, Salvador Dalí, and Lluís Montanyà (the authors of the "Manifiesto Antiartístico Catalán," published earlier in 1928 in *Gallo*); and Rafael Alberti. These "itinerarios" were to form the third volume in the series of Gecé's *Visitas literarias de España*, following volumes dedicated to older figures and, apparently, another intermediate age group. See Giménez Caballero, "Itinerarios" 7; Anderson, *Ernesto Giménez* 185–6.

22 The letters are held in the Centro de Documentación of the Residencia de Estudiantes, Archivo León Sánchez Cuesta. They are dated September 6, 9, and 20, respectively. The book was to include several essays, some of which Bergamín had already published: one on Pedro Salinas; another on Jorge Guillén; a study of "Andalusian idealism" in Rafael Alberti, Vicente Aleixandre, and Manuel Altolaguirre; essays on the theatre of Claudio de la Torre and Federico García Lorca; and more on Gerardo Diego, Dámaso Alonso, Antonio Espina, and Antonio Marichalar. A projected appendix on other writers including Melchor Fernández Almagro, Ernesto Giménez Caballero, and Benjamín Jarnés would round out the collection.

23 Letter of 6 September 1928. Residencia de Estudiantes, Centro de Documentación, signatura 280790340/LSC/3/43/11. In a letter to Arturo Serrano Plaja that he printed in *Cruz y Raya* in 1935, Bergamín reflects on his trip to Moscow and on the link between his admiration for communism and his own Christian faith: "Cuando yo estuve en Rusia, en 1928, traje de aquel rápido contacto vivo una lección moral inolvidable: algo que, como dije entonces, me había enseñado para siempre, aún más que el sabor de la sangre, el gusto y regusto del pan, entero y compartido. Y este gusto o sabor de comunión humana no podré olvidarlo … se adentra y vivifica cada vez más en mi recuerdo; y eso mientras más se acentúa en mí, espiritualmente, el hambre de otro pan imperecedero" ("When I was in Russia, in 1928, I took away from that quick, intense contact an unforgettable moral lesson: something that, as I said then, had taught me forever, even more that the taste of blood, the taste and aftertaste of bread, whole and shared. And I will not forget this taste or flavor of human communion … it deepens and intensifies increasingly in my memory; even as the hunger for another, everlasting bread grows stronger in me") (Bergamín, *Cristal* 76).

24 On Bergamín's political thought and action and their relationship to his interpretation of Christianity, see Arana Palacios; Pérez Gutiérrez, "José Bergamín"; Penalva 82–5; and Mendibourne 75–88.

25 Santiáñez calls *Genio de España* "perhaps the most complete and significant fusion of fascism and avant-gardism in Spain" (34). On *Arte y Estado*, see Santiáñez 46–54.

26 See "Juvenalia" (*OCE* 7:668–70), "La generación de 1931" (3:1243–5), and "Otra vez con la juventud" (8:1227–9).

Conclusion

1 In fact, already in 1928 the publishing house Renacimiento had begun work on an edition of Unamuno's *Obras completas*. An advertisement for it appeared printed below the article by Francisco Ayala on the passing of Spanish literature's youth in 1931.

2 This would no longer be the case in the second edition of *Poesía española*, published in 1934.

3 On Bergamín and the Editorial Séneca, see Santoja.

4 On the Spanish Transition as *Bildungsroman*, see Medina.

Bibliography

Abel, Elizabeth, Marianne Hirsch, and Elizabeth Langland, eds. *The Voyage In: Fictions of Female Development*. Hanover, NH and London: University Press of New England, 1983.

Aibar, Eduardo and Wiebe E. Bijker. "Constructing a City: The Cerdà Plan for the Extension of Barcelona." *Science, Technology & Human Values* 22 (1997): 3–30.

Alas, Adolfo, ed. *Menéndez Pelayo. Unamuno. Palacio Valdés. Epistolario a Clarín*. Madrid: Ediciones Escorial, 1941.

Alberti, Rafael. *La arboleda perdida*. Barcelona: Editorial Planeta, 1977.

Alonso, Dámaso. "Una generación poética (1920–1936)." *Obras completas*. 10 vols. Madrid: Gredos, 1975. 4:653–76.

Altolaguirre, Manuel. *El caballo griego. Reflexiones y recuerdos (1927–1958)*. Ed. James Valender. Madrid: Visor Libros, 2006.

Álvarez Castro, Luis. *La palabra y el ser en la teoría literaria de Unamuno*. Salamanca: Ediciones Universidad de Salamanca, 2005.

– "Miguel de Unamuno, ¿poeta vanguardista?: El diálogo entre teoría y praxis lírica en el *Cancionero*." *Bulletin of Spanish Studies* 86 (2009): 205–25.

– "Nivola y metaficción en la narrativa española de vanguardia." *Ínsula* 807 (2014): 9–13.

Anderson, Andrew A. *El Veintisiete en tela de juicio: examen de la historiografía generacional y replanteamiento de la vanguardia histórica española*. Madrid: Gredos, 2005.

– *Ernesto Giménez Caballero: The Vanguard Years (1921–1931)*. Newark, DE: Juan de la Cuesta, 2011.

Arana Palacios, Jesús. "José Bergamín, un hombre de su siglo." *Revista de Occidente* 166 (1995): 29–52.

Aranguren, José Luis. *La juventud europea y otros ensayos*. Barcelona: Seix Barral, 1965.
Arias Santos, Francisco Javier. "Una nueva visión de Unamuno." *Cuadernos hispanoamericanos* 589–90 (1999): 179–90.
Areilza, José María. "Memorias de un dictador, de Ernesto Giménez Caballero." *Anthropos* 84 (1988): 38–9.
Ayala, Francisco. "Anotación en el calendario." *La Gaceta Literaria*. 1 May 1931: 16.
Azorín. "La generación de 1898." *Clásicos y modernos*. Buenos Aires: Editorial Losada, 1939. 170–87.
Baez Pérez de la Tudela, José. "Movilización juvenil y radicalización verbalista: La Juventud de Acción Popular." *Historia contemporánea* 11 (1994): 83–105.
Benjamin, Walter. *Illuminations*. Ed. Hannah Arendt. New York: Schocken Books, 1969.
– *Selected Writings*. 1. Ed. Marcus Bullock and Michael W. Jennings. Cambridge, MA: Belknap Press, 1996.
Berchem, Theodor, and Hugo Laitenberger, eds. *El joven Unamuno en su época*. Salamanca, Spain: Junta de Castilla y León, 1997.
Bergamín, José. *Caballito del diablo*. Buenos Aires: Editorial Losada, 1942.
– *La cabeza a pájaros*. Madrid: Cruz y Raya, Ediciones del Árbol, 1934.
– *El cohete y la estrella*. Madrid: Biblioteca de Índice, 1923.
– *Cristal del tiempo*. Ed. Gonzalo Santoja. Hondarribia, Basque Country: Hiru, 1995.
– *La decadencia del analfabetismo. La importancia del demonio*. Madrid and Santiago de Chile: Cruz del Sur, 1961.
– *Detrás de la cruz*. México: Editorial Seneca, 1941.
– "Literatura y brújula." *La Gaceta Literaria* 1 February 1929: 1+.
– "Patos del aguachirle castellana." *Verso y Prosa* 1 June 1927: 2.
– "El pensamiento hermético de las artes." *Cruz y Raya* 15 April 1933: 41–66.
– "Signo y diseño de *Cruz y Raya* (1933–1936)." Introduction. *El Aviso de escarmentados del año que acaba y Escarmiento de avisados para el que empieza de 1935. Signo y diseño de Cruz y Raya*. Glashütten im Taunus and Nendeln-Liechtenstien: Verlag Detlev Auvermann KG/Kraus. Reprint, 1974. vii-xiv.
Berman, Marshall. *All That is Solid Melts Into Air: The Experience of Modernity*. New York: Penguin Books, 1988.
Blanco Aguinaga, Carlos. "De nuevo: El socialismo de Unamuno (1894–1897)." *Cuadernos de la Cátedra Miguel de Unamuno* 18 (1968): 5–48.
– "El socialismo de Unamuno." *Revista de Occidente* 41 (1966): 166–84.

Blanch, Antonio. *La poesía pura española. Conexiones con la cultura francesa*. Madrid: Gredos, 1976.

Blasco, Francisco Javier. *La poética de Juan Ramón Jiménez. Desarrollo, contexto y sistema*. Salamanca: Ediciones Universidad de Salamanca, 1981.

Blasco, Javier, María Pilar Celma, and Ramón González. *Miguel de Unamuno, poeta*. Valladolid: Universidad de Valladolid, 2003.

Blázquez González, Jesús Alfonso, ed. *Unamuno y Candamo: Amistad y epistolario (1899–1936)*. Madrid: Ediciones 98, 2007.

Bockus Aponte, Bárbara. *Alfonso Reyes and Spain: His Dialogue with Unamuno, Valle-Inclán, Ortega y Gasset, Jiménez, and Gómez de la Serna*. Austin, TX: University of Texas Press, 1972.

Borzoni, Sandro. "Fajismo y fascismos: Miguel de Unamuno frente a las ideologías totalitarias en la década de los treinta." Ph.D. diss. Universidad de Salamanca, 2009.

Bourdieu, Pierre. *Questions de sociologie*. Paris: Les Editions de Minuit, 1980.

Brémond, Henri. *La Poésie pure*. Paris: B. Grasset, 1926.

Brihuega, Jaime. *Manifiestos, proclamas, panfletos y textos doctrinales (Las vanguardias artísticas en España: 1910–1931)*. Madrid: Ediciones Cátedra, 1982.

Brooke, Rupert. *1914 and Other Poems*. London: Sidgwick & Jackson, 1917.

Burt, Stephen. *The Forms of Youth: Twentieth-Century Poetry and Adolescence*. New York: Columbia University Press, 2007.

Cacho Viu, Vicente. *La Institución Libre de Enseñanza*. 2 vols. Madrid: Ediciones Rialp, 1962.

Calinescu, Matei. *Five Faces of Modernity*. Durham: Duke University Press, 1987.

Cano Ballesta, Juan. *La poesía española entre pureza y revolución (1930–1936)*. Madrid: Gredos, 1972.

– "Poetas celestes, poetas demoníacos: Juan Ramón Jiménez y la generación del 27." In Gilbert Paolini ed., *La Chispa '85: Selected Proceedings*. New Orleans: Tulane University Press, 1985. 49–56.

Cansinos Asséns, Rafael. *La nueva literatura*. 4 vols. Madrid: V.H. de Sanza Calleja, 1917–1927.

– *La nueva literatura: colección de estudios críticos*. Madrid: Editorial Páez, 1925.

Capellán de Miguel, Gonzalo. *La España armónica: El proyecto del krausismo español para una sociedad en conflicto*. Madrid: Editorial Biblioteca Nueva, 2006.

Carden, Ron. *German Policy Toward Neutral Spain, 1914–1918*. New York and London: Garland, 1987.

Cascardi, Anthony and Leah Middlebrook, eds. *Poiesis and Modernity in the Old and New Worlds*. Nashville, TN: Vanderbilt University Press, 2012.

Cate-Arries, Francie. "Poetics and Philosophy: José Ortega y Gasset and the Generation of 1927." *Hispania* 3 (1988): 503–11.
Celma Valero, María Pilar. *Literatura y periodismo en las revistas del fin de siglo: estudio e indices (1888–1907)*. Madrid: Ediciones Júcar, 1991.
Cerezo Galán, Pedro. *El mal del siglo: El conflicto entre Ilustración y Romanticismo en la crisis finisecular del siglo XIX*. Madrid: Biblioteca Nueva, 2003.
– *Las máscaras de lo trágico. Filosofía y tragedia en Miguel de Unamuno*. Madrid: Trotta, 1996.
– ed. *Vieja y nueva política y otros escritos programáticos* by José Ortega y Gasset. Madrid: Biblioteca Nueva, 2007.
Cernuda, Luis. *Prosa completa*. Eds. Derek Harris and Luis Maristany. Barcelona: Barral Editores, 1975.
Ciplijauskaité, Biruté. "Apostilla a una polémica: J. R. Jiménez y los poetas del 27." *Revista Canadiense de Estudios Hispánicos* 21 (1996): 77–85.
– "Los valores fónicos en la poesía de Unamuno." *Hispania* 71 (1988): 31–7.
Cirre, José Francisco. *La poesía de José Moreno Villa*. Madrid: Ínsula, 1963.
Chica, Francisco. "La Málaga de Jiménez Fraud y los malagueños de la Residencia." *Boletín de la Institución Libre de Enseñanza* 78–79–80 (2010): 91–106.
Cobb, Christopher. *Artículos olvidados sobre España y la Primera Guerra Mundial*. London: Tamesis, 1976.
Coke-Enguídanos, Mervyn. "Miguel de Unamuno, the Poet of His Early Essays: 1887–1905." In John Crispin, Enrique Pupo-Walker, and Luis Lorenzo-Rivera, eds. *Los hallazgos de la lectura: Estudio dedicado a Miguel Enguídanos*. Madrid: Porrúa Turanzas, 1989.
"¿Cómo ven la nueva juventud española?" *La Gaceta Literaria*. 1 Mar. 1929: 1+.
Corella Lacasa, Miguel. "Ernesto Giménez Caballero, o la estetización de la política." *Olivar* 1 (2000): 123–42.
Costa, Joaquín, ed. *Oligarquía y caciquismo como la forma actual de gobierno en España: urgencia y modo de cambiarla*. Madrid: Imprenta de los Hijos de M.G. Hernández, 1902.
– *Reconstitución y europeización de España*. Madrid: Imprenta de San Francisco de Sales, 1900.
Crispin, John. *Oxford y Cambridge en Madrid: La Residencia de Estudiantes (1910–1936) y su entorno cultural*. Santander: Sur Ediciones, 1981.
Cruz Mendizábal, Juan. "Unamuno: Ensayista poético y poeta del ensayo." *Cuadernos de Aldeeu* 6 (1990): 165–76.
Davidson, Robert. "Cybernetic Totemism in Giménez Caballero's *Hércules jugando a los dados* (1928)." *Bulletin of Hispanic Studies* 84 (2007): 305–18.

Dennis, Nigel, ed. *El epistolario. José Bergamín. Miguel de Unamuno (1923–1935).* Valencia: Pre-Textos, 1993.
– *José Bergamín: A Critical Introduction, 1920–1936.* Toronto, Buffalo, and London: Toronto University Press, 1986.
– *Perfume and Poison: A Study of the Relationship between José Bergamín and Juan Ramón Jimenez.* Kassel, Germany: Reichenberger, 1985.
De Paepe, Christian. "Aquella intentona de *Intentions*. De *La Jeune littérature espagnole* (*Intentions*, 1924) a *Poesía española. Antología 1915–1931* (G. Diego, 1932)." In *Principios modernos y creatividad expresiva en la poesía española contemporánea*, eds. Elsa Dehennin and Christian de Paepe. Amsterdam and New York: Rodopi, 2009. 239–64.
– "Lorca y *La Jeune littérature espagnole*: Nueva luz sobre el número especial de la revista *Intentions* (París, abril-mayo de 1924)." In Andrés Soria Olmedo, María José Sánchez Montes, and Juan Varo Zafra, eds., *Federico García Lorca, clásico moderno (1898–1998)*. Granada, Spain: Diputación de Granada, 2000. 205–19.
Díaz de Castro, Francisco J., ed. *Los Cuatro Vientos. Madrid 1933.* Facsimile edition. Seville: Renacimiento, 2000.
Díaz Fernández, José. *Prosas*. Ed. Nigel Dennis. Madrid: Fundación Santander Central Hispano, 2006.
Díaz-Plaja, Fernando. *Francófilos y germanófilos. Los españoles en la guerra europea.* Barcelona: Dopesa, 1973.
Díaz-Plaja, Guillermo. *Modernismo frente a noventa y ocho. Una introducción a la literatura española del siglo XX.* Madrid: Espasa-Calpe, 1951.
Diego, Gerardo. "Crónica del centenario de Góngora (1627–1927)." *Lola* 1 and 2. December 1927 – January 1928. 1:1–8, 2:1–7.
– *Obras completas*. Eds. Díez de Revenga, Francisco Javier, and José Luis Bernal. 8 vols. Madrid: Aguilar, 1989.
– ed. *Poesía española: antología, 1915–1931.* Madrid: Signo, 1932.
– "Presencia de Unamuno, poeta." *Cisneros* 7 (1943): 67–8.
– and José María de Cossío. *Epistolario. Nuevas claves de la generación del 27.* Madrid: Ediciones de la Universidad de Alcalá de Henares, 1996.
Dobón, María Dolores. "Sociólogos contra estetas: Prehistoria del conflicto entre modernismo y 98." *Hispanic Review* 64 (1996): 57–72.
D'Ors, Carlos. *El Noucentisme. Presupuestos ideológicos, estéticos y artísticos.* Madrid: Cátedra, 2000.
D'Ors, Eugenio. *Trilogía de la 'Residencia de Estudiantes.'* Ed. Alicia Gómez-Navarro and Ángel d'Ors. Pamplona: Ediciones Universidad de Pamplona, 2000.

Driscoll, Catherine. "Portrait of the Young Man as Artist: Modernism and Adolescence." In *Modernist Cultural Studies*. Gainesville, FL: University Press of Florida, 2010. 45–65.

Eliot, T.S. *Selected Essays: 1917–1932*. London: Faber and Faber, 1999 [1932].

Elizalde, Ignacio. "Fray Luis de León en la poesía de Miguel de Unamuno." In Víctor García de la Concha and Javier San José Lera, eds. *Fray Luis de León: Historia, humanismo y letras*. Salamanca: Ediciones Universidad de Salamanca, 1996. 615–28.

Enciso Recio, Luis Miguel, eds. *Ecos de la generación del 98 en la del 27*. Madrid: Ediciones Caballo Griego para la Poesía, 1998.

Enjuto Rangel, Cecilia. "Góngora, Unamuno y el 27 en clave transatlántica." In Julio Ortega, ed. *Reyes, Borges, Gómez de la Serna: Rutas transatlánticas en el Madrid de los años veinte*. Monterrey, Mexico: Orfila Valentini, 2011.

Escobar Borrego, Francisco Javier. "Acercamiento a un ciclo poético: Los *Salmos* de Miguel de Unamuno." *Philologia Hispalensis* 13 (1999): 197–214.

Espina, Antonio. "José Bergamín: *El Cohete y la Estrella* (Biblioteca de 'Indice')." *Revista de Occidente* 3 (1924): 125–7.

Esty, Jed. *Unseasonable Youth: Modernism, Colonialism, and the Fiction of Development*. Oxford: Oxford University Press, 2011.

Eysteinsson, Astradur and Vivian Liska, eds. *Modernism*. 2 vols. Amsterdam and Philadelphia: John Benjamins Publishing Company, 2007.

Feixa, Carles. *De jóvenes, bandas y tribus. Antropología de la juventud*. Barcelona: Editorial Ariel, 1999.

Fernández Almagro, Melchor. "Nuestra joven literatura." *La Época* 14 June 1924: 5.

Flores Arroyuelo, Francisco José. "'Arte Joven': 1901. Una revista modernistsa." *Monteagudo* 7 (2002): 23–30.

Flores Moreno, Cristina. "Nature Imagined in S.T. Coleridge's 'Meditative Poems' and Miguel de Unamuno's *Poesías*: A Study on Reception." *Journal of English Studies* (La Rioja) 5–6 (2005–2008): 83–103.

Foard, Douglas W. *The Revolt of the Aesthetes: Ernesto Giménez Caballero and the Origins of Spanish Fascism*. New York: Peter Lang, 1989.

Fox, Inman. "'La Generación de 1898' como concepto historiográfico." In John P. Gabriele, ed. *Divergencias y unidad: Perspectivas sobre la Generación del '98 y Antonio Machado*. Madrid: Orígenes, 1990. 23–8.

Franz, Thomas R. "Picasso, *Arte Joven*, and Unamuno's *Niebla*." *Hispania* 92 (2009): 213–22.

Fuente, Ricardo de la and Serge Salaün, eds. En torno al casticismo *de Unamuno y la literatura en 1895*. Valladolid: Universitas Castellae, 1997.

Gajic, Tatjana. "Reason, Practice, and the Promise of a New Spain: Ortega's 'Vieja y nueva política' and *Meditaciones del 'Quijote.'" Bulletin of Hispanic Studies* 77 (2000): 193–215.

García Blanco, Manuel. "Clarín y Unamuno." *Archivum* 2 (1952): 113–40.

– *Don Miguel de Unamuno y sus poesías. Estudio y antología de textos poéticos no incluidos en sus libros*. Madrid: Universidad de Salamanca, 1954.

– "Un hispanista británico olvidado: J.E. Crawford Flitch." *Actas del Primer Congreso Internacional de Hispanistas*. Oxford: Dolphin Book Co. for the International Association of Hispanists, 1964. 289–97.

García Lorca, Federico. *Epistolario completo*. Eds. Christopher Maurer and Andrew A. Anderson. Madrid: Cátedra, 1997.

– *Obras completas*. Ed. Miguel García-Posada. 4 vols. Valencia and Barcelona: Círculo de Lectores/Galaxia Gutemberg, 1996–1997.

– *Poesía inédita de juventud*. Ed. Christian de Paepe. Madrid: Cátedra, 1996.

García Montero, Luis. "La Generación del 27 como razón de Estado." *Ínsula* 732 (2007): 2–3.

García Morente, Manuel. "La poesía de Moreno Villa." *El Liberal* 23 July 1914: 3.

García Sanz, Fernando. *España en la Gran Guerra. Espías, diplomaticos y traficantes*. Barcelona: Galaxia Gutemberg, 2014.

García-Velasco, José. "Alberto Jiménez Fraud y la tradición liberal." *Boletín de la Institución Libre de Enseñanza* 78–79–80 (2010): 29–49.

Geist, Anthony Leo. *La poética de la generación del 27 y las revistas literarias: de la vanguardia al compromiso (1918–1936)*. Barcelona: Editorial Labor, 1980.

– and José B. Monleón, eds. *Modernism and Its Margins: Reinscribing Cultural Modernity from Spain and Latin America*. New York and London: Garland Publishing, 1999.

Getman Eraso, Jordi. "Too Young to Fight: Anarchist Youth Groups and the Spanish Second Republic." *Journal of the History of Childhood and Youth* 4 (2011): 282–307.

Gillis, John R. *Youth and History: Tradition and Change in European Age Relations, 1770–Present*. New York: Academic Press, 1974.

Giménez Caballero, Ernesto. "Carta a un compañero de la Joven España." *La Gaceta Literaria* 15 February 1929: 1+.

– "Colofón." *La Gaceta Literaria* 15 March 1930: 20.

– *Genio de España. Exaltaciones a una resurrección nacional y del mundo*. Madrid: Ediciones de "La Gaceta Literaria," 1932.

– *Hercules jugando a los dados*. Prologue by Inocencio Galindo and Enrique Selva. Zaragoza: Libros del Innombrable, 2000.

– "Itinerarios jóvenes de España: Guillermo de Torre." *La Gaceta Literaria* 15 October 1928: 7.
– *Julepe de menta y otros aperitivos*. Madrid: La Lectura, 1929.
– *Notas marruecas de un soldado*. Barcelona: Planeta, 1983.
– "Pespuntes históricos sobre el núcleo gongorino actual." *La Gaceta Literaria* 1 June 1927: 6–7.
– "Primer amor. Y Góngora en el dancing." *Verso y Prosa* 6 (June 1927): 2.
– *Visitas literarias de España (1925–1928)*. Ed. Nigel Dennis. Valencia: Pre-Textos, 1995.
Giner de los Ríos, Francisco. "Aspectos del anarquismo." *Boletín de la Institución Libre de Enseñanza* 23 (March 1899): 88–90.
– *Por una senda clara (antología)*. Eds. José García-Velasco and Eugenio Otero Urtaza. Seville: Centro Andaluz de las Letras, 2011.
Gómez Molleda, María Dolores. "Juventud y política en la España contemporánea." *Studia historica. Historia contemporánea* 5 (1987): 7–20.
– *El socialismo español y los intelectuales: cartas de líderes del movimiento obrero a Miguel de Unamuno*. Salamanca: Ediciones Universidad de Salamanca, 1980.
Gómez-Santos, Marino, ed. Gerardo Diego, *Autobiografía*. Santander: Fundación Gerardo Diego, 2008.
González, Ángel. *El grupo poético de 1927*. Madrid: Taurus, 1976.
González Calleja, Eduardo. *Rebelión en las aulas: movilización y protesta estudiantil en la España contemporánea, 1865–2008*. Madrid: Alianza Editorial, 2009.
– and Sandra Souto Kustrín. "De la dictadura a la República: orígenes y auge de los movimientos juveniles en España." *Hispania: Revista Española de Historia* 67 (2007): 73–102.
González Muela, Joaquín and Juan Manuel Rozas. *La generación poética de 1927*. Madrid: Istmo, 1986.
Guillén, Jorge. "Su originalidad." *La Gaceta Literaria* 1 June 1927: 2.
Gullón, Ricardo. *Direcciones del modernismo*. Madrid: Gredos, 1963.
– "La invención del 98." *La invención del 98 y otros ensayos*. Madrid: Gredos, 1969. 7–19.
Hall, G. Stanley. *Adolescence: Its Psychology and its Relations to Physiology, Anthropology, Sociology, Sex, Crime, Religion, and Education*. 2 vols. New York and London: D. Appleton and Company, 1904. Rpt. 1921.
Harkema, Leslie J. "Escritura adolescente y anti-textualidad: *Nuevo mundo* de Miguel de Unamuno." *Anales de la Literatura Española Contemporánea* 39 (2014): 33–59.
Harnack, Adolf. *History of Dogma*. Trans. Neil Buchanan. 7 vols. New York: Dover Publications, Inc., 1961.

Harrison, Robert Pogue. *Juvenescence*. Chicago: University of Chicago Press, 2014.

Hegel, Georg Wilhelm Friedrich. *Introductory Lectures on Aesthetics*. New York: Penguin Books, 1993.

Herrera Navarro, Javier. "Unamuno, Picasso y 'Arte Joven.'" *Cuadernos de la Cátedra Miguel de Unamuno* 30 (1995): 163–72.

Hewitt, Andrew. *Fascist Modernism: Aesthetics, Politics, and the Avant-Garde*. Stanford, CA: Stanford University Press, 1993.

Jeschke, Hans. *La generación de 1898 en España (Ensayo de una determinación de su esencia)*. Trans. Y. Pino Saavedra. Santiago, Chile: Ediciones de la Universidad de Chile, 1946.

Jiménez, Juan Ramón. *Guerra en España, 1936–1953*. Ed. Ángel Crespo. Barcelona: Seix Barral, 1985.

– *Leyenda (1896–1956)*. Madrid: Visor Libros, 2006.

Jiménez Fraud, Alberto. *Historia de la universidad española*. Madrid: Alianza Editorial, 1971.

– *Residentes. Semblanzas y recuerdos*. Madrid: Alianza Editorial, 1989.

Jiménez-Landi, Antonio. *La Institución Libre de Enseñanza y su ambiente*. 4 vols. Madrid: Editorial Complutense, 1996.

Johnson, Roberta. *Crossfire: Philosophy and the Novel in Spain, 1900–1934*. Lexington, KY: The University Press of Kentucky, 1993.

Jongh, Elena de. "Don Alberto Jiménez y el viaje de Unamuno a Málaga en 1906." *Ínsula* 382 (1978): 12.

Juaristi, Jon. *Miguel de Unamuno*. Madrid: Taurus, 2012.

Juliá, Santos. "'La charca nacional': Visión de España en el Unamuno de fin de siglo." *Historia y Política* 2 (1999): 149–64.

– "Ser intelectual y ser joven, en Madrid, hacia 1930." *Historia Contemporánea* 27 (2003): 749–75.

Kagan, Richard L. "Prescott's Paradigm: American Historical Scholarship and the Decline of Spain." *The American Historical Review* 101 (1996): 423–46.

Kant, Immanuel. *Anthropology from a Pragmatic Point of View*. Trans. and Intro. Mary J. Gregor. The Hague, Netherlands: Martinus Nijhoff, 1974.

– *Political Writings*. Ed. H.S. Reiss. Cambridge, UK: Cambridge University Press, 1991.

Kaplan, Louis J. "The Inventors of Adolescence: Jean-Jacques Rousseau and G. Stanley Hall." In *Adolescence: The Farewell to Childhood*. New York: Simon and Schuster, 1984. 51–80.

Kermode, Frank. *The Sense of an Ending: Studies in the Theory of Fiction*. London: Oxford University Press, 1966.

Kerrigan, Anthony. "Translator's Foreword." Miguel de Unamuno, *The Tragic Sense of Life in Men and Nations*. Trans. Anthony Kerrigan. Princeton, NJ: Princeton University Press, 1972. vii-xxviii.

Kirkpatrick, Susan. *Mujer, modernismo y vanguardia en España (1898–1931)*. Madrid: Cátedra, 2003.

Krauel, Javier. *Imperial Emotions: Cultural Responses to Myths of Empire in Fin-de-Siècle Spain*. Liverpool: Liverpool UniversityPress, 2013.

– "Visión parcial del enemigo íntimo: La Gran Guerra como antesala de la Guerra Civil." *Vanderbilt e-Journal of Luso-Hispanic Studies* 5 (2009): 55–76.

Labanyi, Jo. "Nation, Narration, Naturalization: A Barthesian Critique of the 1898 Generation." In Mark I. Millington and Paul Julian Smith, eds. *New Hispanisms: Literature, Culture, and Theory*. Ottawa: Dovehouse, 1994. 127–49.

– *Myth and History in the Contemporary Spanish Novel*. Cambridge, UK and New York: Cambridge University Press, 1989.

Laín Entralgo, Pedro. *La generación del 98*. Buenos Aires: Espasa-Calpe Argentina, 1948.

Larra, Mariano José de. *Fígaro. Colección de artículos dramáticos, literarios, políticos y de costumbres*. Ed. Alejandro Pérez Vidal. Barcelona: Crítica, 2000.

Larson, Susan. *Constructing and Resisting Modernity: Madrid 1900–1936*. Madrid and Orlando, FL: Iberoamericana Vervuert, 2011.

– "Unreadable Bodies and Symbolic Violence in Antonio de Obregón's *Hermes en la vía pública*." In *Modernism and the Avante-Garde Body in Spain and Italy*, eds. Nicolás Fernández-Medina and Maria Truglio. New York and London: Routledge, 2016. 54–72.

Levi, Giovanni and Jean-Claude Schmitt, eds. *Stormy Evolution to Modern Times*. 2 of *A History of Young People in the West*. Cambridge, MA and London: Belknap, 1997.

Lewis, Pericles, ed. *The Cambridge Companion to European Modernism*. Cambridge, UK and New York: Cambridge University Press, 2011.

Lissorgues, Yvan. "Unamuno y Clarín: ¿Una amistad frustrada?" *Letras de Deusto* 15 (1985): 87–101.

Litvak, Lily. "La idea de la decadencia en la crítica antimodernista en España (1888–1910)." *Hispanic Review* 45 (1977): 397–412.

Longhurst, C.A. *Modernismo, noventayochismo y novela: España y Europa. Ensayo de literatura comparada*. Oxford: Peter Lang, 2014.

López-Rey, José. *Los estudiantes frente a la dictadura*. Madrid: J. Morata, 1930.

López Frías, María Antonia. *José Moreno Villa: Vida y poesía antes del exilio (1887–1937)*. Málaga: Diputación Provincial de Málaga, 1990.

Lowe, Sid. *Catholicism, War and the Foundation of Francoism: The Juventud de Acción Popular in Spain, 1931–1939*. Brighton, UK and Portland, OR: Sussex Academic Press, 2010.

Mao, Douglas. *Fateful Beauty: Aesthetic Environments, Juvenile Development, and Literature, 1860–1960*. Princeton, NJ: Princeton University Press, 2010.

Machado, Antonio. *Campos de Castilla: 1907–1917*. Ed. Geoffrey Ribbans. Madrid: Cátedra, 2006.

Mainer, José-Carlos. *La Edad de Plata (1902–1939): Ensayo de interpretación de un proceso cultural*. Madrid: Cátedra, 1983.

– *Literatura y pequeña burguesía en España. (Notas 1890–1950)*. Madrid: EDICUSA, 1972.

Mannheim, Karl. *Essays on the Sociology of Knowledge*. Ed. Paul Kecskemeti. London: Routledge & Paul, 1952. Rpt. 1972.

Marichalar, Antonio. "Madrid Chronicle." *The New Criterion* 4 (1926): 357–62.

Martínez-Nadal, Rafael, ed. *Miguel de Unamuno y José María Quiroga Pla. Un epistolario y diez* Hojas libres. Madrid: Editorial Casariego, 2001.

Massis, Henri and Alfred de Tarde (Agathon). *Les Jeunes gens d'aujourd'hui*. Ed. Jean-Jacques Becker. Paris: Imprimerie Nationale Éditions, 1995.

Mateo Gambarte, Eduardo. *El concepto de generación literaria*. Madrid: Síntesis, 1996.

Maurer, Christopher. "*El Cristo de Velázquez*: Creación y creencia." Supplementary study. Miguel de Unamuno, *El Cristo de Velázquez*. Ed. Mario Hernández. Madrid: Imprenta Artesanal del Ayuntamiento de Madrid, 2008.

– "Más allá de Eco y Narciso: J.R.J. y Jorge Guillén." In Javier Diéz de Revenga and Mariano de Paco, eds., *La claridad en el aire. Estudios sobre Jorge Guillén*. Murcia: Caja Murcia, 1994. 207–23.

McFarland, Andrew. "*Regeneracionismo del cuerpo*: The Arguments for Implanting Athletics in Spain." *Sport in Society* 11 (2008): 615–29.

Medina, Alberto. "Over a Young Dead Body: The Spanish Transition as *Bildungsroman*." *Modern Language Notes* 130 (2015): 298–315.

Meier, Elke. "Unamuno, Rubén Darío y el modernismo." *Cuadernos de la Cátedra Miguel de Unamuno* 27 (1983): 135–48.

Mendibourne, Jean-Michel. *José Bergamín. L'écriture à l'épreuve de Dieu*. Toulouse: Presses Universitaires du Mirail, 2001.

Menéndez Alzamora, Manuel. *La Generación del 14: Una aventura intelectual*. Madrid: Siglo XXI, 2006.

Meyendorff, John. *Byzantine Theology: Historical Trends and Doctrinal Themes*. New York: Fordham University Press, 1974.

Meyer, Lothar. *Les Théories modernes de la chimie et leur application à la mécanique chimique [Die modernen Theorien der Chemie und ihre Bedeutung für die chemische Mechanik]*. Trans. M. Albert Bloch. Paris: Georges Carré, 1887–1889.

Morelli, Gabriele. *Gerardo Diego y el III centenario de Góngora*. Valencia: Pre-Textos, 2001.

– *Historia y recepción de la* Antología *poética de Gerardo Diego*. Valencia: Pre-Textos, 1997.

Moreno Villa, José. *Los autores como actores y otros intereses literarios de acá y allá*. México: El Colegio de México, 1951.

– *Memoria*. Ed. Juan Pérez de Ayala. México and Madrid: El Colegio de México/Residencia de Estudiantes, 2011.

– *Poesías completas*. Ed. Juan Pérez de Ayala. México and Madrid: El Colegio de México/ Residencia de Estudiantes, 1998.

Moretti, Franco. *The Way of the World: The* Bildungsroman *in European Culture*. London and New York: Verso, 2000.

Naharro-Calderón, José María. "J.R.J. 'Ma non troppo.'" In Cristóbal Cuevas García, ed. *El universo creador del 27*. Málaga: Congreso de Literatura Española Contemporánea, 1997. 389–402.

Neira, Julio. Litoral: *la revista de una generación*. Santander, Spain: Publicaciones La Isla de los Ratones, 1978.

Neubauer, John. *The Fin-de-Siècle Culture of Adolescence*. New Haven and London: Yale University Press, 1991.

North, Michael. *Novelty: A History of the New*. Chicago and London: University of Chicago Press, 2013.

Nuñez, Diego and Pedro Ribas, eds. *Unamuno y el socialismo. Artículos recuperados (1886–1928)*. Granada: Editorial Comares, 1997.

Onís, Carlos de. "El magisterio de Unamuno en el hispanista Federico de Onís." *Confluencia* 1 (1985): 1–29.

Onís, Federico de. *Disciplina y rebeldía*. Madrid: Residencia de Estudiantes, 1915.

Onieva, Antonio J. "Recuerdos de la Residencia (Fragmentos)." *Revista de Occidente* 66 (1968): 297–306.

Orringer, Nelson R. "Poesía y teología en Unamuno." In José Ángel Áscunce Arrieta, ed. *La poesía de Miguel de Unamuno*. San Sebastián: Universidad de Deusto, 1987.

– *Unamuno y los protestantes liberales (1912). Sobre las fuentes de 'Del sentimiento trágico de la vida.'* Madrid: Gredos, 1985.

Ortega y Gasset, José. *Obras completas*. 10 vols. Madrid: Taurus, 2004–2010.

Palenque, Marta, ed. *La corte de los poetas. Florilegio de rimas modernas*. [1906] Facsimile edition. Seville: Editorial Renacimiento, 2009.

Pao, María T. "A Novel *Nadie*: Benjamín Jarnés Responds to Unamuno and Pirandello." *Bulletin of Spanish Studies* 87.4 (2010): 463–83.

Penalva, Gonzalo. "El clavo ardiendo." *Revista de Occidente* 166 (1995): 65–85.

Pérez de Ayala, Juan. "José Moreno Villa y 'el espíritu de la casa.'" *Boletín de la Institución Libre de Enseñanza* 78–79–80 (2010): 151–65.

Pérez de la Dehesa, Rafael. *Política y sociedad en el primer Unamuno*. Barcelona: Ariel, 1966.

Pérez Ferrero, Miguel. "¿Qué es la vanguardia?" *La Gaceta Literaria* 1 June 1930: 1–2.

Pérez Firmat, Gustavo. *Idle Fictions: The Hispanic Vanguard Novel, 1926–1934*. Durham, NC: Duke University Press, 1982.

Pérez Gutiérrez, Francisco. "La fe y lo religioso en la obra poética de Gerardo Diego: Velo y desvelo de poeta." In *Gerardo Diego: Poeta mayor de Cantabria*. Ed. Rafael Gómez de Tudanca, Rosa Fernández Lera, and Andrés del Rey Sayagués. Santander, Spain: Ayuntamiento-Sociedad Menéndez Pelayo-Biblioteca de Menéndez Pelayo. 153–94.

Pérez Gutiérrez, Francisco. "José Bergamín, un cristiano extraviado en su tiempo (y en el nuestro)." *Boletín de la Biblioteca de Menéndez Pelayo* 80 (2004): 81–110.

Pérez-Villanueva Tovar, Isabel. *La Residencia de Estudiantes: grupo universitario y Residencia de Señoritas, 1910–1936*. Madrid: Residencia de Estudiantes, 2011.

Picasso, Pablo and Fracisco de Assís Soler. "Arte joven." *Arte Joven*, 10 March 1901: 2.

Pino, José M. del. *Montajes y fragmentos: una aproximación a la narrativa española de vanguardia*. Amsterdam and Atlanta, GA: Rodopi, 1995.

"La polémica J.R.J./J.G." *Índice de artes y letras* 30 March 1954: 1, 6–9.

Poggioli, Renato. *The Theory of the Avant-Garde*. Trans. Gerald Fitzgerald. Cambridge, MA and London: Belknap Press, 1968.

Prados, Emiilio and Manuel Altolaguirre, eds. *Homenaje a Don Luis de Góngora. Litoral* 5, 6, 7 (October 1927): 1–65.

Predmore, Michael. *Una España joven en la poesía de Antonio Machado*. Madrid: Ínsula, 1981.

Rabaté, Colette and Jean-Claude Rabaté. *Miguel de Unamuno: biografía*. Madrid: Taurus, 2009.

Rabaté, Jean-Claude. *Guerra de ideas en el joven Unamuno (1880–1900)*. Madrid: Biblioteca Nueva, 2001.

– Introduction. Miguel de Unamuno, *En torno al casticismo*. Madrid: Cátedra, 2005. 9–107.

– coord. *Crise intellectuelle et politique en Espagne à la fin du XIXe siècle*. Paris: Éditions du Temps, 1999.

Ramos-Gascón, Antonio. "Clarín y el primer Unamuno." *Cuadernos Hispano-americanos* 263–4 (1972): 489–95.

Ramsden, Herbert. *The 1898 Movement in Spain*. Manchester: Manchester University Press, 1974.

Rasula, Jed. "Make It New." *Modernism/modernity* 17 (2010): 713–33.

Resina, Joan Ramon. "For Their Own Good: The Spanish Identity and Its Grand Inquisitor, Miguel de Unamuno." In Jesús Torrecilla, ed., *La Generación del 98: Frente al nuevo fin de siglo*. Atlanta: Rodopi, 2000. 235–67.

Ribagorda, Álvaro. "Las publicaciones de la Residencia de Estudiantes." *Iberoamericana* 7 (2007): 43–64.

Ribas, Pedro. "Unamuno y el Marxismo en el período 1891–1900." In Berchem and Laitenberger, 113–22.

Ribbans, Geoffrey. "'Indigesto, mezquino, pedestre, confuso': A Hostile Contemporary Critique of Unamuno's *Poesías* (1907)." *Revista Canadiense de Estudios Hispánicos* 31 (1996): 203–16.

– "Unamuno y 'los jóvenes' en 1904." In *Niebla y soledad: Aspectos de Unamuno y Machado*. Madrid: Gredos, 1971. 45–82.

Ricoeur, Paul. *Lectures on Ideology and Utopia*. Ed. George H. Taylor. New York: Columbia University Press, 1986.

Ripley, W.Z. *The Races of Europe: A Sociological Study*. New York: D. Appleton, 1899. Rpt. New York: Johnson Reprint Corp., 1965.

Roberts, Stephen G.H. *Miguel de Unamuno o la creación del intelectual español moderno*. Salamanca: Ediciones Universidad de Salamanca, 2007.

Robles, Laureano. "La colaboración de Unamuno en *La Lucha de Clases* (octubre 1894–abril 1897)." In Berchem and Laitenberger, 123–96.

– "Doce cartas inéditas de J. Moreno Villa a Unamuno." *Jábega: Revista de la diputación provincial de Málaga* 67 (1990): 57–66.

– "Miguel de Unamuno y Gerardo Diego (Correspondencia)." *Ensayos* 2 (1989): 109–35.

– "Unamuno en Málaga (1906)." *Jábega: Revista de la diputación provincial de Málaga* 66 (1989): 57–66.

– ed. *Epistolario completo Ortega-Unamuno*. Madrid: El Arquero, 1987.

Rodríguez, María Pilar. *Vidas im/propias: Transformaciones del sujeto femenino en la narrativa española contemporánea*. West Lafayette, IN: Purdue University Press, 2000.

Rodríguez García, José María. "Introduction: How 'Modernist' Were Hispanic Literary and Artistic Modernities?" *Modernist Cultures* 7 (2012): 1–14.

Rogers, Gayle. *Modernism and the New Spain: Britain, Cosmopolitan Europe, and Literary History*. New York: Oxford University Press, 2012.

Rojas, Pablo. "Un intelectual en la Talavera de la II República: Ernesto López-Parra (1895–1941). Más allá del ultraísmo." *Cuaderna: Revista de estudios humanísticos de Talavera* 9–10 (2001–2002): 139–65.
Romero Salvadó, Francisco J. *Spain 1914–1918: Between War and Revolution*. London and New York: Routledge, 1999.
Romojaro, Rosa. *Lo escrito y lo leído: ensayos sobre literatura y crítica literaria*. Barcelona: Anthropos, 2004.
Ross, Kristin. *The Emergence of Social Space: Rimbaud and the Paris Commune*. London and New York: Verso, 2008.
Rubio, Adolfo. "Miguel de Unamuno, *Poesías*." *Nuestro Tiempo* 7 (1907): 108–9.
Sáenz de la Calzada, Margarita. *La Residencia de Estudiantes. Los Residentes*. Madrid: Publicaciones de la Residencia de Estudiantes, 2011.
Salcedo, Emilio. *Vida de don Miguel*. Salamanca: Anaya, 1970.
Salinas, Pedro. "El concepto de 'generación literaria' aplicado a la de 98." *Literatura española. Siglo XX*. Madrid: Alianza Editorial, 1970. 26–33.
San José Lera, Javier. "Una clave decisiva de la 'Generación del 28': José María de Cossío." *Ínsula* 545 (May 1992): 9–13, 16–20.
Sánchez, Carmen. "El *Efebo rubio* en la Residencia de Estudiantes. La *paideia* griega." *Boletín de la Institución Libre de Enseñanza* 78–79–80 (2010): 137–49.
Santiáñez, Nil. *Topographies of Fascism: Habitus, Space, and Writing in Twentieth-Century Spain*. Toronto: University of Toronto Press, 2013.
Santoja, Gonzalo. *Al otro lado del mar: Bergamín y la Editorial Séneca (México, 1939–1949)*. Barcelona: Círculo de Lectores/Galaxia Gutenberg, 1997.
Savage, Jon. *Teenage: The Prehistory of Youth Culture, 1875–1945*. New York: Penguin Books, 2007.
Schork, R.J. "Ayala's Joycean 'Portrait': *A.M.D.G.*" *Comparative Literature Studies* 26 (1989): 50–70.
Selva, Enrique. *Ernesto Giménez Caballero: entre la vanguardia y el fascismo*. Valencia: Pre-Textos, 1999.
Sender, Ramón J. *Unamuno, Valle Inclán, Baroja y Santayana. Ensayos críticos*. México: Ediciones de Andrea, 1955.
Shaw, Donald L. *The Generation of 1898 in Spain*. London: Ernest Benn Limited, 1975.
Silver, Philip. "La estética de Ortega y la generación de 1927." *Nueva Revista de Filología Hispánica* 2 (1971): 361–80.
Sinclair, Alison. "'Telling it Like it Was'?: The 'Residencia de Estudiantes' and its Image." *Bulletin of Spanish Studies* 81 (2004): 739–63.
Sobejano, Gonzalo. *Nietzsche en España*. Madrid: Gredos, 1967.

Sody, Ángel. *...Y al final la luz. La polemica entre Juan Ramón Jiménez y Jorge Guillén*. Barcelona: Grupo de Historia José Berruezo, 1999.

Soria Olmedo, Andrés, ed. *Una densa polimorfía de belleza: Góngora y el grupo del 27*. Málaga: Junta de Andalucía, Centro Andaluz de las Letras, 2007.

– "Jorge Guillén y la 'joven literatura.'" In *Jorge Guillén, el hombre y la obra*. Ed. Antonio Piedra and Javier Blasco Pascual. Valladolid: Universidad de Valladolid, Fundación Jorge Guillén, 1995. 257–78.

– ed. *Las vanguardias y la generación del 27*. Madrid: Visor, 2007.

Sotelo Vázquez, Adolfo. *Miguel de Unamuno: Artículos en Las Noticias de Barcelona (1899–1902)*. Barcelona: Editorial Lumen, 1993.

– "Miguel de Unamuno y la génesis del *Romancero gitano*." *Cuadernos Hispanoamericanos* 433–434 (1986): 199–210.

– "Pedro Salinas entre el joven Eliot y el joven Unamuno." *Cuadernos Hispanoamericanos* 514–515 (1993): 239–45.

– "El primer Unamuno y Cataluña." *Cuadernos Hispanoamericanos* 440–441 (1987): 65–88.

Soufas, C. Christopher. *The Subject in Question: Early Contemporary Spanish Literature and Modernism*. Washington, DC: The Catholic Univeristy of America Press, 2007.

Spacks, Patricia Meyer. *The Adolescent Idea: Myths of Youth and the Adult Imagination*. New York: Basic Books, Inc., 1981.

Spires, Robert C. *Transparent Simulacra: Spanish Fiction, 1902–1926*. Columbia, MO: University of Missouri Press, 1988.

Tasende, Mercedes. "*El resentimiento trágico de la vida*: Últimas reflexiones de Unamuno en torno a la Guerra Civil Española." *Anales de la Literatura Española Contemporánea* 34 (2009): 275–304.

Teruel Benavente, José. "Unamuno en Cernuda." In *Miguel de Unamuno. Estudios sobre su obra. II*. Salamanca: Ediciones Universidad de Salamanca, 2005. 399–409.

Thion Soriano-Mollá, Dolores. "La Gente Nueva del fin de siglo." *Actas del XIII Congreso de la Asociación Internacional de Hispanistas. Tomo II*. Madrid: AIH, Editorial Castalia. 1998. 425–33.

– "Gente nueva versus Gente vieja: Martínez Ruiz y los hijos del siglo del Modernismo." In *Azorín et la Génération de 1898: IVème colloque international*. Pau, France: Université de Pau et des Pays de l'Adour, 1998. 147–68.

Thomas, Michael D. *Coming of Age in Franco's Spain. Anti-Fascist Rites of Passage in Sender, Delibes, Laforet, Matute, and Martín Gaite*. New York: Peter Lang, 2014.

Torre, Guillermo de. *Literaturas europeas de vanguardia*. Madrid: Rafael Caro Raggio, 1925.

Trend, J.B. *A Picture of Modern Spain*. Boston and New York: Houghton Mifflin, 1921.

Tuñón de Lara, Manuel. *Costa y Unamuno en la crisis de fin de siglo*. Madrid: Editorial Cuadernos para el Diálogo, 1974.

Unamuno, Miguel de. *Artículos desconocidos en 'El Mercantil Valenciano' (1917–1923)*. Ed. Laureano Robles Carcedo and Manuel María Urrutia León. Valencia: Generalitat Valenciana, 2003.

– "Carta." *Carmen* 5 (1928): 1–2.

– *Cartas del destierro*. Ed. Colette Rabaté and Jean-Claude Rabaté. Salamanca: Ediciones Universidad de Salamanca, 2012.

– "Comentario." *Nuevo Mundo*. 7 April 1924. n. p.

– *De la desesperación religiosa moderna*. Ed. and trans. Sandro Borzoni. Madrid: Trotta, 2011.

– *Diario íntimo*. Madrid: Alianza Editorial, 1998.

– *Ensayos*. 7 vols. Madrid: Residencia de Estudiantes, 1916–1918.

– "Intermedio lírico." *Los Lunes de El Imparcial* 20 January 1913: 3.

– *Manual de quijotismo. Cómo se hace una novela. Epistolario Miguel de Unamuno / Jean Cassou*. Ed. Bénédicte Vauthier. Salamanca: Ediciones Universidad de Salamanca, 2005.

– *Mi confesión*. Ed. Alicia Villar Ezcurra. Salamanca and Madrid: Ediciones Sígueme/Universidad Pontificia Comillas, 2011.

– *Nuevo mundo*. Ed. Laureano Robles. Madrid: Editorial Trotta, 1994.

– *Obras completas*. Ed. Manuel García Blanco. 9 vols. Madrid: Escelicer, 1966.

– *Poesías*. Ed. Manuel Álvar. Madrid: Cátedra, 2009.

– *El resentimiento trágico de la vida*. Ed. Carlos Feal. Madrid: Alianza, 1991.

– "Sobre Góngora." *Helios* May 1903: 475–7.

– "El tiempo material." *Los Lunes de El Imparcial* 17 February 1924: 2.

Unamuno Pérez, María de la Concepción de. *Miguel de Unamuno y la cultura francesa*. Salamanca: Ediciones Universidad de Salamanca, 1991.

Urrutia Jordana, Ana. *La poetización de la política en el Unamuno exiliado.* De Fuerteventura a París *y* Romancero del destierro. Salamanca: Ediciones Universidad de Salamanca, 2003.

Urrutia, Manuel María. *Evolución del pensamiento político de Unamuno*. Bilbao: Universidad de Deusto, 1997.

– "Miguel de Unamuno y la revista *España* (1915–1924) (Textos desconocidos)." *Cuadernos de la Cátedra Miguel de Unamuno* 47 (2009): 113–45.

Valdés, Mario J. Introduction. *Niebla*. By Miguel de Unamuno. Madrid: Cátedra, 1982. 9–58.

Valdés, Mario J. and María Elena de Valdés. *An Unamuno Source Book: Catalogue of Readings and Acquisitions, with an Introductory Essay on Unamuno's*

Dialectical Enquiry. Toronto and Buffalo, NY: University of Toronto Press, 1973.

Valender, James. *El impresor en el exilio: Tres revistas de Manuel Altolaguirre. Atentamente. La Verónica. Antología de España en el Recuerdo*. Facsimiles. Madrid: Residencia de Estudiantes, 2003.

– "A propósito de las *Poesías completas* de José Moreno Villa." *Nueva revista de filología hispánica* 47 (1999): 385–98.

Valente, José Ángel. "Luis Cernuda y la poesía de la meditación." In Derek Harris, ed. *Luis Cernuda*. Madrid: Taurus, 1977.

Vallejo, César. "Estado de la literatura española." *Favorables París Poema* 1 (June 1926): 6–7.

Vanderborght, Paul, ed. *Hommage à Rupert Brooke, 1887–1915*. Brussels: L'Élegantine, 1931.

Vauthier, Bénédicte. *Arte de escribir e ironía en la obra narrativa de Miguel de Unamuno*. Salamanca: Ediciones Universidad de Salamanca, 2004.

Verbeke, Frederik. "Anotaciones sobre Unamuno y su estancia en Bruselas de 1924." In *La cultura del otro: español en Francia, francés en España./La Culture de l'autre: espagnole en France, français en Espagne. Actas del primer encuentro hispanofrancés de investigadores (APFUE/SHF)*. Eds. Manuel Bruña Cuevas et. al. Seville: Universidad de Sevilla, 2006. 721–32. Web. 25 August 2014.

Wahnón, Sultana. "La crítica literaria de la generación del 27: la formación de una minoría literaria." In Cristóbal Cuevas García, ed. *El universo creador del 27*. Málaga: Congreso de Literatura Española Contemporánea, 1997. 131–61.

Williams, Raymond. "The Bloomsbury Fraction." In *Culture and Materialism: Selected Essays*. London and New York: Verso, 2005. 148–69.

Wohl, Robert. *The Generation of 1914*. Cambridge, MA: Harvard University Press, 1979.

Wohlfarth, Irving. "The Politics of Youth: Walter Benjamin's Reading of *The Idiot*." *Diacritics* 22 (1992): 160–72.

Ynduráin, Francisco. "Unamuno en su poética y como poeta." *Clásicos modernos*. Madrid: Gredos, 1969. 59–125.

Zambrano, María. *Unamuno*. Ed. Mercedes Gómez Blesa. Barcelona: Random House Mondadori, 2003.

Zardoya, Concha. "La 'humanación' en la poesía de Unamuno." In *Poesía española contemporánea. Estudios temáticos y estilísticos*. Madrid: Ediciones Guadarrama, 1961. 91–178.

Zubiri, Xavier. "Hegel y el problema metafísico." *Cruz y Raya* 15 April 1933: 11–40.

Zulueta, Carmen de, ed. *Miguel de Unamuno. Luis de Zulueta. Cartas (1903–1933)*. Madrid: Aguilar, 1972.

Zulueta, Luis de. *La edad heroica*. Madrid: Residencia de Estudiantes, 1916.

Index

TORONTO IBERIC

1 Anthony J. Cascardi, *Cervantes, Literature, and the Discourse of Politics*
2 Jessica A. Boon, *The Mystical Science of the Soul: Medieval Cognition in Bernardino de Laredo's Recollection Method*
3 Susan Byrne, *Law and History in Cervantes' Don Quixote*
4 Mary E. Barnard and Frederick A. de Armas (eds), *Objects of Culture in the Literature of Imperial Spain*
5 Nil Santiáñez, *Topographies of Fascism: Habitus, Space, and Writing in Twentieth-Century Spain*
6 Nelson Orringer, *Lorca in Tune with Falla: Literary and Musical Interludes*
7 Ana M. Gómez-Bravo, *Textual Agency: Writing Culture and Social Networks in Fifteenth-Century Spain*
8 Javier Irigoyen-García, *The Spanish Arcadia: Sheep Herding, Pastoral Discourse, and Ethnicity in Early Modern Spain*
9 Stephanie Sieburth, *Survival Songs: Conchita Piquer's* Coplas *and Franco's Regime of Terror*
10 Christine Arkinstall, *Spanish Female Writers and the Freethinking Press, 1879-1926*

11 Margaret Boyle, *Unruly Women: Performance, Penitence, and Punishment in Early Modern Spain*
12 Evelina Gužauskytė, *Christopher Columbus's Naming in the* diarios *of the Four Voyages (1492-1504): A Discourse of Negotiation*
13 Mary E. Barnard, *Garcilaso de la Vega and the Material Culture of Renaissance Europe*
14 William Viestenz, *By the Grace of God: Francoist Spain and the Sacred Roots of Political Imagination*
15 Michael Scham, Lector Ludens: *The Representation of Games and Play in* Cervantes
16 Stephen Rupp, *Heroic Forms: Cervantes and the Literature of War*
17 Enrique Fernandez, *Anxieties of Interiority and Dissection in Early Modern Spain*
18 Susan Byrne, *Ficino in Spain*
19 Patricia M. Keller, *Ghostly Landscapes: Film, Photography, and the Aesthetics of Haunting in Contemporary Spanish Culture*
20 Carolyn A. Nadeau, *Food Matters: Alonso Quijano's Diet and the Discourse of Food in Early Modern Spain*
21 Cristian Berco, *From Body to Community: Venereal Disease and Society in Baroque Spain*
22 Elizabeth R. Wright, *The Epic of Juan Latino: Dilemmas of Race and Religion in Renaissance Spain*
23 Ryan D. Giles, *Inscribed Power: Amulets and Magic in Early Spanish Literature*
24 Jorge Pérez, *Confessional Cinema: Religion, Film, and Modernity in Spain's Development Years (1960-1975)*
25 Juan Ramon Resina, *Josep Pla: Seeing the World in the Form of Articles*
26 Javier Irigoyen-Garcia, *'Moors Dressed as Moors': Clothing, Social Distinction, and Ethnicity in Early Modern Iberia*
27 Jean Dangler, *Edging Toward Iberia*
28 Ryan D. Giles and Steven Wagschal (eds): *Beyond Sight: Engaging the Senses in Iberian Literatures and Cultures, 1200-1750*
29 Silvia Bermúdez, *Rocking the Boat: Migration and Race in Contemporary Spanish Music*
30 Hilaire Kallendorf, *Ambiguous Antidotes: Virtue as Vaccine for Vice in Early Modern Spain*
31 Leslie J. Harkema, *Spanish Modernism and the Poetics of Youth: From Miguel de Unamuno to* La Joven Literatura